Communication and Society
Series Editor: Jeremy Tunstall

The manufacture of news

*This book is the third volume in a series
edited by Jeremy Tunstall and devoted to
explorations of the interrelationships between
society and all forms of communications media.*

STANLEY COHEN AND JOCK YOUNG
Editors

The manufacture of news

a reader

SAGE Publications
Beverly Hills, California

For Information Address
SAGE PUBLICATIONS, INC.
275 South Beverly Drive
Beverly Hills, California 90212

Printed in Great Britain

International Standard Book Number 0-8039-0325-1

Library of Congress Catalog Card No. 73-87747

First Printing

'Up till now it has been thought that the growth of the Christian myths during the Roman Empire was possible only because printing was not yet invented. Precisely the contrary. The daily press and the telegraph, which in a moment spread inventions over the whole earth, fabricate more myths . . . in one day than could have formerly been done in a century.'

KARL MARX·
(writing on atrocity stories in the British
press during the Paris commune –
in a letter to Kugelmann, 27 July 1871)

Acknowledgements

The editors would like to thank the following for their kind permission to reproduce from material mentioned below: Tavistock Publications Ltd for Leslie Wilkins' *Social deviance, social policy, action and research*; Bob Roshier for 'The selection of crime news by the press'; Random House Inc. and Jay K. Hoffman for Robert Cirino's *Don't blame the people*; The International Institute for Peace and Conflict Research for Johan Galtung and Mari Ruge's 'Structuring and selecting news'; Paul Rock for 'News as eternal recurrence'; Collins and Viking Press for Michael Frayn's *The tin men*; Stuart Hall and *New Society* for 'A world at one with itself'; Bernard Berelson, Patricia Salter and *The Public Opinion Quarterly* for 'Majority and minority Americans: an analysis of magazine fiction'; A. S. Linsky and *Public Opinion Quarterly* for 'Theories of behaviour and the image of the alcoholic in popular magazines'; The University of Chicago Press for F. James Davis' 'Crime news in Colorado newspapers'; Holt, Rinehart & Winston Inc. for Jum C. Nunnally's *Popular conceptions of mental health*; Graham Murdock for 'Political "deviance": press presentation of a militant mass demonstration'; Stuart Hall for 'The determinations of news photographs'; Doubleday Inc. for William Braden's 'LSD and the press' which appeared in B. Aaronson and H. Osmond's *Psychedelics*; *Society* and Terry Ann Knopf for 'Sniping—a new pattern of violence?' which appeared in *Transaction*; Eamonn McCann for 'The British press and Northern Ireland'; E. P. Thompson and *New Society* for 'Sir, Writing by candelight . . .'; The Institute of Race Relations for Paul Hartmann's and Charles Husband's 'The mass media and racial conflict' which first appeared in *Race*; Frank Pearce for 'How to be immoral and ill . . .'; Jerry Palmer for 'Mickey Spillane: a reading'; Damien Phillips for 'The press and pop festivals: stereotypes of youthful leisure'; and Allen Lane The Penguin Press and Beacon Press Inc. for extracts from Philip Slater's *The pursuit of loneliness*; also the editors of the *Daily Mail* and *The Guardian* for articles on Sir John Waldron's annual report of 1972.

The editors would also like to acknowledge help received from Dave Chaney, Stuart Hall, Sonny Mehta, Graham Murdock and Jeremy Tunstall.

Contents

8   Contents

Introduction

UNDER THE PAVING STONES THE BEACH	ANGRY BRIGADE: SEX ORGIES AT THE COTTAGE OF BLOOD
CONSUME MORE? THEN YOU LIVE LESS	A DREAM CAR FOR YOU!
THERE'S NOTHING THEY WON'T DO TO RAISE THE STANDARD OF BOREDOM	HAPPINESS IS £ SHAPED
PLAY WITHOUT RESTRAINTS AND LIVE WITHOUT DEAD TIME	NEW 'GET TOUGH' MEASURES ON DRUG PROBLEM
ALL POWER TO THE IMAGINATION	WHO ARE BRITAIN'S SMUT PEDLARS?
BE REALISTIC, DEMAND THE IMPOSSIBLE	'MILITANT TEACHERS INFILTRATING SCHOOLS' CLAIMS HEADMASTER

Two sets of slogans: one found on the walls of Paris in May 1968, the other in the headlines and advertisements carried in our national newspapers every day. They represent not just degrees of bias from a taken-for-granted social reality but – in their very words and syntax – radically alternative and oppositional realities. One conjures up a world that might be and deplores the façade of what is, the other accepts the present façade and its monolithic certainty and caricatures all deviations from it.

Just as the slogans on the Paris walls represent a created image of society, so the mass media are in the business of manufacturing and reproducing images. They provide the guiding myths which shape our conception of the world and serve as important instruments of social control. These processes are, of course, extremely complex: the media neither simply supply information and entertainment nor do they mechanically implant attitudes into the heads of their recipients. Just what effects the mass media do have on attitudes, values and behaviour has been the subject of much popular and scientific debate and this book is not meant to provide a comprehensive or representative selection of such arguments. Even to draw only on sociological work would have meant lumping together an eclectic sample of the vast literature.

Rather, by concentrating on how the media treat certain forms of deviance and social problems, we have chosen to emphasize a particular theoretical perspective. We have deliberately biased the book away from some of the standard questions on the subject, particularly those concerned with the supposed direct effects on behaviour of media exposure: for example, does the viewing of TV violence lead to increased aggressiveness? Instead we have concentrated on a somewhat neglected aspect, but one which we believe to have much greater sociological potential and practical importance, namely: the conceptions of deviance and social problems revealed in the mass media and the implicit view of society behind such conceptions.

The writings on this aspect of the media debate are informed by a number of different theories and rely on different methods of investigation. For our purposes, two polarized traditions are important to distinguish: the Mass Manipulative model and the Commercial Laissez-Faire model. In the Manipulative model, the public is seen as an atomized mass, passive receptacles of messages originating from a monolithic and powerful source. In the left-wing political version of this model, the source is controlled by and represents the interests of the ruling class. Those in power use the media to mystify and manipulate the public. In some right-wing versions, the media are also seen as powerful, but their influence is in the direction of lowering cultural standards and propagating values of permissiveness. A centrist version simply sees the media as a force for unity and cohesion in a divided society. Each of these versions carries its logical implications for how the media *select* and *present* information and for what *effects* this might have on the public.

The Commercial Laissez-Faire model emerged largely as a critique of the manipulative picture: it is mostly adhered to by journalists themselves and it tends to be more optimistic. It argues that there is variety and diversity in information and opinions presented in the mass media and that such variation minimizes the chances of manipulation. Principles such as 'give the public what it wants' (and their commercial implications) rather than some manipulative conspiracy, are what determine how the media select and present information. Indeed the public themselves, as consumers, can actively select or selectively perceive those media (or parts of the media) which already fit existing positions and preconceptions.

The effects of the media then are seen as less awesome than in the Manipulative model: people's opinions might be reinforced, but rarely changed in an opposite direction and moreover the primal source of attitude formation and change is personal experience and face-to-face contact.

Our own position is one that will emerge as we compare how these models 'work' in the three areas of social problem imagery the book covers: *selection, presentation* and *effects*. In the case of selection – Part One of the book – the existing literature is not nearly so comprehensive or relevant as we would like; we include only a few readings, some reprinted and some specially prepared for this volume. These address themselves to the question of how news is selected in the first place. The second Part is the longest and consists of separate case studies – using diverse sources and methods – on the modes of presentation and underlying models of deviance and social problems employed in the media. Most of the articles or extracts refer to Britain or America and most are contemporary or as near to contemporary as we could find.

Part Three is concerned with the likely effects of the mass media both on people's conceptions of social problems and on the groups themselves designated as deviant or socially problematic. It draws upon some of our own work in this area and attempts to pull together some of the arguments advanced in the first two parts of the book.

It would have made our task as editors much easier if we had confronted a field where most of the important areas had been explored and analyzed. But this is not the case – the very fact that we draw so much on our own research in limited areas makes the volume atypical – and our major aim is to point to the areas of media research which have been ignored, despite a proliferation of research institutes, commissions and grants. We hope to interest enough people to fill these gaps and get involved themselves in what is a very open research field. Consequently, the last Part of this book consists of suggestions for do-it-yourself research which can be carried out with very few resources. We believe that much mainstream media research is on the wrong lines; a major objective in putting this volume together is to suggest some new ones.

PART ONE

The process of selection

In terms of the dominant Commercial Laissez-Faire picture of the media, there is a common conception of news as an objective body of events which occur and which the journalist pursues, captures in his notebook or newsreel and takes back triumphantly to his editor. Objectivity consists in reproducing the real world as faithfully as possible. But even within the boundaries of this rather simple conception, it is obvious that it is not technically possible to reproduce all the events, to tell all the stories, to give every bit of information. So some selection must take place. Not all the events in the world, for instance, are of equal interest to the public; the newsman must therefore have a set of criteria, a 'news sense' with which to select his material.

The mass media, then, must operate with certain definitions of what is newsworthy. It is not that instruction manuals exist telling newsmen that certain subjects (drugs, sex, violence) will always appeal to the public or that certain groups (youth, celebrities, immigrants) should be continually exposed to scrutiny. Rather, there are built-in factors, ranging from the individual newsman's intuitive hunch about what constitutes a 'good story', through precepts such as 'give the public what it wants' to structured ideological biases, which predispose the media to make a certain event into news.

Selection according to 'structured ideological biases' is at the heart of the Mass Manipulative model but in the Commercial model and particularly in regard to phenomena classified as deviance or social problems, the criteria are seen to be more *intrinsic* to the material. The two interrelated and apparently simple concepts of 'unusual-ness' and 'human interest' are the most frequently used to explain the quality of the news which does appear. Thus Leslie Wilkins, in his attempt to understand how information modifies the definition of deviance,* states that unusualness is simply a property character-ized by events which deviate to a certain degree from normal

* Where no numbered footnote is indicated, the reference is to the relevant selection in this book. Numbered references appear at the end of each article.

behaviour. With only a slightly different emphasis, Bob Roshier finds that unusualness, seriousness, human interest and drama are the sort of factors involved in the selection of criminal events as worthy of reporting. Clearly, unusualness alone is not sufficient: it might be unusual for red-haired men to appear on drunken driving charges but this is hardly of concern to anyone. The unusual must also be of interest, or judged to be of interest by commercial standards.

The journalist then, in the Commercial model of the media, must ideally reproduce, without bias or personal prejudice, events, information and opinions which are unusual and of interest to his audience. His role is to supply, as efficiently as possible, the demand for news.

Problems occur at this point, though, for who really judges that certain social problems are of 'human interest' and others not? Whose interest is involved and how does one find out about it? And what precisely is meant by such terms as 'unusual'? Robert Cirino, whose case is that the American news media use bias, distortion and censorship to manipulate public opinion, notes that the journalist does not merely make an inspired guess about the potential interest of an item. Powerful commercial and political interests direct his attention to particular issues while shutting out his awareness of others. The massive deaths from lung cancer caused by cigarette smoking, widespread poverty, environmental pollution and the inadequate safety precautions in cars which result in unnecessarily severe road accidents are four of the many areas cited by Cirino as being (presumably) of acute public concern, but which had been systematically ignored by the American mass media. To take an example of a different order from this country: for some two years before the story became big news in the conventional media, most working journalists knew (and *Private Eye* had already published) the information about the Home Secretary Mr Maudling's suspicious financial involvements which was to lead to his resignation in 1972. The more left-wing adherents of the Mass Manipulative model would argue that news is not selected according to public interests but rather delivered in a biased fashion supportive of the *status quo* of power and interest. Many unusual and startling events are concealed for a considerable period of time before other events force some discussion of them, while many 'events' such as comments of politicians, amazing only in their lack of surprise and interest, are reported in great detail. As far as this argument is concerned, there can be little doubt that the degree of oligopolization of the mass media in both this country and the United States is considerable. For example, Graham Murdock[1] in a survey of the British media industry has shown the very high existing concentration of ownership. He calculates that four corporations (Reed International, EMI, ATC, and Beaverbrook Newspapers) closely linked by inter-locking directorships and shareholdings account for:

> 48 per cent of all newspaper circulation; 40·5 per cent of the audience for commercial television; 42 per cent of the total record market; a substantial and growing proportion of film production and exhibition; the only commercial radio station currently in operation; in addition to sizeable interests in paper, print, catering, hotels, theatres, bingo, dancing, gaming, book publishing, electronics and consumer durables.

But to point to the concentration of ownership of the mass media and its overlap with wider industrial and commercial interests is only a partial critique of the Commercial model. The model depends to an extent on the notion of a free market for news, namely that the mass media are merely in the business of supplying the demand for news, and wherever a particular desire for certain information grows to a size that is commercially feasible, a section of the media will develop in order to cater for it. Such competition between news sources cannot occur in a situation where ownership is in a few hands. But – the defenders of the commercial position will retort – such a situation, although real in terms of the limited number of news outlets, does not imply that the various magazines, newspapers and broadcasting stations will not compete among each other in order to increase their respective audiences. The owners are only interested in maximizing specific audiences – and thus advertising revenue – and they maintain a commercial laissez-faire rather than a dictatorial relationship to their editors. Ownership of the means of transmitting news does not imply control of the criteria of the selection of news.

To counter this would demand proof of discernible processes of censorship and control which govern the selection of news and its presentation in ways which are both unvaried and supportive of élite or conservative positions. Some evidence along these lines is provided in an influential article by Johan Galtung and Mari Ruge. They list – eclectically, rather than from a clearly Manipulative model – a series of factors found to be criteria of newsworthiness in the selection of foreign news. Two groups of factors are relevant to our discussion of deviance and social problems: *bureaucratic* and *ideational*.

In terms of bureaucratic criteria Galtung and Ruge state that an item of news is more likely to be reported if its frequency is similar to that of the media. That is, a daily newspaper will preferentially describe stories that occur within a period of a day – or if a news item takes longer to develop it will only report its climaxes. This criterion may be termed *periodicity*. Similarly, definite proportions of a newspaper will be allocated to varying types of news (e.g., crime, foreign, sport): the threshold for incorporating into the paper a particular type of news will depend on the relative scarcity of this sort of news at that time. All in all, the standard *composition* or balance between different types of news will be maintained – despite the variation of occurrences in the real world.

Among the ideational factors of significance are *consonance* and *expectedness*. An item will be more readily assimilated if it is consonant with the mental set or image of the newsman. As a corollary to this, new events without immediate precedent may be assimilated into the frame of reference of earlier accepted images. For example, Galtung cites how the Norwegian Broadcasting Company interpreted the Russian invasion of Czechoslovakia in terms of the previous invasion of Hungary.[2] Similarly, Graham Murdock, in his paper in Part Two of this book, notes how the October 27th 1968 Vietnam demonstration in London was cast in the scenario of the May events in Paris or the demonstrations surrounding the Chicago Convention, both occurring earlier that year. Within the factor of consonance, however, it is the *unexpected* that will be preferentially selected. That is, an unusual event in terms of the media's definition of usualness will find itself in the news.

It is not difficult to apply these bureaucratic and ideational factors to the selection of deviance and social problem news, say about crime, suicide, drug-taking, political corruption, pornography or pollution. What Galtung and Ruge importantly suggest is that the organizational set-up for gathering news has profound effects in determining the acceptability of incoming information. In other words, that bureaucratic exigencies mediate between events and the news. This formulation, however over-mechanistic one might find it, recognizes that journalists are not merely tools in the invisible hand of the newsmarket – as the extreme Commercial model would have it – but play a much more active, selective role. Moreover – to invoke the ideational dimension – they are creatively selecting and interpreting events to fit their preconceived models of the social universe. In a real sense the court correspondent going through the daily list, the crime reporter phoning up the police desk, the London editor of the TV news deciding whether to run an item on a Birmingham bank robbery, the editor selecting a news story on abortion statistics as suitable for an editorial: all are involved in *making* news.

This view of the media as active agents and not passive recipients or gatherers obviously goes against the Commercial model. But equally, it raises problems for the Manipulative model which presents an over-simplified view of the domination of owners and controllers over creators. It, too, ignores the organizational and ideational mediations. Moreover, bias – which no doubt does exist, as our readings in Part Two demonstrate – may not *necessarily* be impelled by a conscious machiavellianism. Along with the more blatant censorship by others – which operates very much in such areas as violence and sex – goes the more important 'self censorship' of the journalist as he systematically attempts to fit events into a particular world view whose basic premises he sees as embodying a faithful portrayal of society. So-called 'objectivity' becomes a matter of interpreting and analysing the event dispassionately in the light of the accepted paradigm of 'how things happen', and 'what the social universe looks like'. That the paradigm itself may be false is a question which occurs on very rare occasions.

Paul Rock, in his paper in this section, explores the nature of news as an organized response to routine bureaucratic problems. He expands on the criteria such as those used by Galtung and Ruge, noting how the demand for a regular news intake of a consistent and reliable nature leads to the mass media feeding off each other. Their shared product becomes reified as possessing an especially 'objective' quality but this is within the series of close relationships between official news generating agencies. Rock illustrates with great clarity how news consists of the unusual event occurring within the rubric of the 'usual' characterizations of journalists and press officers. The paradigm of the usual 'taken for granted' world view of the journalist becomes stylized into a number of almost reflexive clichés evoked effortlessly in the face of the deluge of events which face him in his work. In his fine satirical novel set in some futuristic research institute, Michael Frayn simply carries this notion to its logical conclusion by conjuring up the idea of a digital computer which could effortlessly produce entertaining news without any contact with 'the raw, messy offendable real world' at all.

But, granted that the bureaucratic structure of the media demands a well-timed, correctly phrased product, where does the *content* of the stereotypes used in this selection and packaging of events come from? Stuart Hall tackles this problem of the implicit and unstated rules of journalism, by examining one of its products, the daily radio news, in the light of the ideological significance of its characterizations. Its basic model of society is that of a democratic consensus where a considerable measure of agreement occurs over the legitimate nature of the existing political and economic arrangements. This paradigm might in fact 'work' for many events but the problems and contradictions arise when the media are asked to explain those groups and phenomena which explicitly deny this consensual world view, for example, Black Power, the New Left, unofficial strikes, the Gay Liberation Movement, the formation of prisoners' unions. To face this challenge, the media adopt an analysis – and hence, implicitly, a mode of selection – which defuses the reality of alternative conceptions of social order. It does not allow such phenomena an integrity of their own, but instead characterizes them as 'meaningless', 'immature' or 'senseless', as involving a *misunderstanding* of reality rather than an alternative interpretation of its nature. Thus Hall finds in the structures used to select and analyse events in the mass media important ideological significance for the maintenance of the *status quo* of power and interest.

So the picture that emerges of the selection process is one in which the newsman actively squeezes events into categories suitable for the smooth running of the media bureaucracy as well as ideologically significant in upholding a particular world view. Among the many lines of analysis which are as yet indistinct and conjectural is the socialization of the journalist into this mode of operation. How does he learn the correct methods of analysis? What sanctions and rewards are used to achieve this end? To what extent is he sceptical of his role? To what measure is there a contradiction between his face-to-face contact with events on his journalistic assignments and the standardized news story demanded of him? It is important to understand, for example, the institutionalized bad faith which journalism, perhaps more than any other occupation, is prone to. Over the years we have been interviewed on numerous occasions by reporters on such matters as the 'drug problem' and the 'violence problem'; each time we have been earnestly assured that the reporter privately absolutely agrees with our views, is determined to write up a fair and balanced story, is only taking an aggressive and philistine line of questioning to put himself in the hypothetical position of his readers and viewers, and that any distortion or unfair selection which appears is the fault of sub-editors, producers and other such nasties. And when the highly selective story does appear or the taped interview judiciously edited, we know that it is too simple to dismiss all reporters as either fools or knaves, a judgement which this book certainly does not set out to propagate. But where does the responsibility lie?

These sorts of questions – and their extensions to the organization and other levels[3] – should be priorities in media research as a whole and the problem of selection in particular.

REFERENCES

1. G. Murdock, 'The ownership and control of the mass media in contemporary Britain', unpublished paper.
2. Cited in J. Halloran, P. Elliott and G. Murdock, *Demonstrations and communications* (Harmondsworth, Penguin Books, 1970), p. 26.
3. For a recent study on the organizational experience of journalists, see Jeremy Tunstall, *Journalists at work* (London, Constable, 1971).

Information and the definition of deviance*

LESLIE WILKINS

The experience which forms the basis for classification of usual and unusual events is obtained in different ways and its content will differ. Experience is coded and stored as information, this the mind retrieves from the store as and when required. In the retrieval process the information may become distorted owing to its interaction with other information stored at earlier periods. Some discussion of the ways in which information influences classifications of deviance is necessary in presenting the general theory.

It would appear that information may be classified for the current purpose according to three types of consideration:

      (a) content
      (b) amount
      (c) channel

By 'channel' is meant the different means of receiving information, particularly the difference between directly and indirectly received information. Some information may be regarded as trivial because of its content, or it may have no impact because the amount was small or the channel through which the information was received regarded as unreliable. What is regarded as trivial will relate to the perception of the culture in which the observer lives as much as to the degree of unusualness.

As an example of the trivial, but perhaps also unusual, the following might suffice. If I am unaccustomed to eating without wearing a jacket, I will perceive a person so eating as acting 'abnormally'. According to my interpretation of the action in relation to the culture and my status within the culture I may take a different seat at the restaurant, go to a different restaurant, or demand that the person be arrested! In general the dimension of 'unusualness' and the dimension of triviality will be negatively correlated. It is difficult to think of something that would be defined by every person as a

*Extract from Leslie T. Wilkins, *Social deviance: social policy, action and research* (London, Tavistock, 1964), pp. 59–65.

trivial deviation from normality but that, at the same time, is an extremely rarely observed deviation. If an event or an act committed by any person is *sufficiently* rare, the rare nature of the event would normally be taken to imply lack of triviality. If I have never seen a thing in my life before, and it is very different from anything else I have ever seen, I am not likely to regard the matter as trivial unless I have other information to confirm the triviality.

A shopkeeper who notes that 2 per cent of his annual turnover seems to disappear in unaccountable ways may perceive this as normal, although he may know that it is due to shoplifting and staff pilfering. Depending upon his experience of variation about the 2 per cent, he may define 3 per cent loss as abnormal and take action which could result in an increase in the number of reported crimes, and perhaps also of arrested criminals.

It will be obvious that the hypothetical shopkeeper would adjust his behaviour and his definitions if he had further information regarding his expected losses. If, for example, he knew that the majority of stores in his particular chain experienced, say, only 1 per cent unaccountable loss, he would begin to consider ways and means of reducing his losses (2 per cent) to around the average or adjusted perception of 'normal' figures for his company. If he had other information enabling him to point to other 'abnormalities' in his district or type of trade, it might be possible that the two abnormalities would be perceived to cancel out to a total situation representing 'normality'.

As another example of the influence of information on the perception of normality, consider the following experience of the author. Rather late one Saturday evening he was returning to his home from central London. He joined a bus queue, which seemed to him to consist of some six or seven tough and probably delinquent gang members. He inferred this from the way they stood, and particularly from the manner of their dress. They had not spoken. His knowledge of the delinquent sub-culture did not relieve him of certain feelings of anxiety, or at least of a defensive attitude towards the members of the group. However, immediately they spoke he was able completely to modify his perception of 'abnormality' or deviance of the group – they spoke in French. From his knowledge of the habitual dress of French youth on holiday in England, he was able to fit this apparently 'deviant' behaviour and dress symbolism into a 'normal' or expected context. It would seem, therefore, that we may claim that what is defined as deviant is determined by our subjective experience of 'non-deviant' or 'normal', but that our experience and the resulting classifications can be changed by certain types of information. It would appear that information acts upon our expectations through our storage system and modifies the classifications which provide the basis for our prediction of behaviour.

The amount of information may influence the base against which events are considered with regard to their unusualness. The more odd experiences I may have, the less odd they will seem to be. The quantity of information available to an individual may increase his tolerance because it may increase the range of his experience of all forms of behaviour, or it may decrease his tolerance because his experience has been limited to more of the same kinds of observation. The shopkeeper may, for example, be tolerant of a loss of 2 per cent if he has information that only two or three other stores in his chain have a lower rate, but he may be less tolerant if he has information only from those with the lower rates; in the latter case his information is not only less but also biased. Increase in tolerance of events which would otherwise be defined as deviant is not a direct function of increased knowledge.

In recent years technological advance has mainly resulted in speedier communications between places in different parts of the world; highways, railways, and air travel have increased the range of communications both between nationalities and cultures and between different sub-cultures within the same nation. The shopkeeper of the 2 per cent loss store can no longer be unaware of the loss rate of other stores. The behaviour of people living in groups in what were once far-away mountains is now observable by tourists, administrators, and social agencies. In times gone by, deviant groups were able to establish their own cultures with reference only to their own sets of norms. Except for the intrusion of an occasional itinerant anthropologist they were left without contact with the norms of other societies. There have been numerous cultures where the total definitions of normality were out of accord with existing Western values. It was not until the increase in transportion and the increased speed of movement brought these communities into contact with other communities having different concepts of normality that their deviance was defined. The definition of 'deviance' was, of course, provided by the more powerful forces.

TYPES OF INFORMATION

Let us refer to the analogy of bridges. In total, the experience of bridges possessed by the population in 1600 would be much smaller than the experience of bridges possessed by the population today. The base of experience to which any new bridge could be referred for comparison by persons living in 1600 would be a sample of a much smaller (n) than would be the case now. The increase in speed

of transport has increased the sample of bridges available to the
population. The individual who travels widely will personally travel
over and *directly* experience a large number of bridges in addition to
those he may read about in the press. But the increase in travel may
not be expected to increase his direct experience of crime. This is an
example of a general point. The experience people have of *things* has
tended to increase rapidly – things have to be extremely unusual to
occasion surprise today. But the base of experience of *people* available by which we may be able to assess *people* may have diminished.
In the village community were included all kinds of people, but the
modern housing development tends to be limited in both class structure and age. There are communities where hardly an elderly person
can be seen on the streets, and there are zones where children do not
play in the public places. In the small local communities the farmer
and the labourer and even the slave in feudal times were in direct
contact with each other. Today more selective living is possible.
The middle and upper classes do not necessarily *have* to know how
the working classes live. There is no need even to give them their
orders directly. Intermediary communications systems have been
established so that the direct contact which was essential in earlier
times is not now required.

The telephone makes it possible to talk to people without personally seeing them; the fact that even the lowest social classes can now
be expected to read means that they may be sent letters and forms
to complete. The administration may ask them whether they have a
bathroom or not without seeing (and smelling) for itself. The insane,
the criminal, and the deviant can now be isolated from society so
that the normal members of the culture do not gain any experience
of the non-normal. The unpleasant smell of the bathroomless homes
contaminates a different sector of the town from that where the
authorities concerned are likely to live. Even a world authority in
criminology may not necessarily ever meet a criminal in order to
become informed or to keep up to date.

In earlier times the young and the old were continuously in touch
with each other; youth was aware of the problems of age, and age
was aware of the problems of youth. The village was aware of the
problems of mental deficiency – each village had its village idiot
who was part of the total culture. Everybody knew 'Jack' who stood
at the corner of the cross-roads and drooled. The newcomer to the
village might feel threatened by Jack's behaviour, but immediately
he spoke with a member of the village culture he would be assured,
'Oh! Jack's all right, he's just a little weak in the head – he was
dropped on it when a baby.' Thus, apart from indirect experience
derived from newspapers and other mass media, our modern culture

has led to the isolation (and alienation) of deviant groups. The nature of the information obtained from direct experience and that obtained from mass media differs in both quality and type. The sample of experience obtained in the village contains different information, covers a wider range, and is of a different order from information indirectly obtained in the urban environment.

In urban societies the isolation of deviants has become institutionalized. Even the direct experience of one social class by visits for 'charitable purposes' has been reduced so that the paid social worker, quietly and decently, away from the normal citizen, is charged with the pacification of Jack, and the society has lost its direct information about and feeling for the problems of mental deficiency. The wealthy have moved from the downtown areas and have lost their direct experience of the problems of the idle youth, and so on. This is not merely a replacement of face-to-face communication and the information derived from such situations by other means, but a quantitative and qualitative change in the nature of the information. Clues may be picked up in face-to-face communication covering many dimensions and the information related to the situations which occur in a wide variety of ways. In a real sense members of the urban culture have suffered a *loss of information*, even though Jack may now be better cared for than previously. If it were possible for the urban culture to receive the *same type and quantity* of information regarding deviants as is obtained in the village, it might be possible for the urban cultures to accept a greater range of deviance. But, as will be noted later, the difference between rural and urban communication systems (face-to-face as compared with mass media and the like) necessarily involves also a difference in the type and the quantity of information received.

No value judgements are made here: we merely wish to bring out the point that information is a factor to be considered in explanations of definitions of deviance, and of societies' reactions to it. Value systems come into this discussion when we consider the mechanisms which people have constructed to insulate themselves from information – the ways in which societies' defects and shortcomings may be hidden because the deviants can be isolated and information regarding them rejected and distorted.

If the information individuals within a social system receive about the workings and expectations of the system is biased, they will be robbed of reinforcement of their definitions of normality. The effect of propaganda has been well documented in this regard. The individual's store of information, which serves as the reference for individual definitions of normal and abnormal behaviour, is today easily derived from the mass media. The larger units of society do not provide a set of information sufficiently varied for the individual to rely upon his own direct experience except within some limited range of activities. The average middle-class citizen living in the urban environment may be supposed to have information from his own experience, plus the information he derives from newspapers that is defined by their editors as 'newsworthy'. . . . The model

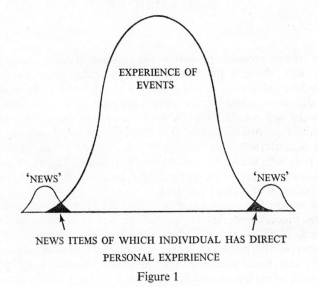

NEWS ITEMS OF WHICH INDIVIDUAL HAS DIRECT PERSONAL EXPERIENCE

Figure 1

used to describe deviant behaviour may perhaps be used to describe the differences between the nature of 'news' and the nature of information derived directly by experience, as shown in *Figure 1*. The region of overlap, where the individual has both direct experience of events and the experience of reading the news presentation of the same event, provides a check on the validity of the press comment and a base-line for the integration of the two types of information into a coherent 'experience' information set against which further events may be matched. Where there is no common ground between the two types of information intake, there may be a tendency to sum them simply together, ignoring the difference.

The selection of
crime news by the press*

BOB ROSHIER

There are two processes at work in the selection of crime news by the press: first, there is the extent to which crime news is actually selected for publication in competition with other categories of news; secondly, there is the way in which particular types of crimes (and criminals) are selected for publication out of the total pool of potentially reportable crime (i.e. officially recorded crime). This study is concerned with both processes. An additional underlying concern is with the impact of this double process of selection on the recipients of crime news, in particular its effect, if any, on public perceptions of crime and criminals.

The reason for these concerns is that they are tied up with the general process whereby the 'official' picture of crime is itself constructed. For the nature of this crime picture is shaped by the decisions of the public to report potential criminal events to the police, and these decisions are obviously influenced by public definitions of the nature and extent of crime. In turn, these definitions are likely to be influenced by the type of information fed back to the public through the mass media (since most people very rarely actually experience crime except in this secondhand way). In other words, it is at least plausible that the selective portrayal of crime in the mass media plays an important part in shaping public definitions of the 'crime problem' and hence also its 'official' definition. This can be explored by comparing the relationship between the three different definitions of the nature of crime and criminals: that shared by the public, that portrayed in the official statistics and that portrayed in the mass media. This study attempts to do this, in a limited way, with reference to press portrayals of crime and criminals.

The first process of selection (of crime news in preference to other types of news) is examined through quantitative measures of the amount of news space devoted to crime. In addition, these measures have been repeated for different time periods when the crime rates were different and moving in opposite directions, in order to see whether these variations were reflected in the levels of crime news

*Paper prepared especially for this volume.

coverage. This was done in order to check one possible manifestation of media influences on public and official definitions suggested
by Leslie Wilkins' concept of *deviance amplification*.[1] One aspect
of this process is that during periods of rising crime rates, feedback
of information about this rise increases public sensitivity to crime
which is reflected in increased reporting, hence amplifying the
initial increase. Since the media are the main source of this information feedback, the theory suggests that rising crime rates should be
accompanied by increased media concern and coverage, and vice-
versa.

The second process of crime news selection is the way in which
particular types of crimes, criminals and circumstances are selected
for reporting. Where possible, the 'facts' portrayed in this way have
been compared with the 'facts' as they appear in the criminal
statistics to see whether there are any consistent variations. In
addition, an attempt is made, through a qualitative analysis, to
assess the common underlying factors which appear to account for
the way in which news items are selected.

The study is based on a content analysis of crime news in the press
(still the most detailed purveyor of crime news) and concentrates on
three national dailies – the *Daily Mirror,* the *Daily Express* and the
Daily Telegraph together with the *Newcastle Journal* (an important
local daily newspaper in the area where this study was carried out).
Some further information was collected from the Sundays, in
particular the *News of the World.* The period covered was September
1967 (September to November for the Sundays). The same information was also collected for the national dailies (and some for the
News of the World) for September 1955 and September 1938.
These two years were chosen to see what quantitative and qualitative
changes in press coverage had taken place since the present post-
war 'crime wave' really got under way, and to test the 'amplification'
hypothesis. 1955 was chosen since it was the last year of a five-year
period during which the crime rate had been declining. Hence this
would give useful comparative information as to how press coverage
was influenced by a downward trend in crime rates. The information
collected was: percentage of news space (i.e., total space minus
advertisements) devoted to crime news, types of crime reported,
stage at which items were reported (pre- or post-arrest), sentences
given and information on offenders (age, sex and social class).
In addition, information was collected on qualitative aspects of
crime reporting. An attempt was made to classify the factors associated with the newsworthiness of crimes, and to assess how factually
or otherwise crime news items were dealt with.

To supplement the content analysis data, a postal questionnaire was sent to a random sample of the adult population of Newcastle upon Tyne. This was used to assess public perceptions of crime and criminals using as far as possible the same variables as were measured in the content analysis. Also, the respondents were asked directly about their perceptions of crime reporting in the newspapers they read.

Finally, the official *Criminal Statistics* for each of the years were used for comparative purposes in relation to both the content analysis data and the survey data.

In the first section of the questionnaire respondents were asked various questions about the crime news in the newspapers they read. They were asked whether they thought their newspapers

(i) contained too much/too little/about right amount of crime news?

(ii) made crime appear attractive and profitable?

(iii) were too sympathetic/too hard/neither/on criminals?

(iv) made heroes out of criminals?

(v) put ideas into people's heads about how to commit crimes?

(vi) increase/decrease/have no effect/on people's tendencies to commit crime?

On all these questions the majority of each readership group (with the exception of *News of the World* readers) took the favourable view of their newspapers. A majority of *News of the World* readers thought that their newspapers contained too much crime and gave people ideas about how to commit crime. On the other variables the majority took the favourable view. These generally favourable findings are in marked contrast to the findings of a recent National Opinion Poll survey which showed, for example, that 70 per cent of respondents thought press coverage of crime increased criminal tendencies.[2] However, there is an important difference: in the National Opinion Poll study respondents were critical of 'the press' in general while in this study they were replying in relation to the newspapers they themselves read (there was evidence in the questionnaires that they differentiated the two). Thus, although people view the press in general unfavourably, they view their own newspapers favourably. Paradoxically, this seems to apply whichever newspapers they read (including the *News of the World* for most of the variables).

The respondents were also asked what crimes they thought their newspapers concentrated on and this was checked against what they actually concentrated on. In most cases there was very little relationship between the two. The exception, once again, were *News of the World* readers who were remarkably accurate (and not just because they got sex crimes right). I will return to this point later.

Finally, the respondents were asked to estimate what percentage of the total news space in their newspapers was devoted to crime news. Interestingly, in all cases the estimates were wildly high. For all readership groups the mean estimate was at least four times the actual figure (this was despite the fact that the legal definition of crime used in this study meant that the newspaper figures were, if anything, an over-estimate since they included a substantial proportion of minor offences which might well not have been viewed as 'crime' by the readers). There is one obvious explanation for this: people perceive more crime in their newspapers than there actually is because they are more likely to read it. In fact, there is some evidence to support this view. In the various 'reading and noting' studies that have been carried out crime items were among those which obtained high 'thorough readership' scores. As James Curran[3] has pointed out, there is a marked discrepancy between what people actually read in their newspapers (human interest items with entertainment value) and what they say, in interviews, they think their newspapers ought to contain (serious social and political news items). This points to an interesting dilemma for the press which is rather well illustrated by the case of *News of the World* readers in this study.

The *News of the World* contained the highest proportion of crime news. Its readers were exceptionally accurate in assessing the types of crimes it reported, suggesting that it caters particularly well for their tastes and hence is read less selectively. This all adds up to a clear impression of a newspaper that knows what its readers want and is giving it to them (as indeed its circulation figures suggest). Yet alone among the newspapers considered, it had a clear majority of its readers who thought it had too much crime news in it. In addition, its readers were noticeably more censorious of the way it reported crime compared with the other newspapers. It seems unlikely that the *News of the World* has recruited among its readers a majority of moral crusaders dedicated to its reform. A more likely conclusion is that there is a discrepancy between what *News of the World* readers say they want of their newspaper with what they actually read in it. Further, it suggests that people feel guilty about what they read in their newspapers and that one of the categories they read and feel guilty about is crime. If this is true it has rather ominous implications for newspaper producers: if they concentrate on what people actually read and hence presumably want to buy, they are likely simultaneously to incur the maximum public disapproval.

These findings have an important implication for the main concerns of this study. That is, whatever the quantity of crime news

contained in the newspapers, it is more significant in terms of readership than the simple quantitative measure suggests. In fact, as can
be seen from the table, the actual percentages are very small for all
the newspapers for all three periods. The exception, once again, is
the *News of the World*, especially in the earlier periods. One criticism
of this type of data is that simple quantitative measures such as
these ignore the prominence that may be given to the items (such as
large headlines and position on front page). Consequently, an
'attention score' (devised by R. Budd)[4] was calculated for each
crime news item. The overall findings were that, on average, crime
news items were not especially prominently displayed in any of the
newspapers.

From the point of view of quantitative coverage the figures give
little support to the amplification hypothesis suggested earlier. The
figures for the dailies seem to have remained surprisingly stable, while
for the *News of the World* there has been a marked decline, particularly since 1955. Thus the post-war 'crime wave' does not seem to
have been accompanied by an increase in press coverage, nor was
the decline in the official rate between 1950 and 1955 accompanied by
a decrease. This, of course, does not deny the amplification hypothesis. However, it does suggest that it is not simply a matter of
feedback of increasing amounts of information in the form of crime
news items.

It has been suggested to me that the small amount of crime in
the national press reflects the fact that it is the local press that is
the main purveyor of crime news. This certainly did not appear to be
the case in this study for the *Newcastle Journal* whose pattern of
crime coverage was very similar to the national press (despite
reporting predominantly crime in the north east). However, the
Journal is an unusual local newspaper in that it is a daily with a
large circulation over a relatively wide area. In these respects it is
closer to a national newspaper than a local. It may well be that the
more directly local press does play this role.

For all the newspapers for all three periods, the relative frequency
with which different types of crime were reported bore no relationship to their relative frequency in the *Criminal Statistics*. This
applied even when motoring offences (which account for two thirds
of official crime) were excluded from both sets of figures. On these
data, an interesting finding was that the types of crime over-reported
remained constant for all newspapers for all three periods. These
were: all crimes against the person, robbery, fraud, blackmail and
drugs (1967 only). However, the only crime very markedly over-
reported was murder (including manslaughter). An important
point is that in all the newspapers a substantial proportion of the

TABLE 1

PERCENTAGE OF TOTAL NEWS SPACE
(MINUS ADVERTISEMENTS) DEVOTED TO
CRIME NEWS, FEATURES AND ARTICLES

Newspaper	Sept. *1938*	Sept. *1955*	Sept. *1967*
Daily Mirror	5·6	7·0	5·6
Daily Express	4·4	5·6	4·4
Daily Telegraph	3·5	3·4	2·4
Newcastle Journal	—	—	2·0
News of the World	17·8	29·1	11·0*

*Sept.–Nov.

total (up to one third) consisted of a wide variety of trivial offences. The only very significant variation between newspapers was the very high proportion of sex crimes in the *News of the World*, although even this was only really marked in 1967 when it accounted for one third of the total (as against less than 5 per cent for all the other newspapers). The general conclusion, however, was that the newspapers do give a distorted impression of the relative frequency of different types of crime and that this distortion is in the direction of over-representation of more serious offences (or offences of serious topical concern in the case of drugs). If this seems a rather obvious finding, it is worth pointing out that this was not found to be the case in a study of Oslo newspapers by Ragnar Hauge.[5]

A unanimous tendency for all the newspapers was to concentrate on solved crimes. In all three periods all the newspapers included far more reports at the post-arrest stage than was warranted from the actual 'clear-up' rate. In addition, where sentences were reported, there was a very marked tendency, again in all cases, to over-report the more serious punishments, particularly imprisonment. In other words, all the newspapers gave an exaggerated impression of the chances of getting caught and, when caught, of getting a serious punishment. This is obviously relevant to the often-voiced view that the press glorifies crime or makes it appear attractive and profitable. From these data the opposite seems to be the case.

Very little information was usually given about offenders. The only information that could be at all consistently collected was sex, age and social class and in the last case this was only possible for the minority of offenders whose occupations were given. However, on these characteristics it was obviously possible for the news-

T.M.O.N.—B

papers to give a false impression of offenders. In fact, once again there was considerable consistency both between newspapers and over the three periods. The sex ratio of reported offenders was very close to the official picture. The age structure, on the other hand, over-represented older, adult offenders. Finally, there was a consistent tendency to over-report higher social class offenders. The last two findings are of particular interest since they are perhaps the opposite of what might be expected from a more jaundiced view of newspapers (although they do fit in with the findings of Ragnar Hauge's study of Oslo newspapers). It seems, then, that the press does not exaggerate the extent of youthful crime, nor does it purvey a lower-class stereotype of offenders as has sometimes been suggested (at least, not in simple quantitative terms).

In general, then, two main conclusions emerge: first, that newspapers do give a distorted impression of crime and criminals through their process of selection (although not always in the way that might be expected): secondly, that these distortions show remarkable consistency both over time and between newspapers.

An attempt was also made to assess some of the qualitative aspects of crime reporting. First, why are some crimes selected in preference to others? What are the factors associated with newsworthiness?

From those aspects which were 'played up' in the reports, it was possible to discern four sets of factors:

(1) The seriousness of the offence. Sometimes this, on its own, would account for the newsworthiness (although usually only in the case of murders or large-scale robberies).

(2) 'Whimsical' circumstances, i.e. humorous, ironic, unusual. Examples are items headed:
'Flower people take blooms in raid on cemetery.'
'Jail man's first job – in a bank!'
'Thief pinches detective car.'
'Bank was tricked by boy of ten.'
This category, perhaps surprisingly, seemed to be probably the most important in relation to crime reporting in general.

3. Sentimental or dramatic circumstances. These could be associated with either the victim or the offender, arousing feelings of either sympathy or outrage:
'Boys take Arthur's budgies. 25 years' work ruined.'
'Mother lied to protect daughter.'
'Man pleads in vain for woman who cheated him.'

4. The involvement of a famous or high status person in any capacity (although particularly as offender or victim).

It is impossible to quantify these categories separately, since they were usually involved in varying mixtures in particular reports. They seem to account for nearly all the reports in the *Daily Mirror* and the *News of the World*, the vast majority in the *Daily Express* and a large proportion in the *Daily Telegraph*. The last mentioned, however, did have a substantial proportion of reports which did not seem to be accounted for by any of these factors or, indeed, by any factors which differentiated them from a multitude of similar offences which were not reported. Interestingly, the categories seemed to apply even more comprehensively in the earlier periods, particularly 1938. The earlier periods were also characterized by a greater concentration on drama and sentiment. This was generally the case, but an interesting example was the very much greater emphasis on suicide reports, with extracts from suicide notes (rarely reported in 1967). Reports with headlines such as: 'I prayed while he attacked me, sobs girl in court' which are difficult, although not impossible, to come by today, were quite commonplace in 1938 (with the exception of the *Daily Telegraph*, although even this newspaper was noticeably different in 1938).

'Sensationalism' in its usual sense of a contrived appeal to the 'baser' human emotions emerges from this as only one aspect of newsworthiness. Trivial, light entertainment is equally if not more important. In fact, anything which has entertainment value and contains human interest in the widest sense (appealing to the nobler as well as the baser human emotions) makes crime newsworthy. Indeed, if the evidence mentioned earlier is correct, this is what people want to read in their newspapers generally.

As this suggests, it is difficult to accuse any of the newspapers of taking a consistent line on crime reporting. There were, however, two notable exceptions: the reporting of drug offences and football hooliganism in all the newspapers in 1967. In these two categories there was a noticeable tendency to dramatize the seriousness and extensiveness of these problems and to publicize 'get tough' statements. In the case of football hooliganism this was achieved through various techniques such as grouping together a large number of separate (often trivial) offences in a wide variety of places into one report with a joint heading, '40 arrested in football riots', and also by publicizing statements from magistrates and football managers saying how serious the problem was and how something needed doing about it. This is not suggesting that there would be no football hooliganism problem without the press. It is suggesting, however, that the press does use the considerable power at its disposal to keep alive, direct and to some extent exaggerate the problem as it is purveyed to the public. Similarly, the approach to drug offences was universally condemnatory using everything from ridicule to spurious 'facts' and unsubstantiated opinions. The idea, again often voiced, that the press aggravates the drug problem by making drug use attractive or exciting did not gain support from a single item in this study. The important point about both these cases is that they suggest that there is a significant distinction between the way the press handles day-to-day, run-of-the-mill crime reporting (which usually includes most crime) and the way it handles areas of particular topical concern (the concern itself being, at least in part, a product of the press).

Another exception to the general points made so far was the *News of the World*. Although in all three periods the *News of the World* contained more sex crimes than the other newspapers, this was by far the most marked in 1967 (although in that year the total amount of crime news was much the lowest). But most interesting was the trend, over the three periods, towards a particularly characteristic style of reporting these crimes which makes it distinctive from all the other newspapers. 'Titillating' is perhaps the term which most people would use to describe this approach and, in fact, this is the term that most readily springs to mind from this study. It is achieved by the use of relatively long reports with a literary style that often carefully unfolds the plot like a novelette, with headlines which are suggestive without giving much away. A few examples from this period are:

LOVE IN THE SAND DUNES

DEEP IN THE SHADOWS SOMETHING STIRRED

THE PLOTTERS IN THE HOUSE OF SIN

THE STRIPPER, A P.C. AND A POWDER PUFF

A note was made of crime news items (and features) which expressed an opinion about the causes of or cures for crime in all the newspapers. The findings were very much in keeping with those of an earlier study by Peter Scott:[6] there is a great variety of often contradictory views expressed within any of the newspapers studied. This is not to deny an overall bais towards punitiveness or otherwise which may characterize particular newspapers. But there is a large amount of evidence today to suggest that people use the mass media selectively in such a way as to reinforce existing attitudes that they hold. The data here suggest that there is sufficient variety of implicit or explicit views in any of the newspapers to reinforce practically any viewpoint (although not always about particular offences, as the earlier data on drugs and football hooliganism suggested). This point is supported later by the lack of relationship between the overall bias of the newspapers studied and the views of their readers.

The final section of this study deals with public perceptions of crime and criminals and how these relate to newspaper presentations on the one hand and the official picture in the *Criminal Statistics* on the other. The overall finding is that public perceptions do not seem to be influenced by the biases in their newspapers but, in fact, are surprisingly close to the official picture.

First, however, respondents were asked what crimes they thought were the most serious. Most of the crimes selected were also those that were over-reported in the newspapers. The exceptions were robbery and fraud which were not rated as particularly serious. In general, though, there was some evidence that the newspapers concentrated on the crimes which their readers view as particularly serious.

Respondents were then asked to rate the relative frequency with which different types of offence occurred. These were then compared with the relative frequencies in the newspapers they read and in the *Criminal Statistics*. In all cases the estimates were very much closer to the official picture (they were surprisingly accurate in this respect). The accuracy was positively related to the socio-economic status of the respondents, but all groups correlated strongly with the official picture. Also, insofar as the different readership groups did differ from the *Criminal Statistics* they were not in the direction that would be expected from their newspapers' deviations.

One area where respondents were closer to their newspapers was in their estimates of the percentage of crimes cleared up. All groups over-estimated the clear-up rate. This is in keeping with the fact that all the newspapers over-represented solved crimes.

On the characteristics of offenders there was again very little relationship between readers' views and their newspapers' presentations. All groups tended to slightly over-estimate the relative frequency of female crime compared with the official picture, while their newspapers did not. Their estimates of the relative propensity of the different age groups to commit crime was close to the official picture, while their newspapers over-represented older offenders. On the social class of offenders, there was some evidence that respondents did over-estimate the extent of crime among the higher status groups (compared with the official picture, although in this case the official picture is not itself very clear). This was in line with their newspaper portrayals, but the tendency was not very marked.

In general, then, on these characteristics public perceptions of crime and criminals appeared to be very more much influenced by the official picture than by their newspapers. This is more or less encouraging depending on how sceptically one views the meaningfulness of the official picture. However, there certainly seems to be very little evidence of any direct influence by the newspapers on their readers' views.

News of the World readers, however, presented an interesting case. They rated sexual crimes as being particularly serious and particularly frequent (there was in fact a general tendency to rate sexual crimes very high on these dimensions, but *News of the World* readers were the most marked). Thus, in one respect they did appear to share their newspaper's relative preoccupation with sex (although, as we saw earlier, they disapproved of this). Whether this reflects an influence by the *News of the World* on its readers, or whether it simply means that the *News of the World* caters particularly well for those who share an extreme form of a general preoccupation is impossible to say. However, in view of the other findings, the latter probably seems more likely.

Respondents were also asked what they thought was necessary to reduce the crime rate. Their answers were rated as 'predominantly punitive', 'predominantly reformative' or 'neutral'. In line with the National Opinion Poll findings the respondents were generally predominantly punitive. This, however, was strongly related to socio-economic status, the lower groups being markedly more punitive. Interestingly, it did not relate directly to the newspapers they read. Thus, for example, *Daily Mirror* readers far more frequently mentioned the need for the return of capital punishment than did *Daily Telegraph* readers despite the opposite policies of the two newspapers on this issue. The difference was entirely accounted for by the different socio-economic status of the readership groups. Once again, then, it appears that newspaper presentations have not been very influential on their readers' views.

Well over 90 per cent of respondents agreed that the crime rate had been rising in recent years and a generally high level of concern about 'the crime problem' was reflected in the answers to the previously mentioned question. This has obvious implications for the 'amplification' question. Although the rising crime rate had not been reflected in increased crime reporting it was clear that the increase had been more than adequately conveyed to the public. This was presumably through the communication of crime trends in the official *Criminal Statistics* (hence the general accuracy of public perceptions). It is still possible, then, that feedback of official information may play a significant amplifying function.

In conclusion, the findings in this study suggest that although the press do present a consistently biased impression of crime and criminals through their process of selection, there is little evidence to suggest that this is very influential on public perceptions of, and opinions about, these phenomena. In general the findings support the view that the simple deterministic conception of the effects of the mass media whether on attitudes, knowledge or behaviour grossly underestimates the abilities of the recipients to differentiate and interpret the information they receive. Not only do they not confuse media fiction with reality but nor, it seems from this study, do they take media presentations of real events to be necessarily representative of reality.

References

1. L. T. Wilkins, *Social deviance* (London, Tavistock, 1964).
2. *National Opinion Poll, Attitudes towards crime, violence and permissiveness in society* (1971).
3. J. Curran, 'The impact of television on the audience for national newspapers 1945–68', in J. Tunstall (ed.), *Media sociology* (London, Constable, 1970).
4. R. W. Budd, 'Attention score: a device for measuring news "play"', *Journalism Quarterly* Vol. 41, No. 2 (Iowa, 1964).
5. R. Hauge, 'Crime and the press', in N. Christie (ed.), *Scandinavian studies in criminology* Vol. 1 (London, Tavistock, 1965).
6. P. D. Scott, 'Public opinion and juvenile delinquency', *British Journal of Delinquency* (July 1950).

Bias through selection and omission: automobile safety, smoking*

ROBERT CIRINO

One of the most effective and easy ways of implanting bias is one that the public could never be aware of. We have no way of knowing what news stories the editors decide not to print on any given day. We cannot see the film or the interview segments that were not selected for inclusion in the day's news. Newspapers handle more news than any other news medium, yet what finally ends up in the paper is only a small portion of the news that is available. A large newspaper will receive more than a hundred photographs a day from the wire services plus many more from local sources and its own staff photographers. Only a few will be chosen as newsworthy: the public has no way of knowing which photographs were excluded. Radio and television must be even more selective than newspapers: naturally they cannot be expected to cover as much as newspapers. A three-minute radio news summary includes a small fraction of the available news; the public will just have to trust that the rest of the news was not as important.

Nobody could expect (or want) newspapers to print, or newscasts to broadcast, every bit of news they receive; it would be lengthy, costly, boring and chaotic. But we-the-public should be aware that many decisions are made by editors who select news in a way designed to support certain viewpoints, to be entertaining at the expense of 'hard' reality or not to antagonize the audience. Regardless of which reason, the bias that results is one that favours conservative view-points and the *status quo*. Chet Huntley admits how subjective these decisions are:

> In our sometimes zeal for shooting film with interesting façades and lovely landscapes, and in our fear of dullness and the low rating, we arbitrarily rule out a long and imposing list of awesome subjects and conclude that they were just not meant for television and radio.[1]

*Extracts from Robert Cirino, *Don't blame the people* (Los Angeles, Diversity Press, 1971).

A study of 1800 news items covered by *Huntley-Brinkley* and *Walter Cronkite* during two months in the summer of 1969 reveals a high percentage of entertaining but unimportant news items. Robert Macneil, former NCB correspondent studied in detail the three network television newscasts for a three-day period in 1967 and concluded:

> They perform wonders of technical competence, but their journalistic achievement is still erratic. Their content demonstrates capricious selection due not only to news judgment, but to the unshakable belief that picture must come first.[2]

One July morning in 1968, famous Hawaii disc jockey Aku-Head Pupule reported 'to the moment, the latest news of the world'. He told his KGMB listeners: 'Not much news. Ky and Johnson to meet – that's all.' On the local scene Aku mentioned that there had been seven traffic accidents. He wrapped it up quickly with a weather report and got back to the commercials and discs. Network news-on-the-hour is unquestionably more responsible than this, but a two-month study of 776 news items from Mutual and ABC shows that their selection of what is newsworthy is very capricious from a journalistic standpoint.

Professor Jack Lyle checked the selection of news by seven different television stations in Los Angeles. He found that together they covered a total of 103 stories, but only 5 of these appeared on all seven stations. Of the 103 stories, 65 were presented on only one station.[3] These different selections by these stations demonstrates clearly the capriciousness of the selections which determine for the public their view of the world for one day.

Our previous examination of the front pages of newspapers for three two-month periods in different years showed that what newspaper editors decide to put on the front page is governed by the same subjective political and commercial considerations that predominate in news broadcasting. The content of the rest of the newspaper is even more whimsically selected than the front page. . . .

In another study, ten daily newspapers together covered 69 different stories of national significance. A majority of the ten papers ran stories on only 7 of the 69 items. Only 3 of the 69 items were covered by all ten newspapers. Three of the ten newspapers decided that news of the physicians' draft was not important enough to mention.[4]

Dr Edward Glick made a study of 22 newspapers to see how they covered health news.[5] He concluded that the majority of 22 newspapers – including all the dailies in seven major cities – did not publish many of the stories made available to them by the Associated Press and UPI. Selection on the part of individual editors varied greatly. While the *Washington Post* and *Washington Star* both printed more than 30 stories each, the *Chicago Tribune* printed only 5. The newspapers studied covered seven cities. Only one newspaper outside Washington D.C. published the AP story reporting the Surgeon General's statement that more than one half of all American children of pre-school age were not adequately protected against polio. Nineteen of the 22 papers, including those in air-polluted Los Angeles, passed up the story of a government report which showed a link between the common cold and air pollution.

Despite complaints of too much coverage of radical dissent at the 1968 Democratic Convention in Chicago, the networks actually devoted very little time to showing the demonstrations. As noted in a staff report to the National Commission on the Causes and Prevention of Violence, CBS allotted 32 minutes to demonstrations out of a total of 38 hours and 3 minutes. Out of 19 hours and 37 minutes of convention coverage, NBC devoted only 14 minutes to film or tape coverage of disorders involving demonstrations and police.

Nevertheless (perhaps due in part to the conservative complaints that too much attention was given to protests at that Convention), the networks used their power of arbitrary selection to ignore dissent that took place along the Presidential Inauguration route. NBC ignored the dissent almost completely; CBS reported some incidents, but repeatedly apologized to its audience for doing so.[6]

Sometimes in their desire to keep ideas they dislike off the air, media owners will conspire to ignore certain events which otherwise would be selected as news. Newpapers, radio and television outlets in Medford, Oregon, in agreement with the state police, suppressed coverage of an anti-Vietnam war vigil in 1967.[7]

Decisions to select items as newsworthy or un-newsworthy must make the total picture of the day's events very biased to begin with. As we try to absorb the numerous images and headlines that compete for our attention, there is no way for us to evaluate this hidden bias, for all we see is what the editors think we should see.

Bias through omission of news

After an editor decides a story shall become news he can give the story a considerable bias merely by omitting the part of the story he doesn't want the reader or listener to know about. The citizen can't possibly be aware of what was left out even if he stopped to analyze the shortened news article. The editors leave no blank spaces.

Dr Jean Meyer, Director of the White House Conference on Food, Nutrition and Health, said on *Meet the Press* in 1969 that one of

the biggest roadblocks to feeding the poor was to get Americans to
be concerned about the issue. He noted that Congress received very
few letters or telegrams urging Congressional action on the matter.
And he noted another roadblock: many politicians were actually
opposed to feeding the hungry. He cited as an example the case of
New Hampshire's State OEO official losing his job because he showed
that there was hunger and malnutrition in the state. In the AP release
sent to newspapers the above points were omitted.[8]

Omission of important points like these and the playing down of
certain news items about hunger keeps the public satisfied with the
status quo, though today 15 million Americans don't have enough
money to buy food for an adequate diet. News of vocal complaints
about the President or local officials doing little or nothing to feed the
hungry is either buried or omitted. On the other hand, to make the
people think that establishment politicians are acting decisively to
meet the emergency, the media gives priority attention and presents
as decisive the stop-gap measures of the President that are seen as
inadequate by critics.

The media gave a big headline on page one to Nixon's proposal
for an increase in the food stamp programme.[9] But six months later
in December 1969, Senator George McGovern in a *Face the Nation*
interview accused the Nixon administration of actively lobbying
against passage of a newly proposed food stamp bill. This was
given only six inches and placed with a very small headline in the
middle of page 26 in the *New York Times*.[10] This is obvious playing
down of the news item. Sunday interview shows usually are priority
news items: *Face the Nation* received first or second-page coverage
in the *New York Times* for all 52 of its interviews in the year ending
June, 1969.[11] Besides burying the McGovern interview on page 26,
the *New York Times* omitted McGovern's statement which summed
up what he thought to be the real reason why the poor were not
being fed:

> We have had the kind of leadership both in the executive branch
> and in the Congress that has been too much concerned about
> special interest in this country and not enough concerned about
> the broad range of human need. That's really the problem.

However, the *New York Times* in this inconspicuous story did
mention McGovern's contention that the administration was
guilty of 'double talk' in that it had actively opposed passage of a
food stamp increase and then applauded when the appropriation
was passed.

The AP dispatch as printed on page 17 of the *Los Angeles Times*
omitted completely any of McGovern's comments about hunger.[12]

Instead it focused exclusively on the other topic covered by McGovern during the interview – the massacre at Songmy. And its coverage of this part of the interview omitted McGovern's strongest statement:

> Now really, what is the difference between a bombing plane or an artillery piece destroying a village and destroying its inhabitants, men, women and children, and what Lt Calley did? The difference, I suppose, is that Lt Calley and his people, if they are guilty as charged, were operating at closer range. But the moral issues, it seems to me, [are] the same.

The *New York Times* report of the interview omitted all of the Senator's comments on the significance of the Songmy incident.

One of the reasons Dr Jean Meyer could truthfully claim the American people are not concerned enough about hunger is because of news coverage that protects from exposure to public view the machinations of politicians who resist measures designed to help feed the hungry. A UPI release in July 1969 told of the Senate Agriculture Committee's rejection of proposals to give free food stamps to families earning less than 40 dollars a month. It included the names of the five committee members voting for the bill but omitted the names of those seven who voted against the bill.[13] The *New York Times* coverage also mentioned the five who voted yes but omitted the names of the other seven.[14] Politicians may now be doing more than ever in combating hunger, but this does not exonerate the past inaction or obstruction by politicians, or media's use of bias to protect those who acted in no great haste as millions of Americans went hungry.

Senator William Knowland in a 1953 *Meet the Press* interview stated that South Korea's Syngman Rhee 'was not sufficiently consulted [on Asian policy matters] during the Truman Administration or during the Eisenhower Administration'. The AP dispatch, omitting the reference to the Eisenhower Administration, reported that Knowland 'said today that we might not be faced with the present "unfortunate" situation in Korea if the Truman Administration had consulted with Syngman Rhee'.[15]

The bias implanted by the wire services is minimal compared to the news agencies they serve. The *Pottstown Mercury* on September 5, 1968, omitted from its published news reports enough statements to make up almost an entire newspaper page. The parts omitted were those critical of the President, the United States Government, the local government and U.S. policy in Vietnam.[16]

Most news agencies use this tool for creating bias less frequently than the above newspaper, but vital information is still omitted from important stories by even the more responsible agencies. In October

1960, Chet Huntley reported: 'Premier Fidel Castro said counter-revolutionaries fighting his regime are stronger than were the Batista forces but he will win.'[17] This report would perhaps lead television viewers to think that there was a substantial opposition to Castro by Cubans inside Cuba – a concept pleasing to the establishment at that time. What Chet Huntley left out was the key part of the news release as received from the wire services. Edward P. Morgan included it as he reported that same evening: 'Fidel Castro *accused the United States of mobilizing* his political enemies into a force more powerful than the Batista dictatorship he overthrew.'[18]

Huntley-Brinkley's 20 million viewers were shown films of President Nixon at his desk up to his knees in the thousands of telegrams that citizens had sent expressing their support for his Vietnam speech.[19] What the audience was not told is that these letters were actively solicited by the Republican National Committee through its newsletter. That same evening *Walter Cronkite* included this information.

When Black Panther leader Bobby Seale was on trial for conspiring to cross state lines with the intent to incite riot, his hands were tied and mouth gagged at the order of Judge Julius J. Hoffman. The Judge had become annoyed by Seale's interruptions of the trial with outspoken demands that he be allowed to defend himself.

After a tireless effort he somehow managed to free a hand, yank off the gag, and shout at the Judge: 'You fascist dog, you. You rotten low life son of a gun.' *Walter Cronkite*, which spent more than two minutes on the episode, omitted these words and merely told its viewers that Seale had yelled 'obscenities' at the judge. *Huntley-Brinkley* apparently didn't consider 'fascist' as obscene; they used the word in describing what Seale had shouted to the judge.[20]

Former Health, Education, and Welfare Secretary Robert Finch's first choice for Assistant Secretary for Health and Scientific Affairs, Dr John Knowles, said in July 1969, that 'the White House under President Nixon is in the grip of the arch-conservatives and progress is at a complete standstill'. KPFK, listener-supported radio in Los Angeles, and the *Los Angeles Times* chose this as the main point of Knowles' statement, but the *New York Times*, which gave more than 40 inches of coverage to the story, omitted it.[21] *Huntley-Brinkley* and *Walter Cronkite* didn't cover the story at all.

In a speech to the National Press Club, Wright Patman, Chairman of the House Banking and Currency Committee said:

> It is an open secret on capital hill that many campaign chests are swelled by contributions from the banks. Members of the House Banking and Currency Committee have been offered huge blocks

of bank stocks free of charge and directorships on bank boards.
Freshmen members have been approached within hours of their
arrival in Washington and offered quick and immediate loans. In
one instance that was reported to me, the bank told the member,
quote, 'just write a check, we will honor it'. . . .
    Today's economy which has the highest interest rates in the
nation's history is largely the result of the banking and monetary
policy written by the special interests for special interests

Patman drew attention to the fact that banks were denying mort-
gages to middle income families at the same time they were

. . . issuing credit cards by the tens of millions, sending them to
people who never asked for them or didn't want them, making
credit easier while all the time claiming to fight inflation. . . .
    Through their newly found toy, the bank holding company, they
are moving into all lines of business using the special privileges of
the bank to force their competitors to the wall. They are now into
everything from pizza parlors to green stamps. This movement,
left unchecked, will change the face of the entire American
economy, sharply concentrating power in the hands of a few. . . .
This new Nazi style economy, should it become a reality would
destroy this nation.

Patman also claimed Federal Reserve Board Chairman William
Martin had cost the American people 300 billion dollars through
his tight money policy.[22]
    Huntley-Brinkley failed to mention the Patman speech. *Walter
Cronkite* took 25 seconds to report briefly Patman's charge that
lobbyists were trying to influence Congress with campaign contributions, but Patman's statements about credit cards, pizza parlours,
William Martin and the Nazi-style economy were omitted. The
New York Times and the *Los Angeles Times* both omitted the same
statements from their coverage.
    President Nixon's trip to India in 1969 was given priority coverage
by the media. Both the *New York Times* and the *Los Angeles Times*
covered his trip on the front page. Television featured satellite-relay
coverage. That same day Mrs Indira Gandhi, Prime Minister of
India, gave a press conference that was attended by members of the
U.S. press. In her talk Mrs Gandhi said she felt the United States
was moving toward India's policy in Vietnam, but then she made
some statements that showed that her thinking about the Vietnam
war was fundamentally different from that of President Nixon. She
commented that she had always felt the Vietnamese should be left
to solve their own problems, that foreign troops should be with-
drawn, and that all outside interference should end. She added:

'Left to themselves, the Vietnamese would not want to be under the Chinese or anyone else.' She emphasized that the strongest force in Asia was nationalism. Another important part of the Prime Minister's speech was covered in a Reuters dispatch as broadcast over KPFK radio:

> She said if the whole of Vietnam went Communist, it would not affect India very much. She said it was up to the Vietnamese to decide on their own government and that there were different forms of communism, some of them even liberalizing.

The *New York Times* mentioned the Prime Minister's press conference but omitted the above statements except the one about the United States moving toward India's policy in Vietnam. The *Los Angeles Times* covered the above statements but buried the coverage at the end of the report on President Nixon's trip to India.[23] *Walter Cronkite* allotted 2·48 minutes on President Nixon in New Delhi but didn't mention a thing about Mrs Gandhi's press conference. *Huntley-Brinkley* alloted 3·40 minutes but omitted all of Mrs Gandhi's comments except the one about the United States moving toward India's policy. Lest you think the story was knocked off the news by other pressing stories, we note that *Huntley-Brinkley* did find time the same day to allot a minute to coverage of a humorous item about a stolen car.

On 11 and 12 July 1969, President Thieu made the front page of almost every newspaper with his proposal that the National Liberation Front join in free elections to decide South Vietnam's future. The proposal was thoroughly covered by the media. Also reported were favourable responses made by several U.S. politicians, but the *New York Times*, the *Los Angeles Times*, and *Huntley-Brinkley* all omitted the controversial response of Senator George McGovern. This should have been the response most significant and newsworthy since the Senator had just spent four hours talking with National Liberation Front delegates in Paris. Senator McGovern said the NLF would not participate in any election with the Thieu–Ky government administration 'holding the ballot boxes'.[24] *Walter Cronkite* newscast, also ignoring McGovern's comments, found time to slip in a hidden editorial by one of its own reporters, Robert Pierpoint, who tried to persuade his 20 million listeners that, 'at least a basis for political negotations have been put on the table and if Hanoi and the NLF refuse to negotiate, they are on the defensive, in Paris and around the world'.

On 9 December 1969, President Thieu, the man Richard Nixon had called one of the four or five *great* statesmen of the world,

attacked three members of the lower house of the South Vietnamese
legislature who had advocated neutralism. He said he might 'cut off
their heads' if they continued their ways.[25] But neither the *Los
Angeles Times* nor *New York Times* readers will ever know about this
great statesman's threat to cut off the heads of his political opponents
because both newspapers omitted that part of President Thieu's
warning.[26] The statement was made available to both newspapers
in a Reuters dispatch.

AUTO SAFETY: A DEADLY, CRIPPLING, DISFIGURING SILENCE

Hunger was allowed to exist because the media, through deliberate
neglect and apathy, kept it from being a national issue of prime
importance until 1968. Hunger in America isn't the only deplorable
situation the media have allowed to go on almost unnoticed for
years. Ralph Nader, in his book *Unsafe at any Speed*, claimed that
the auto industry,

> by dominating the channels of communications through which the
> customer receives his information about automobiles, has obscured
> the relation of vehicle design to life and limb and has kept quiet
> its technical capability of building crash-worthy vehicles.

Noting that pressure can be applied by advertising money and
other subtle forms of pressure, Nader continued: 'It is more than
coincidental that radio, television, newspapers and magazines have
so long ignored the role of vehicle design in producing . . . collisions.'[27] Ironically, as if to prove Nader correct, not even one out of
over 700 newspapers accepted the offer to run a serialization of his
book.[28]

An analysis of how the media treated car design as a possible cause
of accidents and injuries shows Nader correct in blaming media for
failing to inform the people about this issue. This can be seen by
noting how America's best news medium, the *New York Times*,
handled the problem over the years. We can assume, and my
research indicates, that the other 99·9 per cent of the press did even
worse than the *New York Times*.

Writing in the *American Medical Association Journal* in January
1937, Dr Clair Straith, plastic surgeon and nationally recognized
specialist in the treatment of facial injuries caused by automobile
accidents, pointed out that the majority of 'severe, crushing, facial
injuries' were sustained by young women sitting in the seat next to
the driver. With an eye to reducing such injuries and personal trage-

dies that followed disfiguration, he made a few suggestions to automobile manufacturers:

> ... projecting objects on the instrument panel (handles, knobs and cranks) add to the hazard. Elimination of such objects from the passenger's side of the instrument panel should be attempted by motor car engineers. The use of 'crash padding' might do much to minimize the seriousness and extent of these injuries.[29]

The Associated Press sent out a short news release on the article. It was printed on page 2 of the *New York Times*. It reported that Dr Straith 'called facial disfigurement an even more tragic product of auto accidents than sudden death'.[30] But the article contained not even a hint that Straith felt that many cases of disfigurement could be prevented by a better designed car. The press didn't bother to pursue the matter and as a result the people heard nothing about it.

Later in 1937, Dr Straith wrote another article which appeared in the *American Medical Association Journal*. Lamenting injuries caused by machinery, he said: 'Man's ingenuity has enabled him to perfect "Frankenstein's" monster which now turns about to destroy. Mechanical progress has become a double-edged sword.'[31] He then wrote specifically about automobile injuries he knew about from first hand experience. He said that when the

> guest passenger is thrown violently forward against windshield or instrument panel ... crushing of the nose, cheek bones and marillae, facial lacerations and rupture of the eyeballs results. The seriousness of many of these injuries could be greatly minimized if projecting handles, knobs, cranks and other features on the instrument panel and doors could be eliminated entirely in construction. It seems possible that many if not most of these projecting features could be recessed or made flush with the body of the car. ...
> For several years I have had crash padding installed in my own cars to cover prominent portions of the instrument panels for the protection of children and other guest passengers. Designers of automobiles should, I believe, make further efforts to eliminate these hazards by some such means.[32]

To emphasize his point, Dr Straith even included a photograph of the interior of his own car showing the padding that he had installed.

Both the article and the photograph were completely ignored by the *New York Times* and the rest of the media.

Ten years later Dr Fletcher Woodward, who had treated many disfigurements resulting from auto accidents, declared at the 1948 annual session of the AMA that 'automobiles should be redesigned to stress safety rather than speed and appearance'. He recommended padded dashboards, safety belts, safer windows, and the elimination of projecting handles and knobs. The *New York Times* reported this but hid it in a few paragraphs under a large article on page 20 headlined RADAR BEAMS HELD AID IN DIATHERMY.[33]

Later in 1948, Dr Woodward wrote an article in the *American Medical Association Journal* criticizing automotive engineering. He noted that 15 per cent of all accidents involved defects of a mechanical nature and that automobiles could be redesigned to prevent many accidents. Using medical diagnoses of injuries sustained in auto accidents, he described car features which caused the injuries and illustrated in detail the corrections that could be made. He concluded that there was an 'abundance of evidence to render it at present possible to build motor cars capable of withstanding collisions at high speed with greatly reduced likelihood of injury to occupants'.[34] Not a word of this potentially controversial article was printed in the *New York Times*.

There were others who criticized the auto industry. Arthur Stevens, president of the Automobile Safety Association, spoke out many times in an effort to inform the people how the auto industry for years had been disregarding pleas to redesign their cars.[35] He never made priority news in the media. The *New York Times* did publish one of his letters to the editor,[36] but every newspaperman knows that the editorial page is the least read part of a newspaper.

Dr Horace Campbell, speaking before a meeting of the American College of Surgeons in 1955, claimed that for about $30 per car manufacturers could install four safety features that would substantially reduce injuries and deaths. This claim, like those of Drs Straith and Woodward, was certainly a priority news item – worthy, one might think, of waking up the media from its long slumber on the issue. But nothing happened. The speech was entirely ignored by the *New York Times*. Later the *Times* made a reference to the speech on its editorial page: a respectable plea that 'safety, not color and power, should be the outstanding feature of the 1956 automobile'. But in the editorial were statements that revealed the *Times* as an instrument of the auto industry. Noting safety improvements made by the industry, the *Times* stated: 'Certainly American car makers have not been indifferent to the importance of building safety factors into their products.' The *Times* suggested no government or legislative action; instead, it suggested leaving the problem in the hands of those who for twenty years had been the least enthusiastic about safety engineering: 'It would seem that the auto manufacturer is in the best position to give such protection.'[37]

Not all politicians agreed with leaving the people's safety in the hands of such protectors. A few felt the auto manufacturers would never make the needed changes unless forced to by legislative and court actions. A few days after the *New York Times* editorial. Senator Frank Barrett introduced legislation requiring safety belts on all cars sold for interstate travel. To put some teeth in his law, he provided for a $1000 fine or imprisonment for a year, or both, for any person selling a car not equipped with belts. This was one of the first serious congressional attempts to force the auto industry to take safety engineering seriously. Evidently the *Times* didn't think the proposal worthy of bringing to public attention in any big way. The item was given one inch of space at the bottom of page 18.[38]

Was legislation really needed or had the auto industry, as the *Times* claimed, 'not been indifferent to the importance of building safety factors into their product'? The record shows some improvements as having been made, but safety features that could easily have been installed and which would have saved thousands of lives were ignored by the industry. The industry's record on this issue, detailed in the 1966 book *Safety Last*, reveals that Dr Straith, 'as early as 1934 had numerous conferences with the automobile makers, begging them to design and construct the car interior so as to inflict as little injury as possible upon the occupants should crash occur'.[39] Dr Woodward's detailed suggestions of 1948 were also ignored and ridiculed.[40] Two and a half years after Senator Barrett's 1955 attempt to force the industry to adopt seat belts, General Motors, Chrysler, Ford, Studebaker and Packard opposed seat belts as standard equipment.[41] Henry Wakeland, Nash automobile engineer for five years, put most of the blame on General Motors:

> The automobile companies are tightly organized against the rest of the country. They will not compete in safety. But GM is the real foot dragger. If it were not for GM, the rest of the industry would have moved before this.[42]

The Automobile Manufacturers Association in 1961 opposed a bill that would have required car makers to install safety padding on all motor vehicles, saying the requirement was 'impractical and unnecessary'.[43] The same year, the head of General Motors ridiculed what he termed were self-styled experts and amateur engineers by describing their safety suggestions as 'radical and ill conceived'.[44] Despite the manufacturers' record of apathy and opposition to most features, Henry Ford II in opposing safety legislation in 1966 said: 'If these critics who don't really know anything about safety of an automobile, will get out of our way, we can go ahead with our job. . . .'[45] The *Times* in a special report found room to *objectively* report Ford's claim at the top of page one. The industry often explained that they were giving the public what it wanted – that public education was needed first. This was true. But a major reason why the people didn't demand safety features is that the instruments of communication were cooperating with the automobile industry in keeping the problem from becoming the national issue of importance that it deserved to be, and that it later became as the result of Ralph Nader's book. The media kept the people from knowing about unsafe cars just as it had kept them from knowing about hunger in America.

Representative Kenneth Roberts, chairman of the House Subcommittee on Traffic Safety, heard testimony in 1956 from some of the people the head of General Motors had ridiculed as being radical, ill-conceived amateur engineers and self-styled safety experts – the same ones that Henry Ford II claimed didn't know anything about the safety of an automobile. They included spokesmen for the American Public Health Association, The American College of Surgeons, The American Medical Association and several experienced automotive engineers. All emphasized the capability of the automobile industry to make a safer car. These were the same people whose complaints had been ignored or deprecated for years by the media.

It seems reasonable to ask the following: After these critics were finally heard by Congress, why did it take ten more years before Congress passed its first legislation requiring mandatory safety standards? The answer rests with the media's use of bias. Unable to ignore completely the congressional investigation and the increasing clamour of the critics for urgently needed legislation, the press dutifully reported some of what the critics had to say, but in a biased way that did not arouse great public interest or indignation. This is evident in the press treatment which the *Times* gave to a dedicated priest who spent five years building a car he hoped would demonstrate the fact that safer cars could be built. Completing his car in 1957, Father Juliano drove it to New York City in order to put it on display. The car had many mechanical breakdowns on its way. This is the aspect the *Times* jumped on. The story was headlined:

DREAM CAR HERE AFTER 15 MISHAPS, RADICALLY
DESIGNED SAFETY AUTO NEEDS 7 TOWS

A photograph of the car appears above the caption:

DREAM CAR IS A NIGHTMARE ON ROAD

The article went on to say that the car taxed the patience of the policemen and, 'Ironically, the car, which was designed to emphasize safety features, almost became involved in a number of accidents.'[46] The article made no mention whatsoever of the safety features and their purpose, nor did it even hint at why Juliano had bothered to go to all the trouble to demonstrate safety design features in the first place. No statements by Juliano were mentioned or quoted. Readers are left with the impression that Juliano is some kind of a clown with a preposterous idea. Evidently Juliano hadn't considered that whatever he had to communicate to the people about auto safety would have to go through the digestive apparatus of the media.

The American Medical Association made the alarming claim that '10,000 people killed in auto accidents in 1960 would be alive today if they had been wearing seat belts' (based on the conservative estimate that safety belts would have decreased fatalities 25 per cent).[47] This made no headlines. It was included in an article in section III, page 11, of the *New York Times*, in an article that heralded the Ford Motor Company as a great auto safety crusader. Another similar claim made in 1962 was placed in section X without a headline to call attention to it. John O. Moore, a pioneer researcher in seat belt safety, stated that seat belts could make the 'difference between permanent disability and minor hurts for 200,000 people each year'.[48] A 1965 story serves as example of the type of automobile news which the *Times* felt deserved a page-one display. The two-column head-line read:

66 AUTO TO STRESS POWER AND A SPORTS LOOK[49]

In its general tone, this article seems more of an advertisement for the auto industry than a news story. It could well have been written by a public relations firm.

An analysis of the frequency in which the safety engineering issue received priority news treatments also confirms Nader's claim that the communication industry did its best for the auto manufacturers. Neither the *New York Times* nor the *Los Angeles Times* had even one mention of the issue on their front pages in February and March of 1950 or in April and May of 1960. The three network television newscasts, along with the three network radio newscasts mentioned in the previous section, completely ignored the issue for the six-week period preceding the 1960 election.

As we shall see, this record of suppression of news about a life-and-death issue is not an isolated case by any means. Our society is dependent on a communication system dominated by those who have the power and the determination to deny divergent viewpoints an equal chance to be heard. Many are more concerned with money than with saving lives. The result is always the same: The People suffer.

SMOKING: HOW TO PROTECT THE ADVERTISER

Two million Americans quit smoking in 1968 alone, and more than 13 million have quit since 1966.[50] During the first half of 1969, consumption of cigarettes decreased at a rate three times faster than in 1968.[51] Both the consumption per person and total consumption of cigarettes is decreasing.[52] There is little doubt that the decrease in smoking is prompted by the belief that smoking causes lung cancer. A recent Gallup Poll found that 71 per cent of Americans shared this belief.[53] Not everyone who believes smoking is a cause of cancer quits smoking, but many do. Unknown millions never begin smoking because of concern for their health; the drop in the percentage of college freshmen who smoke is one indication of this. As a result of quitting the habit or never beginning in the first place, millions of Americans will have added years to the most precious gift of all – life. I wonder how many millions of Americans would have quit or never begun smoking in the 1940s and 1950s had they been fully aware that cigarettes could take away eight or more years of their life. Consider, now, the fact that information that would have convinced many to quit smoking was available beginning in 1938, but for years such information was censored or played down by the media – to such an extent that even as late as 1958 only 44 per cent of the people thought smoking a cause of lung cancer.[54] Those who would never have begun smoking, or would have quit had they known the health hazards earlier, have cause to blame the media for robbing them of life itself.

The most reliable media, such as the *New York Times*, didn't censor all the information outright. This newspaper merely placed it inconspicuously in the middle or back pages so that it never became the urgent life-and-death matter or the front-page controversy it deserved to be. Outright censorship was often used by the majority of the press and, unfortunately, most Americans got their news from the less reliable media then as they do now. An indication of the extent to which smoking news was censored is seen in the way New York City dailies covered two different stories. An Associated Press story in early 1938 presented the findings of Dr Raymond Pearl of John Hopkins University. Dr Pearl presented life tables showing the relationship between smoking and longevity. The tables showed that 66,564 non-smokers survived to sixty years of age compared to 61,911 moderate smokers and 46,726 heavy smokers.[55] He pointed out that: 'smoking is associated with a definite impairment of longevity'.[56] He noted that the shortening of life was proportional to the amount of tobacco smoked, and that it affects even moderate smokers enough 'to be measurable and significant'. George Seldes checked the New York dailies and discovered that six out of eight of them censored the story completely.[57] Ten years later the media wasn't performing any better. In 1948 an AP story sent out on the wires said: 'The cigarette companies won't like this, but a man who ought to know thinks a lot of citizens are digging their graves with their own lungs.' It added that the man, Dr Alton Ochsner: 'takes a dim view of the cheery, four colour cigarette advertisements'. Soon after sending this out on its wire, the AP sent out a bulletin eliminating the above comments from the story because they were too 'controversial'.[58] Nevertheless the trimmed-down story was still available to the nine New York dailies for their use if they thought it newsworthy. They didn't – eight out of nine declined to print it, including the *New York Times*. The *Times* also neglected to review two books detailing the effect of smoking on life expectancy.[59]

The *New York Times* dutifully printed most stories. I discovered that of the 27 possible news items during the period 1938–53 that related to smoking, the *Times* suppressed only the one AP story mentioned above. Unlike many of the papers that repeatedly censored such news, the *Times* was content to keep the stories on the back pages. An examination of these apparently low-priority news items in the *Times* reveals there were facts here that might have convinced all but the tobacco industry that smoking was definitely linked to lung cancer and a shortened life span. The 1938 article on Dr Pearl was placed on page 19, taking only two inches of a 16-inch story on science and longevity. And although Dr Pearl's tables on longevity were available then, the *Times* did not print them until a year later.[60] In the two and a half years after the initial article on smoking there were five more articles, none of them being placed any further forward than page 15. From October 1940 to July 1944 there were no items at all listed in the *Times* yearly *Indexes*.

Buried in the back of the newspaper next to the marriage announcements, a four-inch article appeared in 1944 describing some surprising actuary statistics made public by the Northwestern Mutual Life Insurance Company. 'Long-term studies of large groups of policy holders', the article related, 'had shown 26 to 100 per cent rises in death rates among heavy smokers in the 30 to 50 age brackets as compared with non-smokers.'[61]

In 1948 the *Times* placed on page 11 an AP story which summarized the findings of tests made at the Mayo clinic. Tests on a thousand patients revealed that 'on the average, smokers were found to get coronary thromboses 10 years earlier than non-smokers'.[62]

In 1949 a Dr E. A. Graham was described as having discovered that 'it has been very rare' to find a man with lung cancer 'who had not been an excessive smoker for years, or at least who had not formerly smoked cigarettes excessively'.[63] This AP story was placed on page 24 of the *Times*, and was so small as to be inconspicuous.

In 1950 many cancer experts assembled in Paris to compare and discuss their findings. Three different groups investigating independently all found that the 'lungs of smokers show far higher incidence of cancer than pipe or cigar smokers', and that 'more women who smoked cigarettes had lung cancer than did women who did not'. The article reporting on this important conference also noted that Dr Morton Levin had found that 14 of 1000 cigarette smokers developed lung cancer as compared to 6 of 1000 non-smokers. This significant news item was placed on page 27.[64]

In 1952 a United Nations group reported a rise in cancer deaths all over the world. The UN group cited the findings of the Medical Research Council of England and Wales which showed that for men above the age of 45 the risk of developing lung cancer 'may be 50 times as great among those who smoke 25 or more cigarettes daily as among non-smokers'. The Council flatly stated: 'Smoking is an important factor in the cause of cancer of the lung.' This information was set forth in one paragraph of a 15-inch article placed on page 26.[65]

Writing in the *British Medical Journal* in 1952, Dr Richard Doll and Professor Bradford Hill stated unequivocally that the association between lung cancer and smoking was 'real'. Supporting this was the statement: 'Similar studies in the United States revealed the same.'[66] This was relegated to page 22.

For anyone in 1953 still entertaining doubts about smoking, it should have been cleared up by an article which summarized various reports presented by medical specialists. Four different medical reports 'stated in strong terms' and 'without qualification' the link between cigarette smoking and lung diseases. Dr Ernest Wynder presented a report of thirteen independent studies which showed that 'the prolonged and heavy use of cigarettes increased up to 20 times the risk of developing cancer of the lung'. One report warned that the 'use of tobacco may mean the difference between life and death for persons with disease of circulation'. The article concluded by taking notice of the fact that 'all speakers agreed that smoking was a causative factor in lung cancer'.[67] This news was placed on page 16 of the *Times*. The *Times* did put one smoking article on page one during this fifteen-year period. It was a December 1953 article implying that there was still a great deal of uncertainty about the link between smoking and disease, and that the government was actively concerned about guarding the people's health.[68]

Even more significant than the playing down of this issue by burying it on the back pages was the scarcity of stories on it that appeared from 1938 to 1953. No articles at all were listed in the *Times' Indexes* for the years 1941, 1942, 1943, 1945 and 1947. Even more noteworthy is that except for the *Reader's Digest* and a few other media agencies, none went out of their way to alert the public. The best media performance seemed merely a dutiful reporting, in an inconspicuous manner, of those stories it might have found difficult to ignore entirely. There were no newspaper crusades to arouse the politicians to pass legislation requiring equal time and space to combat the persuasive power of cigarette commercials. There were no stories of the tragic deaths that were now known to be associated with cigarette smoking. More than 99 per cent of the media have continued to accept advertising without demanding a warning. The media in effect have joined with the tobacco industry in opposing legislation controlling ads. There were no crusades to gradually eliminate the billions of dollars of taxpayers' money being spent to subsidize tobacco growers. There were no crusades against our government spending taxpayers' money to send billions of packs of disease-causing cigarettes to Europeans that were starving in the late 1940s.

Scholars have noted the poor performance of the news media in the area of smoking and health. Writing in the *Columbia Journalism Review*, Arthur E. Rowse analysed the media performance in covering smoking news from 1954 to 1962. He chose 12 major stories and examined how the were covered by 12 highly regarded newspapers including the *New York Times, Baltimore Sun, Washington Post* and *Des Moines Register*.[69] His study revealed that smoking news, finally after 15 years, began to make the front page. In the first four stories, he found that about half the newspapers put them on page one. About 10 per cent of the papers censored the items. The papers did a poor job of covering the congressional hearings on smoking in 1957. Of a total of 72 possible stories in 12 papers (6 possible stories for each paper), only a total of 5 articles made page one, 48 appeared elsewhere and 24 were omitted. Rowse noted that 'nearly every story between 1950 and 1954 contained a Tobacco Institute statement dismissing the evidence as inconclusive'. This tended to mislead the readers into thinking that there was really a genuine difference of opinion among medical experts. This was not true. With few exceptions, the only differences of opinion were between those doctors paid by the cigarette companies and those who had no special interest to serve.

Supported in part by millions of dollars of cigarette advertising money, the broadcasting industry understandably never became a crusader against smoking during these years. For example, from 1938 to 1955 there were no documentaries on the problem. CBS had a programme in 1955. NBC waited until 1962 and ABC waited even longer.[70] News covering was dutiful but never comprehensive or enterprising. A survey of the three network radio newscasts analyzed earlier shows no coverage at all of three events involving smoking and health that occurred during the six-week period preceding the 1960 election. One story reported on the International Cancer Conference held in Tokyo where there was 'considerable agreement that the incident of lung cancer was high among persons who had smoked steadily for 20 years or longer'.[71] Another story announced the American Cancer Society's nationwide campaign to woo teenagers away from smoking. The Society was distributing a chart showing that smoking one half a pack a day increased a person's chance of getting lung cancer 8 times, and two packs, 20 times compared with a non-smoker.[72] The third story ignored by all six major newscasts was an AP release in which Dr Daniel Horn of the American Cancer Society predicted that the then rate of 100 people dying each day from lung cancer would double in ten years. Dr Horn was quoted as saying: 'An attack on teenage smoking is the only way to reduce deaths from lung cancer.'[73] The broadcasters' ignoring of Dr Horn's gruesome prediction certainly didn't help inform teenagers. Nonetheless the broadcasters carried ample smoking news in the form of advertisements – all good news, without a warning, about the wonderful rewards of smoking. At the same time Dr Horn was carrying on his campaign against teenage smoking, four out of the ten favourite programmes of 6–10-year-olds carried cigarette ads and five of the ten most favoured by teenagers were interrupted by a Madison Avenue attempt to sell the smoking habit.[74] It's hardly surprising that Dr Horn failed in his efforts to discourage teenagers from smoking. Today teenage smoking is on the increase[75] and even many grammar school children are smoking.

Here we see how our advanced technology of communication has been put to the service of elements whose interests are diametric to those of the public. A technology that as early as 1938 could have brought home to all Americans the truth about smoking has been used instead to bury this truth for as long as possible. No one can now argue that informing the public wouldn't have made any difference; the 13 million Americans who quit smoking since 1966 are testimony enough to refute this. The media have failed in two important respects on the smoking story: first, in failing to give the people adequate and fair information on the priority basis that the problem deserved; second, in failing to expose through creative reporting the politicians and powers who fought to prevent the government from required warnings on advertisements and equal time and space for anti-cigarette ads – requirements that were justified by scientific findings as early as 1938. It is now clear that had the media done their job in informing the public on the danger of smoking when it should have, countless millions of Americans who died an early death would still be alive today.

REFERENCES

1. *New York Times*, 4 April 1967, p. 87, cited in John Hohenberg, *The news media* (New York, Holt, Rinehart & Winston, 1968), p. 9.
2. Robert Macneil, *The people machine* (New York, Harper & Row, 1968), p. 54.
3. Jack Lyle, *The news in Megapolis* (San Francisco, Chandler Publishing Co, 1967), p. 87.
4. 'What the readers see', *Columbia Journalism Review*, Spring 1962, p. 21.
5. 'Health news', *Columbia Journalism Review*, Spring 1964, p. 29.
6. Marvin Barrett (ed.), *Survey of broadcast journalism, 1968–69*, (New York, Grosset & Dunlop Inc. 1969), pp. 25–6.
7. *Columbia Journalism Review*, Winter 1967–68, p. 7.
8. *Los Angeles Times*, 24 November 1969, p. 4.
9. 6 May 1969.
10. *New York Times*, 1 December 1969.
11. *Survey of broadcast journalism. 1968–69*, pp. 17–18.
12. 1 December 1969.
13. *Los Angeles, Times* 1 July 1969, p. 6.
14. *New York Times,* 1 July 1969, p. 1.
15. Robert Lasch, 'I see by the papers', *Progressive*, November 1953, p. 18.
16. *Columbia Journalism Review*, Fall 1968, p. 30.
17. Senate Committee on Commerce Report 994, *Freedom of communication*, p. 402.
18. Ibid., p. 420.
19. 4 November 1969.
20. 30 October 1960.
21. 8 July 1969.
22. Kpfk newscast, 31 July 1969.
23. Kpfk newscast, 31 July 1969; *Los Angeles Times* and *New York Times*, 1 August 1969.
24. Kpfk newscast, 11 July 1969.
25. Kpfk newscast, 9 December 1969.
26. 10 December 1969.
27. *Unsafe at any speed* (New York, Grossman Publications, 1965), p. 329.
28. Robert K. Baker and Sandra J. Ball, A Report to the National Commission on the Causes and Prevention of Violence (eds.) *Mass media*

and violence, Vol. IX (Washington D.C., U.S. Government Printing Office, 1969), p. 76.

29. 'Management of facial injuries caused by motor accidents', 9 January 1937, p. 103.
30. 8 January 1937.
31. 'Automobile injuries', 18 September 1937, p. 940.
32. Ibid., p. 944.
33. 25 June 1948.
34. 'Medical criticism of modern automotive engineering', 30 October 1948, p. 627.
35. Ibid.
36. *New York Times*, 6 December 1948, p. 24.
37. Ibid., 7 January 1955, p. 20.
38. Ibid., 12 January 1955.
39. Jeffrey O'Connell and Arthur Myers, *Safety last* (New York, Random House, 1966), p. 26.
40. Ibid.
41. *New York Times*, 7 August 1957, p. 39, and 9 August 1957, p. 20.
42. O'Connell and Myers, *Safety last*, p. 29.
43. *New York Times*, 29 March 1961, p. 36.
44. Ibid., 18 October 1961, p. 38.
45. Ibid., 16 April 1966, p. 1.
46. Ibid., 12 November 1957, p. 39.
47. Ibid., 19 March 1962.
48. Ibid., 1 April 1962.
49. 18 April.
50. *New York Times*, 23 May 1969, p. 49, *Los Angeles Times*, 10 September 1970, p. 1.
51. *Los Angeles Times*, 2 January 1970, p. 6.
52. Ibid., 23 December 1969, and 25 June 1969, p. 13.
53. *New York Times*, 4 September 1969, p. 21.
54. Ibid.
55. Ibid., 12 March 1939, p. 4.
56. Ibid., 25 February 1938, p. 19.
57. George Seldes, *Never tire of protesting* (New York, Lyle Stuart Inc. 1968), p. 63.
58. Ibid., p. 68, and *In fact*, 2 August 1948.
59. Dr J. M. Gehman, *Smoke over America* (Paterson, Beoma Publishing House, 1943) and Andrew Salter, *Conditional reflex therapy* (New York, Creative Age, 1949).
60. *New York Times*, 12 March 1939, p. 4.
61. 23 December 1944, p. 11.
62. 27 March 1948.
63. 24 October 1949.
64. 18 July 1950.
65. *New York Times*, 16 July 1952.
66. Ibid., 12 December 1952.
67. Ibid., 9 December 1953.

68. 21 December 1953.
69. 'Smoking and News', *Columbia Journalism Review*, Summer 1963, p. 6.
70. Ibid.
71. *New York Times*, 13 October 1960, p. 38.
72. Ibid., 26 October 1960, p. 41.
73. Ibid., 30 October 1960, p. 84.
74. Rowse, *Columbia Journalism Review*, Summer 1963, p. 6.
75. Westinghouse Broadcasting Company, KFWB, Los Angeles, 16 December 1969.

Structuring and selecting news*

JOHAN GALTUNG and MARI RUGE

Imagine that the world can be likened to an enormous set of broadcasting stations, each one emitting its signal or its programme at its proper wavelength. (Another metaphor might be of a set of atoms of different kinds emitting waves corresponding to their condition.) The emission is continuous, corresponding to the truism that something is always happening to any person in the world. Even if he sleeps quietly, sleep is 'happening'[1] – what we choose to consider an 'event' is culturally determined. The set of world events, then, is like the cacophony of sound one gets by scanning the dial of one's radio receiver, and particularly confusing if this is done quickly on the medium-wave or short-wave dials. Obviously this cacophony does not make sense, it may become meaningful only if one station is tuned in and listened to for some time before one switches on to the next one.

Since we cannot register everything, we have to select, and the question is what will strike our attention. This is a problem in the psychology of perception and the following is a short list of some obvious implications of this metaphor:

(F_1) If the frequency of the signal is outside the dial it will not be recorded.

(F_2) The stronger the signal, the greater the amplitude, the more probable that it will be recorded as worth listening to.

(F_3) The more clear and unambiguous the signal (the less noise there is), the more probable that it will be recorded as worth listening to.

(F_4) The more meaningful the signal, the more probable that it will be recorded as worth listening to.

(F_5) The more consonant the signal is with the mental image of what one expects to find, the more probable that it will be recorded as worth listening to.

(F_6) The more unexpected the signal, the more probable that it will be recorded as worth listening to.

(F_7) If one signal has been tuned in to, the more likely it will continue to be tuned in to as worth listening to.

(F_8) The more a signal has been tuned in to, the more probable

*Extract from 'The structure of foreign news: The presentation of the Congo, Cuba and Cyprus crises in four foreign newspapers', *Journal of International Peace Research*, 1 (1965), pp. 64–90.

that a very different kind of signal will be recorded as worth listening to next time.

Some comments on these factors are in order. They are nothing but common-sense perception psychology translated into radio-scanning and event-scanning activities. The proper thing to do in order to test their validity would be to observe journalists at work or radio listeners operating with the dial – and we have no such data. For want of this the factors should be anchored in general reasoning and social science findings.

The first factor is trivial when applied to radio sets, less so when applied to events in general. Since this is a metaphor and not a model we shall be liberal in our interpretation of frequency and proceed as follows. By the 'frequency' of an event we refer to the time-span needed for the event to unfold itself and acquire meaning. For a soldier to die during a battle this time-span is very short; for a development process in a country to take place the time-span may be very long. Just as the radio dial has its limitation with regard to electro-magnetic waves, so will the newspaper have its limitations, and the thesis is that *the more similar the frequency of the event is to the frequency of the news medium, the more probable that it will be recorded as news by that news medium.* A murder takes little time and the event takes place between the publication of two successive issues of a daily, which means that a meaningful story can be told from one day to the next. But to single out one murder during a battle where there is one person killed every minute would make little sense – one will typically only record the battle as such (if newspapers were published every minute the perspective could possibly be changed to the individual soldier). Correspondingly, the event that takes place over a longer time-span will go unrecorded unless it reaches some kind of dramatic climax (the building of a dam goes unnoticed but not its inauguration). Needless to say, this under-reporting of trends is to some extent corrected by publications with a lower frequency. A newspaper may have a habit of producing weekly 'reviews', there are weeklies and monthlies and quarterlies and yearbooks – and there are *ad hoc* publications. If we concentrate on dailies, however, the thesis is probably valid and probably of some heuristic value when other aspects of news communication are to be unravelled.

The second thesis is simply that there is something corresponding to the idea of 'amplitude' for radio waves. What this says is only that the bigger the dam, the more will its inauguration be reported *ceteris paribus*; the more violent the murder the bigger the headlines it will make. It says nothing about what has greater amplitude, the dam or the murder. It can also be put in a more dichotomous form: there is a threshold the event will have to pass before it will be recorded at all.[2] This is a truism, but an important one.

The third hypothesis is also trivial at the radio level but not at the news level. What is 'signal' and what is 'noise' is not inherent; it is a question of convention,[3] as seen clearly when two radio stations are sending on the same frequency. Clarity in this connection must refer to some kind of one-dimensionality, that there is only one or a limited number of meanings in what is received. Thus interpreted the hypothesis says simply the following: the less ambiguity the more the event will be noticed. This is not quite the same as preferring the simple to the complex, but one precization of it; rather an event with a clear interpretation, free from ambiguities in its meaning, is preferred to the highly ambiguous event from which many and inconsistent implications can and will be made.[4]

The fourth hypothesis also deals with meaning but not with its ambiguity. 'Meaningful' has some major interpretations. One of them is 'interpretable within the cultural framework of the listener or reader' and all the thesis says is that actually some measure of *ethnocentrism* will be operative: there has to be *cultural proximity*. That is, the event-scanner will pay particular attention to the familiar, to the culturally similar, and the culturally distant will be passed by more easily and not be noticed. It is somewhat like the North European radio listener in say, Morocco: he will probably pass by the Arab music and speech he can get on his dial as quaint and meaningless and find relief in European music and French talk.

The other dimension of 'meaningful' is in terms of *relevance*: an event may happen in a culturally distant place but still be loaded with meaning in terms of what it may imply for the reader or listener. Thus the culturally remote country may be brought in via a pattern of conflict with one's own group.[5]

The fifth hypothesis links what is selected to the mental pre-image, where the word 'expects' can and should be given both its cognitive interpretation as 'predicts' and its normative interpretation as 'wants'. A person *predicts* that something will happen and this creates a mental matrix for easy reception and registration of the event if it does finally take place. Or he *wants* it to happen and the matrix is even more prepared, so much so that he may distort perceptions he receives and provide himself with images consonant with what he has wanted. In the sense mentioned here 'news' are actually 'olds', because they correspond to what one expects to happen – and if they are too far away from the expectation they will not be registered, according to this hypothesis of consonance.[6]

The sixth hypothesis brings in a corrective to the fourth and fifth. The idea is simply that it is not enough for an event to be culturally meaningful and consonant with what it expected – this defines only a vast set of possible news candidates. Within this set, according to the hypothesis, the more unexpected have the highest chances of being included as news. It is the unexpected *within the meaningful and the consonant* that is brought to one's attention, and by 'unexpected' we simply mean essentially two things: *unexpected* or *rare*. Thus, what is regular and institutionalized, continuing and repetitive at regular and short intervals, does not attract nearly so much attention, *ceteris paribus*, as the unexpected and *ad hoc* – a circumstance that is probably well known to the planners of summit meetings.[7] Events have to be unexpected or rare, or preferably both, to become good news.

The seventh hypothesis is the idea that once something has hit the headlines and been defined as 'news', then it will *continue* to be defined as news for some time even if the amplitude is drastically reduced.[8] The channel has been opened and stays partly open to justify its being opened in the first place, partly because of inertia in the system and partly because what was unexpected has now also become familiar. Thus F_7 is, in a sense, deducible from F_3 and F_6.

The eighth and final hypothesis refers to the *composition* of such units as evening entertainment for the family around the radio set, the front page of a newspaper, the newscast on radio, the newsreel on TV or in the cinema, and so on. The idea is this: imagine the news editor of a broadcasting station has received only news from abroad and only of a certain type. Some minutes before he is on the air he gets some insignificant domestic news and some foreign news of a different kind. The hypothesis is that the threshold value for these news items will be much lower than would otherwise have been the case, because of a desire to present a 'balanced' whole. Correspondingly, if there are already many foreign news items the threshold value for a new item will be increased.

As mentioned, these eight factors are based on fairly simple reasoning about what facilitates and what impedes perception. They are held to be culture-free in the sense that we do not expect them to vary significantly with variations in human culture – they should not depend much on cultural parameters. More particularly, we would not expect them to vary much along the east–west, north–south or centre–periphery axes which we often make use of to structure the world. In particular, these factors should be relatively independent of some other major determinants of the press. A newspaper may vary in the degree to which it caters to mass circulation and a free market economy. If it wants a mass circulation, all steps in the news chain will probably anticipate the reaction of the next step in the chain and accentuate the selection and distortion effects in order to make the material more compatible with their image of what the readers want. Moreover, a newspaper may vary in the degree to which it tries to present many aspects of the situation, or, rather, like the partners in a court case, try to present only the material that is easily compatible with its own political point of view. In the latter case selection and distortion will probably be accentuated and certainly not decrease.

But there is little doubt that there are also culture-bound factors influencing the transition from events to news, and we shall mention four such factors that we deem to be important at least in the north-western corner of the world. They are:

(F_9) The more the event concerns élite nations, the more probable that it will become a news item.

(F_{10}) The more the event concerns élite people, the more probable that it will become a news item.

(F_{11}) The more the event can be seen in personal terms, as due to the action of specific individuals, the more probable that it will become a news item.

(F_{12}) The more negative the event in its consequences, the more probable that it will become a news item.

Again, some comments are in order.

That news is *élite-centred*, in terms of nations or in terms of people, is hardly strange. The actions of the élite are, at least usually and in short-term perspective, more consequential than the activities of others: this applies to élite nations as well as to élite people. More-over, as amply demonstrated by the popular magazines found in most countries, the élite can be used in a sense to tell about everybody. A story about how the king celebrates his birthday will contain many elements that could just as well have been told about anybody, but who in particular among ordinary men and women should be picked for the telling of the story? Elite people are available to serve as objects of general identification, not only because of their intrinsic importance. Thus in an élite-centred news communication system ordinary people are not even given the chance of representing themselves. *Mutatis mutandis*, the same should apply to nations.

More problematic is the idea of *personification*. The thesis is that news has a tendency to present events as sentences where there is a subject, a named person or collectivity consisting of a few persons, and the event is then seen as a consequence of the actions of this person or these persons. The alternative would be to present events as the outcome of 'social forces', as structural more than idiosyncratic outcomes of the society which produced them. In a structural presentation the names of the actors would disappear much as they do in sociological analysis and for much the same reason – the thesis is that the presentation actually found is more similar to what one finds in traditional personified historical analysis. To the extent that this is the case the problem is *why*, and we have five different explanations to offer:

(1) Personification is an outcome of *cultural idealism* according to which man is the master of his own destiny and events can be seen as the outcome of an act of free will. In a culture with a more materialistic outlook this should not be the case. Structural factors should be emphasized, there will be more events happening to people or with people as instruments than events caused by people.

(2) Personification is a consequence of the need for meaning and consequently for *identification*: persons can serve more easily as objects of positive and negative identification through a combination of projection and empathy.

(3) Personification is an outcome of the *frequency-factor*: persons can act during a time-span that fits the frequency of the news media, 'structures' are more difficult to pin down in time and space.

(4) Personification can be seen as a direct consequence of the *élite-concentration* but as distinct from it.

(5) Personification is more in agreement with modern techniques of news gathering and news presentation. Thus, it is easier to take a photo of a person than of a 'structure' (the latter is better for movies – perhaps), and whereas one interview yields a necessary and sufficient basis for one person-centred news story, a structure-centred news story will require many interviews, observation techniques, data gathering, etc. Obviously, there is an egg-chicken argument implied here since it may also be argued that personification came first and that techniques, the whole structure of news communication, were developed accordingly.

We only offer those explanations without choosing between them; first of all because there is no reason to choose as long as they do not contradict each other, and secondly because we have neither data nor theory that can provide us with a rational basis for a choice. It is our hunch that future research will emphasize that these factors reinforce each other in producing personification.

When we claim that *negative* news will be preferred to positive news we are saying nothing more sophisticated than what most people seem to refer to when they say that 'there is so little to be happy about in the news', etc. But we can offer a number of reasons why this state of affairs appears likely, just as we did for the factor of personification. We shall do so using the other factors relatively systematically:

(1) Negative news enters the news channel more easily because it satisfies the *frequency* criterion better. There is a *basic asymmetry* in life between the positive, which is difficult and takes time, and the negative, which is much easier and takes less time – compare the amount of time needed to bring up and socialize an adult person and the amount of time needed to kill him in an accident: the amount of time needed to build a house and to destroy it in a fire, to make an aeroplane and to crash it, and so on. The positive cannot be too easy, for then it would have low scarcity value. Thus, a negative event can more easily unfold itself completely between two issues of a newspaper and two newscast transmissions – for a positive event this is more difficult and specific. Inaugurating or culminating events are needed. A PR-minded operator will, of course, see to that – but he is not always present.

(2) Negative news will more easily be *consensual and unambiguous* in the sense that there will be agreement about the interpretation of the event as negative. A 'positive' event may be positive to some people and not to others and hence not satisfy the criterion of unambiguity. Its meaning will be blurred by other overtones and undertones.

(3) Negative news is said to be more *consonant* with at least some dominant pre-images of our time. The idea must be that negative news fulfils some latent or manifest needs and that many people have such needs. Of the many theories in this field we prefer the cognitive dissonance version because it is falsifiable. The theory, however, presupposes a relatively high level of general anxiety to provide a sufficient matrix in which negative news can be embedded with much consonance. This should be the case during crises,[9] so a test of this theory would be that during crises news that is not related to the crises tends to be more negative and not more positive (as a theory of compensation rather than of dissonance/reduction would predict).

(4) Negative news is more *unexpected* than positive news, both in the sense that the events referred to are more rare, and in the sense that they are less predictable. This presupposes a culture where changes to the positive, in other words 'progress', are somehow regarded as the normal and trivial thing that can pass under-reported because it represents nothing new. The negative curls and eddies rather than the steady positive flow will be reported. The test of this theory would be a culture with *regress* as the normal, and in that case one would predict over-reporting of positive news. This is exemplified by news about the illness of an important person: the slightest improvement is over-reported relative to a steady decline.

Again we do not have sufficient theory to make a choice between these possible explanations – nor do we have to do so since they do not exclude each other.

As to these last four factors it was mentioned that they seem to be of particular importance in the northwestern corner of the world. This does not mean that they are not operating in other areas, but one could also imagine other patterns of relationship between the set of events and the set of news. Table 1 shows some examples:

TABLE 1

SOME PATTERNS OF NEWS STRUCTURE

Pattern	F_9 nation	F_{10} people	F_{11} personification	F_{12} negativization
I	élite centred	élite centred	person centred	negative centred
II	élite centred	élite centred	structure centred	positive centred
III	élite centred	élite centred	both	negative centred
IV	non-élite centred	élite centred	person centred	positive centred

Pattern I is the pattern we have described above. Pattern II would, where the last two aspects are concerned, be more in agreement with socialist thinking, and where the first two are concerned, with big-power thinking. It might fit the news structure of the Soviet Union, but with the important proviso that one would probably use Pattern III to describe Western powers. Similarly, a newly independent developing nation might use Pattern IV for itself, but also receive Pattern III for former colonial powers. But all this is very speculative.[10]

Let us then list systematically the twelve factors we have concentrated on in this analysis; with subfactors:

Events become news to the extent that they satisfy the conditions of

(F_1) frequency
(F_2) threshold
($F_{2.1}$) absolute intensity
($F_{2.2}$) intensity increase
(F_3) unambiguity
(F_4) meaningfulness
($F_{4.1}$) cultural proximity

($F_{4.2}$) relevance
(F_5) consonance
($F_{5.1}$) predictability
($F_{5.2}$) demand
(F_6) unexpectedness
($F_{6.1}$) unpredictability
($F_{6.2}$) scarcity
(F_7) continuity
(F_8) composition
(F_9) reference to élite nations
(F_{10}) reference to élite people
(F_{11}) reference to persons
(F_{12}) reference to something negative

As mentioned, these twelve factors are not independent of each other: there are interesting inter-relations between them. However, we shall not attempt to 'axiomatize' on this meagre basis.

Let us now imagine that all these factors are operating. This means, we hypothesize, three things:

(1) The more events satisfy the criteria mentioned, the more likely that they will be registered as news (*selection*).
(2) Once a news item has been selected what makes it newsworthy according to the factors will be accentuated (*distortion*).
(3) Both the process of selection and the process of distortion will take place at all steps in the chain from event to reader (*replication*).

Thus the longer the chain, the more selection and distortion will take place according to this – but the more material will there also be to select from and to distort if one thinks of the press agencies relative to special correspondents. In other words, we hypothesize that every link in the chain reacts to what it receives fairly much according to the same principles. The journalist scans the phenomena (in practice to a large extent by scanning other newspapers) and selects and distorts, and so does the reader when he gets the finished product, the news pages, and so do all the middle-men. And so do, we assume, people in general when they report something, and, for instance, diplomats when they gather material for a dispatch to their ministry – partly because they are conditioned by their psychology and their culture partly because this is reinforced by the newspapers.

In general this means that the cumulative effects of the factors should be considerable and produce an image of the world different from 'what really happened' – for instance in the ways indicated by Östgaard.[11] However, since we have no base-line in direct reports on 'what really happened' on which this can be tested we shall proceed in a different direction. Our problem is how the factors relate to each other in producing a final outcome.

NOTES AND REFERENCES

1. For an impression of what sociologists can get out of the condition of sleeping see Vilhelm Aubert and Harrison White, 'Sleep: a sociological interpretation', *Acta Sociologica*, Vol. 4, No. 2, pp. 46–54 and Vol. 4, No. 3, pp. 1–16.

2. This, of course, is a fundamental idea in the psychology of perception. Actually there are two separate ideas inherent here: the notion of an absolute level that must not be too low, and the notion of the increase needed to be noticed – the 'just noticeable differences' (jnd's). The jnd increases with increasing absolute level; the stronger the amplitude, the more the difference is needed to be noticed (whether this is according to Weber's principle or not). This principle probably applies very explicitly to news communication: the more dramatic the news, the more is needed to add to the drama. This may lead to important distortions. The more drama there already is, the more will the news media have to exaggerate to capture new interest, which leads to the hypothesis that there is more exaggeration the more dramatic the event – i.e., the less necessary one might feel it is to exaggerate.

3. N. R. Ashby in *An introduction to cybernetics* (New York, Wiley, 1957) defines noise simply as distortion that may create differences in interpretation at the sender and receiver ends of a communication channel. But one may just as well say that the signal distorts the noise as vice versa.

4. B. Berelson and G. A. Steiner in their *Human behaviour: an inventory of scientific findings* (New York, Harcourt, Brace & World, 1963) mention a number of principles under 'Perceiving', and two of them are (p. 112 and p. 100):

   B7:   The greater the ambiguity of the stimulus, the more room and need for interpretation.

   B3.3a: There may also be decreased awareness of stimuli if it is important *not* to see (perceptual defence).

   What we have been doing is to combine these theorems (but not deductively) into the idea of defence against ambiguity. There are several reasons for this. Modern newspapers are mass media of communication, at least most of them, and publishers may feel (justifiably or not) that increase in ambiguity may decrease the sales. Moreover, to the extent that news shall serve as a basis for action orientation ambiguity will increase rather than reduce the uncertainty and provide a poorer basis for action.

5. The common factor behind both dimensions of what we have called 'meaningfulness' is probably 'identification'.

6. Again, some findings from Berelson and Steiner are useful (op. cit., p. 101 and p. 529):

B3.2:   With regard to expectations, other things equal, people are more likely to attend to aspects of the environment they anticipate than to those they do not, and they are more likely to anticipate things they are familiar with.

B3.3:   With regard to motives, not only do people look for things they need or want; but the stronger the need, the greater the tendency to ignore irrelevant elements.

A1:   People tend to see and hear communications that are favourable to their predispositions; they are more likely to see and hear congenial communications than neutral or hostile ones. And the more interested they are in the subject, the more likely is such selective attention.

7. For a discussion of this see Johan Galtung, 'Summit meetings and international relations', *Journal of Peace Research* (1964), pp. 36–54.

8. For a discussion of this factor see E. Ostgaard, *Nyhetsvandering* (Stockholm: Wahston and Widstrand, 1968), p. 151.

9. Festinger has a very interesting account of how Indians selected rumours following an earthquake, and consistent with the fear provoked by the earthquake: 'Let us speculate about the content of the cognition of these persons. When the earthquake was over they had this strong, persistent fear reaction but they could see nothing different around them, no destruction, no further threatening things. In short, a situation had been produced where dissonance existed between cognition corresponding to the fear they felt and the knowledge of what they saw around them which, one might say, amounted to the cognition that there was nothing to be afraid of. The vast majority of the rumours which were widely circulated were rumours which, if believed, provided cognition consonant with being afraid. One might even call them 'fear-provoking' rumours, although, if our interpretation is correct, they would more properly be called "fear justifying" rumours.' Leon Festinger, 'The motivating effect of cognitive dissonance', in Gardner Lindzey (Ed.), *Assessment of human motives* (New York, Grove Press, 1958), p. 72.

10. As an example some impressions can be given from three months' systematic reading of the Moroccan newspaper *Le Petit Marocain*. In very summarized form: the first page contained news about progress in Morocco, the second about decadence, murder, rape and violence in France – so that anybody could draw his conclusion. Of course, such things will depend rather heavily on the value-systems of the editorial staff – but we nevertheless postulate the existence of general patterns. Ola Mårtensson, in a mimeographed report (in Swedish) of a content analysis of three major papers in the USSR, indicates both personification and élite concentration. Ola Mårtensson, *Pravda, Izvestija och Krasanaja Zvezda under våren hösten 1964* (Lund, Institute for Political Science, Lund University, Sweden, 1965), 26 pp. mimeo.

11. Östgaard, op. cit., pp. 52 ff.

News as eternal recurrence*

PAUL ROCK

News is a peculiar form of knowledge: its character derives very much from the sources and contexts of its production. With few exceptions, those sources and contexts are bureaucratic, and news is the result of an organized response to routine bureaucratic problems. So obvious is this interpretation that it has informed numerous treatments of news. Those treatments have, however, been dominated by one particular perspective on organized communication. The newspaper office has been portrayed as a network of communication channels, and news itself has been explained by concepts which revolve loosely around the cybernetic properties of such channels.[1] This mode of analysis neglects what is distinctive about news as *bureaucratic* knowledge; it fails to recognize that the communications of a newspaper office constitute a special system. In this paper, I shall examine one consequence of knowledge being transformed into a work material that can be practically managed by a complex organization.

The business of any bureaucracy is the routine production of sequences of activity that are anticipated and guided by formal rules. Those rules can never be exhaustive. They explicitly and implicitly define the limits of variation in the material that can be processed by the bureaucracy. When an organization does not exercise total control over that material, there is always the possibility that it will fall outside the defined limits of variation. In such a case, the formal rules are rendered inappropriate. The roles that were established to superintend normal work will lose their usefulness. The understandings that informed activity become irrelevant or misleading. An organization can respond by attempting to force the obdurate materials into a workable form; it may modify some of its practices; it may destroy the materials; or it may simply refuse to handle them. Yet it is apparent that anomalous or ambiguous cases can be disruptive and that some bureaucratic effort must be directed at their control.

The basic product of a newspaper office is knowledge about particular events in the world. Those events must have some extra-

*Paper prepared especially for this book.

ordinary quality that makes them worthy of being reported to a large audience. They may be extraordinary and repetitive like dealings on the stock exchange, or extraordinary and uncommon like a disaster at sea. In either case, their reporting signifies that they have been identified as an important departure from the familiar and the everyday.

It would seem, however, that the identification process is not simple. Journalists and sociologists alike maintain that the world does not appear to reporters as a clearly structured entity.[2] A few of its happenings have become remarkable by convention. Aircraft crashes and elections are routinely reported.[3] Other happenings are so engineered that they become eminently reportable.[4] The rest is ambiguous and perplexing. It is not laid out before the reporter as a landscape composed of transparently ordinary and extraordinary occurrences.

This experience of confusion is compounded by the largely solipsistic nature of the identification process. News is held to be distinguished by its objective facticity. It is a social fact that is not open to much negotiation or manipulation. The readership of a newspaper is taken to be capable of recognizing and demanding accounts of such social facts. Its interest grows and wanes in response to changes in the natural world of social events. The reporter's own perspective on those events acknowledges both their facticity *and* their lack of immediate significance. However, it cannot rely on the public's interpretative procedures for clarification because they tend to be inaccessible to the reporter.[5] In the absence of such directives, the staff of a newspaper office are thrown back on themselves. They become a surrogate for the unreachable public.[6] Thus, while much news becomes what the office has itself decided to treat as news, 'newsworthiness' is still regarded as an independent quality of autonomous events.

The world does not seem to be arranged for reporting purposes, and the strategies which would make it describable reflect its confusion. They are not amenable to reflective analysis by those who use them. Journalists seem unable to explain how they impose order on flux. In consequence, the procedures which are employed to identify and record news are not regulated by formal rules.[7] They are, instead, governed by an interpretative faculty called 'news sense' which cannot be communicated or taught.[8] A newspaper office, then, is regarded by its members as a bureaucracy which cannot generate formal rules for all its important areas of activity. Such a lack of structure creates a great potential for anarchy. The critical task of capturing news is entrusted to an indescribable skill whose workings are uncertain.

The world reported as news is ambiguous and elusive. Unless it can be translated into a succession of coherent events, the entire reporting exercise would fail. The process of translation must, moreover, be mechanical enough to ensure that a constant volume of news is produced at regular and frequent intervals. The organization of newspaper work cannot rely on a random search for news. It cannot permit lengthy explorations which might be fruitless. Certainty must be built into reporting processes.

The apparent formlessness of much journalism is lent a shape by its organizational setting. The explicit rules which fail to emerge in the quest for news are remedied by institutional imperatives that emanate from the more manageable areas of the industry. What seems unregulated is, in fact, controlled. These imperatives relate chiefly to issues of the mapping out and timetabling of newspapers. They give structure to the schemes which journalists use to confront an ambiguous world. They provide the categories that underlie 'news sense'. If journalists themselves are unable to articulate those categories, it is perhaps because they do not fully understand the larger contours of the context in which they work.

SPACE

Policies affecting the layout of a newspaper predetermine what can be reported about the world. They map out the rough system of priorities which will be allocated to the description of unrealized events; decide the proportions that those reports will occupy in the total presentation; and limit the entire volume of events which can evoke a journalistic reaction.[9] Newspapers do not vary substantially in size from day to day; neither do they vary in their composition. The inclusion of photographs, advertising and standardized matter such as cartoons and stock-exchange reports further defines what is recordable. Although policies differ between newspaper organizations, each one imposes a firm grid on the distribution of events that will be recognized. Such a grid enhances the probability that consistent amounts of crime, sport, foreign conflict and so on will journalistically occur. If the anticipated amount does not obviously manifest itself, the definition of what might properly be reported becomes negotiable.[10] The conception of what is newsworthy will grow elastic enough to encompass relatively nebulous or insignificant events. After all, it is this layout policy which supports the journalistic division of labour. Crime reporters, sports commentators and foreign correspondents are occupationally committed to producing a relatively constant output of knowledge about their particular worlds.

Of course, the overall spacing scheme is not immutable. The changing expertise of a newspaper's staff, novel events which seem to be unambiguously important, or perceived changes in a public's demands can all bring about shifts in the scheme. These shifts are, however, likely to be calculated and orderly. Once a newspaper has acquired a new focus, it will tend to retain it for some while. The movement from focus to focus will not minutely reflect the fluid character of the world that is under observation.[11]

Although the scheme organizes journalistic responses, it is evident that the way in which a newspaper allots space is itself based on some initial definition of the absolute and relative importance of different areas. In part, that definition may be explained by convention: newspapers record crime and sport because other newspapers record crime and sport.[12] Indeed, it may be regarded as the essence of a newspaper that it covers such phenomena. Other features of the scheme may be attributed to journalistic understandings of popular morality and culture. For instance, crime news has traditionally been defined as attractive to readers.[13] Yet, in the absence of effective feedback from a readership, the solipsistic element of selection remains and, once formulated, the scheme tends to serve as its own authority. What has been news in the past is likely to be news again.[14]

TIME

Not only are events seen to occur in relatively stable proportions, they are also expected to occur in definite sequences. Newspapers are published in editions which succeed one another in time. Each edition must convey a coherent and persuasive portrait of the world; each must be significantly differentiated from its predecessors and successors; and each one must have some thematic continuity with other editions. The timetable of newspaper production imposes itself upon what can be recorded.

Developments which unfold very gradually tend to be unreportable by the daily press unless some distinctive stage is reached.[15] Phenomena which do not change appreciably have a lesser chance of being recorded unless they were expected to develop.[16] There is thus a constant strain within the reporting enterprise to adapt the world of events to the timetable of the newspaper. Such an adaptation may be achieved by a deliberate scheduling of newsworthy occurrences,[17] by delays in reporting, or by negotiation with those who are responsible for initiating action.[18] Newspapers must demonstrate that significant change has occurred during the time interval that elapsed between editions. This requirement may lead to nothing more than a special selection of what is newsworthy, but it may lead to the imposition of development upon recalcitrant phenomena. Western newspapers are unable to contend with slow-moving historical cycles; they are far better equipped to accommodate rapid, expected change.[19] They are, moreover, generally incapable of reporting what seems to be an indeterminate or fluid situation. Process may be forced on occurrences whose direction is indecisive.[20]

Thus, in the place of random search, newsgathering takes routine forms. Those forms can be continually maintained only if they are supported by a set of operating assumptions about the world and about the newspaper's place in that world. The assumptions transform a possible anarchy into a more or less stable universe of events in which there is some predictability and rationality. The events are linked together in a discernible manner, and their emergent properties observe an established time-scale. These assumptions maintain and are maintained by a corresponding allocation of resources. In the main, journalists position themselves so that they have access to institutions which generate a useful volume of reportable activity at useful intervals. Some of these institutions do, of course, make themselves visible by means of dramatization, or through press releases and press agents.[21] Others are known regularly to produce consequential events. The courts, sports grounds and parliament mechanically manufacture news which is effortlessly assimilated by the press.[22]

When these assumptions are applied, news can acquire a cyclical quality. If resort is made to developments which are institutionalized, predicted, short-lived and in continual production, news will itself become a series of cycles. The content may change, but the forms will be enduring.[23] Much news is, in fact, ritual. It conveys an impression of endlessly repeated drama whose themes are familiar and well understood.[24]

The ambiguity of events is thus considerably dispelled by trapping the activities of reliable and permanent organizations. News is less likely to be made by ephemeral groups of people, by ill-structured groups or by groups whose behaviour does not appear on a suitable schedule.

An interesting consequence of the search for an objectified and sure world of news is that the solipsism of the newspaper office may feed upon itself and transform newspapers into authoritative sources themselves. Once some newspaper ratifies an event as news, others may accept that ratification and treat the event as independently newsworthy. Journalists religiously read their own and others' newspapers;[25] they consult one another;[26] and look for continuities in the emerging world which their reporting has constructed. In this process, a generally consistent interpretation is maintained and built up. It possesses an independent and impersonal quality which makes it seem compelling.

These self-generated paradigms may, in time, become virtually autonomous. They may become progressively detached from their base and then unfold in accord with an internal logic of their own. In this fashion, the press can create 'pseudo-disasters'[27] which may have no discernible relation with events as they are known by outsiders. Pseudo-disasters, crime waves[28] and panics create a reality which is organized by the structure of the newspaper office alone. Most probably, these autonomous news cycles are more conveniently constructed than any other to meet the space and timetabling demands of a newspaper organization. They are likely to be discrete, brief, well structured, and pregnant with intelligible, consistent development.

I have done no more than impose a slightly different construction on themes which are familiar in the writings on newspapers and news. Yet the ritualized and cyclical nature of much reporting is a critical feature of the way in which the world is made known. It conveys an impression of eternal recurrence, of society as a social order which is made up of movement but no innovation. Change occurs in a series of small occurrences of small duration. There is no grand design.

REFERENCES

1. The prototype for such work was D. White, 'The "gatekeeper": a case study in the selection of news', *Journalism Quarterly* (Fall 1950), Vol. 27, No. 4.
2. Cf. J. Carey, 'The communications revolution and the professional communicator', in P. Halmos (ed.), *The sociology of mass-media communicators*, *Sociological Review Monograph*, No. 13, University of Keele (1969), esp. p. 33; J. Tunstall, *Journalists at work* (London, Constable, 1971), esp. p. 6.
3. Cf. B. Cohen, *The press and foreign policy* (New Jersey, Princeton University Press, 1963), esp. p. 55.
4. Cf. D. Boorstin, *The image* (London, Weidenfeld & Nicolson, 1961), esp. pp. 9–11.
5. Cf. W. Gieber, 'News is what newspapermen make it', in L. Dexter and D. White (eds.), *People, society, and mass communications* (New York, Free Press, 1964), p. 176; J. Tunstall, *The Westminster Lobby correspondents* (London, Routledge & Kegan Paul, 1970), p. 67; W. Gieber, 'Two communicators of the news', *Social Forces* (October 1960), Vol. 39, No. 1, p. 80; C. Lindstrom, 'Sensationalism in the news', *Journalism Quarterly* (Winter 1956), Vol. 33, p. 9; W. Gieber, 'Across the desk', *Journalism Quarterly* (Fall 1956), Vol. 33, p. 431.

6. Cf. G. Gerbner, 'Institutional pressures upon mass communicators', in P. Halmos (ed.), op. cit., p. 242; W. Gieber, 'Two communicators of the news', op. cit., p. 80; T. Burns, 'Public service and private world', in P. Halmos (ed.), op. cit., p. 65.

7. Cf. W. Breed, 'Newspaper opinion leaders and processes of standardization', *Journalism Quarterly* (Summer 1955), Vol. 32. p. 282; M. Warner, 'Decision-making in network television news', in J. Tunstall (ed.), *Media sociology* (London, Constable, 1970), p. 63.

8. Cf. B. Cohen, op. cit., p. 54.

9. Cf. R. Casey and T. Copeland, 'Current "news hole" policies of daily newspapers: a survey', *Journalism Quarterly* (Spring 1957), Vol. 34, pp. 175–6; W. Gieber, 'Across the desk', op. cit., pp. 429–30.

10. Cf. W. Breed, 'Social control in the newsroom', *Social forces* (May 1955), Vol. 33, No. 4, p. 331.

11. Cf. B. Cohen, op. cit., p. 99.

12. Cf. W. Breed, 'Newspaper opinion leaders', op. cit., p. 278.

13. Cf. J. Frank, *The beginnings of the English newspaper: 1620–1660*, (Massachusetts, Harvard University Press, 1961), pp. 202, 212, 237.

14. Cf. B. Cohen, op. cit., p. 59.

15. Cf. H. Hughes, *News and the human interest story* (Chicago, University of Chicago Press, 1940), p. 80.

16. Cf. J. Galtung and M. Ruge, 'The structure of foreign news: The presentation of the Congo, Cuba and Cyprus crises in four foreign newspapers', *Journal of International Peace Research*, 1 (1965), pp. 64–90. Extract reprinted in this Reader.

17. Cf. D. Boorstin, op. cit., pp. 9–11.

18. Cf. P. Murphy, 'Police–press relations', in A. Brandstatter and L. Radelet, *Police and community relations* (California, Glencoe Press, 1968).

19. Cf. H. Hughes, op. cit., pp. 55–6; W. Gieber, 'How the "gatekeepers" view local civil liberties news', *Journalism Quarterly* (Spring 1960), pp. 199–205.

20. Cf. S. Cohen, 'Hooligans, vandals and the community' (Unpublished Ph.D. dissertation, University of London, 1969).

21. Cf. W. Lippmann, *Public opinion* (New York, Free Press, 1949).

22. Ibid.

23. Cf. H. Hughes, op. cit., p. 210.

24. Cf. H. Duncan, *Communication and social order* (New York, Bedminster Press, 1962), p. 305.

25. Cf. W. Breed, 'Newspaper opinion leaders', op. cit., p. 278.

26. Cf. D. Grey, 'Decision-making by a reporter under deadline pressure', *Journalism Quarterly* (Autumn 1966), Vol. 43, p. 427.

27. Cf. N. Medalia and O. Larsen, 'Diffusion and belief in a collective delusion: The Seattle windshield pitting epidemic', *American Sociological Review*, Vol. 23, No. 2; D. Johnson, 'The phantom anesthetist of Matoon', *Journal of Abnormal and Social Psychology* (April 1945), Vol. 40; N. Jacobs, 'The phantom slasher of Taipei', *Social Problems* (Winter 1965), Vol. 12, No. 5.

28. Cf. M. Wiseheart, 'Newspapers and criminal justice', in R. Pound and F. Frankfurter (eds.), *Criminal justice in Cleveland* (Cleveland, Cleveland Foundation, 1922); F. Davis, 'Crime news in Colorado newspapers', *American Journal of Sociology* (January 1952), Vol. 57, No. 4.

The complete stylization of news*

MICHAEL FRAYN

The soporific quiet which filled Goldwasser's laboratory in the Newspaper Department was disturbed only by the soft rustle of tired newsprint. Assistants bent over the component parts of the Department's united experiment, the demonstration that in theory a digital computer could be programmed to produce a perfectly satisfactory daily newspaper with all the variety and news sense of the old hand-made article. With silent, infinite tedium, they worked their way through stacks of newspaper cuttings, identifying the pattern of stories, and analysing the stories into standard variables and invariables. At other benches other assistants copied the variables and invariables down on to cards, and sorted the cards into filing cabinets, coded so that in theory a computer could pick its way from card to card in logical order and assemble a news item from them. Once Goldwasser and his colleagues had proved the theory, commercial interests would no doubt swiftly put it into practice. The stylization of the modern newspaper would be complete. Its last residual connection with the raw, messy, offendable real world would have been broken.

Goldwasser picked up a completed file waiting for his attention. It was labelled 'Paralysed Girl Determined to Dance Again'. Inside it were forty-seven newspaper cuttings about paralysed girls who were determined to dance again. He put it to one side. He had picked it up, looked at the heading, and put it to one side every day for a week, waiting for a day when he felt strong.

He picked up the next file instead, labelled 'Child Told Dress Unsuitable by Teacher'. Inside there were ninety-five cuttings about children who had been told their dress was unsuitable by their teacher, an analysis of the cuttings into their elements, and a report from the researcher who had prepared the file. The report read:

'V. Satis. Basic plot entirely invariable. Variables confined to three. (1) Clothing objected to (high heels/petticoat/frilly knickers). (2) Whether child also smokes and/or uses lipstick. (3) Whether child alleged by parents to be humiliated by having offending clothing inspected before whole school.

*From Michael Frayn, *The tin men* (London, Collins, 1965), Chapter 7.

'Frequency of publication: once every nine days.'

Nobbs, Goldwasser's Principal Research Assistant, shambled over and threw some more files on to Goldwasser's desk. He wore a beard, to identify himself with the intelligentsia, affected a stooped, lounging gait to establish parity of esteem with the aristocracy, and called everyone except the Director and Deputy-Director 'mate', to demonstrate solidarity with the proletariat. He had a powerful effect on Goldwasser, causing a helpless panic to seize him.

'Here you are, mate', said Nobbs, ramming the word 'mate' into Goldwasser like a jack-knife. 'I'm just doing the "They Think Britain is Wonderful" file now. Seems all right. Variables are mainly who's doing the thinking – American tourists, Danish *au pair* girls, etc.'

'Are you going to cross-index it with "British Girls Are Best, Say Foreign Boys"?' said Goldwasser, 'I mean, to avoid using them both on the same day?'

'It wouldn't matter, would it, mate?' said Nobbs. 'We're trying for an upbeat tone overall, aren't we?'

'I suppose so,' muttered Goldwasser, unable to bring himself to argue with anyone as horrible as Nobbs. 'But cross-index it with "Boomerang, Bustling Britain", then. We can't have them *all* in on the same day.'

'Your word is law, O master,' said Nobbs. 'Mate.'

O God, prayed Goldwasser humanely, let Nobbs be painlessly destroyed.

'Have you checked "Paralysed Girl Determined to Dance Again" yet?' asked Nobbs.

'Not yet,' said Goldwasser.

'Well, don't blame me when we're a week behind schedule at the end of the month,' said Nobbs. 'That's all I ask, mate. And what about "I Plan to Give Away My Baby, Says Mother-to-be"? We can't do anything more on that until we've got a policy decision from you.'

'I'll look at that now,' said Goldwasser. Nobbs slouched away. Goldwasser lifted his eyes from the pencil jar, where they had taken refuge from the sight of Nobbs, and watched Nobbs shamble back to his office, knocking over chairs and sweeping files off the corners of desks as he went. He turned to the 'I Plan to Give Away My Baby, Says Mother-to-be' file.

'Difficulty here', said the researcher's report. 'Frequency of once a month, but in fifty-three cuttings examined there are no variables at all. Even name of mother-to-be the same. May possibly involve fifty-three different foetuses, but no way of telling from cuttings. Can we use story with no variables?'

Goldwasser put it to one side. One had to wait for decisions as big as that to ambush one unexpectedly. He looked at his watch. He had the impression that he had been working continuously for an exceedingly long time. Perhaps he had earned a break; perhaps he could slip across to play with the loyal leader cards for five minutes.

Goldwasser sometimes took himself out of himself by pretending to be a computer, and going through one of the completed sets of cards observing the same logical rules and making the same random choices that a computer would to compose a story from them. The by-election set and the weather story set soon palled. So did 'I Test New Car' and 'Red Devils Fly In to Trouble Spot'. But the set for composing a loyal leader on a royal occasion seemed to Goldwasser to have something of that teasing perfection which draws one back again and again to certain pictures.

He opened the filing cabinet and picked out the first card in the set. *Traditionally*, it read. Now there was a random choice between cards reading *coronations, engagements, funerals, weddings, coming of age, births, deaths,* or *the churching of women*. The day before he had picked *funerals*, and been directed on to a card reading with simple perfection *are occasions for mourning*. Today he closed his eyes, drew *weddings*, and was signposted on to *are occasions for rejoicing*.

The wedding of X and Y followed in logical sequence, and brought him a choice between *is no exception* and *is a case in point*. Either way there followed *indeed*. Indeed, whichever occasion one had started off with, whether coronations, deaths, or birth, Goldwasser saw with intense mathematical pleasure, one now reached this same elegant bottleneck. He paused on *indeed*, then drew in quick succession *it is a particularly happy occasion, rarely,* and *can there have been a more popular young couple*.

From the next selection Goldwasser drew *X has won himself/ herself a special place in the nation's affections*, which forced him to go on to *and the British people have clearly taken Y to their hearts already*.

Goldwasser was surprised, and a little disturbed, to realize that the word 'fitting' had still not come up. But he drew it with the next card – *it is especially fitting that*.

This gave him *the bride/bridegroom should be,* and an open choice between *of such a noble and illustrious line, a commoner in these democratic times, from a nation with which this country has long enjoyed a particularly close and cordial relationship,* and *from a nation with which this country's relations have not in the past been always happy*.

Feeling that he had done particularly well with 'fitting' last time, Goldwasser now deliberately selected it again. *It is also fitting that,* read the card, to be quickly followed by *we should remember,* and *X and Y are not merely symbols – they are a lively young man and a very lovely young woman.*

Goldwasser shut his eyes to draw the next card. It turned out to read *in these days when.* He pondered whether to select *it is fashionable to scoff at the traditional morality of marriage and family life* or *it is no longer fashionable to scoff at the traditional morality of marriage and family life.* The latter had more of the form's authentic baroque splendour, he decided. He drew another *it is fitting that,* but thinking three times round was once too many for anything, even for a superb and beautiful word like 'fitting', he cheated and changed it for *it is meet that,* after which *we wish them well* followed as the night the day, and the entertainment was over.

What a piece of work had the school of Goldwasser wrought here! What a toccata and fugue! How remote it was from the harsh cares of life!

Goldwasser started all over again with the churching of women. He had got as far as choice between *it is good to see the old traditions being kept up* and *it is good to see old usages brought more into line with our modern way of thinking,* when Nobbs came shambling out of his room, the word 'mate' written all over his face.

'Now look here, mate,' started Nobbs, 'this Paralysed Girl Determined to Dance Again . . .'

But at this point, as it said on one of the cards in the 'They Are Calling It the Street of Shame' story cabinet, *our investigator made an excuse and left.*

A world at one with itself*

STUART HALL

The issue of violence in the mass media has been posed in the familiar terms of the fantasy or fictional portrayal of violence there. But if the media are playing a role in the alleged escalation of social violence, it is almost certainly not *Z Cars, The Virginian, Callan* or *Codename* which are 'responsible'. What is at issue is not the fantasy role of fictional violence, but the alleged real effects of real violence. The area of broadcasting in question is that traditionally defined as 'news/current affairs/features/documentaries'. It is, for example, the only too real bodies of only too real Vietnamese, floating down an all too real Cambodian river, which some as yet unstated informal theory of cause and effect links in the minds of television's critics with question of 'law and order'. Thus it is to the question of *news* that we must turn.

As it happens, news has just undergone an enormous expansion in the new radio schedules. In the philosophy of streamed radio which underpins the BBC's *Broadcasting in the Seventies*, news got a privileged place. Under the new dispensation, the avid listener is never more than half an hour away from the next news bulletin. But the really striking development is the growth of the news-magazine style of programme, on the *World At One* model.

What constitutes the definition of news currently employed on radio programmes of this new type? I put the point in this way, and not in the more familiar terms of 'coverage' or 'bias/objectivity', because this constitutes the heart of the matter. Journalists through-out the media are notoriously slippery and defensive when thus confronted. 'The news', they assume, is clearly what it is: news-worthy people and events, happening 'out there' in the real world, at home and abroad.

The relevant questions are always technical ones: 'How adequately can we cover these events?', 'Is the coverage biased or objective?' This view is legitimated by a body of journalistic folklore, with its ritual references to copy, deadlines and news angles. These sanction professional practice and keep non-professional busybodies at bay.

Of course, newsmen agree, the news can be either 'hard' or 'soft',

*From *New Society* (18 June 1970), pp. 1056–8.

graphically or neutrally presented (sensationalism/objectivity), a report from the front or a background analysis (actuality/depth), But these are matters of treatment – of form and 'flavour' – not of content or substance. It is worth observing that all these routine ways of setting up the problem are drawn from the press, reflecting both the common background of media newsmen in Fleet Street, and, more important, the powerful hold of models borrowed for radio or television from the press.

The notion that the news somehow discovers itself may be of service to the harassed newsgatherers and editors. Such professional 'commonsense constructs', such *ad hoc* routines, are employed in most large-scale organizations. They enable hard-pressed professionals to execute their tasks with the minimum of stress and role-conflict.

These idiomatic shorthands give the professional a map of the social system, just as the categories of classification in mental hospitals (Erving Goffman), the clinical records of hospitals (H. Garfinkel) and the notebooks and case records of police and probation officers (Aaron Cicourel) witness to the moral order and the system of meanings which other professionals use to give sense to their tasks.

But against this defensive strategy, it needs to be asserted that the news is a *product*, a human construction: a staple of that system of 'cultural production' (to use Theodor Adorno's phrase) we call the mass media. Journalists and editors select, from the mass of potential news items, the events which constitute 'news' for any day. In part, this is done by implicit reference to some unstated and unstatable criteria of *the significant*. News selection thus rests on inferred knowledge about the audience, inferred assumptions about society, and a professional code or ideology. The news is not a set of unrelated items: news stories are coded and classified, referred to their relevant contexts, assigned to different (and differently graded) spaces in the media, and ranked in terms of presentation, status and meaning.

The process of news production has its own structure. News items which infringe social norms, break the pattern of expectations and contrast with our sense of the everyday, or are dramatic, or have 'numerous and intimate contacts with the life of the recipients', have greater news salience for journalists than others. As a highly reputable reporter observed to an irate group of student militants, who were questioning her as to why her paper reported every vote cast during the period of a university occupation, but nothing of the weekend teach-in: 'Votes represent decisions: decisions are news: discussion is not.'

The role of the news journalist is to mediate – or act as the 'gate-keeper' – between different publics, between institutions and the individual, between the spheres of the public and the private, between the new and the old. News production is often a self-fulfilling activity. Categories of news, consistently produced over time, create public spaces in the media which have to be filled. The presence of the media at the birth of new events can affect their course and outcome. The news is not only a cultural product: it is the product of a set of institutional definitions and meanings, which, in the professional shorthand, is commonly referred to as *news values*.

Statistics of crime represent not only the real movement of the crime rate, but the changing definition of what constitutes crime, how it is recognized, labelled and dealt with. To label as 'violent' every incident from skinhead attacks on Pakistanis, to Ulster, to protests against the South African tour, is to establish a certain way of seeing and understanding a complex set of public events.

Once the category of 'law and order' has come into existence as a legitimate news category, whole different orders of meaning and association can be made to cluster together. Terms of understanding– such as the criminal categories reserved for acts of collective social delinquency ('hooligans', say, or 'layabouts') – become transferred to new events like the clashes between citizens and the army in Ulster. It may be that there has been some objective increase in real-world violence; but the effect on news values is *even greater* than that would justify.

This shift is difficult to pinpoint in the brief radio or television news bulletin, though if we take a long enough stretch of time, we can observe changes both in the profile and in the style of news reports. But in the format of the radio news magazine, which approximates more closely to the profile and treatment of a daily newspaper, the amplifying and interpretative function of the media comes into its own.

News magazines include studio interviews, reports from correspondents, replies to attacks, features and 'human interest' stories. This is where background classifying and interpretative schemes register most forcefully. In terms of direct bias, there seems less cause for concern. Within its limits, radio shows little direct evidence of intentional bias. It treats the spokesmen of the two major political parties with scrupulous fairness – more, in fact, than they deserve. But the troublesome question is the matter of unwitting bias: the institutional slanting, built-in not by the devious inclination of editors to the political right or left, but by the steady and un-examined play of attitudes which, via the mediating structure of professionally defined news values, inclines all the media towards the *status quo*.

The operation of unwitting bias is difficult either to locate or prove. Its manifestations are always indirect. It comes through in terms of who is or who is not accorded the status of an accredited witness: in tones of voice: in the set-up of studio confrontations: in the assumptions which underlie the questions asked or not asked: in terms of the analytical concepts which serve informally to link events to causes: in what passes for explanation.

Its incidence can be mapped by plotting the areas of *consensus* (where there is a mutual agreement about the terms in which a topic is to be treated), the areas of *toleration* (where the overlap is less great, and the terms have to be negotiated as between competing definitions) and the areas of *dis-sensus* or *conflict* (where competing definitions are in play).

Unwitting bias has nothing directly to do with the style of 'tough' interviewing, since, even in the areas of consensus issues, the professional ethic sanctions a quiet aggressive, probing style (Hardcastle with Heath, Robin Day with Wilson), though the probe does not penetrate to underlying assumptions.

Areas of *consensus* cover the central issues of politics and power, the fundamental sanctions of society and the sacred British values. To this area belong the accredited witnesses – politicians of both parties, local councillors, experts, institutional spokesmen.

Areas of *toleration* cover what might be called 'Home Office issues' – social questions, prisoners who can't get employment after discharge, little men or women against the bureaucrats, unmarried mothers, and so on. The more maverick witnesses who turn up in this group get, on the whole, an off-beat but sympathetic 'human interest' – even at times a crusading – kind of treatment. Guidelines in this sector are less clear-cut. When such topics edge over into the 'permissive' category, they can arouse strong sectional disapproval. But here even the scrupulously objective news editor can presume (again, a matter of negotiation and judgment, not of objective fact) on a greater background of public sympathy, more room for manoeuvre.

Areas of *conflict* have their un-accredited cast of witnesses too: protesters of all varieties; shop stewards, especially if militant, more especially if on unofficial strike; squatters; civil rights activists; hippies; students; hijackers; Stop the Seventy Tour-ers; and so on. In dealing with these issues and actors, interviewers are noticeably sharper, touchier, defending their flanks against any predisposition to softness.

One could plot the hidden constraints of this informal ideology in the media simply by noting the characterististic arguments advanced against each of these groups. Unofficial strikers are always confronted with 'the national interest', squatters with 'the rights of private property', civil rights militants in Ulster with the need for Protestant and Catholic to 'work together', Stop the Seventy Tour-ers with the way their minority actions 'limit the right of the majority to enjoy themselves as they wish'.

I am not arguing here that these arguments should not be accorded some weight. I am remarking how, in the handling of certain issues, the assumptions which shape an interview item are coincident with official ideologies of the *status quo*. I recall numerous instances when Ulster civil rights militants were confronted with the consequences of violence. But I cannot recall a single instance when an Ulster Moderate or politician was confronted with the equally tenable view, succinctly expressed by Conor Cruise O'Brien, that since Ulster society has for long been based on the dominance of a minority over a majority, no fundamental change in that structure can be expected without its accompanying release of the 'frozen violence' inherent in the situation.

I know that Ulster is a particularly sensitive matter, that the BBC's impartiality came under direct fire during the events of September 1969, and that in this period a close executive watch was maintained over the news output. But then, my criticism is not of the wilful, intentional bias of editors and newscasters, but of the institutionalized ethos of the news media as a whole. The influence exerted by this ethos over actual broadcast programmes is precisely to be found on those occasions when men of quite varying temperaments and political views are systematically constrained in a certain direction.

I recall William Hardcastle's phrase, when reporting the American Anti-Vietnam demonstrations last year: 'the so-called Vietnam Moratorium Committee'. William Hardcastle's objectivity is not in question. But I await, without much confidence, the day when *The World At One* will refer to 'the so-called Confederation of British Industries' or the 'so-called Trades Union Congress' or even the 'so-called Central Intelligence Agency'.

The sources for this hidden consensus must be located outside the broadcasting media proper, at the heart of the political culture itself. It is a view of politics based on the relative absence of violence in British political life, the relative degree of integration between the powerful corporate interest groups within the state. This negotiated consensus is both a historical fact and a source of ideological comfort. The sociologist, Paul Hirst, in a recent paper, 'Some problems of explaining student militancy', gave a succinct sketch of this political style:

What is the nature of this consensus? It is that parliamentary democracy is founded upon legitimate procedures of political action, and that primary among these procedures is that parliament is the mode of pursuit and accommodating interests within the society. It provides legitimate means for the pursuance of interests without resort to open conflict . . . British democracy raises the means of political action to the level of ends: the primary values of British political culture are specified by a body of existing institutions. These institutions and their maintenance have become the primary political goals.

We can only understand the limits and constraints within which 'objectivity' functions in the media when we have grasped the true sources of legitimation in the political culture itself.

We are now at the crunch. For the groups and events upon which, increasingly, the media are required to comment and report, are the groups in conflict with this consensual style of politics. *But* these are precisely the forms of political and civil action which the media, by virtue of their submission to the consensus, are consistently unable to deal with, comprehend or interpret. The nervousness one has observed in the treatment of these issues reflects the basic contradiction between the manifestations which the media are called on to explain and interpret, and the conceptual/evaluative/interpretative framework which they have available to them.

Whereas the core value of the political consensus is the adherence to 'legitimate means for the pursuance of interests without resort to open conflict', the highly heterogeneous groups I have mentioned are characterized either by political militancy, leading through extra-parliamentary politics to the varying types of 'confrontation', or by social disaffiliation, leading through collective and expressive acts of rebellion to the various types of civil disturbance. Civil righters, students, Black Power militants, political hijackers and kidnappers, shop stewards fall into the political militancy category. Skinheads, hippies, squatters, soccer hooligans, psychedelic freak-outs fall into the social disaffiliation category.

The collective label of 'violence' – and its twin metaphor, 'law and order' – is, at one and the same time, both a staggering confusion of new and old meanings and a penetrating insight. As symbolic categories they only make sense when the issues they refer to are shifted from the explanatory context of media to the content of *politics*.

The effective question about the role of the media, then, is not Callaghan's – 'Do the media *cause* violence?' – nor Wedgwood Benn's – 'Is politics too important to be left to the broadcasters?' (with its obvious retort); but rather, 'Do/can the media help us to understand these significant real events in the real world?' 'Do the media clarify them or mystify us about them?'

Actuality versus depth is not a simple technical choice. The distinction is already built into the structure of the national press. In the arena of news and foreign affairs, popular journalism does not permit systematic exploration in depth. In the 'quality' press, some measure of background interpretation and analysis is more regularly provided. Both these things are legitimated by the professional folk-wisdom. Thus, for the populars: 'The Great British Public is not interested in foreign news' – though how the regular reader of the *Mirror*, the *Express* or the *News of the World*, our circulation front-runners, could develop an intelligent interest in foreign affairs is a matter for speculation. And for the quality press there is 'the rigid separation of "hard" news from comment'.

Distinctions of format and depth of treatment flow, via the grooves of class and education, into the papers we get, and they are hardened and institutionalized in the social structure of the national press. But the relevance of this fragmented universe of press communication for a medium like radio at this time is highly questionable. The audience for news through the day is far less stratified by class and education than the readership of newspapers. Radio must operate as if its potential audience is *the whole nation*.

It follows that radio must find ways of making *both* the foreground event *and* the background context core aspects of its working definition of the news. Otherwise, the radio audience, whatever its range of interests, will be consigned effectively to getting a perpetual foreground.

This becomes a critical issue when the coverage is of groups and events which consistently challenge the built-in definitions and values enshrined in the political culture of broadcasters and audiences alike. This position redefines the concept of 'public service', in relation to radio, in a way which runs diametrically counter to the philosophy of rationalization which infected *Broadcasting in the Seventies*. The press has little to contribute to the development of appropriate models.

Judged in these terms, the manifest tendencies in radio are not encouraging. A heady, breathless immediacy now infects all of the news-magazine programmes. In terms of their profile of items, these programmes progressively affiliate to the model of the daily newspaper. As events like political confrontation and civil disturbance escalate, so the coverage is doubled, quadrupled. As coverage expands, so we become even more alive to the actual 'violent' events and overwhelmed by the vivid sound and image. But as this coverage takes the characteristic form of *actuality without context*, it directly feeds our general sense of a meaningless explosion of meaningless and violent acts – 'out there' somewhere, in an unintelligible world where 'no legitimate means' have been devised 'for the pursuance of interests without resort to open conflict'.

'Out there', let us note, is a rapidly expanding area, covering most of the rest of the globe – Indo-China, Latin America, the Middle East, Africa, the Caribbean, Berkeley, Chicago, Tokyo – as well as some growing enclaves closer home. Events of this order play straight into an *ideological gap* in the media – and in public consciousness. That gap is not filled by the media – or, rather, it is now being filled in a systematically distorted way.

Let me conclude with two examples. Take the spate of kidnappings of foreign diplomats in Latin America. These events were endlessly covered on radio and television, usually by reporters on the spot. There was some studio discussion; but the thrust was consistently towards actuality coverage: has he been shot? will the government pay the ransom? will West Germany break off diplomatic relations? The model? Essentially: the front page of the *Daily Express*. What this coverage lacked was some framework which would make this bizarre series of events meaningful or intelligible.

I have been told that this kind of 'background piece' would be provided by the longer reports at the weekend by BBC foreign correspondents. But this is like telling a man whose regular and only newspaper is the *Mirror*, 'If you want to understand the politics of Guatemala, read the *Sunday Times*'. The example is not fortuitous. For during the kidnappings the *Sunday Times* did print a fairly full background article on Guatemala – and a hair-raising, all too intelligible, story it turned out to be.

An even better example, and one where the press performed as badly as radio and television (with the exception of *24 Hours*) was the recent Black Power rioting in Trinidad. The most generally agreed judgment among intelligent West Indians about Trinidad and Jamaica is that the political situation there is highly explosive. Indeed, the real question is why either society has not, before now, gone down in a wave of riots by underprivileged blacks against the privileged coloured middle class. The answer is not unconnected with the presence both of Cuba and of the American fleet within easy striking distance of Kingston and Port of Spain.

The background to the foreground-problem of riots in Trinidad is the persistent grinding poverty of the mass of the people, intensified by basic conflicts of interest between the coloured middle class inheritors of the 'end of colonial rule' (one of the most conspicuous-consumption classes anywhere in the Third World) and the mass of peasants, workers and urban unemployed, who also happen to be black. Without this knowledge, the large-scale migration from the Caribbean to Britain, which has occupied so much 'foreground' space in recent months is, literally, unintelligible. It is another of those meaningless events, leading to the expected confrontations, and ultimately to 'violence'.

This gap between the urban and rural masses and a native bourgeoisie, grown flush in the hectic, post-colonial years of neo-imperialism, is *the* political fact about vast tracts of the Caribbean and Latin America. Yet radio discussions in studio uniformity expressed puzzlement at how Black Power could become an organizing slogan in a country where the government is 'black'. The fact which needs clarification, of course, is that in the West Indies (unlike the United States, where the permanent presence of a white power structure creates solidarity between all 'black brothers'), the emergent lines of social conflict are laid down precisely by the over-determined coalescence of class, power and gradations of colour.

Unfortunately, neither of the two accredited witnesses – Sir Learie Constantine, who regarded the riots as inexplicable, and Alva Clark, who regarded them as 'a tragedy' – contributed to this process of conceptual clarification. When faced with this sudden eruption of yet another incidence of political violence, the explanatory concepts of 'neo-colonialism' and 'native bourgeoisie' were not available – nor anything else which could do duty for them – in the world of radio. Instead, the ingredients of the consensual view were quickly wheeled into place: 'The Prime Minister' . . . 'resignations from the government' . . . 'state of emergency' . . . 'small groups of vandals roaming the streets' . . . 'disaffection in the army' . . . 'detachment of marines from nearby Puerto Rico' . . . violence/law and order.

In one event after another, now, the same informal theories – supported by the same ideological commitments, and functioning as an 'objective' set of technical-professional routines – produce the same mysterious product with systematic regularity.

REFERENCES

1. A. Cicourel, *The social organisation of juvenile justice* (New York, John Wiley & Sons, 1968).
2. H. Garfinkel, *Ethnomethodology* (New Jersey, Prentice Hall, 1967).
3. P. Berger and T. Luckmann, *The social construction of reality* (New York, Doubleday Anchor, 1967).
4. R. Clausse, *Les nouvelles* (Brussels, Centre National d'Etude des Techniques de Diffusion Collective, 1963).

5. U. Saxer, 'News and publicity' in *Diogenes*, No. 68 (1969).
6. W. Breed, 'Social control in the newsroom', *Social Forces*, vol. 33 (1955).
7. D. White, ' "The gatekeeper": a case in study the selection of news' in Dexter and White (ed.), *People, society and mass communications* (Glencoe, The Free Press, 1964).
8. K. and G. Lang, 'The inferential structure of political communications' *Public Opinion Quarterly*, vol. 19 (1965).
9. P. Hirst, 'Some problems of explaining student militancy' (paper delivered to the BSA Conference (Durham, 1970) unpublished).
10. W. Breed, 'Analysing news: some questions for research', *Journalism Quarterly*, vol. 33 (1956).
11. H. Hughes, 'The social interpretation of news', *Annals*, vol. 219 (1942).

PART TWO

Modes and models

In Part One we raised some problems about how events are selected by the journalist. We criticized the Commercial Laissez-Faire model of this process for suggesting that news was 'discovered' and that the institutions dealing with the news merely supplied existing public demand. News, rather, is manufactured by journalists through interpreting and selecting events to fit pre-existing categories, themselves a product of the bureaucratic exigencies of news organizations and the particular concentration of media control and ownership. To stress this creative nature of journalism is not to imply a Mass Manipulative model: distortion is not limited to the heavy hand of direct censorship but is a less obvious process – often unconscious and unstated – of interpreting the event in terms of an acceptable world view.

In Part Two, we discuss various ways of analyzing and explaining such world views. What models of society – and specifically, of deviance and social problems – are implicit in the news or stories produced for the media? Our readings fall into three groups: those which limit themselves to a description of the content of media items; those which relate the various items to a coherent image seen as a function of the problems of the journalist as a member of a bureaucracy, and finally those which explain the images as part of an ideological weapon. (We include here a few studies based not on 'nonfictional' news presentation, but on fiction stories carried by mass circulation books and magazines. To stress the creative nature of journalism and the way it moulds events into particular world views is to narrow the distinction between fiction and nonfiction. From this point of view, neither form of writing is inherently 'superior': our critical evaluations do not relate to the actual use of an interpretative paradigm – this is inevitable – but to the content of the models and world views which shape such interpretations, whether by journalist, film producer or novelist.)

THE QUANTITY AND QUALITY OF DEVIANCE AND SOCIAL PROBLEMS

The first set of readings describes the content of the images presented to the public by the mass media, contrasting this, where possible, with evidence from alternative sources. Thus Berelson and Salter in an article written 30 years ago compare the portrayal of minority and majority Americans in magazine fiction. They note how heroes or heroines were almost exclusively of 'pure' American or Anglo-Saxon/Nordic stock and that minority group members played wicked or servile roles. They trace the stereotypical depiction of minority groups and note how their numbers are consistently under-represented. For example, 9·8 per cent of the American population were black yet only 1·9 per cent found roles in these stories. Such fiction portrays a world where good motives, success and decency are the monopoly of the American White who exists in a world where most lower status minority members are servile to or subversive of his interests.

Such research is complementary to the work of F. James Davis who in a classic article on the crime news coverage in Colorado newspapers showed that the quantity of crime news in the news-papers was unrelated to that reflected in the criminal statistics. A similar conclusion was reached by Bob Roshier (in his paper in Part One) who showed in addition that the relative proportions assigned to various types of crimes were considerably unbalanced. The total impression from such studies on both fictional and news sources is of a series of distortions about the quantity and quality of crime and the type of person likely to be criminal.

Two further articles examine other social problem areas, namely mental illness and alcoholism. Nunnally contrasts the stereotype of the mentally ill person as presented in the mass media (using fic-tional and nonfictional material) to that of public and expert opinion. The mass media are found to distort causes, symptoms, methods of treatment, prognoses and social effects of mental illness. The men-tally ill person is cast in a stereotype different from that held both by public and expert opinion (although we do not agree with Nunnally's implication that the experts are 'right'). Linsky makes his comparisons within the media over time, comparing the changes in the explanations of alcoholism between 1900 and 1966. He finds a radical shift from a free will notion of human nature to an extreme determinist conception of the aetiology of social problems. Linsky suggests that the mass media not only provide a system of cate-gorization which delineates the quality and quantity of deviance, they also contain implicit explanatory models of how such deviance came about.

Such elementary content analyses of the mass media, illuminating although they may be, suffer from two major shortcomings. First, they fail to separate out the *total* messages which the media carry. That is, they discuss the stereotype of the deviant in isolation, they do not discuss his relationships to others within the particular universe being considered. This (as Jerry Palmer rightly points out, in his paper later in this Part) has been a failure of much sociological analysis of the media. For it is only by delineating the whole underlying structure of the media's message that we can understand the world view that is being diffused. This relates to the second criticism, namely, that it is necessary to relate this message to its possible ideological implications in the wider society and thus begin to unravel the reasons for its prevalence. One clearly cannot understand, for example, the racial stereotypes which Berelson and Salter describe, without relating them to the actual position of minorities in America.

PERIODICITY AND CONSONANCY

The second group of readings in Part Two attempt to separate out the underlying structures implicit in news items and relate them to the organizational problems of the media. Students of mass communication have only begun to do the sort of research necessary to illuminate just what organizational and professional mediations are involved in presenting certain images to the audience.[1]

We know that one of the central concerns of the journalist is to make sense of the mass of events which confront him. One way of doing this is actively to phase events to fit the time schedules of the news organization (*periodicity*); another is to draw on existing analytical models to interpret the events (*consonancy*). The daily periodicity of a newspaper will result in what Graham Murdock calls an event-orientation: information which can be gathered, processed and dramatized within a 24-hour cycle stands a better chance of being incorporated than news which is gradual and undramatic. Murdock's example is the coup or assassination attempt compared to the drawn out guerilla war. But even if the phenomenon does not 'naturally' present itself in a series of dramatic events, the mass media may well create such events. Even if *nothing happens*, what Daniel Boorstin calls 'our extravagant expectations' about the amount of novelty in the world, will ensure that something is turned into news.[2] One technique of presenting such 'pseudo events' is to run a story which has died or even a non story by extracting the maximum drama through varying the headlines. This common practice is satirized in the technique of 'Unit Headline Language' invented by Michael Frayn's computer expert, Goldwasser. The 'event orientation' of the media closely relates to another tendency, that of personalizing the news. This, as Galtung and Ruge (Part One) indicate, is not an absolute characteristic of the mass media but a function in part of cultural idealism. That is, events are seen to occur because of the intervention of important figures while collective action and wider social determinants are ignored. These event and personality orientations vary widely within the media, showing again that they are not just inevitable bureaucratic tendencies. Thus many papers or feature programmes make worthy attempts to 'fill in' the background for the reader or viewer. A brief comparison between the contrasting styles of, say, the *Sun* and *The Guardian* makes this clear.

All in all, then, the argument that the images presented in the mass media are a function of technical/bureaucratic problems *in the abstract* ignores the fashion in which the analytical models (in the examples we have cited culturally idealist, event-oriented and personalized) transfigure this process. Similarly, in the case of consonancy there are undoubtedly weighty bureaucratic forces which impose upon the journalist the need to make snappy last minute analyses of events. But whereas, this will create a tendency to utilize unreflectingly a preconceived stereotype, this does not explain, just as the notion of periodicity fails to do, the content of that stereotype nor the pressures against the journalist changing the model he uses. To take an example: when marijuana use was first reported in the British newspapers (in the 'fifties) it was categorized in terms of the 'dope fiend', a stereotype based on opiate addicts. Because of this, certain items of information were more readily assimilated and accredited as truthful (e.g., craving, eventual death from use), while others were more readily ignored (e.g., aesthetic pleasure, harmlessness). A new 'social problem' was squeezed, pummelled and distorted into the already grotesque and inaccurate category of 'dope fiend'. No sooner was the word 'drug' mentioned than the well-trained journalist proceeded to search for the exploitative pusher (the corrupter) in order to complete the *Gestalt* – the total world view – that his story demanded.

William Braden, a reporter for the *Chicago Sun-Times*, presents us with an illuminating illustration of this process. LSD was first categorized in the early 'sixties as a 'miracle drug' used in the treatment of alcoholism, drug addiction and mental illness, and only later as a 'killer drug' similar to other illicit psychotropic substances. Braden notes how the transition between these two stereotypes corresponded to the increasing advocacy of LSD as a 'consciousness-expander'. The ineffable mystical feeling claimed to be experienced by LSD users could not be easily categorized as a product of a therapeutic 'miracle drug' or as being within the realm of 'normal' religious experience. For a while, the drug's qualities did not fit existing media categories and caused a degree of unease. The arrival at last of 'proof' that it was dangerous in terms of chromosome damage and its suicidogenic qualities, came as a relief to the journalists who could now easily place it within the 'killer drug' category.

Such examples illustrate the fashion in which consonancy operates and underlies media stories. But they stop short of explaining why particular paradigms are utilized and what is the motivation behind the journalist's reluctance to change directions and reconceptualize the phenomenon that he faces. Graham Murdock's paper starts to do this. By showing how underlying structural and ideological factors shape the journalist's definition of the situation when faced with the phenomena of political deviance and mass demonstrations, it provides a link between our earlier group of papers (which are descriptive or leave explanations at the bureaucratic level) and our later group which moves to the ideological level. A similar link is provided by Stuart Hall's account of the determination of news photos. He discusses both the 'operational practices which allow editors, working over a set of prints, to select, rank, classify and elaborate the photo in terms of his "stock of knowledge" as to what constitutes "news" ' and the further determinants which exist at an ideological level.

Another way of leading up to the same problem is through uncovering the mythical elements contained in the media presentation of deviance and social problems. Once the subject of the story is fixed, its subsequent shape is determined by certain recurrent processes of news manufacture. Halloran, Elliot and Murdock refer to the development of an *inferential structure*. This is not intentional bias nor simply selection by expectation, but '. . . a process of simplification and interpretation which structures the meaning given to the story around its original news value'.[3] The conceptual framework they use to locate this process is Boorstin's notion of the *event as news*. That is to say, the question 'Is it news?' becomes as important as 'Is it real?' The argument is that:

> . . . events will be selected for news reporting in terms of their fit or consonance with pre-existing images – the news of the event will confirm earlier ideas. The more unclear the news item and the more uncertain or doubtful the newsman is in how to report it, the more likely it is to be reported in a general framework that has been already established.[4]

This is not to imply that the images are wholly fictitious; Mods and Rockers, Teddy Boys, Skinheads, violent criminals, hippies, drug addicts are after all not just inkblots on to which fantasies are projected. Thus, as Terry Ann Knopf's article on distortions in press reports of racial violence in America (in the direction of grossly exaggerating supposedly 'new' elements of planning, organization, sniping and leadership) concludes:

> Unwittingly or not, the press has been constructing a scenario on armed uprisings. The story line of this scenario is not totally removed from reality. There *have* been a few shoot-outs with the police, and a handful may have been planned. But no wave of uprisings and no set pattern of murderous conflict have developed – at least not yet.

Using the notion of a 'constructed scenario' Cohen compares what happened at the initial Mods and Rockers events with their fantasy portrayal in the mass media. He suggests that much of the inventory of qualities ascribed to these actors was putative: that is, it had little foundation in their actual behaviour. None of these readings – and this is particularly clear in Murdock's and Hall's articles – argues that there is nothing 'out there', that the journalist sits in his office wilfully and maliciously inventing stories. What is being scrutinized is the process of construction which transforms what happens 'out there' into news. The wider societal reasons for such constructions bring us to our last group of readings.

MASS MEDIA AND THE SOCIAL CONSENSUS

In discussing the relationship between the internal dynamics of the news organization and the events which it confronts, we argued that an additional explanatory point outside the bureaucracy was necessary for an adequate explanation of the particular images and the selection procedures used. The Commercial Laissez-Faire model would imply that such a point exists simply in terms of the demands of the audience. The Mass Manipulative model, in contrast, would insist that the images are those selected, and moulded to fit the interests of a ruling élite or class. To test such propositions we must examine the implicit functions of the world view carried by the mass media. Do they, in fact, merely reflect a variety of conflicting interests as one might expect if they are a simple product of audience demands? Or do portrayals of social problems relate to conservative consensual models of society and thus uphold the *status quo* of power and interest?

In Part One we quoted 'bias through selection' and 'bias through omission' from Robert Cirino's 'Catalogue of Hidden Bias'. When he goes on to analyze how the news is then structured, his argument is even more explicitly – some might say more crudely – directed towards showing how this structure rests on support of the politically and commercially powerful. Here are some of the items from his catalogue:[5]

1. *The art of interviewing:* interviews are conducted and presented in such a way as to clearly favour one side's position. Even when an 'even number' from each side is interviewed the result is determined by the format of a story or programme. Cirino quotes Malcolm X:

> I don't care what points I made in interviews, it practically never got printed the way I said it. I was learning under fire how the press, when it wants to, can twist and slant. If I said 'Mary had a little lamb', what probably would have appeared was 'Malcolm X lampoons Mary' . . . I developed a mental image of reporters as human ferrets – steadily sniffing, darting, probing for some way to trick me, somehow to corner me in our interview exchanges.

2. *Bias through placement:* some events occur which are too big to ignore – to do so would lose one's audience credibility – but their significance can be minimized by placing them on back pages, giving them only 5 or 10 seconds on a newscast or sandwiching them between other favoured items. The mere appearance of an item on the front or back pages in its itself persuades the reader of its importance. Cirino also discusses a technique found by Cohen in the Mods and Rockers inventory: bias through 'co-incidental' placement. He quotes examples which particularly occur at election time: 'An editor chooses a headline or photograph that is favourable to one candidate and right next to it, on the same or next page, he places a headline or photograph unflattering to another candidate.'

3. *Bias in the headlines:* for many members of the public, headlines constitute a *total* impression of the news. Headlines also set the tone and value position of the newspaper and can critically influence readership.[6] Stories about deviance and social problems demand particularly a subjective choice on the part of the headline writer. Cirino quotes the different treatment given to a United States Department of Agriculture assessment of the defoliation programme in Vietnam. The report was vague enough to leave this sort of freedom to the copy editor:

Los Angeles Times	*New York Times*
STUDY FINDS NO LASTING	STUDY FINDS
HARM FROM DEFOLIATION	ECOLOGY HURT

4. *Bias in words and images:* organizations, policies or people can be discredited or exalted through the words and images chosen in news reports. Certain stock phrases and scenes can be used – as the reading from Frayn shows – to create a sameness in emotions and

values. Cirino quotes the deliberate use of certain words in Vietnam war stories: 'body counts'; Vietnamese family huts described as 'v.c. structures'; sampans as 'waterborne logistic craft'. The enemy are always mobs, rioters or terrorists, one's allies are freedom fighters, the forces of law and order or disciplined troops. One classic study[7] showed how the dominant mood conveyed by the TV coverage of General MacArthur's welcome-home parade conveyed by its verbal imagery ('you can feel the tenseness in the air . . . Never such a thrill') a sense of hero-worship which was not at all the dominant one in the crowd.

5. *Bias in photograph selection and captions:* here, as with words and images in the stories themselves, deliberate choices have to be made in terms of presentation, and photos probably receive more attention than the actual news items. Stuart Hall's article specifically deals with this subject.

6. *The use of editorials to distort facts and the hidden editorial:* The function of editorial and other comment is explicitly to interpret the news; clearly this allows the possibility of bias. Less clearly recognized are hidden editorial comments in the stories themselves.

Cirino's case, then, is that in these and many other ways, the news media 'clearly and unmistakenly' distort material to give establishment positions a decided competitive advantage over all others. The images of favoured politicians are carefully nurtured, the correct photograph selected, the advantageous quotation and interview used, the headlines and images judiciously manipulated.

We refer again to Graham Murdock's paper for a case study and a theoretical elaboration of an argument something like this. He also presents an explicit view of the role of the media in managing conflict and dissent – a view even more obviously brought out in Eamonn McCann's pamphlet – from which we reprint extracts – on the coverage by the British press of the Northern Ireland conflict. The British soldiers can do no wrong, while the 'rioters' or the 'mob' are vicious and cowardly, 'almost depraved in their bloodlust'. The consensus is reinforced by the images.

E. P. Thompson, in his analysis of the letters chosen by the press to depict public attitudes to the 1970 power workers' strike, develops the same theme. He detects a scenario created by the media which caricatures the strikers as irrational and ignorant and the effect of their strike as being directed against the *whole* of the nation and causing casualties among the *weak*. Class conflict becomes recast into the conservative imagery of a small group of men trampling on the poor and damaging the national interest. The vast majority of men are seen to agree with the economic system as it stands, disturbances are due to the machiavellianism of a few. Real conflict of interests *is* possible in this model but it tends to be reserved for those cases where the 'real' indigenous population is portrayed as being threatened by the 'alien' members in their midst. Thus Hartmann and Husband note the constant depiction of race relations in terms of this sort of conflict. The media's handling of the 'invasion' by the Ugandan Asians in 1972 reflects a similar image.

An even more explicit attempt to relate media models to broader societal conflict is made in Frank Pearce's analysis of the media's characterization of homosexuality. Only the normal categories of sexuality relating to male and female are allowed. Homosexuality is a deviant form which violates the male/female bifurcation and is grouped as an aberration, as an almost non- or semi-human activity. Pearce thus attempts to explore the total *structure* of sexual categorization utilized rather than merely depict the appearance of each category.

Jerry Palmer's article is one of the few studies of fiction included in this volume. Micky Spillane's best-selling novels, centred on his hero Mike Hammer, are mass media in their own right. Palmer extracts from them an underlying structure which implicitly tackles from a conservative vantage point the problem of order in modern societies. Mike Hammer represents a solution to the contradiction between social order and the competitive individualism posed by such ideology. The unpalatable truth of the war of all against all is rendered palatable by making the process of competition heroic. That is, Hammer's very ruthlessness is represented as social in that its goal is the preservation of order.

Young in his study of the mass media representation of drug takers, finds a similar contradiction being worked out. The media must solve the problem of advocating a consensus model yet explain the prevalence of widespread deviation, for example, drug use, strikes, student militancy. The solution is to suggest that deviancy is never freely chosen. It is either the result of sickness, or if it is widespread, a function of the corruption of the ignorant or innocent by a wicked minority. The typical citizen is thus represented as freely choosing normality – i.e., the *status quo* – and the deviant as ineluctably impelled by forces beyond his knowledge or control into transgression. A morality play unfolds where the normal is seen to prosper and the abnormal inevitably to suffer pain and hardship.

This framework is applied by Damien Philips to a study of the coverage of pop festivals. Society views hedonistic activity with ambivalence: it is only justified if it is seen as a deserved reward for hard work and if such leisure is in itself capable of being managed as a commercial enterprise.[9] The adherence of youth to a strongly hedonistic pop culture virtually places pop festivals into a deviant category. As such the elements of conflict and perceived amorality are heightened. Yet a contradiction occurs, for it is inconceivable, given a consensus model, that such a vast number of young people can be deviant. A process of *normalization*, therefore, occurs as the news of the festival unfolds itself. Namely, the majority of youngsters are pictured as decent fun-loving kids indulging in respectable leisure but all this has been tarnished by a minority who give the others a bad name.

Such studies of the mass media move from a mere description of the *dramatis personae* involved in what is categorized as a social problem to a study of the play itself, examining its implicit structures and tracing the fashion in which it justifies the world 'as it is'.

REFERENCES

1. For an excellent case study of how a television documentary – in this case, on the nature of prejudice – was made, from the emergence of the idea to its ultimate realization in the studio, see Philip Elliott, *The making of a television series: a case study in the sociology of culture* (London, Constable, 1972).
2. Daniel J. Boorstin, *The image* (Harmondsworth, Penguin, 1963). For numerous examples, see particularly Chapter 1 entitled 'From news gathering to news making: a flood of pseudo events'.
3. James D. Halloran, Philip Elliott and Graham Murdock, *Demonstrations and communications* (Harmondsworth, Penguin, 1970), pp. 215–16.
4. Ibid., p. 26.
5. Robert Cirino, *Don't blame the people* (Los Angeles, Diversity Press, 1971), pp. 147–79. Cirino's evidence and examples cover mainly American political reporting.
6. For some evidence on this, see Percy H. Tannenbaum and Jean S. Kerrick, 'Effects of Newscast Item leads upon listener interpretation', *Journalism Quarterly* (Winter 1954), p. 3, and 'The effect of headlines on the interpretation of news stories', *Journalism Quarterly* (Spring 1953), p. 189.
7. K. Lang and G. E. Lang, 'The unique perspective of television and its effect: a pilot study', *American Sociological Review*, Vol. 18 (1953), pp. 3–12.
8. For a more comprehensive discussion, see Jock Young, 'The consensual myth: the portrayal of the drugtaker in the mass media' in P. Rock and M. McIntosh (eds.), *Deviance and social control* (London, Tavistock Publications, 1973). For a more general critique of absolutist thought, see Jack Douglas, *The American social order* (New York, The Free Press, 1971), Chapter 2, and J. Young, *The drugtakers: the social meaning of drug use* (London, Paladin, 1971), Chapter 3.
9. See Young, op cit. (1971) Chapter 6 for an analysis of the relationship between work and leisure in advanced industrialized societies.

Majority and minority Americans: an analysis of magazine fiction*

BERNARD BERELSON and PATRICA J. SALTER

Prejudice against minority peoples in this country is widespread. It embraces a large number of groups: American Negroes and Jews are disapproved; Mexicans, Italian-Americans, Japanese-Americans are rejected as 'out-group'; and even Irish-Americans are sometimes not accepted as 'good Americans'. Common to all these prejudices against minorities is the other side of the coin – prejudice in favour of the majority and approval of the '100 per cent Americans'.

Discrimination based upon these prejudices is expressed in many ways. Negroes are often the last to be hired and the first to be fired; people of 'pure American stock' – white, Protestant, Anglo-Saxons – often have the best chance at better jobs. The Epsteins and the Goldbergs are often barred from hotels which are glad to welcome the Smiths and the Joneses. The sons of South European or Oriental parents are less apt to be put up for Congress than their '100 per cent American' neighbours.

The fight against prejudice and discrimination is most likely to take place in areas where they are the most overt and intentional. But it is not only these overt and intentional areas of attack upon minority groups and support of 'Americans' which serve as sources of such discrimination. Prejudice also finds its way into innocuous areas where people are exposed to them without consciousness that an ethnic problem is being raised at all.

This is a study of the latter kind of exposure to anti-minority and pro-majority discrimination: the treatment of majority and minority groups in the popular fiction appearing in mass magazines. How do people meet the various ethnic and religious groups of this country in this channel of communication, which reaches a large number of people in their relaxed, leisure hours? Are some groups presented as more important or more personable or wealthier than others? Do some groups in these stories get more of society's rewards, such as love or high position? What picture is presented of the relationships

*Extracted from Bernard Berelson and Patricia J. Salter, 'Majority and minority Americans: an analysis of magazine fiction', *Public Opinion Quarterly* Vol. 10 (1946), pp. 169–90.

between different ethnic groups? In short, what kinds of people appear in typical magazine short stories in terms of their racial, religious, and national backgrounds, and how are they treated?

THE SAMPLE AND THE STORIES

The sample: The object of analysis was a sample of 198 short stories published in eight of the country's most widely read magazines in 1937 and 1943: The magazines included in the study are the following:

General weeklies:	*Saturday Evening Post*
	Collier's
General monthlies:	*American*
	Cosmopolitan
Women's:	*Woman's Home Companion*
	Ladies' Home Journal
Confessionals:	*True Story*
	True Confessions

The years 1937 and 1943 were selected in order to investigate the effect of World War II upon the fictional treatment of various groups. The standard analysis was done for a total of 185 stories – those with a United States locale or a 'transferred' U.S. locale (i.e., the fifteen or so stories laid outside the United States but containing a predominantly American cast of characters). A special analysis was done for the thirteen stories in the sample which were laid in foreign countries and peopled with predominantly foreign characters. For each magazine for each year, four issues were selected at regular intervals (in order to avoid the possible bias of seasons or events), and the first, third, and fifth short stories were analysed in each of the selected issues (in order to avoid the possible bias of placement in the magazine). Serials and 'short short stories' were omitted altogether. . . .

THE METHOD

The analysis procedure: The central problem of the study was to investigate the existence and nature of differential treatment accorded various ethnic groups in magazine fiction. The procedures and techniques of the analysis can be described in the following stages, listed here in roughly chronological order.

(1) On the basis of general knowledge of such stories, supplemented by the focused reading of a few of them, a set of hypotheses dealing with the problem at hand was formulated. For the sake of

simplicity, the hypotheses were formulated in terms of two major groups – the 'Anglo-Saxons' and the 'foreigners' – with the understanding that the actual analysis would establish empirically the ethnic composition of these two groups in the stories. The hypotheses dealt with the frequency of appearance of various groups, their characteristics, cultural contributions, relative status positions, and social interaction. In addition, hypotheses on time and locale differences were also formulated. From time to time during the study, some of the hypotheses were modified and a few were added.

(2) The conversion of the hypotheses into analytic operations took two forms, based upon two different units of analysis. The first unit was a character in the story and the second was the story as a whole.

The first called for the coding of eight characteristics for each of the speaking characters (or groups) in the story. The eight characteristics for which data were secured whenever possible were the following: *Role* in the story (major, submajor, minor; hero, heroine, villain); *Sex; Status position* (occupation, economic status, educational level, class); *Social origin* (nationality, race, religion); *Personality traits; Goals or values* (the ends the characters were trying to realize, such as economic advancement, romantic love, settled marriage state, social position, etc.); *Plus-minus position* (the approval or disapproval of the character: sympathy-hostility, liking-disliking, desirability-undesirability, pleasantness-unpleasantness, etc.); *Summary identification* by ethnic groups (using both explicit and implicit indicators).

The analysts not only checked each of these categories for each speaking character, whenever applicable, but also documented their entry with a brief summary of or quotation from the appropriate story content, which were used to standardize the indices used by the analysts for certain categories.

The second form of analysis dealt with the story as a whole. The hypotheses not covered directly by the character analysis – e.g., the hypothesis that the stories do not *explicitly* deal with problems of ethnic relationships in American life – were listed, with five possible entries for each: confirmed; refuted; both confirmed and refuted in the same story; indeterminate as between confirmation and refutation; not applicable. An entry for each hypothesis for each story was required, together with full documentation of the basis for decision.

(3) After a period of instruction in the procedures of the study, the eight analysts coded the same story. Differences in interpretation were discovered and minimized through re-definition of the disputed categories. In addition, the supervisor of the analysts checked a

random sample of each analyst's work during the early stages of the study and standardized analytic procedures among the workers.

(4) After the analysis of the story had been completed, codes were inductively constructed for the 'open' categories in the character analysis, such as goals and traits. The codes were based upon a total of about a third of the analysis sheets; at about that point, additional analyses failed to yield additional categories for the code. The character analysis was coded for transfer to punch cards. The story analysis was hand-tallied because of the progressive re-definition of hypotheses in the course of the study and the necessity for standardization.

So much for the procedures. Now let us turn to the findings of the study. Did magazine short stories 'prefer' some kinds of people to other kinds? If so, how did such preferential treatment operate? We shall present the results of our analysis in five main sections:

> The distribution of the characters
> Their role
> Their appearance
> Their status
> Their goals

DISTRIBUTION OF CHARACTERS

What was the composition of the fictional population? What groups of people appeared more and less frequently in the stories? The brief answer is that characters identifiable only as 'Americans' more than filled the centre of the stage.

The 'Americans' and the field
Of all the identifiable speaking characters, fully 84 per cent were presented just as 'Americans' (Table 1). The others were about equally divided between the various American minorities on the one hand and various foreign groups on the other. The nearly 200 stories, containing nearly 900 identifiable characters, included only 16 Negroes and only 10 Jews. On the whole, this small number of minority and foreign characters is spread very thin throughout the stories. Very seldom did more than one of them appear in a single story. They typically filled isolated roles in order to provide background or 'tone' or some other specialized function within the stories. The 'Americans', on the other hand, appeared not only in almost every story but also in whole aggregates of characters.

But what about the ethnic composition of the characters as compared to the ethnic composition of the people of the United States?

TABLE 1

MINORITY AND FOREIGN GROUPS IN MAGAZINE
STORIES ARE DWARFED BY THE 'AMERICAN' GIANT*

	Per cent	*Per cent*
'Americans'		84·0
American Minorities		8·5
Anglo-Saxon and Nordic hyphenates	3·0	
Other hyphenates	2·5	
Negroes	2·0 −	
Jews	1·0 +	
Foreigners		7·5
Anglo-Saxon and Nordic groups	4·0	
Other foreign groups	3·5	
Total number of identifiable characters	889	100

* Since relatively few of the characters were explicitly identified by national origin, it was necessary to classify them by other indicators. The following sources of identification were used (the total is more than 100% because some characters were identified in more than one way):

Explicit identification		21%
Identified by:	Name	58
	Language	21
	Appearance	17
	Position	8
	Other indicators	2

Examples of names used for purposes of identification:

American: Julie Britton, Eleanor Madison, Doris Baldwin, Martha Langford, Dorothy Green, Dick Ferris, Steve Kennedy, Perry West, Bill Davis, Joe Blake. *Italian:* Mr. Casparri, Marty Spinelli, Louis di Paolo. *Jewish:* Max Betterman, Chick Bernstein. *Scandinavian:* Sven Borsen, Fred Gorse. *Irish:* Marty Flanagan, Officer Flaherty. *German:* Adolph Hertz. *Polish:* Anna Krupek. The assumption here is that such names would be similarly identified by typical readers.

In both the American minority and the foreign groups the following classification is used:

Anglo-Saxon and Nordic: English, Irish, Scotch, Canadian, Scandinavian (Norwegian, Swedish, Finnish, Danish).

Other: German, Polish, Italian, Russian, Austrian, Czech, Portuguese, Spanish, Latin American, Oriental.

Perhaps the distribution of the fictional characters simply reflected census statistics. Actually, however, census data only accentuate the differential treatment accorded 'natives' and 'minorities' in the stories. Although the 'minorities' (as here defined) make up 40 per cent of the population of the United States, they make up only

10 per cent of the population of the short stories (Chart 1). Every 'minority' group appears less frequently in the stories than in the country. Only the 'Americans' appear more frequently.

Thus we start with a fundamental conclusion: in popular magazine short stories laid in the United States, minority and foreign groups were seldom represented. The American minorities appeared much less frequently in magazine fiction than in the population. Overwhelming attention was given to the 'Americans'. The stage and the spotlight belonged to them.

The three basic groups of characters

Three ethnic groups of characters in these stories were accorded differential treatment. The first group is composed of *the Americans* – white Protestants with no distinguishable ancestry of foreign origin. They are called *the Americans* here because that is the stereotypic designation for this type of 'unadulterated' person.

Not all the non-Americans were treated alike, and the other two groups are composed of sub-groups within the minorities, and foreigners. The basic distinction is *not* that between all American minorities on the one hand and all foreigners on the other; these two groups were approved and disapproved to the same extent. Rather, the important distinction appeared between those American hyphenates and foreigners with Anglo-Saxon and Nordic backgrounds, on the one hand, and the Jews, the Negroes, and the hyphenates and foreigners with other European, Latin-American, and Oriental backgrounds, on the other. On all the important considerations, the former group showed up to better advantage than the latter.

Accordingly, the findings shall be presented as comparisons of these three groups:

The Americans – 84 per cent of the total group of characters

Anglo-Saxon and Nordic minorities and foreigners (abbreviated *the AS & Ns*) – 7 per cent of the total

Other minorities and foreigners – Jews, Negroes, Italians, Germans Poles, Orientals, etc. (abbreviated *the others*) – 9 per cent of the total

Since World War II did not serve to increase or otherwise modify the treatment of minority and foreign characters in these stories, the data reported in this study include both the 1937 and the 1943 samples.

CHART 1

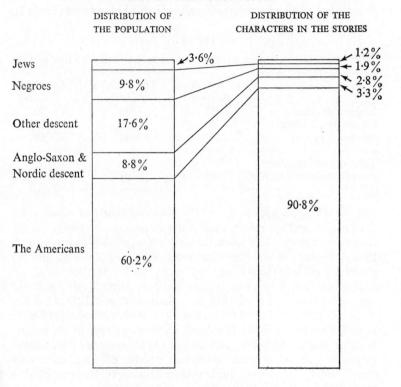

DISTRIBUTION OF
THE POPULATION

DISTRIBUTION OF THE
CHARACTERS IN THE STORIES

Jews

Negroes

Other descent

Anglo-Saxon &
Nordic descent

The Americans

3·6%

9·8%

17·6%

8·8%

60·2%

1·2%
1·9%
2·8%
3·3%

90·8%

THE ROLES OF THE CHARACTERS

The characters in these stories play all sorts of parts, ranging from
the central and highly approved figure appearing throughout the
action to the marginal and unsympathetic figure appearing only for a
few lines. What about the importance to the story of our three basic
groups of characters?

The majors and the minors

The characters in these stories can be conveniently classified into
three groups – major, sub-major, minor – in terms of their importance to the story (as measured by the amount of attention given
to them). Those playing the most important roles, i.e., given the
most space, are the major characters. The characters given a medium

amount of space in the stories are the sub-major and those who appear in incidental roles are the minor characters.

The Americans appeared as major characters just over half the time and as minor characters only about a third of the time (Table 2).

TABLE 2

'THE AMERICANS' APPEARED MORE OFTEN IN THE MAJOR ROLES

	The Americans	The AS & Ns	The others
	Per cent	*Per cent*	*Per cent*
Major characters	52	38	30
Sub-major characters	16	18	14
Minor characters	32	44	56
Total no. of identifiable characters (equalling 100%)	745	61	77

But *the AS & Ns* appeared slightly more frequently in minor roles than major, and *the others* much more frequently. Not only did *the Americans* appear more often than the rest, but they also got more than their share of the important roles. When *the AS & Ns* and *the others* did get into the stories, they were placed in smaller roles.

The heroes and heroines occupy the best roles of all. Again *the Americans* furnished more than their share, and so did *the AS & Ns*. About 35 per cent of all *the Americans* and 31 per cent of *the AS & Ns* were heroes or heroines, as against only 10 per cent of *the others*. In other words, the heroes and heroines in these stories were almost exclusively either of 'pure' American or else of Anglo-Saxon or Nordic stock. *The others* – Italian-Americans, Jews, Negroes, et al. – rarely reached such lofty positions.

The approved and the disapproved

Similarly, the characters can be differentiated on the basis of the approval or disapproval attached to their roles in the stories. The approved characters were likeable, personable, wise, desirable, respectable, honest, upright; the disapproved characters were the opposite. In such 'light' fiction as these magazine stories – which are entertaining and pleasant rather than 'realistic' or 'serious' – the large majority of the characters are approved. This was true, in this sample, for all three groups – but not equally true (Table 3). Here *the Americans* and *the AS & Ns* were approved more often than *the others*. Incidentally, the heavy appearance of neutral characters among the minority and foreign groups reflects the colourless roles to which they were assigned.

This tendency of the minority and foreign groups to draw minor, less approved roles and seldom to reach the positions of hero or heroine obviously places serious limitations on the extent to which their personalities can be developed. Space limitations, together with

TABLE 3

THE CHARACTERS WERE DIFFERENTIATED BY THEIR APPROVAL IN THE STORIES, WITH '*the others*' THE LEAST APPROVED OF ALL

	The Americans *Per cent*	The AS & Ns *Per cent*	The others *Per cent*
Approved characters	80	78	62
Neutral characters	4	14	14
Disapproved characters	16	8	24
Total no. of identifiable characters (equalling 100%)*	726	60	77

* These figures are not exactly alike from table to table because of varying numbers of indeterminate characters for the different categories.

the general lack of sophistication of these stories, impose a low level of complexity for all characters, and have a particularly strong impact upon the minority and foreign groups. Since they were more often hand-maidens to the plot, they must more often be one-dimensional in personality. They were usually developed only in that aspect of their personalities necessary to their dramatic function, namely, the most obvious or stereotypic aspect which made the author's point facilely and quickly.

Indeed, some of the minor non-Americans, falling even lower on a scale of personalities-in-their-own-right, came to serve the function of *things* in the stories. That is, they merely provided atmosphere and mood or dramatized the broadminded or cosmopolitan nature of *the Americans*. A typical case, for example, was the American heroine who was seen 'talking charmingly to the quaint Italian flower vendor', who in that sentence fulfilled his role in the story.

THE APPEARANCE OF THE CHARACTERS

By its nature, this sort of magazine fiction capitalizes on quick stereotypic delineations of characters. Such delineations apply to most of the characters in the stories – whether major or minor, approved or disapproved, American or not. The easy description of personality *types* which are considered desirable or acceptable, rather than the difficult and complicated elaboration of an individual *personality*, is the custom. As a result, some facets of the characters – those which are thought to be representative or at least familiar to a wide audience – are often made to serve as the complete personality.

For example, the American heroes in the stories were typically tall, blond, and handsome in the best Hollywood tradition, and the American heroines were stereotyped in similar fashion. Other American characters were similarly drawn from standard patterns – the 'darling' Southern girl, the 'stalwart' college athlete, the 'efficient' career girl, the 'modern' housewife and mother. However, such stereotypes are seldom invidious or even implicitly disparaging and, more important, they are not attached to socially distinctive groups in the sense in which that term applies to Negroes or Jews or Italian-Americans.

But this function of the stereotype to compress the members of a group into a common mould operates in these stories not only artistically as the enemy of individuality in fictional characters. When the stereotype applies to ethnic groups like Negroes or Jews or Italian-Americans, it also operates socially as a stimulus of xenophobia. Studies of popular attitudes have repeatedly shown that people hold certain settled opinions about the traits and behaviour of members of 'out-groups' – mental pictures of what other 'different' kinds of people believe and do. Such stereotypes, to which they think the others actually correspond, may arise from personal contact with some individuals in the other group, or from general hearsay, or from reading and listening, or from some other source. But whatever their source, their function is to label the 'outsider' as an outsider, so that he may be easily identified, appropriately reacted to, and conveniently rejected.

Minority and foreign characters described stereotypically

The representatives of minority and foreign groups were usually tailored to the stereotypic dimensions of their respective groups. Of all the stories including one or more minority or foreign characters, familiar and usually disparaging stereotypic descriptions were employed in fully three-quarters.

Stereotypes were found for virtually every minority and foreign group in the fictional population. The Negro, the Irishman, and the Italian appeared most frequently in this connection, but many others were given the same sort of treatment: Jews, Poles, Filipinos, French, Chinese, Scandinavians, and even South Sea island natives. (Of the very few non-stereotypic descriptions, half involved Canadians, the out-group closest to *the Americans*.) The following are only a few examples of the stereotypic treatment found in the sample of stories:

The amusingly ignorant Negro: Rosemary is a 'generously up-holstered' maid who 'cackles' and 'rocks back and forth from her rounded hips'. Her 'golden eye-teeth' reveal themselves 'in an affectionate smile, her flat feet toed out at a forty-five degree angle, her bulgy body solid enough but looking perilously safety-pinned together'. She leaves a note for her mistress: ' "I taken the gray evening dress like you said. Will leave it at the diars on my way home tonite. I allso taken some of your lonjourey and your lecktrick ion because I got time to do some wash on my oather job. Will bring the ion in the mourning. If you needed it tonite you find me att my oather place till 8 o'clock." '

The Italian gangster: Louie di Paolo, an amiable racketeer with a debt of loyalty to an heiress, furnishes her with money and a kidnapping so that she can get her own way with a young man. Louie is 'a sinister-looking individual with a white scar over one eye . . . known as Blackie, Two Rod, and Smart 'Em Up in various police precincts, and among the underworld citizenry. . . .' Says he: ' "Beer was my racket. I made my pile and been layin' low ever since. If you want twenty-five G's all I got to do is stick up my own safe-deposit box." ' He drives 'a coupe with bullet-proof glass and a specially built steel body, ready for anything'.

The sly and shrewd Jew: Jew Jake, manager of a troop of barn-storming stunt flyers, shows greater concern for money than for the safety of his employees. He has an 'ungainly and corpulent figure' and he rubs his hands 'in a familiar and excited gesture'. In answer to his question, 'Maybe you'd like to make five bucks easy?', the hero says: 'Jake, you would not put out five bucks for anything less than a suicide.' Another character says: 'You ought to know the way Jake is. He'd like it better if I did not pull it (the parachute cord) at all. It would give the customers a thrill.'

The emotional Irish: Ellen, an Irish cook, is overwhelmed by her first sight of the new baby: 'Ellen – who, being a Celt, was easily moved – flew out of the kitchen, saw a fraction of David's face, and burst into a flood of tears.'

The primitive and 'backward' Pole: A Polish-American girl thinks of escape from her national community. 'I began to despise our way of life. . . . The American men did not value a wife who could work all day on her knees at his side, taking only a day or two off to bear a child. They love the weakness, not the strength in their women; love the job of looking after and supporting them.'

The patronized native of a Pacific island: The orientation of a white planter in the Pacific world is set at the beginning of the story. After a few years on an island, the planter learns the native patois, 'mixed with a smattering of Mother English to justify their white skins'. Then, 'after the coconut planter completes the metamorphosis, he takes on a native mistress who develops gradually into a native wife. Still more gradually the house begins to fill with brown mestizo children. Upon reaching this stage of little brown souvenirs of his exile, the planter passes into that broad classification of "one who has missed too many boats". Eventually he misses his final boat.'

In addition to these, there are the humorous Chinese servant, the correct Filipino houseboy, the volatile Latins, the extravagantly romantic Frenchman, the hard-working and thrifty Scandinavian. And in most of the cases, there is also a patronizing tone in these stereotypic descriptions of minority and foreign characters.

THE STATUS OF THE CHARACTERS

Now let us turn to the characters' position in the socio-economic hierarchy. Did differences appear between *the Americans* and the rest in the possession of man's wordly goods? What kinds of jobs were held by what kinds of people? What sort of social interaction, if any, occurred between different groups of characters?

Status – possessed and deserved

The general economic level of characters in these stories was assessed as an interviewer for an opinion survey would assess the economic level of a respondent – by the person's appearance, clothes, home, possessions, etc. The characters were classified on four levels, designated A, B, C, and D. The A people have the most money, influence and prestige and the D people have the least.

Again, *the Americans* showed to better advantage than *the AS & Ns* or *the others* (Table 4). Almost three-quarters of the former fell on the upper two levels of this status index as against less than half of the latter. This simple index reflects substantial differences in characters' standards of living. *The Americans* lived better in various ways: they ate better food, wore better clothes, resided in better homes, and generally enjoyed more material conveniences and luxury possessions.

Not only that, they also seemed to *deserve* their higher status; it was usually taken for granted. People can achieve wealth, power and prestige in a variety of ways – through fortunate birth or fortunate marriage or hard work or crooked dealing or luck. In these stories, only infrequently were the sources of *the Americans'* high status positions explicitly mentioned. However, when the representatives of minority and foreign groups appeared in high status positions, *their* paths to power – whatever they were – were more often

TABLE 4

'THE AMERICANS' ENJOYED HIGHER SOCIO-ECONOMIC
STATUS THAN THE REST*

Socio-economic status	The Americans	The AS & Ns	The others
	Per cent	*Per cent*	*Per cent*
A	39	24	16
B	33	18	28
C	23	49	37
D	5	9	19
Total no. of identifiable characters (equalling 100%)	722	55	76

* These status differences are not simply a reflection of the differences in role
among our three basic groups of characters. The status differences remain even
when role is held constant. The data:

	Percentage with A & B status:	
Role	*The Americans*	*The AS & Ns* and *The others*
Major	71% (387)	58% (46)
Sub-major and minor	68% (353)	32% (94)

There was thus a stronger association between *the Americans* and high status
than between major role and high status. Similarly, it can be shown that *the
AS & Ns* and *the others* were approved less than *the Americans* when status is
held roughly constant; thus, the fact that they were approved less is not simply
the result of their lower status. (Although similar control tables do not appear
in the text in connection with other tables, the differences have all been tested in
this way.)

explicitly mentioned (Table 5). In other words, the claim of *the
Americans* on society's rewards was presented much less as a matter
for explanation or justification. Their acceptance at the top, without
elaboration, subtly suggested that they belonged there. But when the
rest appeared at the top, their rise had to be explained more often,
because they did not belong there.

Occupational level – 'positions' and 'jobs'
The Americans also engaged in pleasanter and more desirable work
than the members of minority and foreign groups. For the sake of
convenience, the occupations have been grouped in a few major
categories. Once more *the Americans* came off best, *the AS & Ns*
next, and *the others* worst (Table 6). Not only did *the others* contain
many more characters in illegal and 'suspect' occupations, in addition,
they were more likely to be enlisted men rather than officers in the
armed forces (two-thirds of *the others*, one-half of *the AS & Ns*, and
one-fourth of *the Americans*). Thus the distinctions among the groups
extend even into the military hierarchy.

TABLE 5

FEWER EXPLANATIONS WERE FORTHCOMING OF
'THE AMERICANS' HIGH STATUS POSITIONS

	The Americans	The AS & Ns/The others
	Per cent	*Per cent*
Source of high status not explained in the story	78	43
Source of high status explained in the story	22	57
Total no. of stories with characters in high status positions (equalling 100%)	93	14

TABLE 6

'THE AMERICANS' HAD MORE DESIRABLE OCCUPATIONS
THAN THE OTHER GROUPS*

	The Americans	The AS & Ns	The others
	Per cent	*Per cent*	*Per cent*
High occupations	59	29	20
Middle occupations	19	23	20
Low occupations	11	27	36
Illegal and 'suspect' occupations	1	2	15
Members of the armed forces	10	19	9
Total no. of identifiable characters (equalling 100%)	602	52	66

* *The high occupations:* Business executives; the 'idle rich'; parent-supported college students; lawyers, doctors, professors, ministers, architects, artists, musicians, and other professions; entertainers; major government officials; 'luxury' housewives.

The middle occupations: White-collar workers, minor government officials, small businessmen, farmers, housewives who do their own housework.

The low occupations: Fishermen, skilled labourers, servants, building maintenance workers, unskilled labourers.

The illegal and 'suspect' occupations: Racketeers, thieves, gamblers, night club proprietors (suspect in these stories).

Social interaction – the upper and the lower
These stories contain whole networks of personal interactions, some conducted on a basis of equality but others serving to place one character in a lesser position relative to another. Such social interaction varies from the intimate to the incidental; that is, two characters can marry each other or they can have a chance meeting in a restaurant when one serves the other. How did such social interaction take place among our groups of characters?

The distribution of occupations suggests the answers. Whenever social interaction in these stories occurred *on the job*, it was the members of minority and foreign groups who were found in the subordinate roles. They were the servants, the dressmakers, the liverymen, the restaurateurs, the peddlers. The 'quaint flower vendor' was Italian; Mr Beilstein was a butcher; Mr Casparri ran a restaurant; Silva was a Filipino houseman; Ella was an Irish cook and Hong a Chinese cook; Rosemary and Bessie and Sidonia, and many others, were Negro servants. They worked for, and served, *the Americans*.

In some cases, the minority and foreign representatives appeared subordinate to *the Americans* in non-occupational roles. For example, an Irish mother pleaded with a wealthy American for her criminal son; an Italian gangster was slavishly devoted to an American heroine who once helped him; Tanya Verriki was an inmate of a home for delinquent girls where all the staff members were Americans. And when social interaction between *the Americans* and the rest did occur on a basis of equality, it was usually *the AS & Ns* who participated. The English girl entertained American soldiers; British army officers (aristocrats) were invited to dinner; the Irish-American flyer became his ship's hero; the Scotch-American photographer won the motion picture actress; the Irish sea captain was fully accepted and admired by his American fellows. Only occasionally did *the Americans* associate with *the others* on an equal basis and even in such cases it was usually the former who monopolized the spotlight.

But the acid test for personal relations is courtship and marriage. Who married whom in these stories? What boys won what girls? The distribution of marriages and successful courtships in these stories, closely paralleling the distribution of characters, reveals the slight extent to which *the Americans* courted or married members of

TABLE 7

ON THE WHOLE, COURTSHIP AND
MARRIAGE WERE INTRA-GROUP

Love or marriage partners	Frequency Per cent
The Americans – the Americans	85
The Americans – the AS & Ns	5
The Americans – the others	4
The AS & Ns – the AS & Ns	3
The AS & Ns – the others	2
The others – the others	1
Total identifiable courtships and marriages (equalling 100%)	153

minority and foreign groups (Table 7). It also shows the still smaller extent to which either *the Americans* or *the AS & Ns* courted or married *the others*. Inter-love and inter-marriage were not sanctioned in magazine fiction.

In sum, then, not only did *the Americans* play the leading roles in the stories. In addition, they were also represented as getting more of the world's material values and they occupied the superordinate roles in most of the human relationships. They made more money, lived more comfortably, had better occupations, gave more orders. In these stories, the world belonged to them, and they ran it.

THE GOALS OF THE CHARACTERS

Finally, what were the different groups of characters striving for in these stories? What did they want from life? People in magazine fiction pursue a variety of goals – romantic love, settled marriages, money, power, prestige, idealism, and a few more. These goals were classified into two broad categories – 'heart' goals, which are emotional and affective, and 'head' goals, which are rational and calculating. These specific goals subsumed under each category, and the frequency with which they appeared, are these:

'Heart' goals	*'Head' goals*
Romantic love (231)	Solution of an immediate concrete problem (94)
Settled marriage state (190)	Self-advancement (92)
Idealism (74)	Money and material goods (58)
Affection and emotional security (62)	Economic and social security (51)
Patriotism (57)	Power and dominance (22)
Adventure (20)	
Justice (9)	
Independence (8)	

The 'heart' goals are 'in the clouds' and the 'head' goals are 'down-to-earth'. In these stories, *the Americans* were less encumbered with such down-to-earth goals (Table 8). Their goals were more frequently pleasant and idealistic and 'pure'. Particularly *the others* were bound to mundane and calculating aims.

SUMMING UP

This concludes the analysis of the differential treatment of characters in magazine fiction. On the whole, life in the United States as reflected in these stories was lived differently by our three basic

TABLE 8

'THE AMERICANS' PURSUE 'HEART' GOALS MORE
THAN THE OTHER TWO GROUPS

	The Americans *Per cent*	The AS & Ns *Per cent*	The others *Per cent*
'Heart' goals	69	61	49
'Head' goals	31	39	51
Total no. of identifiable goals (equalling 100%)	793	57	53

groups. On almost every index – frequency, role, delineation, status, goals – *the Americans* received better treatment, both qualitatively and quantitatively, than the minority and foreign groups. And within the latter, a preference operated in behalf of *the AS & Ns*. The rules seem to be that the character receives better treatment the closer he is to the norm of *the American*, i.e., white, Protestant, English-speaking, Anglo-Saxon. Common ancestry and common characteristics are decisive.

And even within *the others* some kinds of people came off better than others. The minority and foreign groups from the other European and Oriental countries, deprived as they were, received preferential treatment in these stories over two critical American minorities – the Negroes and the Jews. On several characteristics this distinction held up. The Negroes and Jews never appeared as heroes and heroines. No Negroes or Jews were depicted as members of the armed forces. They had the lowest occupational rating. They constituted the only group with more disapproved than approved traits. In short, of all the distinguishable groups of characters in magazine fiction, the Negroes and the Jews were depicted least favourably.

INTENT AND EFFECT

Such a description of magazine fiction (or of any other communication content) supports two sets of interpretations. One set deals with the *intent* behind the communication; how did it get that way? The second set deals with the *effects* of the communication; what difference does it make in the readers' attitudes? The communication itself – in this case short stories in popular magazines – occupies a midway position between the writers and the readers.

Presumable intents
How do these stories happen to be written in this way? We can undoubtedly discount at once any malice on the part of the writers and editors responsible for these stories.

First, it is a convenient method of writing. Such short stories call for brief, compact plots in which the action begins immediately and moves rapidly, and any techniques which facilitate 'getting the character across' easily and immediately are at a premium. Thus, many stock roles must be filled by stock characters, and they are often conveniently found in minority groups. For example, whenever the plot requires a gangster it is the simple and 'natural' thing to cast an Italian in the role and put it up to the reader to fill in the overtones for himself on the basis of the familiar stereotypes. Although this practice makes for shallow and cliché-filled writing, it does save time and space in the development of the story.

Secondly, the standard pattern for such short stories demands, and gets, conformity. Inertia on the one hand and fear of changing a 'successful' formula on the other, combine to keep the stories within designated bounds. Just as certain language is proscribed, so are certain ('controversial') topics and certain uses of fictional characters. An editor or publisher who would eagerly accept another variant of the typical boy-meets-girl story starring Julie Britton and Bill Davis would not consider printing the same story if the leading figures in it were called Sadie Horowitz and Abe Goldstein, or Lorenzina Sereno and Sebastian de Grazia.

Further, the heterogeneity of the audience to whom such stories are directed may necessitate the use of the broadest symbols of identification. As the types of readers in an audience increase in diversity, both the variety and the complexity of communicable ideas decrease. Heterogeneity breeds generality, and thus the leading characters become members of the dominant and presumably the best-recognized group.

Finally, insofar as the leading roles are taken by members of probably the most respected and certainly the most envied group in the community, these stories correspond to the historical bias of literature in centring upon the economic-, prestige-, and power-élites of every age. On the one hand they have traditionally been considered the people most worth writing about, and on the other hand, as the people most deferred to, they present a convenient focus of attention for large groups of readers who seek to identify themselves with the rich and the powerful.

Presumable effects

These stories are probably offered and accepted purely as entertainment. Their typical effect upon readers is a respite effect; that is, they normally provide a satisfying and enjoyable vacation, from daily routines and daily cares. That may be the typical effect, but it is certainly not the only one. Many communications have other than their intended effects upon readers or listeners and this is probably such a case. In all likelihood, the consistent deprivation of *the AS & Ns* and especially *the others* in these stories, over a long period of time, serves to activate the predispositions of a hostile or even an indifferent audience. Readers with latent tendencies to assign the usual stereotypic descriptions to groups whom they do not know, or toward whom they are unsympathetic, or with whom they do not come in personal contact, can find support for their convenient tags, labels, and aggressions in such magazine fiction. And this is all the more striking as a result of the implicit comparison with *the Americans*. Thus the condition and behaviour of fictional characters can readily be used to 'prove' that the Negroes are lazy or ignorant, the Jews sly, the Irish superstitious, the Italians criminal, and so on.

THE IMPLICIT YES AND THE EXPLICIT NO

The nature of these stories, then, tends to perpetuate the myth of the '100 per cent American' by differentiating, subtly and consistently, between *the Americans* and the representatives of other groups. Such differentiation in itself constitutes an implicit recognition of a 'minority problem' in this country. What about the *explicit* handling of the problem in these stories? Was the direct relationship between various ethnic groups overtly discussed in these stories, and if so, how?

One of this country's favourite ideologies claims equality for the diverse national, racial, and religious strains which make up the United States. In one sense, it is 'immoral' to suggest that inequality actually exists or, if that is acknowledged, that it cannot be attributed to biological factors or individual inadequacies. This ideology is not challenged in these stories. Minority differences are regularly recognized but the minorities are not *overtly* depreciated.

Of our sample of 185 stories, only four contained a direct reference of any kind to this problem area in American life. Only four brought the issue into the open:

An Indian girl is subject to conflict between loyalty to and marriage into her own people and assimilation into the American culture. Her ambivalence is resolved by acceptance of Indian social life (marriage to an Indian) and by acceptance of material conditions characteristic of American life (clothes, household appliances, etc.). Caste lines are maintained.

A Polish girl rebels against the traditional life of the American-Polish community, notably by dating an outsider. She is shamed by her people, almost loses her fiancé, acknowledges her mistake, and ends by accepting the traditional life of her community.

An upper-class American girl tries to evade jury duty and is chastised: 'This country would get into a pretty mess if a girl of the more intelligent class, why, she just checked aside and let the foreign element administrate justice in our courts.'

An 'American-born' man protests against being identified with French-Canadians living in New England: 'But I'm an American.' A character refers to such French-Canadians as 'kind of American – but ain't'.

The latter two references were only incidental comments on the problem. Only the first two – involving the adjustment problems of the Indian and Polish girls – contained 'serious' and extended considerations of the problem itself. And in each case, the 'out-group' heroine solved her problem by remaining within her own group. In each case, social assimilation was unsuccessful – although in each case the material trappings of American civilization, such as washing machines and radios, were secured. The moral for these stories was sounded by an Indian character: 'We want to win a place among the white people by our efforts and our determination, but we can never hope to be accepted socially.'

Thus the consistent deprivation of the minority groups is indirect; it is present in the stories but only seldom is it directly acknowledged or its implications discussed. The readers of short stories in popular magazines are constantly exposed, implicitly, to the prejudices and stereotypes attached to minority problems in the United States. But they are almost never exposed to serious and direct presentation of the problems themselves. Minority representatives are consistently deprived within an atmosphere which acknowledges no basis for such deprivation.

Minority problems in the United States are serious and deep-rooted. They will not be solved by symbols alone, but symbols will help. So will recognition of the pervasiveness of the problems. Even here, in ephemeral fiction fashioned of sweetness and light and designed purely for entertainment and divertissement, a subtle discrimination against minorities and foreigners has found its way. Even here, there are different classes of citizenship for different classes of people.

Crime news in Colorado newspapers*[1]

F. JAMES DAVIS

The study here reported was designed to test two hypotheses: (1) there is no consistent relationship between the amount of crime news in Colorado newspapers and the state crime rates, either for (*a*) total crime or for (*b*) various types of crime, and (2) public opinion about Colorado crime trends reflects trends in the amount of newspaper coverage rather than in actual Colorado crime rates.

The first hypothesis seemed plausible in the light of studies such as Wiseheart's,[2] which show that newspapers may increase their crime coverage out of all proportion to increases in crime in the belief that a 'crime wave' is occurring. The second hypothesis is consistent with the general thesis that newspapers mould their readers' opinions rather than reflect them, or at least that they influence readers' opinions under certain conditions.

METHODS

Three sources of data were utilized: (1) column-inch measurement of crime news in four Colorado newspapers from 1 January 1948 to 1 July 1950; (2) a state-wide public opinion poll, taken in July 1950; and (3) the *Uniform Crime Reports* of the Federal Bureau of Investigation for 1948, 1949, and 1950.

For purposes of the newspaper content analysis, crime was defined in the legal sense. All news items from any part of the country that in any way pertained to a municipal, state, or federal crime were measured, irrespective of what stage in criminal law procedure was involved.[3] Legislative investigations into alleged Communist party activities were excluded, as also were accounts of international crimes.

Tabulations were made both for news about total crime and for three types of crime – stealing, rape, and violent crimes. Stealing was defined to include robbery, burglary, larceny, and auto theft,

*From F. James Davis, 'Crime news in Colorado newspapers', *American Journal of Sociology*, LVII (June 1952), pp. 325–30.

each as defined by the Federal Bureau of Investigation in its *Uniform Crime Reports*. Violent crimes included murder, non-negligent manslaughter, and aggravated assault, each as defined in the *Uniform Crime Reports*.

Crime news in the entire paper was measured rather than just that on the front page.[4] Streamers, headlines, and photographs were included in the measurement on the assumption that the reader considers them an integral part of the crime story and is influenced by them considerably.[5]

A sample of every sixth newspaper was used for the measurement rather than the complete files. For the sake of convenience the first day of each month was used, the seventh day, and so on. All four newspapers have Sunday editions, and Sunday was counted like any other day. This sampling procedure was not decided upon arbitrarily: different types of samples were experimented with, and before the sample was settled upon it was tested for each of the four newspapers as follows.

The crime news for two months, one early in the two-and-one-half-year period and one late, was measured in entirety and the mean for each month computed. Then the sample of every sixth day was taken for each of these months as described above and the means computed. Tests were then made for the significance of the differences between the universe means and the sample means,[6] and in all cases the differences were not significant at the ·05 level.

The opinion poll was taken by Research Services, Inc., of Denver, an organization which regularly conducts state-wide polls in Colorado. The area sample plan was used,[7] and numerical estimates of crime trends were elicited. For example, the question pertaining to total crime was: 'If Colorado had 100 crimes of all types in a certain period back in 1948, how many crimes would you guess we have *in the same period of time now*?' Similar questions were asked for each of the three types of crime except that 10 was used as a base figure instead of 100.[8] This may seem a questionable procedure, but the pretext results were much more favourable for it than for percentage questions. All interviewers were trained, regular members of the staff of Research Services, Inc., and they were furnished with a set of special instructions designed to help them obtain the estimates in the desired form without suggesting particular figures. However, a good many of the 435 interviewees were unable to make numerical estimates (see Table 4 for the number of 'Don't Know' answers for each crime category). Both hypotheses required time-series analysis, as will be explained.

FINDINGS

The first hypothesis necessitated a comparison of changes in newspaper crime coverage and changes in Colorado crime rates.[9] The semiannual *Uniform Crime Reports* figures were used, and, in order to have comparable periods, it was necessary to compute six-month moving averages of the column inches of crime news.[10] Because of the difficulty of interpreting this information, January–June, 1948, was used as a base period, and percentage changes from the base period were computed for each of the other six-month periods.

TABLE 1

PERCENTAGE CHANGES IN TOTAL CRIME AND IN
TOTAL CRIME NEWS

Period	Changes in total crimes from Jan.–June 1948 total*	Changes from Jan.–June 1948 average of total crime news†			
		Denver Post	Rocky Mountain News	Daily Sentinel	Gazette-Telegraph
	%	%	%	%	%
July–Dec. 1948	+ 4·8	− 3·1	+ 0·8	+ 13·2	−15·2
Jan.–June 1949	+ 8·0	+10·0	+10·7	+ 66·5	−32·2
July–Dec. 1949	+28·7	− 1·7	+ 9·6	+ 55·4	−35·3
Jan.–June 1950	+21·8	+ 6·4	+26·7	+159·6	+44·9

*Cf. *Uniform Crime Reports*. There were 1341·14 crimes per 100,000 inhabitants during this period. Six types of crime included are murder and non-negligent manslaughter, robbery, aggravated assault, burglary, larceny, and auto theft.

* The January–June 1948, averages were: *Denver Post*, 66·74 column inches; *Rocky Mountain News*, 46·26; *Daily Sentinel*, 7·26; *Gazette-Telegraph*, 24·96.

These percentage changes, for total crime, appear in Table 1, which shows that there is marked lack of association between the percentage changes in total Colorado crime and in newspaper coverage. Percentage changes in crime coverage are entirely out of proportion with percentage changes in crime and are frequently in the opposite direction. Also, percentage changes in crime news vary tremendously from one newspaper to another.[11] Thus the evidence for total crime seems to bear out Hypothesis 1 (*a*). Tables 2 and 3 show similar comparisons for two of the newspapers[12] for stealing and violent crimes[13] and apparently verify Hypothesis 1 (*b*).

The first step in testing the second hypothesis was to analyze the opinion poll data, summarized in Table 4. It is apparent that the range of the estimates is great, that the estimates for different types

TABLE 2

PERCENTAGE CHANGES IN STEALING CRIMES AND IN
NEWS ABOUT STEALING

| Period | Changes in stealing crimes from Jan.–June 1948 total* | Changes from Jan.–June 1948 average of news about stealing† | |
		Denver Post	Rocky Mountain News
	%	%	%
July–Dec. 1948	+ 4·7	− 37·4	− 45·1
Jan.–June 1949	+ 7·9	+ 3·6	− 1·6
July–Dec. 1949	+ 28·3	− 13·1	− 5·1
Jan.–June 1950	+ 22·1	+ 3·7	+ 44·1

* There were 1320·5 stealing crimes per 100,000 inhabitants during this period. The semi-annual totals for stealing were obtained by adding the figures in the *Uniform Crime Reports* for robbery, burglary, larceny, and auto theft.

† The January–June 1948, averages were: *Denver Post*, 14·2 column inches; *Rocky Mountain News*, 9·4.

TABLE 3

PERCENTAGE CHANGES IN VIOLENT CRIMES AND IN
NEWS ABOUT VIOLENT CRIMES

| Period | Changes in violent crimes from Jan.–June 1948 total* | Changes from Jan.–June 1948 average of news about violent crimes† | |
		Denver Post	Rocky Mountain News
	%	%	%
July–Dec. 1948	+ 16·9	+ 41·0	+ 20·6
Jan.–June 1949	+ 12·6	+ 48·5	+ 57·3
July–Dec. 1949	+ 53·2	+ 1·6	+ 14·3
Jan.–June 1950	+ 5·5	+ 10·9	+ 63·2

* There were 20·6 violent crimes per 100,000 inhabitants during this period. The semi-annual totals for stealing were obtained by adding the figures in the *Uniform Crime Reports* for murder and non-negligent manslaughter and aggravated assault.

† The January–June 1948, averages were: *Denver Post*, 23·6 column inches; *Rocky Mountain News*, 16·0.

of crime are quite different, and that the bulk of the sample believed crime had increased considerably.

Tests were made of the significance of age and sex differences in the estimates made by the poll sample. The median estimate of the '40 and over' group was a little larger than that made by the '21–39' group, for all crime categories, but none of the differences was significant at the ·01 level. The differences between the estimates made by males and females were much larger, and in all four instances

TABLE 4

ESTIMATES OF CRIME-RATE CHANGES, 1948–50

Estimate*	Total crimes		Crime category					
			Stealing		Rape		Violent crimes	
	No.	%	No.	%	No.	%	No.	%
Increased 100 per cent or more	58	13·3	127	29·2	77	17·7	56	12·9
Increased 50 to 99 per cent or more	56	12·9	85	19·5	71	16·3	51	11·7
Increased 1 to 49 per cent	195	44·9	96	22·1	94	21·6	110	25·3
No change	58	13·3	67	15·4	116	26·7	152	35·0
Decreased	30	6·9	15	3·5	25	5·8	27	6·2
Don't know	38	8·7	45	10·3	52	11·9	39	8·9
Total	435	100·0	435	100·0	435	100·0	435	100·0

*Interviewees did not make percentage estimates. See text for the explanation of method.

the females made the greater estimates. The largest difference was for rape; the median male estimate was a 9·2 per cent increase, while that of the females was a 26·4 per cent increase. However, none of these sex differences proved to be significant at the ·01 level.

The test of the second hypothesis rested on the assumption that newspaper readers' estimates of crime trends vary with the *total impact* of the press rather than on the assumption that each reader is directly influenced only (or mainly) by the particular paper(s) he reads.[14] Newspapers have, it was assumed, both a direct and an indirect effect. Thus, the column inches of crime news in the different papers were *added* for this analysis.

In order to make the necessary comparisons, a base period different from that used in testing the first hypothesis had to be used. It will be recalled that the interviewees were asked to compare a 'certain period back in 1948' and 'now', which was mid-year in 1950. Thus the crime rates and column inches of crime news for the entire year of 1948 were divided by two and the result compared with figures for the first half of 1950[15] and with the interviewees' median estimates of changes in crime rates.

The three sets of data are compared in Table 5. It was assumed that the second hypothesis would be substantiated if the top row of figures (estimates) and the bottom row (crime news) corresponded very closely, while the middle row (crime rates) differed considerably

TABLE 5

MEDIAN ESTIMATES OF CRIME-RATE CHANGES AND
PERCENTAGE CHANGES IN CRIMES AND IN CRIME NEWS*

	Total crimes	Stealing	Rape	Violent crimes
Median percentage estimates of crime-rate changes†	+23·5	+47·2	+2·04	+11·1
Percentage changes in crimes	+19·0	+19·3	−36·2	− 2·4
Percentage changes in crime news	+29·1	+67·5	−72·1	+13·5

* For total crimes the averages of all four newspapers were combined by addition. For the three types of crime only the *Post* and *News* averages were added (see n. 12).
† Interviewees did not make percentage estimates. See text for the explanation of method.

from the other two. It would appear, then, that the data on violent crimes support the hypothesis very well, that the data on stealing support it fairly well, that the data for total crimes are inconclusive, and that the data on rape are contrary to the hypothesis.

It should be noted that the marked decrease in news of rape is due mainly to the sharp decrease made by the largest newspaper, the *Denver Post*. The *Post* had a flood of news about a University of Colorado 'sex murder' during the latter part of 1948 and early part of 1949, and it is possible that this sustained publicity sensitized *Post* readers (and perhaps most Coloradoans) to such news for a considerable time thereafter.[16] Consideration should also be given to the fact that the entire year of 1950 had to be used for rape in the comparison in Table 5 and that the final figures for 1950 involved a different population base (see note 14). Perhaps, then, the data on rape can be explained away, but even so the second hypothesis is not convincingly verified.

Even if Table 5 fitted the expected pattern perfectly, the question of whether newspaper coverage *caused* the estimates to be what they were would still have to be answered, since association does not prove causation. In the attempt to bridge this hazardous gap, the polling interviewers were instructed to ask this open-ended question: 'Concerning crime, what do you base your opinions on; that is, where do you get your information?' Eighty-six per cent included 'newspapers' in their answers to this question, and 24·3 per cent gave 'newspapers' as the sole response. This finding apparently strengthens the case for Hypothesis 2, but it is valid only to the degree that people are aware of the sources of their own opinions.

CONCLUSIONS

The findings of this study bear out the hypothesis that there is no consistent relationship between the amount of crime news in newspapers and the local crime rates. Semiannual percentage changes in crime coverage by Colorado newspapers were found to be at marked variance with Colorado crime trends, both for total crime and for selected types of crime. The four newspapers studied also varied markedly from each other in percentage changes in crime coverage. Evidently the amount of crime news in any one of these newspapers varies independently of both the amount of crime in the state and the amount of crime news in the other newspapers.

The findings lend some support to the hypothesis that public opinion reflects trends in the amount of crime news rather than in actual crime rates, but some of the evidence is inconclusive and some seems contrary to the hypothesis. This evidence would seem to warrant more definitive research, especially since the question involved bears upon the important problem of the relationship of newspapers and public opinions. This study dealt with the total column inches of crime news, and it is possible that a closer association might be found if only front-page news were used. Or investigation might be limited to the influence of the eye-catching devices – streamers, headlines, and pictures. Also, content analysis other than column-inch measurement might prove useful in studying the problem.

NOTES AND REFERENCES

1. The writer wishes to thank President P. P. Mickelson of Western State College of Colorado for a generous grant of money which made the study possible. Invaluable assistance was rendered by William N. McPhee of Research Services, Inc., Denver; Gordon

M. Connelly, research analyst, the *Denver Post*; and students Lester
W. Turner and Virginia Kreger Christensen.

2. M. K. Wiseheart, 'Newspapers and criminal justice', in *Criminal
   justice in Cleveland* (Cleveland, Cleveland Foundation, 1922),
   pp. 544–6.

3. Thus, first accounts of crimes prior to arrest, news about criminal
   'manhunts', arrests, fines, interrogation during detention, grand
   jury hearings, trials, incarceration, prison breaks, release of notorious
   offenders, criminal statistics, and public statements about crime were
   all included. See Frank Harris, *Presentation of crime in newspapers*
   (Minneapolis, Sociological Press, 1932), pp. 6–7, where he upholds
   the use of a very narrow legal definition of crime for this purpose,
   saying that a news story should be considered crime news only when
   legal probes result in indictments. It seems unlikely that the reading
   public draws such a fine line as this.

4. Ibid., pp. 48–62. Harris found a fairly high degree of correspondence
   between crime coverage on the front page and in the entire paper
   but not high enough for very accurate prediction from one to the
   other.

5. In his study Harris included streamers, headlines, and photographs
   (ibid., p. 27). See also Malcolm M. Willey, *The country newspaper:
   A study of socialization and newspaper content* (Durham, University
   of North Carolina Press, 1926), p. 47, for his explanation as to why
   headlines should be included.

6. The procedure followed is outlined in Frederick E. Croxton and
   Dudley J. Cowden, *Applied general statistics* (New York, Prentice-
   Hall, Inc., 1941), pp. 307–11. The *t* table was used for reasons given
   ibid., pp. 325–9.

7. The plan involved random selection of counties, towns and rural
   places, blocks, households, and individual persons with households.
   Seventy-five per cent of the original random sample was successfully
   interviewed. Dates of field work were roughly 25 June to 20 July.

8. This was done in order not to give a false impression of the extent of
   violent crimes and rapes.

9. Why compare crime figures for Colorado with news about crimes
   committed anywhere in the United States? First, most crime news
   in these papers is about Colorado crimes, so results probably would
   be similar if only news about Colorado were used. Second, it was
   assumed that readers form generalized opinions about crime and
   would make similar estimates for national and state trends. Comparisons with national trends may be made by consulting Table 2 in
   the 1949 semiannual bulletin and Table 1 in the 1950 semiannual
   bulletin of *Uniform Crime Reports*. These tables show that total crime
   increased 2·7 per cent from January–June 1948, to January–June
   1949, and increased 1·9 per cent from January–June 1949, to January–
   June 1950. Both for total crime and types of crime the national
   percentage changes during the period studied were much smaller
   than Colorado changes. This may be due to sustained drives against

crime in Colorado during the period. The increase in Colorado's police department employees, however, was only slightly larger than for the nation.

10. Harris, op. cit., pp. 5–6. Because of large variations in the amount of crime news when days and months were used, Harris adopted the year as the basis for comparing shifts in crime coverage. Harris' finding that 'crime news appears to be concentrated at irregular and unpredictable periods of time' is consistent with the findings of the present study.

11. During this period the *Denver Post* gradually grew larger. In the four six-month periods following January–June, 1948, the *Post*'s total editorial column inches showed these percentage increases from the base period: 5·7, 6·1, 10·1 and 14·8. These calculations are based on information in a letter dated 23 February 1951, from Gordon M. Connelly, research analyst for the *Post*. These increases cannot account for the percentage changes in the *Post*'s crime news. No check of changes in newspapers' size was made for the other papers.

12. The column inches of the three types of crime were recorded only for the *Post* and *News*. Only total crime coverage was recorded for the other two papers because of their relatively small size. The *Gazette-Telegraph* (Colorado Springs) ranks a very poor third in the state in circulation; the *Daily Sentinel* (Grand Junction) is sixth.

13. Semiannual figures for rape are not available, so no such comparisons were made for rape crimes.

14. Certain comparisons involving the latter assumption were made, however. The evidence for the *News* appeared fairly consistent with the hypothesis, while that for the *Post* was largely inconsistent with it. Since the *News* usually devotes the front page to one story – chiefly to streamers, headlines, and pictures – and since these often constitute the bulk of a crime story, it is conceivable that the direct influence of eye-catching devices on opinions about crime trends is great.

15. Except that the rape rate used was for the entire year of 1950, since semiannual rates for rape were unavailable. At the end of 1950, twenty-three cities reported crimes known to the police, as against eighteen cities in 1948.

16. By semiannual periods the percentage changes from the January–June 1948, average of 1·66 column inches of rape news in the *Post* were: +635·4, +630·1, −48·8, and −68·8.

Mental illness:
what the media present*

JUM C. NUNNALLY

The media of mass communication are commonly thought to exert a powerful influence on what the general public feels and believes. Consequently, we studied presentations dealing with mental-health phenomena in the mass media and the impact of the media on public opinion. This chapter will describe a content analysis of the mass media.

CONTENT-ANALYSIS PROCEDURE

Our content analysis counted the number of times that particular points of view about mental health were portrayed in samples of mass media presentations.

Coding categories

In a content analysis, the people who do the counting are referred to as *coders* and the things that they count are referred to as *coding categories*. Usually coding categories are determined *a priori*, or 'rationally', rather than deduced from empirical observations. Our content analysis departed from the customary dependence on 'rational' categories. One of the principles which guided our study of information held by our three sources (the public, the experts, and the media) was that comparable measures should be used for all three. Consequently, the ten information factors that were used to study the public and the experts were also used to study the content of the media.

How the information factors were used to analyse the content of media presentations can be illustrated with one of the television programmes 'caught' in our sample. The programme was a 15-minute crime drama. As the scene opens, a thief is sneaking through a clock shop. The shop is filled with ticking clocks and swinging pendulums. The thief enters a barred enclave in the room where the safe is placed. The barred door accidentally closes and locks, and

*Extracted from Jum C. Nunnally, *Popular conceptions of mental health* (New York, Holt, Rinehart & Winston, 1961).

the unfortunate thief must spend the night looking at and listening to a room full of clocks. When the proprietors arrive in the morning, the thief is staring glassy-eyed and mumbling incoherently. In the final scene he is carted away to a mental hospital.

How the content of this television presentation was analysed will illustrate our general procedures. It was first necessary to decide whether any relevant material occurred. (How relevance was determined will be discussed later.) Relevant material was then coded on the ten information factors. A judgment was made as to whether the material affirmed each factor, repudiated each factor, or portrayed a neutral viewpoint (a neutral presentation either said or portrayed nothing relating to the ten factors or was a balance of pro and con). Scores of plus, minus, and zero were given for the results.

The television drama described above is relevant to our problem because the thief was referred to several times as being 'out of his mind' and because he was placed in a mental hospital. The presentation was particularly relevant to two of our factors, 'look and act different' (Factor I) and 'immediate external environment versus personality dynamics' (Factor VII). The thief assumed a very bizarre appearance, which, if characteristic of the mentally ill at all, would be found only in the most severely ill. Consequently, the programme was scored plus on Factor I. In the drama, the thief was 'driven mad' by the ticking clocks. He entered the shop an apparently normal person (except for an unfortunate occupation) and left with a severe mental illness. The lesson that people might learn from this (fortunately people know better) is that one harrowing experience will bring on mental illness. Consequently, the programme was scored 'plus' on Factor VII. The details of the programme supplied information enough to score some of the other information factors as either plus or minus, and zeros were given to the remaining information factors because no related ideas were presented.

In addition to the ten factors, five supplementary content categories were employed. Counts were made of the number of portrayals of *supernatural* causes and cures associated with mental-health problems. Although supernatural explanations were generally rejected by the public, it was thought that some of the media presentations might deal with evil omens, visions, magic spells, and the like. The second supplementary category concerned the *approval of mental-health professions and facilities*. A plus was recorded if the portrayal suggested, for example, that psychiatrists usually do an effective job. An example of a minus situation is one in which the psychiatrist was in league with crooks and used his position to confine hapless victims in a mental hospital. Similarly, codings were made of portrayals relating to psychotherapy, mental hospitals, and specific forms of treatment. The third supplementary category concerned the *incidence* of mental-health problems: whether or not the presentation suggested that mental-health problems occur frequently in our society. For the fourth supplementary category, *methods of prevention and treatment*, coders simply listed all the suggested methods encountered in the media presentations. For the fifth supplementary category, *whom to approach for help* when mental problems occur, coders listed the kinds of persons suggested in the media presentations, such as ministers, psychiatrists, and lawyers.

In addition to the content categories, coders applied a number of space and time categories. For the printed media, the coders determined the amount of space taken up by each relevant message. For radio and television, coders noted the amount of time consumed by each relevant presentation – an hour, a half-hour, or only five minutes. The space and time categories were broken down in terms of the places in which relevant material appeared. For example, in the analysis of newspapers, each relevant item was classified into one of the following 'location' categories: (1) news stories, features, and pictures, (2) paid advertising, (3) entertainment such as fiction, comics, and puzzles, (4) personal-advice columns on health and psychology and for the 'lovelorn', (5) editorials, including political cartoons and 'letters to the editor', and (6) all factual 'how to' items, such as recipes, financial guides, and home-repair columns.

The ten factors and the supplementary categories were intended to measure the information stated and implied by mass media presentations. In addition to these information-type measures, part of the content analysis was concerned with the attitudes suggested by the media presentations. For this, coders were asked to make judgments about the portrayals of the mentally ill and the persons who treated the mentally ill. Each character appearing in the media was rated on a series of seven-step attitude scales. The scales were bounded by polar adjectives such as safe-dangerous, strong-weak, and valuable-worthless. . . . The coders were not asked to rate their personal reactions to the characters portrayed but to try to make impartial judgments about the nature of the portrayals themselves.

Coder selection and training
The main job of the coders was to analyse media content on the basis of the ten information factors. Consequently, the coders had to be familiar with psychological concepts. . . . The meanings of the information factors were explained in detail. One form of practice was to make a 'blind' sorting of the 180 information items (the ones used in the original factor analysis) into their proper

factors. Thus, given a statement like 'The eyes of the insane are glassy', the coders had to guess the corresponding factor (in this case the correct answer was Factor I, 'look and act different'). On the average the coders assigned 75 per cent of the items correctly, giving us some confidence in their understanding and use of the factors. As another form of practice, the coders made content analyses of excerpts from newspaper articles and of contrived written messages. The results were compared with the codings made by psychologists on the research staff, which resulted in more exact specification of the procedures of analysis and continued training for coders.

Media samples

A truly representative sampling of the content of the mass media would be an enormous research undertaking. Not only are there numerous arms of the media (films, books, newspapers, radio, television, and others), but there are numerous classifications of each. Even a representative sample of one arm alone, such as magazines, would require a diverse and extensive collection. In comparison with a truly representative sampling of media content, our sample was relatively weak.

Television. Television coverage was the most restricted of our media samples, because of the difficulties and expenses of content-analysing television programmes as compared with newspapers, magazines, and other media. The television sample was restricted to the total output – about 111 hours of transmission time – of a single VHF station, WCIA in Champaign, Illinois, for one full week, 31 January to 6 February 1955. In addition to local productions, this station offered more than 100 CBS, nearly 20 NBC, and several DuMont programmes.

As was true in all of the content analyses, every minute of the telecasting was considered for material relevant to mental health. Thus our coders watched such apparently unrelated presentations as basketball games, stock-market quotations, and commercials, but we did not want to judge in advance where relevant presentations would be found.

Coders worked in shifts to analyse television programmes, with one shift of three coders watching at all times. A room equipped with clocks, two television sets (in case one fell into disrepair), and partitions separating the coders from one another was specially prepared for the analysis. Supervisors were available to distribute and collect coding sheets and to answer coders' questions about technical procedures.

Radio. The radio sample consisted of one week's total broadcasting by four stations, affiliated with four different networks, in four widely separated geographic areas of the United States. The broadcasts had been recorded in November and December 1953 for another project. It proved much less tedious to analyse the radio recordings than it was to analyse 'live' television. The coders were also able to play back portions of the programme recordings to help them form judgments about the content categories.

Magazines. In this sample were 91 different magazines, one issue of each, which were displayed on news-stands at about the same time in March 1955. These included comic books, news, pictorial, digest, 'quality', health, women's, men's, teenage, sports, farm, romance and confession, detective, film, and other magazines. We tried to gather as diverse a collection as possible, excluding only such highly specialized magazines as photography and 'how to' publications. About 351,000 column inches of space were included.

Newspapers. Our newspaper sample was both the most extensive and the most representative for the country as a whole. The sample consisted of one week's home editions of 49 daily newspapers. The newspapers were proportionately representative of the geographic regions in the United States and proportionately representative of circulation size. The issues were spread over the month of October 1954. Involved were 317 separate issues with a total of 12,419 pages, containing approximately 2,086,423 inches – and every inch was searched for material relating to mental health.

Confession magazines. In gathering the magazine sample discussed above, we found that 'confession' magazines are saturated with material relating to mental illness, neurosis, and emotional disturbance. Consequently, a separate study was made of the mental-health content of confession magazines. Different methods of content analysis were used on the confession magazines and the results were not combined directly with those from our four other media samples. . . .

CONTENT-ANALYSIS RESULTS

How seriously can the results of the content analysis be taken? We have pointed out some of the frailties of the procedures that were used. Much of the data is judgmental and is no better or no worse than the subjective processes of the coders. Also, the content samples were, at best, only moderately representative of the media as a whole. In spite of the limitations of the content analysis and the modest proportions of our media samples, however, the results are so lopsided that we can reach some strong conclusions about the mental-health content of the mass media.

Time and space

Seeking material directly related to mental-health problems (as we defined them) in the mass media is like looking for a needle in a haystack. If you search every inch of space in three different daily newspapers, the odds are that you will find only one item which is relevant. To find one relevant item it would be necessary to read, on the average, the entire content of two magazines. If you listened to one entire day of broadcasting of a radio station, you would, on the average, find about 2·3 programmes with information or portrayals relevant to mental-health problems. An almost identical number of relevant programmes would be expected in the entire daily telecasting of one station – 2·4 programmes which in some way relate to mental-health problems. Thus we can conclude that: *Information concerning mental illness appears relatively infrequently in mass media presentations.*

The findings here contradict our original estimates of the prevalence of mental-health presentations in the mass media. We had guessed that relevant material was presented more frequently than it is. Before doing the study we tried to recall the number of presentations relating to mental-health issues that we had seen recently in newspapers, television, and the other media, but in so doing we did not fully consider the many programmes that were irrelevant. Consequently, we overestimated, percentagewise, the occurrence of related material.

In all of the media samples combined, we found a total of 202 relevant items (items being defined as separate whole programmes in radio and television and as columns, stories, and features in the printed media). Of the total, we found 120 items in newspapers, 49 in magazines, 16 in radio, and 17 in television. There were not enough items for us to compare their content similarities and differences or to demonstrate differences among subclassifications of the media. For example, it would have been interesting to determine whether the mental-health content of newspapers is generally different from that of television programmes or whether the mental-health content of television news programmes is different from that of evening drama programmes. Because there were not enough relevant items to analyse separately, all of the relevant material was lumped together, providing an average profile of the information presented in the mass media.

Although we did not study the issue directly, it seemed to us that information relating to 'physical' disorders – cancer, heart trouble, physical injury, and so forth – appeared more frequently than information relating to mental health. Perhaps the apparent relative scarcity of information relevant to mental-health problems is related to the findings that public information is unstructured and uncrystallized. Problems of mental health may not be discussed sufficiently in the media, in schools, and in private conversation to permit the individual to develop a firm system of beliefs. More research is needed, however, to determine the amount of mental-health information in the media and, if, as our data indicate, such information is relatively scarce, to test the effect of this scarcity on public beliefs.

The information factors

To review: Two out of three coders had to be in agreement before material was classed as relevant and before content was coded on the information factors. Although basing the analysis on majority decisions reduced the total amount of data, it probably produced a more valid set of results.

While the data on the information held by the public and the experts was in seven-step-scale form and could be compared directly, the data from this content analysis had to be converted to the seven-step scale for comparison purposes. The data consisted of ratings by coders of the number of times that one pole of a factor was portrayed as compared with the other pole. For example, 80 instances were found in which the 'immediate external environment' (Factor VII) was portrayed as being at the root of particular mental disorders. The opposite pole of the factor, 'personality dynamics', was portrayed only 29 times. Thus Factor VII was attributed to be the cause in 73 per cent of the classified presentations. Percentages of this kind were then converted to a seven-point scale (see Nunnally, 1957, for a description of the scaling procedure used). From these converted results we were able to compare the results from the mass media with the opinions held by the public and the experts (see Figure 1).

The scaled factor scores for the media, represented by circles, are shown in Figure 1. Three factors (will power, sex distinction, and age function) occurred less than ten times in the media presentations and consequently offered insufficient grounds for making comparisons. The factor scores for the media are compared with the average responses given by experts and by members of the general public. The results are quite clear. Not only are the views that the media present generally incorrect according to expert opinion but they are also far less accurate than the beliefs of the average man. *The media of mass communication generally present a distorted picture of mental-health problems.*

Although some mass media presentations, especially those specifically designed to convey information about mental health, provide a valid picture of mental illness, the number of such programmes is very small in comparison with those which incidentally portray mental illness in a misleading light. An individual is more likely to see some aspect of neurotic behaviour portrayed on television in an evening drama programme than in a public-information programme.

FIGURE 1

COMPARISONS OF EXPERTS, THE PUBLIC, AND THE MASS MEDIA ON THE TEN INFORMATION FACTORS

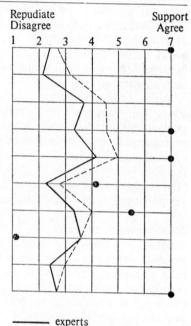

1 Look and act different

2 Will power

3 Sex distinction

4 Avoidance of morbid thoughts

5 Guidance and support

6 Hopelessness

7 External causes vs. personality

8 Non-seriousness

9 Age function

10 Organic causes

——— experts

----- pubic opinion

● mass media

In general, the causes, symptoms, methods of treatment, prognoses, and social effects of mental illness portrayed by the media are far removed from what the experts advocate. . . . In particular, media presentations emphasize the bizarre symptoms of the mentally ill. For example, information relating to Factor I was recorded 89 times. Of these, 88 affirmed the factor, that is, indicated or suggested that people with mental-health problems 'look and act different'; only one item denied Factor I. In television dramas, for example, the afflicted person often enters the scene staring glassy-eyed, with his mouth widely agape, mumbling incoherent phrases or laughing uncontrollably. Even in what would be considered the milder disorders, neurotic phobias and obsessions, the afflicted person is presented as having bizarre facial expressions and actions.

The occurrence of mental disorder is explained in the media most often by pressures in the immediate external environment (Factor VII). The soap-opera heroine develops a neurosis because her husband dies in a plane crash, her little daughter is afflicted with an incurable disease, and all the family savings are lost in a fire. The 'neurosis' goes away with a brighter turn of events. If the pressures of the immediate external environment are not brought in as causal explanations, organic factors are cited. A magazine fiction story might explain neurotic or psychotic behaviour in terms of an old battlefield injury, a head wound in childhood, or physical privation such as thirst or hunger.

In the media, the person with a mental disorder most often receives help from some strong person in the environment who lends guidance and support. The strong individual may be a person who is professionally trained – a psychiatrist, 'doctor', or nurse; equally often the guiding hand is that of a homespun philosopher who manages to say the right thing at the right time. Such cogencies as 'The world is what you make of it' and 'The past cannot hurt you' are portrayed as profoundly influencing the course of a disorder.

Supplementary categories

Because only a few examples of the items in the media contained material which was related to the supplementary categories, there is little to report. For example, in the category 'whom to seek for advice', we found that only eight psychiatrists, two 'doctors', one psychologist, and one nurse were mentioned. These categories did provide one interesting bit of negative evidence: Although we had thought that the media might portray religion as being related to mental-health issues, it was seldom mentioned as an important variable. The same results held in a separate study of confession magazines. In this case, the media are in line with public opinion: our studies show that very few people associate mental-health phenomena with religion.

Attitude ratings

The media samples portrayed 41 persons who could be classified as mentally ill. Of these, 21 displayed typical neurotic symptoms and 20 displayed typical psychotic symptoms. Three coders made attitude ratings of the 41 portrayals, and the median rating of the three coders on each Semantic Differential scale was used in the analysis. The resulting profile of the mentally ill in the mass media closely resembles the public's attitudes toward the mentally ill. Both psychotics and neurotics are portrayed as relatively ignorant, dangerous, dirty, unkind, and unpredictable. Neurotics are pictured as less dangerous, dirty, and unkind than psychotics, the latter being pictured as stronger and more active.

For what they are worth, the coders also made attitude ratings of the portrayals of the 12 'therapists' mentioned above. The resulting average profile is much the same as the attitude profile of the general public toward psychologists and psychiatrsists. The media portrayals depict the therapist as being intelligent, kind, and valuable.

SUMMARY

Our results point to a seeming paradox: the ideas about mental health portrayed in the mass media are less 'correct' compared with expert opinion than are the beliefs of the public at large. Where then did the public get its present body of information? Certainly not from an uncritical acceptance of media presentations. Perhaps, as has been suggested, the public is able to discriminate between 'valid' information and unrealistic portrayals. If this is so, then the public probably does learn something from the 'better' media presentations, although the number of such programmes is relatively small.

The media are, of course, commercial ventures whose policies and presentations are determined in part by their internal needs. Presentations related to mental health are shaped by numerous hands – writers, editors, directors, media executives, commercial sponsors, and others. Perhaps it is necessary to emphasize bizarre symptoms in order to make the presentations more exciting and to enlarge their audience appeal. Perhaps the relatively restricted time period or space available is responsible for much of the oversimplified treatment of mental disorders. If the media took the time to illustrate the complexities of the learning processes that experts deem to be the important components in personality disorders, they might produce some very dull programmes.

The communications media have adopted a stylized picture of mental-health problems which distorts reality, but is a useful device in drama, comedy, and other programmes for the public. It would be a great waste, however, if the communications media did not eventually help to promote a healthy set of public attitudes and improve public understanding of mental-health phenomena. It is also to be hoped that more accurate information can be incorporated into effective forms of entertainment. Our content analysis was performed in 1954 and 1955. Presentations in the mass media may have begun to incorporate more adequate viewpoints about mental health since then.

Theories of behaviour and the image of the alcoholic in popular magazines 1900–1966*

ARNOLD S. LINSKY

In his satirical novel *Erewhon*, Samuel Butler describes a mythical society in which criminals are sympathetically treated in hospitals at the public expense while diseased persons are sent to prisons and punished according to the seriousness of their illness.[1] Butler's satire illustrates the tenuous linkage which may exist between the form of deviance and public definitions and response to that deviance.

The changes in public views of alcoholism during the twentieth century provide a graphic illustration of how a form of deviance may be rapidly redefined. This shift of 'moral passage' does not make alcoholism unique among forms of deviance, but in this case the shift has begun so recently and advanced so rapidly the possibility exists for objectivity charting its course.[2] These changes are believed to reflect both the specific moral history of alcohol problems as well as basic cultural changes in popular conceptions of man's nature and his social relationships which go far beyond the problems of alcohol and which affect views of both normal and abnormal behaviour.

The current study investigates changes in public views on alcoholism during the last seven decades through content analysis of popularly oriented magazine articles dealing with alcohol problems. Popular magazines have long exhorted and advised the public on a variety of social problems, including alcoholism. It is assumed that positions expressed in these magazines are broadly consistent with or at most slightly in advance of beliefs held by their readership, in keeping with the need of such magazines for wide reader acceptance.

The study examines first changes in the methods of treatment advocated and in the aetiological theories of alcoholism presented. Secondly, the study attempts to bring some empirical data to bear on Charles Y. Glock's thesis that a quiet revolution has been occurring

* From Arnold S. Linsky, 'Theories of behaviour and the image of the alcoholic in popular magazines 1900–1966', *Public Opinion Quarterly* 34 (Winter 1970–1), pp. 573–81.

with respect to man's view of human nature.[3] Glock posits a shift away from a moralistic and 'free will' conception of human nature which has traditionally informed American public opinion toward a more deterministic and naturalistic view.

The universe for the present study consists of articles on the subject of alcoholism and alcohol problems listed in *Reader's guide to periodic literature* from 1900 to 1966. Random samples of thirty articles were drawn from each of the six decades from 1900 through 1959, and 60 articles were drawn for the seven-year period 1960–1966. Each article was rated independently on several dimensions by at least two judges.

CAUSAL THEORIES OF ALCOHOLISM

Causal theories presented in articles are classified according to two central dimensions: (1) a *locational* dimension, i.e. whether the causal agent is seen as inside the alcoholic or located in his environment; (2) and a *moral* dimension, i.e. whether the causal agent is evaluated moralistically in the article or interpreted naturalistically, i.e. in scientific terms.[4]

Each article was rated independently on both locational and moral dimensions from (1) to (5). On the locational dimension a rating of (1) indicates that the cause is viewed as exclusively within the individual, while a (5) indicates that the cause is completely external. On the moral dimension (1) represents a highly moralistic evaluation of the causal agent while (5) represents an entirely naturalistic orientation.[5]

Locational dimension
Table 1 indicates important shifts in the perceived locational origins of alcoholism. For the first three decades of the twentieth century the causal agent was seen as clearly outside of the alcoholic, resting in environmental forces. A decisive change occurred by the 1940s when the focus shifted to factors inside the alcoholic, principally psychological. Since the 1940s there appears to be a moderate trend away from strictly internal explanation, with articles often citing both internal and external factors.

The types of external causes cited in the 1950s and 1960s, however, differed from types cited earlier in this century. Current articles citing external causes focus on diffuse cultural and social patterns such as cocktail parties, tensions of fast-paced living, and breakdown of social controls, as opposed to the liquor traffic, the tavern, the poverty of the working class focused on by earlier articles.

Moral dimension

Attribution of moral blame to the agent causing alcoholism has declined steadily over the last seven decades. The most decisive decline occurred between the decades 1930–1939 and 1940–1949. It is evident from Table 1 that this period also witnessed the major changes on the locational dimension. Later articles for the most part either denied the relationship of alcoholism to moral weakness or ignored the question of the moral responsibility of the causal agent.

TABLE 1

EXPLANATIONS OF ALCOHOL PROBLEMS IN POPULAR
MAGAZINES: LOCATION AND MORAL DIMENSION BY
DECADE (MEDIAN RATINGS)

Decade	Number of articles	Location score* (internal–external)	Moral score† (Moralistic–naturalistic)
1960–66	60	2·77	4·44
1950–59	30	2·50	3·50
1940–49	30	2·17	3·50
1930–39	30	3·76	2·50
1920–29	30	4·20	2·14
1910–19	30	3·83	2·13
1900–09	30	4·20	2·04

* Ratings may range from (1) (inside the alcoholic) to (5) 'outside the alcoholic'.
†Ratings may range from (1) 'moralistic' to (5) 'naturalistic'.

Complete causal theories

Most articles on alcoholism include both a stand on the location of the causal agent and a moral evaluation of that agent. The foregoing analysis has focused on the trend for the locational and moral dimensions separately. The distribution of articles on both dimensions jointly is considered in this section. These two dimensions dichotomously treated result in four possible combinations. Each combination, represented by a cell in Figure 1, contains a logically distinct aetiological theory of alcoholism.

Cell (a) represents the traditional free-will theory which holds that the cause of alcoholism is internal to the alcoholic and that he is morally at fault for his condition. Cell (b) represents the social criticism approach which views morally corrupt individuals, groups, and institutions in the external social environment of the alcoholic as the cause of alcoholism. In cell (c) psychological and biological theories are represented, which explain alcoholism on the basis of

FIGURE 1

THEORIES OF THE AETIOLOGY OF ALCOHOLISM BY
MORAL AND LOCATIONAL DIMENSIONS

Moral dimension	Locational dimension	
	Within the alcoholic	External to alcoholic
Moralistic	(a) Traditional free will position	(b) Social criticism
Non-moralistic (or naturalistic)	(c) Psychological and biological explanation	(d) Sociological explanation

internal but naturalistic factors, such as emotional, genetic, or physio-chemical agents, without blaming the alcoholic. Finally, cell (d) represents sociological explanation, which, like cell (b), explains alcohol problems as originating in the social environment of the alcoholic, but unlike (b) views these environmental factors within a morally neutral, naturalistic framework.

Table 2 presents the distribution of these four aetiological positions for four consecutive time periods. The social criticism approach dominated the explanation of alcoholism during the first twenty years of the century. The cause of alcoholism was placed clearly in the alcoholic's environment, and these environmental agents were unequivocally condemned. Explanations emphasizing the free will of the alcoholic were second in importance, but ran far behind the social criticism approach.

By 1940 a significant shift had occurred toward naturalistic internal explanations of alcoholism. Almost 72 per cent of articles written during this period fell within cell (c), psychological-biological explanation. This continued to be the dominant category of explanation during the 1960s.

There is some evidence that a further shift toward sociological explanation has been occurring since the 1940s but psychological explanations still predominate. Naturalistic explanations, cells (b) and (d) together, account for 81·3 per cent of the articles written between 1940 and 1959, and 86·4 per cent written between 1960 and 1966.

TABLE 2

AETIOLOGICAL THEORIES OF ALCOHOLISM AND ALCOHOL
PROBLEMS PRESENTED IN POPULAR MAGAZINE ARTICLES
BY PER CENT OF TOTAL ARTICLES* IN FOUR PERIODS†

	Period			
Theoretical position‡	1900–1919	1920–1939	1940–1959	1960–1966
	%	%	%	%
'Free will'	11·1	5·6	6·2	8·1
Social criticism	75·0	58·3	12·5	5·4
Psychological and biological explanation	5·6	16·7	71·9	54·0
Sociological explanation	8·3	19·4	9·4	32·4
Number of articles	36	36	32	37

* The number of articles is less than the 60 original articles for each period since articles which received a rating of 3 on either the locational or the moral dimension could not be sorted into the dichotomized table and were excluded from this analysis.
† Decades are consolidated into 20-year periods because of small frequencies in some cells.
‡ See Figure 1 for the derivation of these positions.

RECOMMENDATIONS FOR DEALING WITH ALCOHOL PROBLEMS

Treatment recommendations changed markedly during the period covered. Table 3 contains a detailed analysis of these changes. A sharp increase in advocacy of rehabilitation-reform measures is evident for the period of study. Rehabilitation-reform refers to attempts to control the alcohol problem by bringing about changes within the alcoholic himself. Within this major category, therapeutic measures have shown the most dramatic increase. For the most recent decade Alcoholics Anonymous was the most frequently endorsed method of treatment, followed by psychiatric care, medical care, and clinical-institutional care. Neither the traditional measures, such as will power and religious conversion, nor punitive measures have ever assumed major importance in popular articles of this century.

Suggestions oriented toward preventing alcoholism, such as education, social change, and control of the availability of alcohol, have declined, especially since 1939. In the prevention group, only education on alcoholism has gained increased endorsement during the twentieth century. Advocacy of prevention by control of alcohol itself, through moderation, abstinence, and Prohibition, has declined

TABLE 3

METHODS ADVOCATED FOR DEALING WITH ALCOHOLISM
AND ALCOHOL PROBLEMS DURING FOUR PERIODS,
BY PER CENT*

Method	1900–1919	1920–1939	1940–1959	1960–1966
	%	%	%	%
REHABILITATION-REFORM	11·2	19·4	62·9	62·0
Therapeutic	5·6	8·8	52·8	53·0
Alcoholics Anonymous	—	—	14·6	20·0
Medical	2·8	3·5	12·4	11·0
Psychiatric	—	1·8	19·1	15·0
Clinical-institutional	2·8	3·5	6·7	7·0
Traditional (will power, moral change, religious)	5·6	5·3	9·0	6·0
Punitive (jails, fines, social pressure)	—	5·3	1·1	3·0
PREVENTION	81·9	73·6	32·5	31·0
Social and cultural change	23·6	17·5	10·1	9·0
Educational	8·3	14·0	11·2	16·0
Control of alcohol	50·0	42·1	11·2	6·0
Moderation	8·3	15·8	1·1	2·0
Abstinence	11·1	1·8	9·0	3·0
Prohibition	30·6	24·6	1·1	1·0
OTHER	6·9	7·0	4·5	7·0
Total per cent	100·0	100·0	100·0	100·0
Number of treatments suggested	72	57	89	100

* Some articles suggest no treatments, others may suggest more than one.
Percentages are based on total number of methods suggested. Chi-square
equals 107·05 with 15 degrees of freedom, $p < ·001$ (based on four categories:
rehabilitation-reform, social and cultural change, education, and control of
alcohol).

markedly from 50 per cent for the period 1900–1919 to 6 per cent
for 1960–1966.[6]

INTERPRETATION

Mass media have undoubtedly played a part in changing public
opinion on alcoholism. A community survey by the author found
evidence that exposure to mass media was directly related to 'en-
lightened' attitudes on alcoholism among the public.[7] Any changes

that occur in the mass media, however, should be considered instrumental rather than basic causes of change in public attitudes, since both the reasons for changes in content and the reasons for public receptivity remain unexplained.

Despite the rapid growth of scientific research on alcoholism during the last three decades, neither the aetiology of alcoholism nor the efficacy of modern therapeutic treatment has been established. Current views of alcoholism would seem to derive more from broad social and philosophical considerations than from scientific evidence.

Earlier in this paper it was suggested that changes in public attitudes on alcoholism might be related to a changing view of human nature. According to Glock, the basic factor governing the images of man that have prevailed historically is how much free will man is believed to have.[8] He maintains that the traditional image of man, a view grounded in the history of Western theological thought, sees him as possessing almost unlimited free will and thereby in no sense '. . . a victim of his environment'.

Glock sees a decline in this view beginning in the nineteenth century and accelerating in the last three or four decades. Under the influence of the behavioural sciences this traditional view has, according to Glock, been modified to the view that man cannot entirely escape the influence of his inherited attributes and his social environment. Among the consequences of this shift in the image of man Glock includes the changes in attitudes toward Negroes, and toward such deviants as the delinquent, the poverty stricken, the mentally ill, and the criminal.

Our data have some bearing on Glock's thesis. A somewhat restricted view of Glock's free-will orientation would equate it with cell (a) in our Figure 1. We reserved this cell for inside-moralistic explanations, where the cause is seen as within the alcoholic himself, and he is held morally responsible for his condition. According to Glock's thesis we would expect the free-will position to be relatively important for the early period surveyed, but declining in importance in more recent years. The findings in Table 2 indicate that this interpretation was employed more frequently in the period 1900–1919 than in subsequent periods, but there is no consistent trend over the four periods covered in Table 2. Even during the period 1900–1919 only 11·1 per cent of the articles represented the free-will view, compared with 75 per cent which took the social criticism approach. Our findings do not exclude the possibility that the free-will orientation was dominant at some point prior to the beginning of the twentieth century.

A somewhat broader interpretation of Glock's free will versus determinism dimension would equate it with the moralistic-naturalistic dimension of this study. Explanations of behaviour are considered naturalistic in our study if they employ a natural science frame of reference, i.e. alcoholism is viewed as the consequence of preceding events and conditions such as the genetic, biochemical, and psychological make-up of the individual and his social and cultural environment.

Under this broader definition our findings support Glock's thesis. The evaluation of drinking problems was highly moralistic in the first decade of the study but became progressively more naturalistic with each succeeding decade. For the latest period, the years 1960–1966, the average ratings for the 60 articles surveyed approached the naturalistic end of the continuum.

The timing of the change also supports Glock's contention that this change accelerated approximately 35 to 40 years ago. The dramatic shift that occurred during the period roughly between the 1930s and 1940s is evident in Table 1.

In summary, this study has traced broad changes in public views of alcoholism, alcohol problems, and treatment as presented in popular magazines during the twentieth century. The pattern of changes found is interpreted as reflecting in part cultural changes in popular conceptions of man's nature and social relationships which go far beyond the problems of alcohol, and which affect views of both normal and abnormal behaviour.

NOTES AND REFERENCES

1. Samuel Butler, *Erewhon* (London, Cape, 1922).
2. The term 'moral passage' refers to a transition of a behaviour from one moral status to another. Gusfield argues in a recent essay that drinking has undergone two such passages since the early nineteenth century: first from the 'repentant drinker' to the 'enemy drinker' and from the 'enemy drinker' to the 'sick drinker'. Joseph R. Gusfield, 'Moral passage: The symbolic process in public designations of deviance', *Social Problems*, Vol. 15 (1967), pp. 175–88. See also Harold Pfautz, 'The image of alcohol in popular fiction: 1900–1904 and 1946–1950', *Quarterly Journal for Studies on Alcoholism*, Vol. 23 (1962), pp. 131–46.
3. Glock, 'Images of man and public opinion', *Public Opinion Quarterly*, Vol. 28 (1964), pp. 539–46.
4. The following quotes illustrate 'internal' explanations. At this point only the location dimension is considered; the moral dimension is temporarily ignored:

> (1) '. . . drinking is only a symptom of a deeper-seated malady, the source of which is a maladjustment in the drinker's personality, that is in the full circle of his physical, mental, emotional make-up.'

(2) 'Long days of soul searching followed his recognition that the causes of his excessive drinking were wrong moral values and character defects.'

Following are examples of the 'external' orientation:

(3) 'According to one pub manager, the British working man used to drink to forget his hardships. Today the labourer boasts a much better standard of living.'

(4) 'Two great factors contribute toward alcoholism, says Dr Block. One is the necessity for drinking, almost an obligation on the part of a person to drink in our culture. . . . The second factor seems to stem from the extreme toleration on the part of the general American public for drunken behavior.'

It should be remembered that articles are judged independently on both moral and locational dimensions. Some examples of the moral orientation include:

(5) '. . . but drunkenness being an insanity deliberately induced carries a moral stigma'.

(6) 'The booze traffic has been driven underground. It is surreptitious, predatory, evil. The potency of its evil, the weight of the menace it exerts, cannot be determined definitely. . . . The illnesses due to illicit liquor are not made public.'

Two examples of statements reflecting morally neutral or naturalistic explanations follow:

(7) 'Alcoholism is not a vice but a disease. The alcoholic is not a moral weakling. He is tragically ill with a mental malady.'

(8) 'Causes may come under such headings as psychological, medical, economic, and sociological.'

5. Reliability of ratings between the two principal judges on locational dimensions was tested in two pretests of 30 articles each. Gamma between judges for the two samples was ·73 and ·70. In the first sample 40·0 per cent of the items were identically rated by both judges while a total of 93·3 per cent were rated within one point of each other. On the second sample 51·7 per cent of the ratings were identical, while a total of 89·7 per cent fell within one rating of each other.

Reliability on the moral dimension for the two pretest samples is indicated by a gamma of ·74 and ·75. In the first sample 53·3 per cent of ratings were identical by both judges while a total of 86·6 per cent of the ratings were within one point of each other. In the second sample 69·0 per cent of ratings were identical by both while 89·7 per cent of ratings were within one point.

Inter-judge reliability, although reasonable, was undoubtedly reduced by the method of assigning a single rating to an entire article, rather than rating sentences. Many articles were internally inconsistent in the explanations which they used. In a few cases a causal sequence was not directly articulated, but implied.

6. This decline corresponds with Joseph Gusfield's report of the collapse of broad-based middle-class support for the Prohibition movement after repeal of the 18th Amendment in 1933. See his *Symbolic crusade: Status politics and the American temperance movement* (Urbana, The University of Illinois Press, 1963).

7. Arnold S. Linsky, 'Changing public views on alcoholism', *Quarterly Journal of Studies on Alcoholism*, in press.

8. Glock, op. cit., pp. 540–1.

Political deviance: the press presentation of a militant mass demonstration*

GRAHAM MURDOCK

CONSENSUS, CONFLICT AND COINCIDENCE

For much of the post-war period, British political life was under-pinned by the proposition that fundamental conflicts of interest arising out of historically structured inequalities in the distribution of wealth and power were a thing of the past. It was supposed that full employment and rising real wages had brought about a coinci-dence of interests between workers and owners, rulers and ruled, in which both parties had an equal stake in increasing the 'rate of economic growth' and raising the general level of 'affluence'. Once this basic framework of agreement on ends had been assumed, it followed that the only legitimate area for dissent was on the question of means. Consequently, 'politics' was identified with the procedures of parliamentary debate and trade union negotiation through which elected representatives debated the 'issues' and arrived at 'business-like' compromises. Together, these notions served to define the period as one of 'consensus politics'.

Increasingly, during the last five or six years, however, various groups have rejected some or all of the basic notions of 'consensus politics'. Instead they have begun to define their situation in terms of fundamental conflicts of interest which cannot be satisfactorily articulated or resolved through the existing machinery of political and industrial representation. Increasingly, therefore, these groups have turned to direct forms of political action. Examples include: the urban guerilla insurgency and bombing of Ulster; the occupa-tion of work places; student sit-ins; squatting and rent strikes; together with militant industrial strikes and mass demonstrations. In varying degrees, each of these actions presents a radical challenge to both procedures and underlying assumptions of 'consensus politics', a challenge which those in power must actively contest and overcome, and labelling these actions as illegitimate and 'deviant'

* Paper prepared especially for this volume.

is a necessary part of this process. Labelling serves a dual function; first, it reasserts the existence of a basic set of shared assumptions and interests, and secondly, it clarifies the nature of 'consensus' by pointing to concrete examples of what it is not. Both these elements, the celebration of consensus and the denigration of dissent, are indispensable to the process through which power is legitimated in corporate capitalist states. Edward Heath's prime ministerial broadcast following the settlement of the miners' strike in February 1972 provides a good example.

> In the kind of country we live in there cannot be any 'we' or 'they'. There is only 'us'; all of us. If the Government is 'defeated', then the country is defeated, because the Government is just a group of people elected to do what the majority of 'us' want to see done. That is what our way of life is all about.
>
> It really does not matter whether it is a picket line, a demonstration or the House of Commons. We are all used to peaceful argument. But when violence or the threat of violence is used, it challenges what most of us consider to be the right way of doing things. I do not believe you elect any government to allow that to happen and I can promise you that it will not be tolerated wherever it occurs.[1]

Once a definition of the situation in terms of the absence of basic structural conflicts and the presence of a common community of interests is accepted, the specific elements involved in the labelling of radical direct action fall into place. Given a basic agreement on ends and on the framework within which means should be debated, any redefinition of either or both must inevitably appear as an essentially transitory 'deviation' by a minority. Secondly, if there are no structured inequalities in the distribution of wealth and power, there can be no fundamental reason for radical action. Consequently, attention is directed away from the underlying issues and the definitions of the situation proposed by radical groups, and fixes instead on the forms which this action takes. The 'issue' therefore becomes one of forms rather than causes. Again, given that the process of 'peaceful argument' within the electoral/representative system is sufficient to resolve the disagreements which might arise, any basic challenge to this system necessarily appears as potentially 'violent'. Despite this concentration on form, the problem of explaining causes still remains. The solution, however, is simple. If radical activity is not generated by contradictions within the system, it must originate outside. In his speech, Mr Heath talked of an 'invisible danger' which is 'undermining our way of life'. Other politicians have been more specific and have located the gene-

sis of radical action either among groups from outside (e.g., foreign
infiltrators) or among groups who identify themselves with non-
British 'ways of doing things' (e.g., Communist subversives).
Together these elements form a coherent definition of the situation
which serves to label radical activities as an essentially transitory
deviation by a small minority of outsiders. Further, by segregating
and ostracizing these groups and defining them as a threat, the act
of labelling prepares the way for controlling action.

The definitions provided by the legitimated holders of power
appear in the national press in three forms. First, the political
speeches are themselves widely reported; secondly, many of the basic
themes are reiterated in editorials, and, thirdly, the underlying
definition of the situation permeates the texture of news reporting.
This paper is concerned with the mechanisms involved in this last
process.

It is all too easy to look for a conspiracy. Certainly, newspapers
are enmeshed in the present economic and political system both
directly through interlocking directorships and reciprocal shareholdings, and indirectly through their dependence upon advertising.
They therefore have a vested interest in the stability and continuing
existence of the present system. However, the links between this
general framework and the day-to-day business of gathering and
processing news material are oblique rather than direct. Journalists,
in fact, explicitly define themselves in terms of their autonomy and
independence of vested political and economic interests, and stress
the role of the press as the tribune of the people. Neither is this
argument entirely without foundation. Newspapers frequently do
expose corruption, graft and miscalculation among the powerful and
rich. Nevertheless, despite this element of autonomy, the basic
definition of the situation which underpins the news reporting of
political events, very largely *coincides* with the definition provided
by the legitimated power holders. In order to explain how this
coincidence comes about it is necessary to examine the process
through which events come to be selected for presentation as 'news'
and the assumptions on which this process rests.

This paper approaches this general problem through an analysis
of the way in which one particular incidence of radical political
activity – the mass demonstration against the Vietnam War in
London on 27 October 1968 – was presented in the national press.[2]
As with all case studies, this research can be accused of picking on
an atypical incident to illustrate a general case and it is always
possible to find other cases which don't seem to fit. One commen-
tator, for example, has contended that the Demonstration study
over-emphasized the 'sensational' elements in the reporting, and

that by contrast the coverage of the Aberfan disaster was character-ized by 'restraint'.[3] This is to miss the basic point that the Demon-stration was an explicitly political event whereas Aberfan was not. A senior *Guardian* reporter recognized this when he remarked that the two biggest news stories he could remember in recent times were the Demonstration and the General Election. This is not accidental, for both stories are fundamentally related to the defini-tion of consensus in a period of increasing conflict. The Election coverage celebrated participation, acceptance and the management of disagreement, while the Demonstration story served to define and explain the dynamics of militant refusal.

The events of 27 October

The main demonstration on 27 October was organized by a com-mittee representing a coalition of various student, trade union, relig-ious, peace and anti-war groups. The publicity and manifestoes issuing from the militant core of this organizing committee clearly challenged the basic assumptions of consensus politics. First, they asserted that there were fundamental conflicts of interest arising out of economic exploitation and the inequalities in the distribution of power and argued that these constituted the true locus of 'violence' in the system. Secondly, they maintained that the 'failure' of the Labour govern-ment had demonstrated the impossibility of initiating structural change through the parliamentary system and proposed that left-wing groups should unite to form an extra-parliamentary opposition. The 'militant' solidarity of the demonstration was seen as a first step in this long-term strategy. In terms of the immediate tactics of the situation, however, the organizers explicitly rejected a policy of direct confrontation with the police. Consequently, on the day, the demonstration followed the pattern established by the Campaign for Nuclear Disarmament and an estimated 70,000 people marched peacefully along the agreed route through central London to a rally in Hyde Park.

The organizers of the breakaway march to Grosvenor Square also rejected the tactics of confrontation but announced their intention of registering their protest by their physical presence outside the American Embassy, and by the burning of an American flag. This they did. Of the estimated 3000 people who went to Grosvenor Square, approximately 50, supported by a further 200 pushing from behind, attempted to break through the police cordon around the Embassy.

The events of 27 October were situated at a point of transition for the British Left. Following the disillusionment with the 1966 Labour government, young radicals were increasingly moving away from the 'reformism' of the Labour Left and of the Peace Movement, and moving towards the more radical perspectives developed by the international student and anti-war movements. This process was by no means complete by 27 October, however, and consequently, both the consciousness of the participants and the form of events were characterized by an uneasy and essentially ambivalent amalgam of reformist, radical and revolutionary elements. However, it is exactly this ambivalence which makes the Demonstration story a particularly interesting case study. For as Stuart Hall has pointed out, the role of the media in the labelling process is at its maximum in situations which are unfamiliar or ambiguous.[4]

THE DEVELOPMENT OF THE DEMONSTRATION STORY

On 5 September, over one and a half months before the event, *The Times* carried a front-page story headed, MILITANT PLOT FEARED IN LONDON, describing how detectives had discovered that 'militant extremists' planned to use the main march as a cover for attacks on police and public buildings. The plotters were identified as anarchists and American students and the expected level of violence was explicitly compared to the situation in Paris in May. Several elements in this initial story are worth noting. First, the peaceful nature of the main march is contrasted with the expected violent behaviour of 'militant extremists'. This definition of the situation served to concentrate attention on the form of actions to the neglect of underlying causes. More particularly, the implicit equation of militancy with violence bypassed the counter-definitions of these terms offered by the participants. In this way the march was emptied of its radical political content and the way was left open for its appropriation into the consensus on the grounds of its peaceful form. This same exclusive attention to form also characterized the choice of the May *événements* as a context within which to situate the events of 27 October. At the level of form both situations are linked by the image of street fighting between police and student demonstrators, but at the level of underlying causes these are crucial differences. The immediate point is that the fighting in Paris originated in a 'police riot' in which police attacked a peaceful student demonstration with tear gas and baton charges, whereas in London the demonstrators were expected to initiate the confrontation. More fundamentally, however, the Paris street fighting was only one manifestation of a widely based opposition to De Gaulle's government which culminated in a general strike. In *The Times* story, however, this crucial context was cut away, leaving only the image of street fighting. This same basic image was further re-

inforced and amplified by the reference to American students studying in Britain. This simultaneously served to evoke the police–demon-
trators confrontations at the Democratic Party Convention in
Chicago which had occurred a few weeks before in August, and to
attribute the violence expected in London to the intervention of
outsiders. These elements were reiterated and confirmed when
The Guardian published essentially the same story on 11 October.
From this point on, the press coverage was devoted to extending and
amplifying these basic themes.

The main preoccupations of the press coverage in the two weeks
preceding 27 October were summed up in the heading of a *Guardian*
feature, THE WHO AND THE HOW OF PROTEST. What was missing was
any consideration or analysis of the historical context or of the
political perspective offered by the organizers. Instead, attention
concentrated on the likely form of events, on how much violence
could be expected, and on the identity of the organizers. It was
made clear that the 'militants' came from 'outside' Britain and
therefore outside the consensus. A great deal was made of the fact
that French students were expected to participate in the Demonstration, and it was repeatedly pointed out that the leading organizers
of both the main and breakaway marchers, Tariq Ali and Abhi-
manya Manchanda, were not English. The Demonstration was also
firmly linked to the Student Movement through the attention given
to the planned occupation of the London School of Economics.
This stress on students to the neglect of other groups involved served
to define the event as essentially part of a passing fashion, rather
than as arising out of permanently structured conflicts of interest.
The *Daily Express* extended this theme with a story headed, MISS
TIMPSON: DEB DEMONSTRATOR, about a débutante who saw the main
march as a new and fashionable addition to the 'season'. She was
not against the Vietnam War, she told reporters, only against the
Wealth Tax. This idea that participants were essentially play-acting
and had no consistent political perspective was reinforced by the
frequent use of imagery from the cinema and theatre, viz.: '. . . the
Leading Performers', 'supporting cast' (*Daily Express*) 'a Hollywood
mock-up' (*The Guardian*).

The image of the event presented by the national press on 26
October was essentially that set out in the original *Times* story. The
'newsworthiness' of the event was identified with the expectation that
'militant students' led by 'foreign agitators' would use the cover of
the main march to engage in extensive street fighting with the police
and to attack public buildings. The main march itself was emptied
of its radical political content and defined as a performance – bizarre,
but essentially within the framework of consensus politics.

On the day there were relatively few incidents of confrontation between police and demonstrators but having committed themselves to a news image based on this expectation, the newspapers proceeded as though the event had been characterized by street fighting. Of the six national dailies studied in detail, *The Times*, *Daily Express*, *Sun* and *Daily Sketch* devoted over 60 per cent of their coverage to the events in Grosvenor Square, the *Daily Mirror* 55 per cent and *The Guardian* 41 per cent. Further, events were described in terms of how the police, representing 'us', the consensus, faced and overcame the violent challenge of militant outsiders.

Headlines included:

POLICE WIN BATTLE OF GROSVENOR SQUARE AS 6,000 ARE REPELLED
(*The Times*)

FRINGE FANATICS FOILED AT BIG DEMONSTRATION – WHAT THE BOBBIES
FACED (*Daily Express*)

THE DAY THE POLICE WERE WONDERFUL (*Daily Mirror*)

This definition of the situation was underlined by a news photograph of a policeman apparently being held by one demonstrator and kicked in the face by another. All the papers except *The Times* featured this picture on the front page. Despite this concentration on confrontation, the newspapers recognized that there was a considerable gap between the prediction and the actuality. As the *Daily Mirror* caption to the 'kick' picture put it:

> the boot goes in on a policeman already bent almost double as he grappled with a demonstrator. Provocative incidents like this . . . were not commonplace.

Two explanations were provided for the relative infrequency of confrontation. It was argued that the police had been both more efficient and more restrained than those in Paris or Chicago, and secondly it was suggested that the majority of demonstrators had rejected the violent tactics advocated by the 'militants' and foreign elements and had accepted the 'British way of doing things' through peaceful protest.

Summing up we may say that the image and explanation of the event presented by the news coverage coincided and served to reinforce the more general definition of the overall political situation elaborated by parliamentary politicians and other legitimated holders of political power. Further, it is important to recognize that, despite difference of emphasis and presentation, the same basic news image of the event was shared by all the Fleet Street dailies. It cut

right across the conventional, 'quality/popular', 'Right/Left' distinctions. It was also shared by both television networks.

THE ORGANIZATION OF THE NEWS PROCESS: SOURCES OF COINCIDENCE

Journalists generally resist any suggestion that there is an underlying
pattern to news production. As one reporter commented on the
Demonstration study:

> Our product is put together by large and shifting groups of people,
> often in a hurry, out of an assemblage of circumstances that is
> never the same twice. Newspapers and news programmes could
> almost be called random reactions to random events. Again and
> again, the main reason why they turn out as they do is accident –
> accident of a kind which recurs so haphazardly as to defeat
> statistical examination.[5]

The results of the Demonstration study, however, clearly contradict
this viewpoint. From observation of the cumulative process of
selection and interpretation which precedes the final news presentation, it is clear that far from being 'random reactions to random
events', the selections made are the logical outcome of particular
ways of working and of a shared set of criteria of what makes
material newsworthy. These routines and assumptions are common
to all newsmen and combine to produce both the basic uniformity
of news output and the coincidence between the news image of
political events and the more general definition of the situation as
one of consensus. This section is therefore devoted to examining
these routines and criteria of news value.

The first determinant of the news process is the fundamental fact
that newspapers operate on a 24-hour cycle. This means that situations about which information can be gathered and processed during
this time space, stand a much better chance of being selected for
presentation as news than situations which take longer to unfold.
This 'event orientation' of news has several important consequences.
First, it means that certain aspects of a situation pass the news
threshold while others remain more or less permanently below it.
A coup or an assassination attempt in a developing country, for
example, is far likelier to be reported than a continuing guerilla
war. Similarly, the 27 October Demonstration passed the news
threshold whereas the gradual development of disillusionment with
the parliamentary process among an increasing number of radicals
did not. Secondly, by focusing attention on the immediate form of

contemporary events, on what happened and who was involved, news ignores the underlying content of the situation. The coverage of the Demonstration, for example, focused almost entirely on incidents of violence and on the personalities involved, and by-passed completely any consideration of the demonstrators' political perspective. Thirdly, the 'event orientation' of news means that the situations portrayed inevitably appear to be short-lived and transitory. Lastly, in the absence of any analysis of the underlying structural preconditions, events are presented as being 'caused' either by the intervention of natural forces (e.g., floods, earthquakes) or by the immediately preceding actions of particular individuals or groups. As a consequence of the 'event orientation' therefore, the definitions and explanations of situations offered by news presentation coincide with those provided by the political élite. Thus, radical political activity appears as essentially ephemeral, and confined to a small group of outsiders, rather than as the product of historically structured and continuing inequalities in the distribution of wealth and power.

Because it offers no analysis of the relationship between particular events and underlying structural processes, news is fundamentally ahistorical. However, this does not mean that news contains no view of the relationship between events occurring at different times. On the contrary it presents a very specific version of these links. In order to explain this news version of history, however, it is necessary to turn to the other major factor governing the news process – the newspapers' need to attract readers.

In order to remain commercially viable in an increasingly competitive situation it is not enough for a newspaper to reproduce itself once a day, it must also offer a product which is attractive to sufficient readers to maintain sales and advertising revenue. This need to produce something which is both intelligible and interesting to readers, therefore, becomes the main criterion governing the selection and presentation of material.

The need to render information intelligible to the reader means that despite their fundamentally ahistorical nature news stories cannot be presented in a complete vacuum. The journalist must therefore situate the event within a framework which is already familiar to the reader. This is especially necessary if the situation is new or ambiguous as was the case with the Demonstration. As Galtung put it, all 'news' is to some extent 'olds'.[6] Thus, the Dominican crisis of 1965 was approached from within the image of Cuba; Prague in 1968 was translated into Hungary in 1956,[7] and the Attica prison shootings were seen as another 'Riot in Cell Block 11'. In each case, both the structural preconditions of the situation and the political perspectives of the participants were cut away leaving only the immediate image. In the case of Attica for example, the news coverage bypassed the fact that the situation was part of the long-term politicization of American prisons and that the demands of the Attica inmates were explicitly radical (e.g., free passage to a non-Imperialist country), and concentrated instead on the familiar scenario of guards, shotguns and rioting prisoners.[8]

The choice of the May events in Paris, and later the Chicago riots, as a context for the Demonstration story, had several obvious advantages in news terms. First, their comparative recency guaranteed that they were still both familiar and salient to readers. Secondly, they encapsulated all the essential themes of the Demonstration story – street fighting, students and foreign militants – in a single dramatic image which made immediate sense of an ambiguous situation. The news process therefore establishes its own links between situations, links not at the level of underlying structures and processes but at the level of immediate forms and images. Situations are identified as the same if they look the same. In this way news rewrites history for immediate popular consumption.

Having selected a basic framework within which to interpret an event, the next problem is to capture the readers' interest. The solution is to present the material as a dramatic performance in which the action is unfolded through the actions and speech of certain central characters and the conflicts between them. Readers are therefore placed in the role of spectators, encouraged to participate vicariously in the performance through projecting themselves into the situation and/or identifying with the central characters. In many ways therefore newspapers are part of the entertainment business. Certainly, there is a constant and unending search for the offbeat, the bizarre, the 'new', the spectacular, but like the pornography trade, the number of basic situations and plots offered by news presentations is strictly limited.

The presentation of events in terms of the theatrical and spectacular follows logically from journalists' conceptions of what attracts their readers, but it nevertheless has important consequences. As noted above, by presenting the Demonstration participants as performers within a spectacle, the press coverage emptied their actions of their radical political content. For once the Demonstration was conceived as play-acting and therefore both transitory and 'not for real', it became simultaneously both entertaining and capable of being contained and assimilated. To some extent the problem is implicit in the form of mass demonstrations. As John Berger has pointed out, militant mass demonstrations are intended as dramatic 'rehearsals of revolutionary awareness' expressions of 'political ambitions before the political means necessary to realize them have been created'.[9] This was certainly the case with the 27 October Demonstration. However, by choosing to work through the medium of public spectacle, demonstrations invariably open themselves to the possibility that they will be appropriated as entertainment.

The conception of news as dramatic entertainment working through the presentation of personalized conflict is certainly not novel, but it has recently been considerably reinforced by changes in the general economic situation of the national daily press.

The mid-1950s saw the simultaneous ending of wartime restrictions on newsprint and the introduction of commercial television as an alternative news medium and advertising outlet. As a result newspapers, especially the 'populars', found themselves involved in an increasingly stringent competition for a declining number of readers aganst a background of steadily rising costs. In order to survive, therefore, newspapers had to broaden their readership base. This had a number of consequences.

In order to attract readers with a wide range of political views, papers could not afford to be too obviously partisan. This meant that newspapers like the *Daily Mirror* and *Daily Herald* which had hitherto supported the Labour Party, the trade unions and the Co-operative Movement ceased to ventriloquize these sections of working-class interests and sought instead to attract new consumer groups.[10] This competition for the 'middle ground' readership had several consequences for the content and presentation of material. In the first place emphasis shifted away from the public sphere of production to the private sphere of consumption and leisure. There were fewer political stories and more human interest items and more attention was given to areas such as fashion, holidays and entertainment.[11] Thus, newspapers became more and more a part of the entertainment business, part of the society of the spectacle. This shift coincided with the general ideological proposition that in an era of full employment and increasing leisure, the primary focus of social life and interests was no longer the work place but the privatized family.

In addition to this shift in emphasis, the search for new readership, also reinforced the notion of news as the 'objective' reporting of a pre-existing and definable social reality. This notion had long been a component of the journalistic ethos but was greatly strengthened by the fact that when television news was introduced both channels were placed under a statutory obligation to be impartial. Increasingly, therefore, newspapers were obliged to work within this definition of news. Inevitably 'objectivity' in newspaper terms boiled down to an increased concentration on events as this avoided the partisanship implicit in the consideration of underlying issues. Thus, the presentation of stories in terms of 'Us' (the workers and people) versus 'Them' (the bosses and politicians) was replaced by a definition in terms of 'The National Interest'. Only the *Morning Star* retained its political affiliations and with them the rhetoric of conflict. The difference is evident from the following two extracts from editorials on the clash between the Government and railwaymen over the use of the Industrial Relations Act during the rail go-slow in April 1972.

The Tories have decided on a showdown with the Unions to try to safeguard and increase the profits of Big Business. This is what lies behind all their talk of 'the public interest'. (*Morning Star*).

We are not confronted with a case of the Government versus the Unions but of the People versus the People – confrontation in which all will equally suffer. (*Daily Mirror*).

The *Morning Star* was the only national daily to reject the prevailing news image of the Demonstration and to give extended coverage to both the underlying causes of the situation and to the political perspective of the participants. As we have seen the other papers avoided any discussion of these aspects and concentrated instead on the form of events and the issue of violence. This stress follows logically from the notion of 'objectivity' and the perceived need to avoid partisanship, but it nevertheless coincides with the fundamental proposition of consensus politics – that there are no longer any fundamental conflicts of interest.

Finally, the fact that newspapers are increasingly in competition for an overlapping audience tends to increase the similarities in their reporting. The development of the Demonstration story, for example, shows a clear pattern in which one paper followed another by carrying the latter's story either in its own late editions or on the following day. There is an almost obsessive concern with being scooped. The printing of the original *Times* story, for example, was stimulated by the fact that the London *Evening News* had carried a similar story the previous evening. As the *Evening News* does not have a complete national circulation this did not constitute a full scoop and consequently *The Times* gave essentially the same story a front-page splash the following day. This element of competition means that newspapers, especially those with a small reporting staff relative to the space that has to be filled, will print a story while it is still 'soft', i.e., still at the stage of rumour and probability rather than 'hard fact'. During the development of the Demonstration story, for example, *The Guardian* consistently picked up stories a day or so before the other papers. Having once appeared in print however, both the basic themes of the story and the context within which it is interpreted become 'set' and subsequent coverage is obliged to work within this framework. This was clearly the case with the Demonstration story. Only those elements that fitted the image presented in the original *Times* story were selected for printing. In this process newspapers become locked in a cycle of self-infatuation which takes them further and further from the underlying reality of the situation.

Important as reader interest is, however, as Jeremy Tunstall has pointed out, it is not the only criterion governing news selection, for some areas of news bear little or no direct relationship to revenue.[12] Foreign correspondents, for example, are expensive to maintain and the stories which they provide have only limited appeal to the general reader. Yet, in May 1971, of the two leading popular dailies, the *Daily Express* had twenty foreign correspondents (the same number as *The Times*) and the *Daily Mirror* had thirteen.[13] Similarly, compared with sports and crime news, parliamentary stories are known to have low reader appeal. Yet, within the newspapers themselves, foreign and Lobby correspondents have the highest status and are disproportionately represented among editors.[14] Thus a hierarchy of newsworthiness is established in which the actions of members of the legitimated political élites have the highest rank. There are a number of obvious advantages in a newspaper concentrating on the actions and speeches of politicians. Firstly, they conserve the organization's resources and they can be comfortably handled within the daily cycle of news production. In fact most politicians actively attempt to gear their actions and speeches to newsroom deadlines. Secondly, they can be defined as events and presented in terms of personalized conflicts within and between the two major parties epitomized in the gladiatorial combat between the two leaders: HEATH SLAMS WILSON, WILSON ACCUSES HEATH. Thirdly, the structure of parliamentary politics, of dissent and debate within and between the parties, fits perfectly into the structure of news, of drama and conflict within a familiar framework, of 'news' within 'olds'. In fact the one is an analogue of the other. Fourthly, reporting political speeches, shifts the responsibility for the accuracy of the substantive content away from the newspaper and on to the source. On Wednesday 16 October, for example, *The Guardian* carried a report that Mr Arthur Carr (prospective Conservative candidate for East Ham South) claimed to have information from 'impeccable sources' that students on three educational flights from Britain to Cuba were in fact going 'to learn the techniques of insurrection and sabotage'. Thus, the fact that a political figure with high credibility had made this accusation, enabled the paper to print a highly newsworthy story without having to take the responsibility for its substantive accuracy. Lastly, the feeling of 'being where the action is' reinforces newspapers' image of themselves as being both an indispensable and influential channel of political communication and a necessary watchdog on the abuses of power. These factors therefore combine to make parliamentary events and diplomatic exchanges prominent categories of news. However, simply by defining parliament as the focus of power and political action and by identifying parliamentary debate as the most appropriate and efficient way of resolving issues and managing dissent, news coverage reinforces the essential definitions of consensus politics. Of course the press is not an entirely passive channel for parliamentary opinion. Its persona as the Fourth Estate stimulates a continual search for corruption and miscalculation. However, exposés are as event- and personality-oriented as any other sort of news story. Consequently, corruption is presented as the result of the personal failings or machinations of particular individuals or groups, and the solution offered is to replace the bad apples with good ones. In this way the consensus is presented as self-regulating, as much able to identify and deal with threats from within as challenges from outside. The labelling process is essentially the same in both cases and the end result is to leave the basic framework of assumption undisturbed.

The various criteria and assumptions underlying the definition of news are not generally made explicit within the news organization, but remain as the implicit basis of daily decision making. Hence they are absorbed gradually and more or less unconsciously through the process of building successful careers as a journalist. A reporter must constantly 'second guess' what the editor wants, and each time he sees his copy being accepted, modified or 'spiked' he learns a little more about what it means to be a reporter. More specifically, he learns what it means to work for a particular paper with a particular image of itself. An interesting example of inadequate 'second guessing' occurred during the actual Demonstration.

The *Daily Mirror* had drafted in a *Sunday Mirror* reporter to do a background 'colour' story on the rally in Hyde Park. Unfortunately, his ideas of what was worth selecting and presenting did not coincide with those of the *Mirror* news desk. Because there is always far more copy than space to print it, reporters are expected to provide basic information which the sub-editor can then re-arrange or re-write as a coherent story. The house reporting style therefore tends toward the deadpan, and questions of style and presentation are considered a matter for the 'subs'. Unfortunately, the *Sunday*

Mirror reporter was not aware of this basic but unwritten rule, and turned in a piece full of 'purple patches' viz:

> Here and there boys and girls began to neck on the littered bruised grass and lips that had shortly before spat out the four letter words now pressed against other lips in the dark.

This piece was politely but firmly rejected. At a paper like *The Guardian* with more news space to fill and a much smaller staff, reporters are required to present completed stories and consequently they are expected to pay more attention to style. Despite these differences of emphasis, however, the basic assumptions which guide the selection and presentation of material are shared by both types of paper. Even before he gets to Fleet Street, a young reporter on a local paper is likely to absorb a number of crucial tenets. The stress on competency with shorthand, for example, implies not only an attachment to formal accuracy but also to the notions of 'objectivity' and personalization.[15] More importantly, the self-image of local papers as representing the interests of the local community implies an acceptance of the central notion of consensus.[16] On graduating to Fleet Street the young reporter finds himself in increasingly stringent competition for a declining number of prestigious jobs as specialist correspondents or editors. Promotion therefore involves the internalization of the norms of these élite news groups, and as we have suggested, these tend to coincide with those of the political élite.

This socialization process is not entirely automatic, however, for a number of reporters are aware of the dynamics involved and in varying degrees resist the role they are expected to play. This may lead to a prolonged guerilla war between reporters and editors. During the Demonstration for example, a senior *Daily Mirror* reporter sent to cover Grosvenor Square refused to phone any copy to the news desk. This he argued demonstrated his independence of the editorial staff and their essential dependence on him. However, as a reporter's career prospects depend largely on his ability to get the story before, or at least at the same time as, his rivals, the tactic of withholding information is of limited applicability. Another possible tactic is for a reporter to get his own view of the situation across by 'playing the system'. Gaye Tuckman relates how by manipulating the criteria of objectivity and putting quotation marks around terms such as 'New Left', a radical young American reporter managed to persuade the conservative news editor to print an account of a draft resistance demonstration.[17] This tactic is ultimately self-defeating however, for the quotation marks still serve to cast doubt on the legitimacy and status of the radical groups involved, and the event-orientation still excludes consideration of the underlying issues and causes. The possibilities of 'playing the system' are limited, however, and, ultimately, a reporter who remains in Fleet Street is likely to resolve the contradictions between his professional role and his personal convictions through resort to self-censorship. As one reporter explained to Eamonn McCann:

> No journalist I have met writes what he knows will be cut. What would be the point? If he has a story which he knows will cause controversy back at the news desk he will water it down to make it acceptable.[18]

Some of this self-censored material finds its way into publications like *Private Eye* or *Open Secret*, but more often than not it is forgotten. He may not like this situation but if he is to be successful as a journalist working for a capitalistically based national daily, he must eventually accept it. As Marx complained to Engels, about the *New York Tribune*, 'It is really loathsome to have to think oneself lucky that a filthy rag like that takes one on . . .' but 'For all the talk about independence one is tied to the newspaper and its public, especially if one gets paid cash as I do.'[19]

TOWARDS THE AUDIENCE

I have argued that various general factors within the process of news production served to bring about a coincidence between the news image of the 27 October Demonstration and the more general definition of the political situation evolved by the political élite, with the consequence that the two became mutually reinforcing. It now remains to see how far this definition of the situation was accepted first by the participants (the police and the demonstrators) and secondly by the general public.

Certainly on 27 October both the police and the demonstrators expected violence, and these expectations found their concrete expression in the very extensive police preparations and in the establishment of a medical centre at the London School of Economics, then occupied by the demonstrators. However, although there was a general acceptance of the likely form of events there were diametrically opposed views of the likely causes. Thus, the police prepared on the assumption that the demonstrators would initiate violence, while the marchers assumed that the violence was likely to come from the police, as it had in Paris and Chicago. At a more general level, however, evidence suggests that a sizeable proportion of the marchers rejected the overall definition of the situation provided by the news media and the political élite and accepted instead the radical political perspectives of the organizers. The question remains, however, as to how long radical groups can continue to act both within and against the spectacle without internalizing and acting out their ascribed role as 'deviants' and outsiders and hence reinforcing the very processes they are seeking to challenge? In order to answer this question we need to study the development of radical groups over time in order to see how far they take the news presentation of themselves and their motivations into account when formulating their strategy.

As part of the Demonstration study, a small survey was undertaken to see how a sample of non-participants received the story. Despite the many limitations of the resulting information, there were clear indications that these members of the audience, at least, defined and interpreted the event from within the framework provided by the news coverage. Recent studies of white adolescents' definitions of race relations in Britain, and of adults' images of crime and criminals, have produced similar findings.[20] Again these results are indicative rather than conclusive, but the evidence now beginning to accumulate strongly suggests that the news media do provide many people with the framework of definitions and explanations with which they approach situations. Further, this process is self-perpetuating. Thus, the fact that particular images and definitions are known to have wide popular currency makes them more likely to be selected by news organizations as a framework within which to present novel or ambiguous situations. This in turn serves to amplify these images and to keep them circulating as part of the common pool of available stereotypes. On 7 February 1972 for example, over three and a half years after the Demonstration, the *Sun* ran a feature on police heroism in the face of criminal violence. This feature was headed by the 'kick' picture from Grosvenor Square, thus both evoking and further reinforcing the original news image of the event as a confrontation between police and violent extremists. It also served to underline the identification of 'militant' political action with both violence and criminality.

CONCLUSION

In this paper I have argued that the image of the 27 October Demonstration coincided with, and reinforced, the more general definition of the political situation evolved by the political élite and that in this way the press played an indispensable role in the process of managing conflict and dissent, and legitimating the present distribution of power and wealth within British capitalism.

However, I have also suggested that this coincidence is best explained as the result not of any direct collusion or conspiracy between the press and the politicians, but as the logical outcome of the present organization of news gathering and processing and the assumptions upon which it rests. This is not to say that legitimated power holders do not exercise any direct control over the news process: they do. In the first place, legal restrictions such as the Official Secrets Act, 'D' notices and *sub judice* rulings impose considerable limitations on what newspapers can print and when. In addition there are undoubtedly occasions when politicians bring various forms of moral suasion to bear on newspapermen. These occasions are relatively rare, however, and in most cases are strongly resisted. Certainly they are neither sufficiently frequent nor sufficiently widespread to account for the consistency of newspaper coverage. Rather, the resort to direct intervention may be seen as indicative of a breakdown in the 'normal' working relationship between journalists and politicians through which information and 'stories' are exchanged for coverage and publicity. This day-to-day reciprocity is maintained because it is functional for both parties, newspapers need information and politicians need publicity, but it nevertheless serves to sustain and reinforce the coincidence between the definitions of the situation given by the legitimated politicians and those presented in the national press.

This paper has dealt exclusively with newspapers, but the Demonstration study clearly showed that television news tends to work within the same basic framework of routines and assumptions. This is scarcely surprising since most television newsmen have worked on newspapers. However, the fact that television is first and foremost a visual medium means that television news output is primarily determined by the availability of film footage and that the commentary is written around the screen images. Consequently, television news coverage tends to be even more 'event-oriented' than the corresponding press coverage. Interestingly enough, this limitation is often elevated to a virtue by stressing the immediacy of television coverage as against the *déjà vu* of newspaper reporting. Any discussion of television news would be incomplete without an analysis of the unique position of the BBC and more particularly of the nature of the 'special relationship' between the corporation and the government of the day. Such an analysis is however beyond the scope of the present paper.

I have attempted to illustrate some general points with examples drawn from one particular case study and it may well be that this case was to some extent atypical. However, recent studies of newspaper and television news output on race relations, industrial strikes, student sit-ins and drug taking[21] suggest that many of the forms of presentation discussed in this paper are common to a whole range of news stories and may be a feature of 'news' *per se*. Whether or not this is the case is a question which deserves urgent study.

REFERENCES

1. Quoted in *The Times*, Monday, 28 February 1972, p. 2.
2. The research reported here is part of a larger study which is fully reported in *Demonstrations and communication: A case study* (Harmondsworth, Penguin Books, 1970). This study was the result of a collaborative effort by members of the Centre for Mass Communication Research at Leicester University. I am particularly indebted to my co-authors, Professor James D. Halloran and Philip Elliott, for their comments on the press study. I am also indebted to Peter Golding Stan Cohen and Jock Young for their comments on previous drafts of this present paper.
3. Jeremy Tunstall, *Journalists at work* (London, Constable, 1971), pp. 264–5.
4. See: Stuart Hall 'Watching the box', *New society*, No. 411, 3 August 1970, pp. 295–6. Also Stuart Hall, 'Deviancy, politics and the media', in *Deviance and social control*, M. McIntosh and P. Rock (eds.) (London, Tavistock Publications, 1973).
5. John Whale, 'News', *The Listener*, 15 October 1970, Volume 84, No. 2168, p. 510.
6. Johann Galtung and Mari Ruge (1955) 'The structure of foreign news', *Journal of International Peace Research*, No. 1, 1965, pp. 64–90. Extract reprinted in this Reader.
7. Theodore Draper, 'The Dominican Crisis', *Commentary*, December 1965, J. Galtung (1968) *The role of television in the time of international crisis*, Paper given at September 1968 seminar on Television as a Political Power Factor, at Hanko.
8. The example of the Attica shootings was suggested by Stan Cohen.
9. John Berger, 'The nature of mass demonstrations', in *Selected articles and essays: The look of things* (Harmondsworth, Penguin Books, 1972), pp. 246–8.
10. See for example, Mark Abrams, *The newspaper reading public of tomorrow* (London, Odhams Press Ltd., 1964).
11. This shift was pointed out by Mr James Curran of the Open University during a discussion of his recent research on the British press since 1945.
12. Jeremy Tunstall (1971), op. cit., p. 7.
13. Philip Elliott and Peter Golding, *The news media and foreign affairs* (University of Leicester, centre for Mass Communication Research, mimeo, 1971), p. 15.
14. Jeremy Tunstall (1971), op. cit., p. 47 and Table 3:13, p. 110.
15. Oliver Boyd-Barrett, 'Journalism recruitment and training: problems

in professionalization', in Jeremy Tunstall (ed.) *Media sociology* (London, Constable, 1970), pp. 181–201.

16. Ian Jackson, *The provincial press and the community* (Manchester University Press, 1971), pp. 40, 87.
17. Gaye Tuckman, *Objectivity as strategic ritual: An examination of newspapermen's notions of objectivity.* (Paper presented to the 66th Annual Meeting of the American Sociological Association, 1971).
18. Quoted in Eamonn McCann, *The British press in Northern Ireland* (Northern Ireland Socialist Research Centre, 1971), p. 26. Extract reprinted in this Reader.
19. Quoted in Werner Blumberg *Karl Marx* (London, New Left Books, 1972), p. 127.
20. Paul Hartmann and Charles Husband, 'The mass media and racial conflict', *Race*, XII (January 1971), pp. 267–82. Reprinted in this Reader. The findings on images of crime result from the as yet unpublished research of Mr Paul Croll of the Leicester Centre.
21. See Stuart Hall (1973) op. cit., Jock Young, 'Mass media drugs and deviancy', in McIntosh and Rock, *Deviance and social control;* John Downing, *'Class' and 'Race' in the British news media* (unpublished mimeo communication, 1971).

The determinations of news photographs

STUART HALL

I. THE LEVEL OF SIGNIFICATION IN PHOTOGRAPHS

In the modern newspaper, the text is still an essential element, the photograph an optional one. Yet photographs, when they appear, add new dimensions of meaning to a text. As Roland Barthes has observed, 'pictures . . . are more imperative than writing, they impose meaning at one stroke, without analysing or diluting it'.[1]

II. THE CODES OF CONNOTATION

First, we must turn to the *codes* which make signification possible. It is principally codes of connotation which concern us here. Connotative codes are the configurations of meaning which permit a sign to signify, in addition to its denotative reference, *other, additional implied meanings*. These configurations of meaning are forms of social knowledge, derived from the social practices, the knowledge of institutions, the beliefs and the legitimations which exist in a diffused form within a society, and which order that society's apprehension of the world in terms of dominant meaning-patterns. Codes of denotation are precise, literal, unambiguous: the photo-image of a sweater *is* (denotes) an object to be worn, recognizable as a sweater and not as a coat, a hat or a walking stick. Codes of connotation are more open-ended. In the connotative domain of everyday speech *sweater* may also connote 'keeping warm', a 'warm garment' – and thus by further elaboration 'the coming of winter', a 'cold day', and so on. But in the domain of the specialized discourse (sub-code) of fashion, *sweater* may connote 'a fashionable style of *haute couture*', a certain 'informal style' of dress, and so on. Set against the right background, and positioned in the domain of romantic discourse, *sweater* may connote 'long autumn walk in the woods'.[2]

* Extracts from 'The determinations of news photographs' by Stuart Hall which appeared in *Cultural Studies*, no. 3 (Centre for Cultural Studies, University of Birmingham).

At the expressive level, the photo signifies within the lexicon of expressive features distributed throughout the culture of which the reader is a member. This lexicon is not restricted to photography, or indeed to the domain of visual representation. The same 'cues' which allow us to decode the expressive features of the photographed subject are also employed by almost everyone when they 'read' everyday subjects and occasions in an expressive way. Expressive codes depend on our competence to resolve a set of gestural, non-linguistic features (signifiers) into a specific expressive configuration (signified) – an accomplishment which is cultural, not technical. It is part of the 'social stock of knowledge at hand' in any culture that a set of bodily or physical features serves as indices of recognizable expressions. Members of a culture are competent to use this 'knowledge' whether face-to-face with the living subject or a visual transcription of it. The main difference is that in social situations we have available to us a richer set of signifying cues from which to distinguish an expressive pattern: in addition to body position, facial expression, gesture, we have movement, situation, interaction and speech. The photograph therefore represents *a truncated version* of this cultural code.

The front-page photos of Mr Maudling on the day of his resignation over the Poulson affair provide us with a good example of this. The *Daily Mail*, for example, interpreted Mr Maudling as 'angry': MAUDLING – THE ANGRY MAN. The photo – head on hands only – certainly supports this reading, though other descriptions are equally plausible: 'thoughtful', for example, or 'listening patiently'. The interpretation is therefore strengthened by a caption – *Mr Reginald Maudling – angry, disgusted, strongly resentful*. Here the captions selects and prefers one of the possible readings, then amplifies it. The *Sun*, however, interprets Mr Maudling's resignation as 'tragedy': THE TRAGEDY OF MR MAUDLING. It is almost the same photo as the *Mail*'s – certainly the same occasion (a Tory Party Conference?). But a tilt in the angle, a shift of the position of the head, above all, a lowering of the eyes and a slight suggesting of 'misting over', tilts the reading from 'anger' to 'tragedy'. The *Express* story has overtones of tragedy too – *Reginald Maudling sacrificed his political career yesterday* . . . – but its headline and sub-head is more non-committal: I'LL QUIT – MY WAY. *Exit – Alone in a Car*. The photo – of Maudling 'exiting alone in a car' – reads less tragically than the *Sun* photo – tense, abstracted, looking 'to one side', preoccupied by inner turmoil. But the 'tragic' face on the *Express* front page is not Maudling's but Heath's! *Mr Heath After His Commons Announcement* (caption, below an extremely solemn Heath photo – this time it is the Prime Minister's eyes which tend to 'mist over with emotion'). The *Mirror* and the *Telegraph* use the same photo: the *Telegraph* denotatively, the *Mirror* to support a 'reading'. But since this photo is generalized enough to be linked with a vast range of expressions, it requires, in the *Mirror*, an extra linguistic anchor, which the caption supplies: *A look of resignation . . . from Maudling.* It is a very common practice for the captions to news photographs to tell us, in words, exactly how the subject's expression *ought to be read.*

In all five instances, the type of exposition is 'head-and-shoulders-only', enlarged. Both the composition – excluding other inessential details of body and setting – and the enlargement – which highlights the face and eyes, the most expressive parts of the body – enhance the power of the expressive dimension. This has an ideological significance, since its function is to exploit the expressive code in such a way as to inflect or displace the story, away from its political point, towards some aspect of Maudling, *the man*. The exposition seems to pose an implicit question – 'what do we most want to know about the Maudling affair at this moment?' – and answers it implicitly: 'how does *he* feel?', 'how is *he* taking it?' The exception to this treatment is *The Times*, which produces a version of the now-classic photo of 'public figure relaxing at home after momentous decision'. Mr Maudling, himself, gave the lead to this angle, with his reference, in his resignation letter, to 'the glare of publicity which . . . engulfs the private life even of [my] family'. *The Times*, then, picks up this interpretation, and elaborates it. Its photo – of *Mr Maudling, who resigned yesterday as Home Secretary, photographed last year with his wife in their home at Essendon, Hertfordshire* shows him in short-sleeved check shirt, standing with his wife, who is holding the cat, in their breakfast room before a table laden with fruit, peppers etc. This photo, rich enough in connoted social detail, also makes an ideological point: it produces the classic counterposition – public figure/private man – which is such a central myth in our learned wisdom about men weighed-down-by/freed-from the cares and burdens of high office. It generates what we might call the *sentimental effect*, one of the most compelling ties which bind the governed to the governors.

In each case, then, the newspaper has slightly inflected the story towards a different 'news-angle' by exploiting the expressive code. But each is an inflection on a single, common theme: the displacement or mystification of the political event 'through the category of the subject'. This is the essence of the ideology of personalization. Expressive codes are one of the most powerful vehicles in the rhetoric of the news-photo for the production of *personalizing transformations*.

DAILY MAIL

Photo: Associated Newspapers

SUN

Photo: United Press International

DAILY EXPRESS

Photo: London Express

DAILY MIRROR

DAILY TELEGRAPH

Photo: United Press International

THE TIMES

Photo: The Times

III. THE SIGNIFICATION OF NEWS

It is necessary to distinguish *two aspects* to the signification of news. The first is the *news value* of the photographic sign. The second is the *ideological level* of the photographic sign. 'News value' consists of the elaboration of the story (photo + text) in terms of the professional ideology of news – the common-sense understandings as to what constitutes the news in the newspaper discourse. The ideological level consists of the elaboration of the story in terms of its connoted themes and interpretations. *Formal* news values belong to the world and discourse of the newspaper, to newsmen as a professional group, to the institutional apparatuses of news-making. *Ideological* news values belong to the realm of moral-political discourse in the society as such. Ideological themes will be inflected in different ways according to the particular construction which each newspaper selects. This *inflection* will, in turn, be governed by the newspaper's policy, political orientation, its presentational values, its tradition and self-image. But behind the particular inflections of a particular news 'angle' lie, not only the 'formal' values as to 'what passes as news in our society', but the ideological themes of the society itself. Thus the death of the Duke of Windsor meets the requirement of 'formal news values' because it is unexpected, dramatic, a recent event, concerning a person of high status. But, at the ideological level, this event connotes a powerful, resonant 'set' of themes: 'Prince Charming', the 'King with the people at heart', the monarch who 'gave up the throne for the woman I love', the celebrity life of the Windsors in retirement, the late reconciliation with the Queen, the death and national burial – 'the King who came Home'.

Different newspapers will inflect the news-story differently, by picking up one or more of these ideological themes. Nevertheless, in general, *any* of these particular 'news angles' intersects directly with the great ideological theme: *the Monarchy itself*. This is a point which that great chronicler of the British ideology, Bagehot, would have relished:

> The best reason why Monarchy is a strong government is that it is an intelligible government. The mass of mankind understand it, and they hardly in the world understand any other. It is often said that men are ruled by their imaginations; but it would be truer to say they are governed by the weakness of their imaginations. . . . We have no slaves to keep down by special terrors and independent legislation. But we have whole classes unable to comprehend the idea of a constitution – unable to feel the least attachment to impersonal laws. . . . A republic has only difficult ideas in government; a Constitutional Monarchy has an easy

idea too; it has a comprehensible element for the vacant many, as well as complex laws and notions for the inquiring few.[3]

The structure of 'news values' appears as a neutral, operational level in news production. It 'naturally' connects stories and events with persons: it attaches qualities, status, positions in the social world to anonymous events: it searches out the 'drama', the 'human interest', behind impersonal historical forces. Yet, these operational values are not, in the end, neutral values. As Althusser has argued, it is precisely by operating with 'the category of the *subject*', and by producing in the reader 'familiar recognitions', that a discourse becomes ideological.[4]

It appears, then, that the news-photo must lend itself to exploitation at the level of what we have called 'formal news values' first, before – secondly – it can signify an ideological theme. Thus the photo of a demonstrator kicking a policeman has news value because it witnesses to a recent event, which is dramatic, unusual, controversial. It is then possible, by linking this so-to-speak 'completed message' with an interpretation, to produce 'second-order meanings' with powerful ideological content: thus AND THEY TALK ABOUT PROVOCATION! (*The Sketch*), WHAT THE BOBBIES FACED (*Express*), VICTORY FOR POLICE (*Telegraph*), THE DAY THE POLICE WERE WONDERFUL (*Mirror*). Halloran, Elliott and Murdock[5] note how this 'kick-photo' (taken by a free-lance photographer for Keystone Agency) selectively reinforced both a previous interpretation – that the demonstration against the Vietnam War would be a 'violent' one – and a specific 'news angle' – 'the editorial decision to make the police the centre of the story'.[5] In news-value terms, the police are signified as the 'centre' of the story – that is its *formal* news exploitation, grounded by the 'Kick-Photo'. In ideological terms, the police are signified as the *heroes* of the story – an interpretation connotatively amplified by the photo.

In practice, there is probably little or no distinction between these two aspects of news production. The editor not only looks at and selects the photo in terms of impact, dramatic meaning, unusualness, controversy, the resonance of the event signified, etc. (formal news values): he considers at the same time how these values will be treated or 'angled' – that is, interpretatively coded.

It is this double articulation – formal news values/ideological treatment – which binds the inner discourse of the newspaper to the ideological universe of the society. It is via this double articulation that the institutional world of the newspaper, whose manifest function is the profitable exchange of news values, is harnessed to the latent function of reproducing 'in dominance' the major ideo-

THE KICK-PHOTO

Photo: Keystone Agency

logical themes of society. The formal requirements of 'the news' thus appears as 'the operator' for the reproduction of ideology in the newspaper. Via 'news angles', the newspaper articulates the core themes of bourgeois society in terms of *intelligible representations*. It *translates* the legitimations of the social order into faces, expressions, subjects, settings and legends. As Bagehot observed, 'A royal family sweetens politics by the seasonable addition of nice and pretty events. It introduces irrelevant facts into the business of government, but they are facts which speak to "men's bosoms" and employ their thoughts.'

Newspapers trade in news stories. But though the need to harness a multitude of different stories and images to the profitable exchange of news values is 'determining in the last instance', this economic motive never appears on its own. The ideological function of the photographic sign is always hidden within its exchange value. The news/ideological meaning is the *form* in which these sign-vehicles are exchanged. Though the economic dialectic, here as elsewhere, determines the production and appropriation of 'symbolic' values, it is 'never active in its pure state'. The exchange value of the photographic sign is thus, necessarily, over-determined.

News values

By news values we mean the operational practices which allow editors, working over a set of prints, to select, rank, classify and elaborate the photo in terms of his 'stock of knowledge' as to what constitutes 'news'. 'News values' are one of the most opaque structures of meaning in modern society. All 'true journalists' are supposed to possess it: few can or are willing to identify and define it. Journalists speak of 'the news' as if events select themselves. Further, they speak as if which is the 'most significant' news story, and which 'news angles' are most salient are divinely inspired. Yet of the millions of events which occur every day in the world, only a tiny proportion ever become visible as 'potential news stories': and of this proportion, only a small fraction are actually produced as the day's news in the news media. We appear to be dealing, then, with a 'deep structure' whose function as a selective device is un-transparent even to those who professionally most know how to operate it.

A story, report or photo which has the potential of being used to signify the news, seems, in the world of the daily newspaper, to have to meet at least *three* basic criteria. The story must be linked or linkable with an event, a happening, an occurrence: the event must have happened recently, if possible yesterday, preferably today, a few hours ago: the event or person 'in the news' must rank as 'newsworthy'. That is to say, news stories are concerned with *action*, with *'temporal recency'* and *'newsworthiness'*.

These three basic rules of *news visibility* organize the routines of news gathering and selection. They serve as a filter between the newspaper and its subordinate structures – special correspondents, agencies, 'stringers' in far-away places. Once these ground-rules have been satisfied, a more complex set of parameters come into play. These govern the elaboration of a story in terms of *formal news values*. Formal news values have been widely discussed in recent years, but almost always in terms of a simple list of common attributes. Thus Ostgaard[6] suggests that the most newsworthy events are unusual, unexpected events with a problematic or unknown outcome. Galtung and Ruge's[7] list is longer. It includes recency, intensity, rarity, unpredictability, clarity, ethnocentricity: also more presentational features, such as continuity, consonance, 'élite' persons and 'élite' nations, personalization, and so on. These lists help us to identify the formal elements in news making, but they do not suggest what these 'rules' index or represent. News values appear as a set of neutral, routine practices: but we need, also, to see formal news values as an ideological structure – to examine these rules as the formalization and operationalization of *an ideology of news*.

News values *do* have something to do with 'what is not (yet) widely known': with the scarce, rare, unpredictable event. In French the news – *les nouvelles* – means literally 'the new things'. This suggests that news values operate against the structured ignorance of the audience. They take for granted the restricted access of people to power, and mediate this scarcity. News stories often pivot around the unexpected, the problematic. But an event is only unexpected because it 'breaches our expectations about the world'. In fact, most news stories report minor, unexpected developments in the expected continuity of social life and of institutions. They *add to* what we already know or could predict about the world. But, whether the news dramatizes what we really do not know, or merely adds an unexpected twist to what is already known, the central fact is that news values operate as a foreground structure with a hidden 'deep structure'. News values continually play against the set of on-going beliefs and constructions about the world which most of its readers share. That is, news values require *consensus knowledge* about the world. The preoccupation with change/continuity in the news can function at either a serious or a trivial level: the breaking of the truce by the IRA or the latest model on the bonnet of the latest model at the Motor Show. Either the wholly a-typical (the IRA) or the over-typical (the Motor Show) constitute 'news' because, at the level of 'deep structure' it is the precariousness or the stability of the social order which most systematically produces visible news stories.[8]

Without this background consensus knowledge – our 'routine knowledge of social structures' – neither newsmen nor readers could recognize or understand the foreground of news stories. Newspapers are full of the actions, situations and attributes of 'élite persons'. The prestigious are part of the necessary spectacle of news production – they people and stabilize its environment. But the very notion of 'élite persons' has the 'routine knowledge of social structures' inscribed within it. Prime Ministers are 'élite persons' because of the political and institutional power which they wield. Television personalities are 'newsworthy' because celebrities serve as role-models and trend-setters for society as a whole. 'Elite persons' make the news because power, status and celebrity are monopolies in the institutional life of our society. In C. Wright Mills' phrase, 'élite persons' have colonized 'the means of history making' in our society.[9] It is this distribution of status, power and prestige throughout the institutional life of class societies which makes the remarks, attributes, actions and possessions of 'élite persons' – their very being-as-they-are – naturally newsworthy. The same could be said of 'élite nations'. If we knew nothing about Britain's historical connections throughout the world, or the preferred map of power relations, it would be difficult to account for the highly skewed structure to the profile of foreign news in British newspapers. In setting out, each day, to signify the world in terms of its most problematic events, then, newspapers must always *infer what is already known*, as a present or absent structure. 'What is already known' is not a set of neutral facts. It is a set of common-sense constructions and ideological interpretations *about* the world, which holds the society together at the level of everyday beliefs.

Regularly, newspapers make news values salient by *personifying* events. Of course people are interesting, can be vividly and concretely depicted in images, they possess qualities and so on. Personalization, however, is something else: it is the isolation of the person from his relevant social and institutional context, or the constitution of a personal subject as exclusively the motor force of history, which is under consideration here. Photos play a crucial role in this form of personification, for people – human subjects – are *par excellence* the content of news and feature photographs. 'There is no ideology except for the concrete subjects, and this destination for ideology is only made possible by the subject: meaning, *by the category of the subject* and its functioning.'[10] A newspaper can account for an event, or deepen its account, by attaching an individual to it, or by bringing personal attributes, isolated from their social context, to bear on their account as an explanation. Individuals provide a universal 'grammar of motives' in this respect – a grammar which has as its suppressed subject the universal qualities of 'human nature', and which manipulates subjects in terms of their 'possessive individualism'.[11]

The most salient, operational 'news value' in the domain of political news is certainly that of *violence*. Events not intrinsically violent can be augmented in value by the attribution of violence to them. Most news editors would give preference to a photo signifying violence in a political context. They would defend their choice on the grounds that violence represents conflict, grips the reader's interest, is packed with action, serious in its consequences. These are formal news values. But at the level of 'deep structure', political violence is 'unusual' – though it regularly happens – because it signifies the world of politics *as it ought not to be*. It shows conflict in the system at its most extreme point. And this 'breaches expectations' precisely because in our society conflict is supposed to be regulated, and politics is exactly 'the continuation of social conflict without resort to violence': a society, that is, where the legitimacy of the social order rests on the absolute inviolability of 'the rule of law'.

Formal news criteria, though operated by professionals as a set of 'rules of thumb', are no less rooted in the ideological sphere because these transactions take place out of awareness. Events enter the domain of ideology as soon as they become visible to the news-making process. Unless we clarify what it is members of a society 'normally and naturally' take as predictable and 'right' about their society, we cannot know why the semantization of the 'unpredictable' in terms of violence, etc., can, in and of itself, serve as a criterion of 'the news'.

The ideological level

This brings us directly to the second aspect of news construction – the elaboration of a news photo or story in terms of an interpretation. Here, the photo, which already meets and has been exposed within the formal criteria of news, is linked with an interpretation which exploits its connotative value. We suggest that, rhetorically, the ideological amplification of a news photo functions in the same manner as Barthes has given to the exposition of 'modern myths'.[12] By ideological elaboration we mean the insertion of the photo into a set of thematic interpretations which permits the sign (photo), via its connoted meanings, to serve as the index of an ideological theme. Ideological news values provide a second level of signification of an ideological type to an image which already (at the denotative level) signifies. By linking the completed sign with a set of themes or concepts, the photo becomes an ideological sign. Barthes' example is of a Negro soldier in a French uniform, saluting, his eye fixed on the tricoleur. This sign already conveys a meaning: 'a black soldier is giving the French salute'. But when this complete sign is linked with ideological themes – Frenchness, militariness – it becomes the first element in a second signifying chain, the message of which is 'that France is a great Empire, that all her sons, without colour discrimination, faithfully serve under her flag, and that there is no better answer to the detractors of an alleged colonialism than the zeal shown by this Negro in serving his so-called 'oppressors'. The photographic sign serves, then, both as the final term of the visual/denotative chain, and as the first term in the mythical/ideological chain. On this model, all news photos use the signifiers of the photographic code to produce a sign which is the denotative equivalent of its subject. But for this sign to become a news commodity, it must be linked with a concept or theme, and thus take on an interpretative or ideological dimension.

We may take two examples here. (i) The photo of the Nixons, arm in arm, walking in the White House garden. The President is smiling, giving an 'it's O.K.', 'spot on' gesture. Here the ideological message requires little or no further elaboration. The President's in a happy mood: a figure of world prominence relaxes just like other men: Nixon's on top of the world. There is no accompanying text, only a caption: and the caption, apart from identifying the actors and occasion (their daughter Tricia's wedding), redundantly mirrors the ideological theme: 'Everything in the garden's lovely'. This is very different from (ii) the 'kick-photo', where the denoted message – 'a man in a crowded scene is kicking a policeman' – is ideologically 'read' – 'extremists threaten law-and-order by violent acts', or 'anti-war demonstrators are violent people who threaten the state and assault policemen unfairly'. This second-order message is fully amplified in the captions and headlines. But note also that it is slightly inflected to suit the position, presentational tradition, history and self-image of each individual newspaper. It is the linking of the photo with the themes of *violence, extremists and law-and-order, confrontation* which produces the ideological message. But this takes somewhat different forms in each paper: *The Times* inflects it *formally* – POLICE WIN BATTLE OF GROSVENOR SQUARE; the *Express* inflects it *sensationally*, accenting the 'marginal' character of the demonstrators – FRINGE FANATICS FOILED AT BIG DEMONSTRATION; the *Mirror* inflects it *deferentially* – THE DAY THE POLICE WERE WONDERFUL. Here the text is crucial in 'closing' the ideological theme and message.

It is difficult to pin down precisely how and where the themes which convert a photo into an ideological sign arise. Barthes argues that 'The concept is a constituting element of myth: if I want to decipher myths, I must somehow be able to name concepts.' But he acknowledged that 'there is no fixity in mythical concepts: they can come into being, alter, disintegrate, disappear completely'. This is because the dominant ideology, of which these themes or concepts are fragments, is an extremely plastic, diffuse and apparently a historical structure. Ideology, as Gramsci argued, seems to consist of a set of 'residues' or preconstituted elements, which can be arranged and rearranged, *bricoleur*-fashion, in a thousand different variations.[13] The dominant ideology of a society thus frequently appears redundant: we know it already, we have seen it before, a thousand different signs and messages seem to signify the same ideological meaning. It is the very mental environment in which we live and experience the world – the 'necessarily imaginary distortion' through which we continually represent to ourselves 'the [imaginary] relationship of individuals to the relations of production and the relations that derive from them'.[14] The ideological concepts embodied in photos and texts in a newspaper, then, do not produce new knowledge about the world. They produce *recognitions* of the world as we have already learned to appropriate it: 'dreary trivialities or a ritual, a functionless creed'.

Barthes suggests[15] that we can only begin to grasp these ideological concepts reflexively, by the use of ugly neologisms: e.g. 'French-ness', 'Italian-ness'. Or by the naming of very general essences: e.g. militarism, violence, 'the rule of law', the-state-of-being-on-top-of-the-world. Such concepts appear to be 'clearly organized in associative fields'. Thus 'Italian-ness' belongs to a certain axis of nationalities beside 'French-ness', 'German-ness' or 'Spanish-ness'. In any particular instance, then, the item – photo or text – perfectly indexes the thematic of the ideology it elaborates. But its general sphere of reference remains diffuse. It is there and yet it is not there. It appears, indeed, as if the general structure of a dominant ideology is almost impossible to grasp, reflexively and analytically, *as a whole*. The dominant ideology always appears, precisely, diffused in and through the particular. Ideology is therefore both the specific interpretation which any photo or text *specifies*, and the general ambience within which ideological discourse itself is carried on. It is this quality which led Althusser to argue that, while ideologies have histories, ideology as such has none.

Ideological themes exhibit another quality which makes them difficult to isolate. They appear in their forms to link or join *two* quite different levels. On the one hand they classify out the world in terms of immediate political and moral values: they give events a specific ideological reference in the here-and-now. Thus they ground the theme *in* an event: they lend it faces, names, actions, attributes, qualities. They provide ideological themes with actors and settings – they operate above all in the realm of the *subject*. The photo of the demonstrators and the policeman is thus *grounded* by its particularity, by its relation to a specific event, by its temporal relevance and immediacy to a particular historical conjuncture. In that photo the general background ideological value of the 'rule of law', the generalized ethos of attitudes against 'conflict by violent means' were *cashed* at a moment in the political history of this society when the 'politics of the street' was at its highest point, and where the whole force of public discourse and disapproval was mobilized against the rising tide of extra-parliamentary opposition movements. Yet, in that very moment, the ideological theme is distanced and universalized: it becomes *mythic*. Behind or within the concrete particularity of the event or subject we seem to glimpse the fleeting forms of a more archetypal, even archaeological-historical, knowledge which universalizes its forms. The mythic form seems, so to speak, to hover within the more immediate political message. The smiling face of Nixon is of that very time and moment – an American President at a particular moment of his political career, riding the storms of controversy and opposition of a particular historical moment with confidence. But, behind this, is the universal face of the home-spun family man of all times, arm in arm with his lady-wife, taking a turn in the garden at his daughter's wedding. In the handling of the 'kick-photo', *The Times* picks out and specifies the immediate political ideological theme – POLICE WIN BATTLE OF GROSVENOR SQUARE. But, within that message, the *Mirror* glimpses, and elaborates, a more mythic, universal theme – one which may underpin a hundred different photographs: the myth of 'our wonderful British police'.

We seem here to be dealing with a double movement within ideological discourse: the movement towards propaganda, and the movement towards myth. On the one hand, ideological discourse shifts the event towards the domain of a preferred political/moral explanation. It gives an event an 'ideological reading' or interpretation. Barthes puts this point by saying that the ideological sign connects a mythical schema to history, seeing how it corresponds to the interests of a definite society. At this level, the rhetoric of connotation saturates the world of events with ideological meanings. At the same time, it disguises or *displaces* this connection. It asks us to imagine that the particular inflection which has been imposed on history *has always been there*: is its universal, 'natural' meaning.

Myths, Barthes argues, dehistoricize the world so as to disguise the motivated nature of the ideological sign. They do not 'unveil historical realities': they inflect history, 'transforming it into nature'. At the ideological level, news photos are continually passing themselves off as something different. They interpret historical events ideologically. But in the very act of grounding themselves in fact, in history, they become 'universal' signs, part of the great storehouse of archetypal messages, nature not history, myth not 'reality'. It is this conjuncture of the immediate, the political, the historical and the mythic which lends an extraordinary complexity to the deciphering of the visual sign.

News photos have a specific way of passing themselves off as aspects of 'nature'. They repress their ideological dimensions by offering themselves as literal visual-transcriptions of the 'real world'. News photos witness to the *actuality* of the event they represent. Photos of an event carry within them a meta-message: 'this event really happened and this photo is the proof of it'. Photos of people – even the 'passport' type and size – also support this function of *grounding and witnessing:* 'this is the man we are talking about, he really exists'. Photos, then, appear as records, in a literal sense, of 'the facts' and speak for themselves. This is what Barthes calls[16] the 'having-been-there' of all photographs. News photos operate under a hidden sign marked, 'this really happened, see for yourself'. Of course, the choice of *this* moment of an event as against that, of *this* person rather than that, of *this* angle rather than any other, indeed, the selection of this photographed incident to represent a whole complex chain of events and meanings, is a highly ideological procedure. But, by appearing literally to reproduce the event as it *really* happened, news photos suppress their selective/interpretive/ideological function. They seek a warrant in that ever pre-given, neutral structure, which is beyond question, beyond interpretation: the 'real world'. At this level, news photos not only support the credibility of the newspaper as an accurate medium. They also guarantee and underwrite its *objectivity* (that is, they neutralize its ideological function). This 'ideology of objectivity' itself derives from one of the most profound myths in the liberal ideology: the absolute distinction between fact and value, the distinction which appears as a common-sense 'rule' in newspaper practice as 'the distinction between facts and interpretation': the empiricist illusion, the utopia of naturalism.

The ideological message of the news photo is thus frequently displaced by being *actualized*. At first this seems paradoxical. Everything tends to locate the photo in historical time. But historical time, which takes account of development, of structures, interests and antagonisms, is a different modality from 'actuality time', which, in the newspaper discourse, is foreshortened time. The characteristic *tense* of the news photo is the *historic instantaneous*. All history is converted into 'today', cashable and explicable in terms of the immediate. In the same moment, all history is mythified – it undergoes an instantaneous mythification. The image loses its motivation. It appears, 'naturally', to have selected itself.

But few news photos are quite so unmotivated. The story of the Provisional IRA leader, Dutch Doherty, under the headline ULSTER WANTS DOHERTY EXTRADITED, speculates within the story-text on moves against IRA men in the Republic, pressures on the Lynch Government not to shelter wanted men, and so on: but it carries only a small, head-and-shoulders 'passport-photo' of the man in question, with the simple caption *Anthony 'Dutch' Doherty*. Yet the 'passport photo', with its connotation of 'wanted men', prisoners and the hunted, is not without ideological significance. This photo may not be able, on its own, to produce an ideological theme. But it can *enhance, locate* or *specify* the ideological theme, once it has been produced, by a sort of reciprocal *mirror-effect*. Once we know who the story is about, how he figures in the news – once, that is, the text has added the themes to the image – the photo comes into its own again, refracting the ideological theme at another level. Now we can 'read' the meaning of its closely-cropped, densely compacted composition: the surly, saturnine face: the hard line of the mouth, eyes, dark beard: the tilted angle so that the figure appears hunched, purposefully bent: the black suit: the bitter expression. These formal, compositional and expressive meanings reinforce and amplify the ideological message. The ambiguities of the photo are here not resolved by a caption. But once the ideological theme has been signalled, the photo takes on a signifying power of its own – it adds or situates the ideological theme, and grounds it at another level. This, it says, is the face of one of the 'bombers and gunmen': this is what today's headline, of another 'senseless' explosion in downtown Belfast is all about. This its subject, its author. It is *also* a universal mythic sign – the face of all the 'hard men' in history, the portrait of Everyman as a 'dangerous wanted criminal'.

REFERENCES

1. Roland Barthes, 'Myth today', *Mythologies* (London, Cape, 1972).
2. The example is from Barthes, *Elements of semiology* (London, Cape, 1967).
3. Walter Bagehot, 'The English constitution'. *Walter Bagehot,* ed. N. St John Stevas (London, Eyre & Spottiswoode, 1959).

Unit headline language*

MICHAEL FRAYN

If Goldwasser was remembered for nothing else, Macintosh once told Rowe, he would be remembered for his invention of UHL.

UHL was Unit Headline Language, and it consisted of a comprehensive lexicon of all the multi-purpose monosyllables used by headline-writers. Goldwasser's insight had been to see that if the grammar of 'ban', 'dash', 'fear', and the rest was ambiguous they could be used in almost any order to make a sentence, and that if they could be used in almost any order to make a sentence they could be easily randomized. Here then was one easy way in which a computer could find material for an automated newspaper – put together a headline in basic UHL first and then fit the story to it.

UHL, Goldwasser quickly realized, was an ideal answer to the problem of making a story run from day to day in an automated paper. Say, for example, that the randomizer turned up.

STRIKE THREAT

By adding one unit at random to the formula each day the story could go:

STRIKE THREAT BID

STRIKE THREAT PROBE

STRIKE THREAT PLEA

And so on. Or the units could be added cumulatively:

STRIKE THREAT PLEA

STRIKE THREAT PLEA PROBE

STRIKE THREAT PLEA PROBE MOVE

STRIKE THREAT PLEA PROBE MOVE SHOCK

STRIKE THREAT PLEA PROBE MOVE SHOCK HOPE

STRIKE THREAT PLEA PROBE MOVE SHOCK HOPE STORM

* Chapter 13 of Michael Frayn, *The tin men* (London, Collins, 1965).

Or the units could be used entirely at random:

LEAK ROW LOOMS

TEST ROW LEAK

LEAK HOPE DASH BID

TEST DEAL RACE

HATE PLEA MOVE

RACE HATE PLEA MOVE DEAL

Such headlines, moreover, gave a newspaper a valuable air of dealing with serious news, and helped to dilute its obsession with the frilly-knickeredness of the world, without alarming or upsetting the customers. Goldwasser had had a survey conducted, in fact, in which 457 people were shown the headlines.

ROW HOPE MOVE FLOP

LEAK DASH SHOCK

HATE BAN BID PROBE

Asked if they thought they understood the headlines, 86·4 per cent said yes, but of these 97·3 per cent were unable to offer any explanation of what it was they had understood. With UHL, in other words, a computer could turn out a paper whose language was both soothingly familiar and yet calmingly incomprehensible.

Goldwasser sometimes looked back to the time when he had invented UHL as a lost golden age. That was before Nobbs had risen to the heights of Principal Research Assistant, and with it his beardedness and his belief in the universal matehood of man. In those days Goldwasser was newly appointed Head of his department. He had hurried eagerly to work each day in whatever clothes first came to hand in his haste. He had thought nothing of founding a new inter-language before lunch, arguing with Macintosh through the midday break, devising four news categories in the afternoon, then taking Macintosh and his new wife out to dinner, going on to a film, and finishing up playing chess with Macintosh into the small hours. In those days he had been fairly confident that he was cleverer than Macintosh. He had even been fairly confident that Macintosh had thought he was cleverer than Macintosh. In those days Macintosh had been his Principal Research Assistant

It was difficult not to believe the world was deteriorating when one considered the replacement of Macintosh by Nobbs. Goldwasser sometimes made a great effort to see the world remaining – as he believed it did – much as it always was, and to see Nobbs as a potential Macintosh to a potential incoming Goldwasser. It was not easy. Now that Macintosh had gone on to become Head of the Ethics Department, Goldwasser no longer invented his way through a world of clear, cerebral TEST PLEA DASH SHOCK absolutes. Now his work seemed ever more full of things like the crash survey.

The crash survey showed that people were not interested in reading about road crashes unless there were at least ten dead. A road crash with ten dead, the majority felt, was slightly less interesting than a rail crash with one dead, unless it had piquant details – the ten dead turning out to be five still virginal honeymoon couples, for example, or pedestrians mown down by the local J.P. on his way home from a hunt ball. A rail crash was always entertaining, with or without children's toys still lying pathetically among the wreckage. Even a rail crash on the Continent made the grade provided there were at least five dead. If it was in the United States the minimum number of dead rose to twenty; in South America 100; in Africa 200; in China 500.

But people really preferred an air crash. Here, curiously enough, people showed much less racial discrimination. If the crash was outside Britain, 50 dead Pakistanis or 50 dead Filipinos were as entertaining as 50 dead Americans. What people enjoyed most was about 70 dead, with some 20 survivors including children rescued after at least one night in open boats. They liked to be backed up with a story about a middle-aged housewife who had been booked to fly aboard the plane but who had changed her mind at the last moment.

Goldwasser was depressed for a month over the crash survey. But he could not see any way of producing a satisfactory automated newspaper without finding these things out. Now he was depressed all over again as he formulated the questions to be asked in the murder survey.

His draft ran:

1. Do you prefer to read about a murder in which the victim is (*a*) a small girl (*b*) an old lady (*c*) an illegitimately pregnant young woman (*d*) a prostitute (*e*) a Sunday school teacher?

2. Do you prefer the alleged murderer to be (*a*) a Teddy boy (*b*) a respectable middle-aged man (*c*) an obvious psychopath (*d*) the victim's spouse or lover (*e*) a mental defective?

3. Do you prefer a female corpse to be naked, or to be clad in underclothes?

4. Do you prefer any sexual assault involved to have taken place before or after death?

5. Do you prefer the victim to have been (*a*) shot (*b*) strangled

LSD and the press*

WILLIAM BRADEN

There is a legend, hallowed in journalism, about a newspaper
photographer who was assigned to cover an anniversary of the first
sustained nuclear reaction at the University of Chicago. Arriving
on campus, the photographer addressed himself to the assembled
scientists, including Vannevar Bush, Enrico Fermi, Arthur H.
Compton, and Harold C. Urey. 'Now, fellows,' he said, 'I got three
pictures in mind. First, you guys putting the atom in the machine.
Then splitting the atom. And finally all of you grouped around
looking at the pieces.'

I had always supposed the story was apocryphal – until just the
other day, when I was approached by an excited photographer who
works for the same Chicago newspaper I do. 'I've got a terrific
idea,' he said. 'You take me out some night to one of those LSD
parties. I'll set up my camera and take pictures of the whole thing.
All this weird stuff that happens. Who knows? We might come back
with a picture of God.'

I like to think he was putting me on. Taken together, however, the
two anecdotes provide a reasonably accurate idea of the befuddled
manner in which the press has often groped to understand anything
radically new and complex – including nuclear energy, space flight,
and now psychedelic drugs.

We are able now to cover the atom and space beats with a high
degree of competence and sophistication, due in large part to the
development of specialist reporters. At my own newspaper, for
example, we do not have simply a science writer: we have one
reporter who is assigned exclusively to the physical sciences and a
second reporter assigned to the biological sciences. A third reporter
is a nationally respected authority on evolution and DNA.

It seems fair to say, however, that the nation's newspapers as a
whole are still befuddled about LSD. And there are several reasons
for this state of affairs.

Consider first the plight of a typical city editor. Assuming he
wants to provide responsible coverage of LSD phenomena, who
might he assign to the job?

* Extracted from William Braden, 'LSD and the press' in B. Aaronson and
H. Osmond (eds.) *Psychedelics* (New York, Doubleday, 1970).

The medical writer? Perhaps. But that would certainly limit the scope of the investigation, and the writer would probably tend to reflect the attitudes and concerns of the medical establishment.

The religion editor? Well, he or she is pretty busy as it is putting together the Saturday church page and trying to deal with the day-to-day hard news generated by the ecumenical movement and squabbles over birth control and priestly celibacy. The overworked religion editor seldom has the time, space, or inclination to dabble in metaphysics.

The police reporter at detective headquarters? Unfortunately, he is often enough the final choice. But obviously not a very good one.

What about that new cub reporter with the degree in sociology? He could explore the subject from the standpoint of its social impact and social origins. Not a bad idea maybe. But again, too limited.

The travel editor? He's never taken that kind of trip.

The difficulty with the psychedelics, of course, is that they cut across so many areas – law and psychology, physiology and philosophy, Eastern and Western religions. As a result, the city editor may decide to fall back on the talents of that jack-of-all-knowledge, the general-assignment reporter.

In the old days, any reporter worth his pay cheque was supposed to be capable of handling any story on any subject. The theory was that he would ask himself the same questions that the uninformed layman would ask, and that he would supply the answers in terms that could be understood by a Kansas City milkman or a little old lady in Dubuque. For years, reporters all over America were writing stories with these two mythological readers in mind. And the theory in fact was not such a bad one, until we got quite deep into the twentieth century. I still remember, however, the night the first Sputnik flashed across our innocent Western skies. There was turmoil in the city room as the general-assignment reporters placed frantic telephone calls to sleepy astronomers and physicists. We didn't even know what questions to ask. After only a few days of struggling with apogees and perigees, it became all too evident that we needed our own rocket expert, and in time a top investigative reporter was groomed to take over the field. I don't know if the little old lady in Dubuque can understand every word he writes, but she can rest assured at least that her information is accurate.

The late Professor Jacob Scher used to tell his journalism students: 'Do all you can to simplify. But keep in mind there are some things that are just damned hard to understand. They're difficult. And if you simplify beyond a certain point, you won't be telling the truth about them.' Obviously the issues raised by the psychedelics are incredibly complex and damned hard to understand. A general-assignment Da Vinci would have trouble enough explaining all of them, if he understood them himself, and here again it is clear that complexity demands at least a degree of specialization and a fundamental background in a number of areas.

Newspapers in recent years have produced their experts on outer space, as well as education, labour, politics, urban planning, and human relations, to the point where major city rooms have come to resemble mini-universities. As yet, however, they have not developed any comparable authorities on inner space, if such a thing is possible, and it must be admitted in consequence that newspapers in general have done a bum job in telling the many-faceted story of LSD.

Some patterns are revealed by a visit to a newspaper morgue, where the files contain hundreds of clippings about LSD. The clippings were scissored from newspapers across the country, and there are very few of them that date prior to 1963. The few early ones are optimistic, and they tend to treat LSD as a possible new wonder drug:

DRUG HELPS MENTALLY ILL RECALL PAST (1960)

HOW 'NIGHTMARE' DRUG AIDS ADDICTION FIGHT (1961)

As early as 1951, readers of the Chicago *Daily News* were informed that a psychiatrist had told 'how a white powder given in so tiny an amount it could not be seen by the naked eye transformed normal people into strange, psychotic-like individuals in thirty minutes [and] hinted at the exciting possibility that mental illness could be caused by a toxic substance produced in the bodies of people who have broken down under stress'. A NEW SHOCK DRUG UNLOCKS TROUBLED MINDS, readers of the *This Week* newspaper supplement were told in 1959. 'It has rescued many drug addicts, alcoholics, and neurotics from their private hells – and holds promise for curing tomorrow's mental ills.' It has 'excited psychiatric workers all over the world'.

By 1963, however, the pattern had shifted, and the volume of stories since then has appeared to multiply almost in geometric progression. It is not a coincidence, moreover, that 1963 was the year Dr Timothy Leary took his departure from Harvard University. That was the year the press really discovered LSD, having first discovered Dr Leary, and until recently there has been little success in divorcing the one subject from the other. As far as the drug is concerned, the change in emphasis can be detected from a sampling of 1963 headlines:

A WARNING ON LSD: IT CARRIES WILD KICK

DRUG BRINGS HALLUCINATIONS; USE IS GETTING OUT OF HAND

MEDICS WARN THRILL DRUG CAN WARP MINDS AND KILL

Of psychedelic drugs in general, readers of the *Washington Post* learned in 1963: 'They have been blamed for at least one suicide, and for causing a respectable married secretary to appear nude in public.' Since that year, newspaper readers on the whole have learned very little else of consequence about the drugs; the coverage by and large has been of the cops-and-robbers variety, concentrating on police raids, drug-control bills, suicides, and fatal plunges.

As indicated, this sort of treatment can be attributed in part to a lack of reportorial expertise. Before taking a closer look at news-paper handling of the subject, however, another important factor should be pointed out.

It might be argued that the current emphasis on the negative aspects of LSD is at least partially inherent in the very nature of that curious stuff we call 'news'.

There is a common complaint that every newspaperman must have heard at least a thousand times in his lifetime. It goes something like this: 'Why do you always print bad news? Why is the front page always full of war and crime, murders and disasters? Why don't you print some of the *nice* things that happen? Why don't you write stories about all the good people who lead decent lives?'

'Because you wouldn't buy our paper any more' is an obvious and an honest answer. 'You'd run right out and buy some other paper.' And why? Because a newspaper is supposed to print the news, and news is based on conflict. Dog bites man: that's news. More to the point, news deals with *exceptions*. Its stock in trade is the exceptional event that runs counter to ordinary experience, and that is why man bites dog is *really* news. In the same sense, war, crime, and disasters are all exceptions to the normal rule, and there-fore they are news. If a man rises in the morning and does not murder his wife, that is not news. If people live in harmony and do good works, that also is not news. I believe a satirist once wrote a Walter Lord type of book titled *The Day Nothing Happened*, offering an hour-by-hour chronicle of events in some hypothetical American city. One by one, with murderous suspense, these ordinary events built up to a shattering climax in which the sun went down and everybody went peacefully to bed. I can't imagine the book sold very well, but there is probably a lesson in it for those people who complain about news content.

Many complain that the 'good teenager' has had a bad press, that his image has been ruined by a few bad teenagers. The fact is that the good teenager is not news, because he is not exceptional. By the same coin, a good trip on LSD is not news either. But a bad trip: that's news. And a bad trip that ends in suicide or a psychotic break: that's really news.

Newspapers since World War II have been giving more and more space to interpretation of news events – to what is known in the business as 'think pieces'. But their primary function, as it has always been, is still to tell the news – to record the daily glut of occurrences; and since news by definition is almost certain to be bad, it is perhaps unfair to fault the newspapers too much for doing what they are supposed to do.

Having said this, however, I must add that the run-of-mill coverage of LSD has more often than not been superficial at best and violently distorted at worst. Since 1963, the newspapers had had almost nothing to say about the potential benefits of psychedelics in psycho-therapy and related fields, including the treatment or alcoholism. As evidence of the breakdown in communications, reflecting also the breakdown in legitimate research in this country, witness this pathetic little column-closer, which was filed in 1967 by an Associated Press reporter in Germany:

HAMBURG (AP) – The hallucinatory drug LSD is being used by Czech authorities as a possible cure for alcoholism, according to Radio Free Europe monitors.

End of story, in the paper where I read it. Americans can no doubt be thankful at least that they still have Radio Free Europe to keep them posted.

Two news stories in particular were probably of major importance in turning the tide of public opinion decisively against LSD. They broke within a week of each other, in April of 1966. One involved a five-year-old Brooklyn girl who suffered convulsions after swallowing an LSD sugar cube that had been left in a refrigerator by her uncle. The other concerned a former medical-school student, Stephen H. Kessler, who was charged with the stabbing to death of his mother-in-law, also in Brooklyn. 'Man,' he told police, 'I've been flying for three days on LSD. Did I rape somebody? Did I kill my wife?' (It was at this point that Sandoz Pharmaceuticals withdrew its new-drug application, citing unfavourable publicity, and thus cut off most legitimate LSD research in this country.)

Kessler vanished into Bellevue Hospital for mental tests, and that was the last news I have seen about him. But the case since then has been cited repeatedly in newspaper columns to support the assertion that LSD 'can lead to murder'. *Post hoc, ergo propter hoc,* of course. If indeed it was a case of *post hoc.*

Later in the year, in a story on the League for Spiritual Discovery, writer Thomas Buckley noted rather wistfully in the *New York Times,* '. . . the increasing use of LSD poses social, medical, and religious questions that do not seem to be receiving the attention they deserve'. Soon after that, however, the drug was to receive considerable attention in the very influential pages of the *Times:*

LSD SPREAD IN U.S. ALARMS DOCTORS AND POLICE

AUTHORITIES SEE EDUCATION AS KEY HOPE IN
CURBING PERIL OF THE HALLUCINATORY DRUG

Under the three-column headline, in a lengthy story that attracted widespread attention, Gladwin Hill wrote on 23 February 1967, that LSD had become 'the nation's newest scourge'. Setting out to prove it, he reported some horrifying examples – including the case of a teenage driver whose car had crashed into a house and killed a child; in a trancelike state, trying to climb the walls of his cell, the youth shouted: 'I'm a graham cracker. Oops, my arm just crumbled off.' There was no reference to any possible beneficial uses of LSD. As for the drug's supposed consciousness-expanding qualities, the article quoted an expert on the subject, California's Attorney General Thomas Lynch, who said that LSD represents 'a flight from reality'. Lynch did not say what reality is; but then Hill apparently neglected to ask him.

Reporters who wonder if LSD has any mystical or insight-producing properties can always find out by asking a cop, a doctor, or a legislator. Illinois State Senator Robert Cherry, for example, has been quoted as stating, 'This drug puts these people in the world of nothing'. Dr J. Thomas Ungerleider has said flatly, 'There is no basis in fact for their claims'. John Merlo, an Illinois state representative, has observed that the mystical claims for LSD are 'pure bunk', which he may have picked up from Commissioner James L. Goddard of the Food and Drug Administration, who told a House Government Operations subcommittee in Washington that mind-stretching claims for LSD are 'pure bunk'. (Presumably it takes a subcommittee to study a subculture.)

If there are no experts available, the reporter can always decide for himself. Thus, one reporter gave the subject a fair shake recently. He watched an LSD party and even went so far as to listen to a Jefferson Airplane record, all of which led him to conclude concerning 'the mystique' of LSD, 'Tomorrow will come, and that other world

– the straight world, the world of reality – will take over.' Or as another reporter saw it, the hippies take LSD 'to elude a world they don't like, and to create an artificial one in which they feel more comfortable'. Nobody has yet suggested that hippies may take LSD to elude reporters.

The newspapers indeed are full of news about psychedelics:

MYSTERY OF NUDE COED'S FATAL PLUNGE

NAKED IN A ROSE BUSH

HER SON'S TRAGIC TRIP

STRIP-TEASING HIPPIE GOES WILD IN LAKESPUR ON LSD

'NIGHTMARE' DRUG PERIL GROWS

HOME DRUG LAB RAIDED IN BRONX

BOBBY BAKER KIN IN TREE NUDE

BANANA SMOKING UNDER U.S. STUDY

Some terrible things are reported. A team of investigators in California, for example, came across a former disc jockey who said he had lost his job after taking LSD, and what's more, he didn't care. A medical man found: '. . . LSD users are suddenly overcome with religion.' As far back as 1960, *This Week* had recovered from its original optimism, and Dr Franz E. Winkler was warning readers of the supplement that he had detected certain 'ominous symptoms' in some LSD users. 'LSD', the doctor noted,

breaks the fetters of our disenchanted existence and releases the mind to a flight into a fairyland sparkling with colours and sounds and sensations of unearthly beauty. Under its influence, all confinements and separations fade, and the world becomes a place in which individuals need no longer be lonely but become members of an all-encompassing whole. Under such influences, people receive creative inspirations, become inclined to accept the reality of a spiritual world, and at times, even sense the existence of a supreme being.

And this is all wrong and immoral, of course. Because it's too easy. In fact, it's a sin.

Parents, do you know the danger signs? You do if you read a 1967 syndicated series by Ann Honig, which ran among other places in *Chicago's American:*

Parents who suspect their offspring are turned on via LSD should be suspicious if the youngsters suddenly espouse a oneness with

God and the universe, if they are suddenly superknowledgeable about life and love, if they hear and see things no one else does, if their pupils are dilated.

Of course there are real LSD tragedies, and nobody should minimize them. Certainly the press cannot be accused of minimizing them.

BAD LSD TRIPS INCREASE, the headline over an Associated Press story reported in May of 1967. And so they probably had. But this raises an interesting possibility I remember discussing one time with Jean Houston, and I believe we agreed that the press might be partly responsible for creating a sort of self-fulfilling prophecy. One dimly recalls a halcyon time, in the beginning, when nobody spoke much about bad trips, and the psychedelic experience was almost always very nice and rewarding. Perhaps that was never the case, or it could be that fewer bad trips in the past were merely a result of a smaller drug population and/or far less publicity. But the other possibility remains.

Just suppose. Here all of a sudden is this Greek chorus of doctors and psychiatrists warning young people to avoid LSD: it might drive them crazy. And the warnings are dutifully passed on by the press. This doesn't stop the young people from taking LSD, of course; but it could possibly create a subliminal anxiety that results in either a bad trip or in a panic reaction at some later date. Since LSD subjects are so highly suggestible, as is well known, it could be that they oblige the doctors and the press by doing exactly what they were told they would do. They flip out.

In my own case, I was having dinner one night with a bearded psychiatrist of formidable appearance. This was some months after I had participated in a legal psychedelic experiment at a psychiatric hospital, for a newspaper story, and while the trip had not been a pleasant one, I had not given it any thought for some time, and I had not been worried about it in any way. Between courses, the psychiatrist declared: 'The real tragedy of LSD has only now come to light. People think they might have a bad trip for a few hours, and that's all they have to worry about. But we now know the frightening truth that *nobody comes back unharmed.* In *every* case there is some degree of brain damage.' Oh? And where had the good doctor heard that? Well, he said, he had heard it just the other day at a medical-school symposium. And whom had he heard it from? He had heard it from this doctor sitting right next to him at the symposium, he forgot his name. And where had *he* heard it? He had heard it on a recent visit to the West Coast, where the research had been done. Where on the West Coast? My dinner companion didn't know. Who had done the research, and how was it done? He didn't know that either. He called for the dessert menu.

Driving home, like the man in the joke, I kept telling myself: 'Now is not the time to panic. Now is not the time to panic.' And then, finally: 'Now. *Now* is the time to panic!' Without dwelling on the details, I will say only that I spent a very bad week, and I can certainly understand now those stories about rational Westerners who mentally disintegrate under the suggestive curse of an African witch doctor. In my own mind at least, the experience lends credence to the hypothesis that the press and the medical profession between them may have contributed to a similar situation by continually emphasizing the dangers and negative aspects of the psychedelic experience.

One might ask why the press has been so willing to go along with the doctors in this connection, to the point of distorting the overall truth about LSD. There is in fact a fundamental dilemma involved here, and it is one that editors run into rather frequently. In short, should a newspaper tell the truth, or whole truth, when the public safety might be better served by silence or half-truths?

An obvious example is the development of a riot situation in a community. Should the local newspapers call attention to the situation and thereby possibly aggravate it by directing other malcontents to the scene? In most cases, newspapers withhold such stories during the early stages of mob action, and especially so if the disorder is still on a relatively small scale.

It would be hard to argue with that decision. But I recall a less-obvious version of the same basic problem. A rare solar eclipse was soon to occur, and our newspaper was flooded with urgent messages from individuals and organizations dedicated to the prevention of blindness. We were urged to tell our readers there was no safe way to look directly at the eclipse. It so happens that a safe eclipse viewer can be made with exposed photographic negatives, but the anti-blindness lobby said the procedure was too complicated, and many people undoubtedly would botch the job. Well, what should we do? Should we, in effect, fib and play it safe? Those who wanted us to do so were interested only in preventing blindness – not an unworthy motive, certainly – but the eclipse, on the other hand, was a pheno-menon of considerable interest. Did we have the right to deny people the experience of seeing it and studying it? In the end, we decided to tell the truth. We published carefully worded instructions telling how to construct a safe viewer. (To my knowledge, nobody went blind.)

The parallel to psychedelic drugs is obvious. Medical men quite properly are interested in the prevention of suicide and psychosis, and there are strong pressures on a newspaper editor to conform. Besides, there is no foolproof method to guarantee a safe view of the psychedelic world, and editors, in addition, are often cowed by the medical profession. If a doctor says LSD is a deadly peril, how is an editor to argue with him? The result sometimes is a certain timidity on the part of the press in any situation involving a medical judgment. It is understandable, then, if many editors decide to play it safe and treat LSD simply as something that flew out of Pandora's box.

Still, there is no obligation to overdo it.

There was widespread rejoicing when the first study was published in 1967 indicating that use of LSD might result in abnormal chromosome breakage. That would certainly solve the problem very neatly, obviating the necessity to deal with all those sticky questions the psychedelics had raised, and the press in some cases did its best to improve upon the findings. The syndicated series by Ann Honig began with the observation, 'LSD may cause cancer in drug users – and deformity and death in their children.' But the series itself was relatively restrained in comparison with the headlines and advertising that accompanied it in *Chicago's American*. There was an interesting escalation from story to headline to promotional copy. For example the headline:

LSD: FOR THE KICK THAT CAN KILL

Then the printed advertising blurbs:

LSD: THE 'FLY NOW, DIE LATER' DRUG

Although many acid-users have committed suicide or murder while high on LSD, an even grimmer indictment has been placed against it. A well-known genetics expert has found that 'harmless' LSD damages human chromosomes . . . and eventually causes cancer! Find out the frightening facts. Read 'LSD: The Tragic Fad' starting Sunday in *Chicago's American*.

Why does a young person suddenly want to jump out of a window? Or shoot a number of people? Or eat the bark from a tree? Learn what the use of the drug LSD can do to a person. . . .

And finally the spot radio announcements, prefaced with the remark that acid-heads think LSD is harmless:
'Well, they're wrong – *dead wrong*. People who take LSD eventually get cancer.'

In the series, writer Honig sought to analyse why so many young people turn to LSD. The conclusion: 'LSD offers a new mystique, a new entrée to the in-group, a new rebellion against their elders, a new thrill. Also it's cheap, easy to make.' And so much for that. The writer went on to comment upon the experience of a San Mateo high school superintendent who raised $21,000 to finance an 'anti-LSD film' and then asked the students 'whom they would trust as the narrator'. He was 'shocked' by their answer.

'Nobody', said the students.

Small wonder, one might add.

This isn't to say that all newspapers in all cases have taken a limited and wholly negative view of psychedelics. There have been thoughtful pieces, here and there, now and then. My own newspaper, for example, devoted a four-page section to the religious implications of LSD experience, and it also offered vigorous editorial opposition to proposed legislation making LSD possession a crime in Illinois. Occasionally one comes across an isolated headline:

LSD CHEERS UP DYING PATIENT,
DOCTOR FINDS DRUG BRINGS A NEW ZEST FOR LIFE

There has, however, been very little of substance printed. Seldom is any attempt made to explain the nature of the LSD experience, except in terms of the acting-out behaviour it sometimes produces. Even in the *New York Times*, one may be told simply that LSD '. . . produces hallucinations or alters thought processes in various ways'. At best, a reader may find that the experience enhances sensory perception – pretty colours are seen – and sometimes he is told that the experience breaks down the ego and produces a 'mystical' state of mind. But what constitutes a mystical state of mind is left to the imagination. Now and then a perceptive reporter notices that LSD cultists talk a lot about Hinduism and Buddhism. They are interested in something called Zen, and they like to read *The Tibetan Book of the Dead*. But the implications of all this are not pursued; no effort is made to explore or explain the Eastern ideas that hold such fascination for the drug takers. The newspapers report that young drug users are in revolt; they do not say precisely what values are challenged by that revolt, and they do not say what alternatives exactly are offered by the drug movement. This is partly the fault of the cultists themselves – 'mumblers about Reality', a *Life* reporter called them – and it is also due in part to the ineffable character of the psychedelic experience. But it is the fault, too, of the press. It is easy to see why the attractions of LSD seem so inexplicable to those puzzled adults who get all their information from the newspapers. There is one LSD question that is rarely asked in the press, and when it is asked it isn't answered in any depth. In the case of psychedelics, many reporters seem to remember only Who? What?

Where? and When? They forget the most important question of all, which is Why?

One split-off of this has been the emergence of the underground press to represent the non-straight viewpoint – the San Francisco *Oracle*, the Berkeley *Barb*, the *Seed* in Chicago, and the *East Village Other* in New York, to name but a few. These improbable newspapers even have their own Underground Press Syndicate (ups) to service them with news and features. Colourful sheets, sometimes highly original in their content and design, they are of course just as much out of balance on the one side as the regular press is on the other. But if nothing else, they indicate that newspaper readers abhor a vacuum just as much as nature does, and reporters who are still concerned about the fifth W might find a few clues in the pages of the underground journals. (I did like the classified ad I saw in one of them: 'You're welcome, St Jude.')

Recently, a modification in press attitudes seems to have occurred, with the development of a distinct drug subculture focused in such areas as San Francisco's Haight-Ashbury, New York's Greenwich Village, and Chicago's Old Town. The newspapers in these cities have been fascinated by the psychedelic hippies, and at times the fascination has verged on obsession. In New York, the *Times* has devoted many columns of newsprint to their doings, and in San Francisco, the *Chronicle* sent a bearded reporter out to spend a month prowling the acid dens. (You guessed it: 'I Was a Hippie.') Even the 78-year-old historian Arnold Toynbee showed up mingling with the flower children of Haight-Ashbury, where he wrote a series of dispatches for the London *Observer*.

In general, the tone of most stories has been sympathetic. United Press International produced a long feature that compared the hippies favourably with their beatnik predecessors, and a similar piece by the Associated Press seemed to agree with the assessment of a San Francisco florist it quoted: 'These kids are good kids. They don't steal and they don't fight. But they should wash their feet more often.'

Toynbee thought the hippies were just splendid, seeing in them certain similarities to St Francis. I think seriously that the flowers had a lot to do with taming the savage press – it's hard to bad-mouth a little girl who hands you a posy – but even more important perhaps is the fact that the concentration of amiable hippies has taken the publicity spotlight off Dr Leary, on whom it had been shining almost exclusively. He's a very nice fellow. But no single individual can dominate a situation without rubbing many people the wrong way, and he is perhaps a trifle old for his role. The kids as a whole come off better.

In any case, the press at times has seemed on the verge of suggesting that the hippies might just possibly have something to say. They have nudged at least a few observers to inquire into their motivations – 'Why do they act like that?' – and the newspapers have actually reported a few efforts to answer that question. Toynbee said that the hippies are rebelling against American conformism, which he blamed partly on the Puritans and partly on Henry Ford (a nation of car drivers has become habituated to regimentation by traffic cops, who tell them where and how they may drive). One columnist concluded that hippies '... suffer from something the more fashionable sociologists call "anomie"'. And of course somebody, in this case a psychiatrist, had to drag Marshall McLuhan out of the wings: 'We must understand that we are dealing with the first generation raised on TV, and everything is instant. It is a generation that expects instant gratification.'

Not very good, so far. But better than nothing.

So much for the newspapers. Summing up, we have suggested that the essentially negative attitude toward LSD in this area may be attributed to three primary factors: (1) no experts, (2) the nature of news, (3) eclipse syndrome. And we have proposed that newspapers may be partly responsible for the bad trips and panic behaviour they fill their pages with.

Turning briefly to radio and television, there is little to say, since these media have virtually ignored the drug movement. The one important exception has been the 'talk shows', both on radio and television. Some of the talk programmes run up to three hours or longer, often with audience participation by telephone, and they have produced many excellent debates and discussions by experts representing every conceivable point of view on psychedelics. In other areas of programming, however, one would never guess that such a thing as LSD existed. I have never seen or heard any reference to it in a dramatic presentation, and that is understandable perhaps when you consider the fire television comes under when it shows a young person smoking even a Lucky Strike. In fact, the only substantial network show I recall on LSD was the CBS documentary, narrated by Charles Kuralt, on the psychotherapeutic sessions at the Spring Grove (Maryland) State Hospital. That was very good. But, also, that was in May of 1966. And, to my knowledge, there has been nothing since.

It is painful to admit that the major magazines have probably done a better job than newspapers in reporting on LSD, and that *Time* and *Life* between them have possibly done the best job of all. Between 1963 and 1967, *Life* carried at least ten pieces on LSD, including an important cover story on 25 March 1966. (Another

cover story, on psychedelic art, appeared on 9 September 1966.)
Time discovered LSD in 1954 and has since published at least eighteen
pieces on the drug. Other major stories have appeared in such
magazines as *Newsweek, Look, Playboy, Reader's Digest, The
Saturday Evening Post, The Nation, New Republic, The Atlantic*, and
Harper's. In fact I recall the first time I learned about LSD – in a
1963 article by Noah Gordon in *The Reporter* magazine.

With some exceptions, the magazines have plumbed the subject
to a far greater depth than most newspapers have. They, too, have
given heavy play to the dangers involved – as the *Reader's Digest*
saw it, 'LSD will remain about as safe and useful as a do-it-yourself
brain surgery kit for amateurs' – but they also have been willing to
examine psychedelics from other viewpoints, and in general they
have treated the drugs with a balanced perspective. To my knowledge,
incidentally, *Look* senior editor Jack Shepherd did the one thing
journalistic reporters on LSD almost never do: he took the drug
himself (and had a detestable trip).

A curious and significant by-product of the fuss over LSD came in
1967 in the form of a widespread effort, especially in the magazines,
to give a better image to marijuana, the psychedelic near beer. The
proliferation of articles provoked a suspicious complaint from a
hippie friend of mine who prefers his fruit forbidden: 'Man, are you
aware there's a *conspiracy* in the magazines to make pot legal?' And
indeed I could appreciate his growing paranoia on the subject;
in July alone, *Life, Newsweek,* and *Look* carried stories sharply
questioning the wisdom of a marijuana penalties, and *Newsweek*
devoted a cover story to the issue.

Life has described marijuana as 'a mild euphoric drug', adding:
'Pot is not physically addicting, nor need it lead to crime, immorality,
or stronger drugs.'

Newsweek: 'Indeed, the prohibitive laws against marijuana in
America today, like those against alcohol in the 1920s, have not
significantly diminished its use and, in fact, may have increased it.'

Look: 'The severity of the Federal marijuana law far exceeds the
danger of the drug. The law needs an overhaul, with smoking
marijuana reduced from a felony to a misdemeanour, as with LSD.'

The Nation: 'It is difficult to fashion a serious case against smoking
marijuana, except that a user will find himself in serious trouble with
the police.'

New Republic: 'The worst thing about marijuana is the laws
against it, which should be repealed.'

While the magazines outshine the newspapers in reporting on
LSD, their coverage is good only by comparison, and nobody could
truly grasp all the varied implications of the psychedelics just by

flipping through the slicks. In the last analysis, however, anybody in America today who is really interested in the subject can learn what is accurately known about it, which isn't much, by reading both the magazines and the newspapers (underground and above), by listening to the radio and television discussions, by dipping into the large number of books such as this one. And that, perhaps, is all one can ask. As for those who are not really interested, they will resist the best efforts of the media to inform them. As somebody has said, you can't reason people out of an opinion they did not arrive at by reason to begin with.

Sniping – a new pattern of violence?*

TERRY ANN KNOPF

On 23 July 1968, at 2.15 p.m., Cleveland's Mayor, Carl B. Stokes, who was in Washington, D.C., that day, made what he expected to be a routine telephone call to his office back home. He was told of information from military, FBI, and local police intelligence sources indicating that an armed uprising by black militants was scheduled to take place at 8 a.m. the next day. According to the reports, Ahmed Evans, a militant leader who headed a group called the Black Nationalists of New Libya, planned to drive to Detroit that night to secure automatic weapons. There were further reports that Evans' followers had already purchased bandoliers, ammunition pouches, and first-aid kits that same day. Simultaneous uprisings were reportedly being planned for Detroit, Pittsburgh, and Chicago.

At 6 p.m., in response to these reports, several unmarked police cars were assigned to the area of Evans' house. At about 8.20 p.m. a group of armed men, some of whom were wearing bandoliers of ammunition, emerged from the house. Almost at once, an intense gun battle broke out between the police and the armed men, lasting for roughly an hour. A second gun battle between the police and snipers broke out shortly after midnight about 40 blocks away. In the wake of these shoot-outs, sporadic looting and firebombing erupted and continued for several days. By the time the disorder was over, 16,400 national guardsmen had been mobilized, at least nine persons had been killed (including three policemen), while the property damage was estimated at $1·5 million. Police listed most of their casualties as 'shot by sniper'.

Immediately, the Cleveland tragedy was described as a deliberate plot against the police and said to signal a new phase in the current course of racial conflict. *The Cleveland Press* (24 July 1968) compared the violence in Cleveland to guerilla activity in Saigon and noted: '. . . It didn't seem to be a Watts, or a Detroit, or a Newark. Or even a Hough of two years ago. No, this tragic night seemed to be part of a plan.' Thomas A. Johnson writing in the *New York Times* (28 July 1968) stated: '. . . It marks perhaps the first documented

* From Terry Ann Knopf, 'Sniping – a new pattern of violence?' *Transaction* Vol. 6 No. 9 (July/August, 1969), pp. 22–9.

case in recent history of black, armed, and organized violence against the police.'

As the notion that police were being 'ambushed' took hold in the public's mind, many observers reporting on the events in Cleveland and similar confrontations in other cities, such as Gary, Peoria, Seattle, and York, Pennsylvania, emphasized that the outbreaks had several prominent features in common.

The first was the element of planning. Racial outbursts have traditionally been spontaneous affairs, without organization and without leadership. While no two disorders are similar in every respect, studies conducted in the past have indicated that a riot is a dynamic process that goes through stages of development. John P. Spiegel of Brandeis' Lemberg Center for the Study of Violence, has discerned four stages in the usual sort of rioting: the precipitating event, street confrontation, 'Roman holiday', and siege. A sequence of stages is outlined in somewhat similar terms in the second of the Kerner Report on 'the riot process'. It is significant, however, that neither the Lemberg Center nor the Kerner Commission found any evidence of an organized plan or 'conspiracy' in civil disorders prior to 1968. According to the Kerner Report: '. . . The Commission has found no evidence that all or any of the disorders or the incidents that led to them were planned or directed by any organization or group – international, national, or local.'

Since the Cleveland shoot-out, however, many observers have suggested that civil disorders are beginning to take a new form, characterized by some degree of planning, organization, and leadership.

The second new feature discerned in many of 1968's summer outbreaks was the attacks on the police. In the past, much of the racial violence that occurred was directed at property rather than persons. Cars were stoned, stores were looted, business establishments were firebombed, and residences, in some instances, were damaged or destroyed. However, since the Cleveland gun battle, there have been suggestions that policemen have become the primary targets of violence. A rising curve of ambushes of the police was noted in the 7 October 1968 issue of the *U.S. News & World Report* which maintained that at least 8 policemen were killed and 47 wounded in such attacks last summer.

Finally, attacks on the police are now said to be *regularly* characterized by hit-and-run sniping. Using either home-made weapons or commercial and military weapons, such as automatics, bands of snipers are pictured initiating guerilla warfare in our cities.

This view of the changing nature of racial violence can be found across a broad spectrum of the press, ranging from the moderately

liberal *New York Times* to the militantly rightist *American Opinion*.
On 3 August 1968, the *New York Times* suggested in an editorial:

> ... The pattern in 1967 has not proved to be the pattern of 1968.
> Instead of violence almost haphazardly exploding, it has sometimes
> been deliberately planned. And while the 1967 disorders served
> to rip away false façades of racial progress and expose rusting
> junkyards of broken promises, the 1968 disorders also reveal a
> festering militancy that prompts some to resort to open warfare.

Shortly afterward (14 August 1968), *Crime Control Digest*, a
biweekly periodical read by many law-enforcement officials across
the country, declared:

> The pattern of civil disorders in 1968 has changed from the
> pattern that prevailed in 1967, and the elaborate u.s. Army,
> National Guard and police riot control programme prepared to
> meet this year's 'long hot summer' will have to be changed if this
> year's type of civil disturbance is to be prevented or controlled.

This year's riot tactics have featured sniping and hit-and-run
attacks on the police, principally by Black Power extremists, but
by teenagers in an increasing number of instances. The type of crimes
being committed by the teenagers and the vast increase in their
participation have already brought demands that they be tried and
punished as adults.

On 13 September 1968, *Time* took note of an 'ominous trend' in
the country:

> Violence as a form of Negro protest appears to be changing from
> the spontaneous combustion of a mob to the premeditated shoot-
> outs of a far-out few. Many battles have started with well-planned
> sniping at police.

Predictably, the November 1968 issue of *American Opinion* went
beyond the other accounts by linking reported attacks on the police
to a Communist plot:

> The opening shots of the Communists' long-planned terror
> offensive against our local police were fired in Cleveland on the
> night of 23 July 1968, when the city's Glenville area rattled with
> the scream of automatic weapons. ... What happened in Cleve-
> land, alas, was only a beginning.

To further emphasize the point, a large headline crying TERRORISM
was included on the cover of the November issue.

Despite its relative lack of objectivity, *American Opinion* is the only publication that has attempted to list sniping incidents. Twenty-five specific instances of attacks on police were cited in the November issue. Virtually every other publication claiming a change in the nature of racial violence pointing to the 'scores of American cities' affected and the 'many battles' between blacks and the police has confined itself to a few perfunctory examples as evidence. Even when a few examples have been offered, the reporters usually have not attempted to investigate and confirm them.

Without attempting an exhaustive survey, we at the Lemberg Center were able to collect local and national press clippings, as well as wire-service stories, that described 25 separate incidents of racial violence in July and August of last summer. In all these stories, sniping was alleged to have taken place at some point or other in the fracas, and in most of them, the police were alleged to have been the primary targets of the sharpshooters. Often, too, the reports held that evidence had been found of planning on the part of 'urban guerillas', and at times it was claimed that the police had been deliberately ambushed. Needless to say, the spectre of the Black Panthers haunts a number of the accounts. Throughout, one finds such phrases as these: 'snipers hidden behind bushes . . .', 'isolated sniper fire . . .', 'scattered sniping directed at the police . . .', 'exchange of gunfire between snipers and police . . .', 'snipers atop buildings in the area. . . .' It is small wonder that the rewrite men at *Time* and other national magazines discerned a new and sinister pattern in the events of that summer. Small wonder that many concerned observers are convinced that the country's racial agony has entered a new phase of deliberate covert violence.

CONSPIRATIONAL PLANNING OF INCIDENTS

But how valid is this sometimes conspirational, sometimes apocalyptic view? What is the evidence for it, apart from these newspaper accounts?

Our assessment is based on an analysis of newspaper clippings, including a comparison of initial and subsequent reports, local and national press coverage, and on telephone interviews with high-ranking police officials. The selection of police officials was deliberate on our part. In the absence of city or state investigations of most of the incidents, police departments were found to be the best (and in many cases the only) source of information. Moreover, as the reported targets of sniping, police officials understandably had a direct interest in the subject.

Of course, the selection of this group did involve an element of risk. A tendency of some police officials to exaggerate and inflate sniping reports was thought to be unavoidable. We felt, though, that every group involved would have a certain bias and that in the absence of interviewing every important group in the cities, the views of police officials were potentially the most illuminating and therefore the most useful. Our interviews with them aimed at the following points: (1) evidence of planning; (2) the number of snipers; (3) the number of shots fired; (4) affiliation of the sniper or snipers with an organization; (5) statistical breakdowns of police and civilian casualties by sniping; and (6) press coverage of the incident.

As the press reports showed, a central feature in the scheme of those alleging a new pattern involves the notion of planning. Hypothesizing a local (if not national) conspiracy, observers have pictured black militants luring the police to predetermined spots where the policemen become the defenceless victims of an armed attack. No precipitating incident is involved in these cases except perhaps for a false citizen's call.

Despite this view, the information we gathered indicates that at least 17 out of the 25 disorders surveyed (about 70 per cent) *did* begin with an identifiable precipitating event (such as an arrest seen by the black community as insulting or unjust) similar to those uncovered for 'traditional' disorders. The figure of 70 per cent is entirely consistent with the percentage of known precipitating incidents isolated by researchers at the Lemberg Center for past disorders (also about 70 per cent).

In Gary, Indiana, the alleged sniping began shortly after two young members of a gang were arrested on charges of rape. In York, Pennsylvania, the violence began after a white man fired a shotgun from his apartment at some blacks on the street. Blacks were reportedly angered upon learning that the police had failed to arrest the gunman. In Peoria, Illinois, police arrested a couple for creating a disturbance in a predominantly black housing-project area. A group of young people then appeared on the scene and began throwing missiles at the police. In Seattle, Washington, a disturbance erupted shortly after a rally was held to protest the arrest of two men at the local Black Panther headquarters. Yet the disorders that followed these incidents are among the most prominently mentioned as examples of planned violence.

Many of the precipitating events were tied to the actions of the police and in some instances they were what the Kerner Commission has referred to as 'tension-heightening incidents', meaning that the incident (or the disorder itself) merely crystallized tensions already existing in the community. Shortly before an outbreak in Harvey-Dixmoor, Illinois, on 6–7 August, for example, a coroner's jury had ruled that the fatal shooting by police of a young, suspected car thief one month earlier was justifiable homicide. It was the second time in four months that a local policeman had shot a black youth. In Miami, the rally held by blacks shortly before the violence erupted coincided with the Republican National Convention being held about 10 miles away. The crowd was reportedly disappointed when the Reverend Ralph Abernathy and basketball star Wilt Chamberlain failed to appear as announced. In addition, tensions had risen in recent months following increased police canine patrols in the area. Although no immediate precipitating incident was uncovered for the outbreak at Jackson, Michigan, on 5 August, it is noteworthy that the disorder occurred in front of a Catholic-sponsored centre aimed at promoting better race relations, and several weeks earlier, some 30 blacks had attempted to take over the centre in the name of 'a black group run by black people'.

Let us turn briefly to the eight disorders in which triggering events do not appear to have occurred. Despite the absence of such an incident in the Chicago Heights–East Chicago Heights disorder Chief of Police Robert A. Stone (East Chicago Heights) and Captain Jack Ziegler (Chicago Heights) indicated that they had no evidence of planning and the disorder was in all probability spontaneous. In particular, Chief Stone indicated that the participants were individuals rather than members of an organization. The same holds true for the 'ambuscade' in Brooklyn, New York, which the district attorney said at the time was the work of the Black Panthers. Although no precipitating event was uncovered, R. Harcourt-Dodds, Deputy Commissioner for Legal Matters in the New York City Police Department, indicated there was no evidence of planning by anyone or any group. In Jackson, Michigan, as previously noted, tensions in the community had increased in recent weeks prior to the August disorder over a controversial centre which some members of the community thought they should control. Thus the absence of precipitating events in at least three cases does not appear to be significant, least of all as evidence of a deliberate conspiracy to kill.

An assessment of the other five cases is considerably more difficult. In Inkster, Michigan, where four nights of isolated sniper fire were reported in August, Chief of Police James L. Fyke did not identify any precipitating event with the disorder and indicated that the state planned to make a case for conspiracy at a forthcoming trial. On the grounds that the two disorders in this city were under police investigation, Lieutenant Norman H. Judd of the Los Angeles Police Department declined to comment on possible triggering events. In San Francisco, Chief of Police Thomas J. Cahill said there was evidence of planning. He said that 'a firebomb was ignited and the shots were fired as the police vehicle arrived at the scene'.

This brings us to Cleveland and Ahmed Evans, the fifth case in this instance. Because of the dramatic nature of the events and the tremendous amount of attention they received in the national press, any findings concerning Cleveland are of utmost importance. It is significant, therefore, that more recent reports have revealed that the July bloodletting was something less than a planned uprising and that the situation at the time was considerably more complicated than indicated initially.

A series of articles appearing in the *New York Times* is instructive. At the time of the disorder, in an account by Thomas A. Johnson, entitled THIS WAS REAL REVOLUTION, the *New York Times* gave strong hints of a plot against the police: 'Early indications here were that a small, angry band of Negro men decided to shoot it out with the police. . . .' The article dwelt upon past statements of Ahmed Evans predicting armed uprisings across the nation on 9 May 1967 (they never materialized); rumours of arms caches across the country, and the revolutionary talk of black militants. No mention was made of any precipitating event, nor was there any reference to 'tension-heightening incidents' in the community at the time.

One month later, in early September, the *New York Times* published the results of its investigation of the disorder. The report was prepared by three newsmen, all of whom had covered the disorder earlier. Their findings shed new light on the case by suggesting that a series of tension-heightening factors were indeed present in the community at the time of the disorder. For one thing, Mayor Stokes attended a meeting with police officials several hours before the first outbreak and felt that the information about a planned uprising was 'probably not correct'. Ahmed Evans himself was seen, retrospectively, less as the master-mind of a plot than as just another militant. Anthony Ripley of the *New York Times* wrote of him: 'Evans, a tall, former Army Ranger who had been dishonourably discharged after striking an officer, was not regarded as a leading black nationalist. He was an amateur astrologer, 40 years old, given more to angry speeches than to action.' Numerous grievances in the community – particularly against the police – which had been overlooked at the time of the disorder, were cited later. For example, it was noted that there were only 165 blacks on a police force of more than 2,000 officers, and there was a deep resentment felt by blacks towards their treatment by the police. The reporters also turned up the fact that in 1966 an investigation committee had given a low professional rating to the police department.

Ahmed Evans himself had some more specific grievances, according to Thomas A. Johnson's follow-up article. He noted that Evans had arranged to rent a vacant tavern for the purpose of teaching the manufacture of African-style clothes and carvings to black youths but that the white landlady had changed her mind. He said that Evans had been further angered upon receiving an eviction order from his home. The Ripley article noted that, two hours before the shooting began, Evans said he had been asleep until his associates informed him that police surveillance cars had been stationed in the area. (Evans was accustomed to posting lookouts on top of buildings.) According to Evans, it was then that the group made the decision to arm.

Did the presence of the police in the area serve to trigger the gun battle that followed? What was the role of the civilian tow-truck driver wearing a police-like uniform? Did his hitching up an old pink Cadillac heighten tensions to the breaking point? Were intelligence reports of a plot in error? Why were arms so readily available to the group? What was the group's intention upon emerging from the house? These questions cannot be answered with any degree of absolute certainty. Nevertheless, it is significant that the earliest interpretations appearing the the *New York Times* were greatly modified by the subsequent articles revealing the complexities of the disorder and suggesting it may have been more spontaneous than planned. As Ripley wrote in his 2 September article:

> The Cleveland explosion has been called both an ambush of police and an armed uprising by Negroes. However, the weight of evidence indicates that it was closer to spontaneous combustion.

More recent developments on the controversial Cleveland case deserve mention also. On 12 May 1969, an all-white jury found Ahmed Evans guilty of seven counts of first-degree murder arising out of four slayings during the disorder last July. Evans was sentenced to die in the electric chair on 22 September 1969.

Then, on 29 May 1969, the National Commission on the Causes and Prevention of Violence authorized the release of a report entitled *Shoot-Out in Cleveland; Black Militants and the Police: July 23, 1968* by Louis H. Masotti and Jerome R. Corsi. The report was partially underwritten by the Lemberg Center. Its findings confirmed many of the results of the *Times* investigation and provided additional insights into the case.

Doubt was cast on prior intelligence reports that the Evans group had been assembling an arsenal of handguns and carbines, that Evans planned a trip to Detroit to secure weapons, and that simultaneous outbreaks in other northern cities were planned. ('The

truth of these reports was questionable.') Further, it was revealed
that these reports came from a single individual and that 'other
intelligence sources did not corroborate his story'. In addition, the
Commission report underscored certain provocative actions by the
police:

> It was glaringly evident that the police had established a stationary
> surveillance rather than a moving one. In fact, another surveillance
> car was facing Ahmed's apartment building from the opposite
> direction. . . . Both cars contained only white officers; both were
> in plain view of Ahmed's home. . . . Rightly or wrongly, Ahmed
> regarded the obvious presence of the surveillance cars over several
> hours' time as threatening.

The report stressed that 'against theories of an ambush or well-
planned conspiracy stands the evidence that on Tuesday evening
[23 July 1968] Ahmed was annoyed and apprehensive about the
police surveillance'.

The *Times* experience, together with the report of the National
Commission on the Causes and Prevention of Violence, strongly
suggest that the assumption that the Cleveland disorder was planned
is as yet unproved.

It may be significant that 14 out of the 19 police officials who
expressed a view on the matter could find no evidence of planning
in the disorders in their respective cities. In another instance, the
police official said the disorder was planned, but he could offer no
evidence in support of his statement. If this and the Cleveland case
are added, the number of outbreaks that do not appear to have
been planned comes to at least 16 out of 19.

In their assertions that police are now the principal targets of
snipers, some observers give the impression that there have been
large numbers of police casualties. In most cases, the reports have
not been explicit in stating figures. However, as mentioned earlier,
U.S. News & World Report cited 8 police deaths and 47 police
woundings this past summer. In order to assess these reports, we
obtained from police officials a breakdown of police casualties as a
result of gunfire.

What we learned was that a total of four policemen were killed
and that each death was by gunfire. But three of these occurred in
one city, Cleveland; the other was in Inkster, Michigan. In other
words, in 23 out of 25 cases where sniping was originally reported,
no policemen were killed.

POLICE CASUALTIES

Our total agreed with figures initially taken from local press reports. However, our count of four dead was only half the figure reported in *U.S. News & World Report*. We learned why when we found that the story appearing in that magazine originally came from an Associated Press 'roundup', which said that eight policemen had been killed by gunfire since 1 July 1968. But four of these eight cases were in the nature of individual acts of purely criminal – and not racial – violence. On 2 July a Washington, D.C., policeman was killed when he tried to arrest a man on a robbery complaint. A Philadelphia policeman was killed 15 July while investigating a $59 streetcar robbery. On 5 August in San Antonio, a policeman was killed by a 14-year-old boy he had arrested. The youth was a Mexican-American who had been arrested on a drinking charge. And, in Detroit, a policeman was shot to death on 5 August following a domestic quarrel. The circumstances concerning these four cases in no way display the features of a 'new pattern' of violence.

The question of how many police *injuries* came from sniper fire is more complicated. A total of 92 policemen were injured, accounting for 14 out of 25 cases. Almost half the injuries – 44 – came from gunfire. In some instances, our findings showed a downward revision of our earlier information. In Gary, for example, somebody reportedly took a shot at Police Chief James F. Hilton as he cruised the troubled area shortly after the disturbance began. However, when interviewed, Chief Hilton vigorously denied the earlier report. In Peoria, 11 police officers were reportedly injured by shotgun blasts. However, Bernard J. Kennedy, Director of Public Safety, indicated that initial reports 'were highly exaggerated' and that only seven officers were actually wounded. In East Point, Georgia, a white policeman had reportedly been injured during the disorder. Yet Acting Police Chief Hugh D. Brown indicated that there were no injuries to the police. In Little Rock, a policeman swore that he had been shot by a sniper. However, Chief of Police R. E. Brians told us that there was no injury and no broken skin. The Chief added that the policeman had been new and was not of the highest calibre. In fact, he is no longer with the department.

In addition, a closer look at the data reveals that the highest figures for numbers of policemen wounded by gunfire are misleading and need to be placed in perspective. Let us examine the three cases with the highest number of injuries: Cleveland with 10 policemen wounded by gunfire; Peoria, with seven; and Harvey-Dixmoor, Illinois, also with seven.

In Peoria, all seven policemen were wounded by the pellets from *a single shotgun blast*. In an interview, Safety Director Kennedy stressed that 'none of the injuries incurred was serious'. The Harvey-Dixmoor incident was similar. There, five out of the seven injured were also hit by a single shotgun blast. Chief of Police Leroy H. Knapp Jr informed us that only two or three shots were fired during the entire disorder. (A similar scattering of pellets occurred in St Paul, where three out of four policemen hit by gunfire received their injuries from one shotgun blast.)

SNIPING VS. ACCIDENTAL SHOOTING

In Cleveland, almost every injury to a policeman came as a result of gunfire. However, it is not at all clear whether snipers inflicted the damage. In the chaos that accompanies many disorders, shots have sometimes been fired accidentally – by both rioters and policemen. Ripley's 2 September article in the *New York Times* stated the problem very well: 'Only by setting the exact position of each man when he was shot, tracing the bullet paths, and locating all other policemen at the scene can a reasonable answer be found.' Thus far, no information concerning the circumstances of each casualty in the Cleveland disorder has been disclosed, and this goes for deaths as well as injuries.

Moreover, what applies to Cleveland applies to the other disorders as well. The Little Rock case illustrates the point. Chief of Police Brians verified the shooting of a national guardsman. However, he also clarified the circumstances of the shooting. He said that during the disorder a group of people gathered on a patio above a courtyard near the area where the national guard was stationed. One individual, under the influence of alcohol, fired indiscriminantly into the crowd, hitting a guardsman in the foot. Chief Brians added: 'He might just as easily have hit a [civil-rights] protester as a guardsman.' What is clear is that the circumstances concerning all casualties need to be clarified so as to avoid faulty inferences and incorrect judgments as much as possible.

Concerning the amount of sniping, there were numerous discrepancies between early and later reports, suggesting that many initial reports were exaggerated.

According to the police officials themselves, other than in the case of Cleveland where 25 to 30 snipers were allegedly involved, there were relatively few snipers. In 15 out of 17 cases where such information was available, police officials said there were three snipers or less. And in 7 out of 17 cases, the officials directly contradicted press reports at the time and said that no snipers were involved!

As for the number of gunshots fired by snipers, the reality, as reported by police, was again a lot less exciting than the newspapers indicated. In 15 out of 18 cases where information was available, 'snipers' fired fewer than 10 shots. In 12 out of 18 cases, snipers fired fewer than five. Generally, then, in more than one-quarter of the cases in which sniping was originally reported, later indications were that no sniping had actually occurred.

In Evansville, initial reports indicated that a minimum of eight shots were fired. Yet Assistant Chief of Police Charles M. Gash told us that only one shot was fired.

A more dramatic illustration is found in the case of East Point, Georgia. Although 50 shots were reportedly fired at the time, Acting Chief of Police Hugh Brown informed us that no shots were fired.

In York, 11 persons were wounded in a 'gun battle' on the first night. However, it turns out that 10 out of 11 persons were civilians and were injured by shotgun pellets. Only two snipers were involved, and only two to four shots were fired throughout the entire disturbance.

In Waterloo, Iowa, Chief of Police Robert S. Wright acknowledged that shots were fired, but he added: 'We wouldn't consider it sniper fire.' He told us that there was 'no ambush, no concealment of participants, or anything like that'. Moreover, he stated that not more than three persons out of a crowd of 50 youths carried weapons and 'not a great number of shots were fired'. The weapons used were small handguns.

In St Paul, where 10 shots were reportedly fired at police and four officers were wounded by gunshots, Chief of Police Lester McAuliffe also acknowledged that though there was gunfire, there 'wasn't any sniper fire as such'.

A similar situation was found in Peoria. Safety Director Kennedy said that the three shots believed fired did not constitute actual sniping.

In Little Rock, Chief Brians discounted reports of widespread sniping and indicated that many 'shots' were really firecrackers.

In Gary, early reports were that Chief of Police James Hilton had been fired upon and six persons had been wounded by snipers. Assistant Chief of Police Charles Boone told us that while a few shots might have been 'fired in the air', no actual sniping occurred. No one was shot during the disturbance, and no one was injured. Chief Hilton indicated that the fireman who was supposed to have been hit during the outbreak was actually shot by a drunk *prior* to the disorder.

In a few instances, discrepancies between first reports and sober

reappraisal can be traced to exaggerations of the policemen themselves. However, most of the discrepancies already cited throughout
this report can be attributed to the press—at both the local and
national level. In some instances, the early press reports (those
appearing at the time of the incident) were so inexplicit as to give the
impression of a great deal of sniping. In other instances, the early
figures given were simply exaggerated. In still other instances, the
early reports failed to distinguish between sniper fire and other forms
of gunplay.

THE ROLE OF THE PRESS

Moreover, the press generally gave far too little attention to the
immediate cause or causes of the disturbance. Even in the aftermath
of the violence, few attempts were made to verify previous statements
or to survey the tensions and grievances rooted in the community.
Instead, newspapers in many instances placed an unusually heavy
(and at times distorted) emphasis on the most dramatic aspects of
the violence, particularly where sniping was concerned.

A look at some of the newspaper headlines during the disorders
is most revealing, especially where the 'pellet cases' are involved.
As mentioned earlier, large numbers of casualties were sustained
from the pellets of a single shotgun blast—in Peoria, seven policemen; in Harvey-Dixmoor, five policemen, and in York, 10 civilians
were injured in this way; the most commonly cited examples of a
'new pattern' of violence. Unfortunately, inaccurate and sensational
headlines created an impression of widespread sniping, with the
police singled out as the principal targets. A few individual acts of
violence were so enlarged as to convey to the reader a series of
'bloodbaths'. In some cases, an explanation of the circumstances
surrounding the injuries was buried in the news story. In other cases,
no explanation was given. In still other cases, the number of casualties was exaggerated.

Distorted headlines were found in the local press:

RACE VIOLENCE ERUPTS: DOZEN SHOT IN PEORIA
(Chicago (Ill.) *Tribune*,
31 July 1968)

6 COPS ARE SHOT IN HARVEY STRIFE
(Chicago *Sun-Times*,
7 August 1968)

20 HURT AS NEW VIOLENCE RAKES WEST END AREA
11 felled by gun fire, four firemen injured fighting five blazes
(York (Pa.) *Dispatch*,
5 August 1968)

These distortions were transmitted on the wire services as well. For example, in Ann Arbor, Michigan, readers were given the following accounts of Peoria and Harvey-Dixmoor in their local newspapers The first account was based upon a United Press International news dispatch; the second is from an Associated Press dispatch.

10 POLICEMEN SHOT IN PEORIA VIOLENCE

> (By United Press International
> Ann Arbor (Mich.) *News*,
> 30 July 1968)

Ten policemen were wounded by shotgun blasts today during a four-hour flareup of violence in Peoria, Ill. . . .

EIGHT WOUNDED IN CHICAGO AREA

> (Ann Arbor *News*,
> 7 August 1968)

Harvey, Ill. (AP) – Sporadic gunfire wounded seven policemen and a woman during a disturbance caused by Negro youths, and scores of law enforcement officers moved in early today to secure the troubled area. . . .

Finally, they were repeated in headlines and stories appearing in the national press:

GUNFIRE HITS 11 POLICEMEN IN ILL. VIOLENCE

> (*Washington Post*,
> 31 July 1968)

SHOTGUN ASSAULTS IN PEORIA GHETTO WOUND 9 POLICEMEN

> (*The Law Officer*,
> Fall, 1968)

Chicago – On August 6, in the suburbs of Harvey and Dixmoor, seven policemen and a woman were shot in Negro disturbances which a Cook County undersheriff said bore signs of having been planned.

> (*U.S. News & World Report*
> 19 August 1968)

In all probability, few newspapers or reporters could withstand this type of criticism. Nevertheless, it does seem that the national press bears a special responsibility. Few of the nationally known newspapers and magazines attempted to verify sniping reports coming out of the cities; few were willing to undertake independent investigations of their own; and far too many were overly zealous in their reports of a 'trend' based on limited and unconfirmed evidence. Stated very simply: The national press overreacted.

For some time now, many observers (including members of the academic community) have been predicting a change from spontaneous to premeditated outbreaks resembling guerilla warfare. Their predictions have largely been based upon limited evidence such as unconfirmed reports of arms caches and the defiant, sometimes revolutionary rhetoric of militants.

And then came Cleveland. At the time, the July disorder in that city appeared to fulfil all the predictions – intelligence reports of planning prior to the disorder, intensive sniping directed at the police, the absence of a precipitating incident, and so on. Few people at the time quarrelled with the appraisal in the *New York Times* that Cleveland was 'perhaps the first documented case' of a planned uprising against the police. Following the events in Cleveland, disorders in which shots may have been fired were immediately suspected to be part of a 'wave'.

Unwittingly or not, the press has been constructing a scenario on armed uprisings. The story line of this scenario is not totally removed from reality. There *have* been a few shoot-outs with the police, and a handful may have been planned. But no wave of uprisings and no set pattern of murderous conflict have developed – at least not yet. Has the press provided the script for future conspiracies? Why hasn't the scenario been acted out until now? The answers to these questions are by no means certain. What is clear is that the press has critical responsibilities in this area, for any act of violence easily attracts the attention of the vicarious viewer as well as the participant.

Moreover, in an era when most Americans are informed by radio and television, the press should place far greater emphasis on interpreting, rather than merely reporting, the news. Background pieces on the precipitating events and tension-heightening incidents, more detailed information on the sniper himself, and investigations concerning police and civilian casualties represent fertile areas for the news analyst. To close, here is one concrete example: While four policemen were killed in the violence reviewed in this article, at least 16 civilians were also killed. A report on the circumstances of these deaths might provide some important insights into the disorders.

SUGGESTED FURTHER READING

Richard Hofstadter, *The paranoid style in American politics and other essays* (New York, Knopf, 1966). A historian looks at the receptiveness of Americans to conspiratorial theories.

Louis H. Masotti and James J. Corsi, *Shoot-out in Cleveland; Black militants and the police: July 23, 1968.* A report of the Civil Violence

Research Center (Cleveland, Ohio, Case Western Reserve University, submitted to the National Commission on the Causes and Prevention of Violence, 16 May 1969). This is an in-depth account of the background, nature, and circumstances of the July 1968 disorder.

National League of Cities, Department of Urban Studies, Public information and civil disorders (Washington, D.C., July, 1968) contains recommendations concerning the activities of the news media during civil disorders.

Report of the National Advisory Commission on Civil Disorders (Washington, D.C., Government Publishing Office, 1968). Chapter 15 evaluates the media coverage of civil disorders during the summer of 1967.

Mods and Rockers:
the inventory as manufactured news*

STANLEY COHEN

The scene for the first Mods and Rockers 'event', the one that was to set the pattern for all the others and give the phenomenon its distinctive shape was Clacton, a small holiday resort on the East Coast. This was the traditional gathering place over Bank Holiday weekends for kids from the East End and the North East suburbs of London.

Its range of facilities and amusements for young people is strictly limited and Easter 1964 was worse than usual.

It was cold and wet, and in fact Easter Sunday was the coldest for 80 years. The shopkeepers and stall owners were irritated by the lack of business and the young people had their own boredom and irritation fanned by rumours of café owners and barmen refusing to serve some of them. A few groups started scuffling on the pavements and throwing stones at each other. The Mods and Rockers factions – a division initially based on clothing and life styles, later rigidified, but at that time only vaguely in the air – started separating out. Those on bikes and scooters roared up and down, windows were broken, some beach huts were wrecked and one boy fired a starting pistol in the air. The vast number of people crowding into the streets, the noise, everyone's general irritation and the actions of an unprepared and undermanned police force had the effect of making the two days unpleasant, oppressive and sometimes frightening.

Immediately after a physical disaster there is a period of relatively unorganized response. This is followed by what disaster researchers call 'the inventory phase' during which those exposed to the disaster take stock of what has happened and of their own condition. In this period, rumours and ambiguous perceptions become the basis for interpreting the situation. Immediately after the Aberfan coal tip disaster, for example, there were rumours about the tip having been seen moving the night before and previous warnings having

* This is an abbreviated form of material that appears in Chapter 2 of *Folk devils and moral panics: The creation of the Mods and Rockers* (London, Mac-Gibbon & Kee, 1972).

been ignored. These reports were to form the basis of later accusations of negligence against the National Coal Board, and the negligence theme then became assimilated into more deep-rooted attitudes, for example, about indifference by the central government to Welsh interests.

I am concerned here with the way in which the situation was initially interpreted and presented by the mass media, because it is in this form that most people receive their pictures of both deviance and disasters. Reactions take place on the basis of these processed or coded images: people become indignant or angry, formulate theories and plans, make speeches, write letters to the newspapers. The media presentation or inventory of the Mods and Rockers events is crucial in determining the later stages of the reaction.

On the Monday morning following the initial incidents at Clacton, every national newspaper, with the exception of *The Times* (fifth lead on main news page) carried a leading report on the subject. The headlines are self-descriptive: DAY OF TERROR BY SCOOTER GROUPS (*Daily Telegraph*), YOUNGSTERS BEAT UP TOWN – 97 LEATHER JACKET ARRESTS (*Daily Express*), WILD ONES INVADE SEASIDE – 97 ARRESTS (*Daily Mirror*). The next lot of incidents received similar coverage on the Tuesday and editorials began to appear, together with reports that the Home Secretary was 'being urged' (it was not usually specified exactly by *whom*) to hold an enquiry or to take firm action. Feature articles then appeared highlighting interviews with Mods or Rockers. Straight reporting gave way to theories especially about motivation: the mob was described as 'exhilarated', 'drunk with notoriety', 'hell-bent for destruction', etc. Reports of the incidents themselves were followed by accounts of police and court activity and local reaction. The press coverage of each series of incidents showed a similar sequence.

Overseas coverage was extensive throughout; particularly in America, Canada, Australia, South Africa and the Continent. The *New York Times* and *New York Herald Tribune* carried large photos, after Whitsun, of two girls fighting. Belgian papers captioned their photos, 'West Side Story on English Coast'.

It is difficult to assess conclusively the accuracy of these early reports. Even if each incident could have been observed, a physical impossibility, one could never check the veracity of, say, an interview. In many cases, one 'knows' that the interview must be, partly at least, journalistic fabrication because it is too stereotypical to be true, but this is far from objective proof. Nevertheless, on the basis of those incidents that were observed, interviews with people who were present at others (local reporters, photographers, deck-chair attendants, etc.) and a careful check on internal consistency, some estimate of the main distortions can be made. Checks with the local press are particularly revealing. Not only are the reports more detailed and specific, but they avoid statements like 'all the dance halls near the seafront were smashed' when every local resident knows that there is only one dance hall near the front.

The media inventory of each initial incident will be analysed under three headings: (i) Exaggeration and distortion, (ii) Prediction, and (iii) Symbolization.

EXAGGERATION AND DISTORTION

Writing when the Mods and Rockers phenomenon was passing its peak, a journalist recalls that a few days after the initial event at Clacton, the Assistant Editor of the *Daily Mirror* admitted in conversation that the affair had been 'a little over-reported'.[1] It is this 'over-reporting' that I am interested in here.

The major type of distortion in the inventory lay in exaggerating grossly the seriousness of the events, in terms of criteria such as the number taking part, the number involved in violence and the amount and effects of any damage or violence. Such distortion took place primarily in terms of the mode and style of presentation characteristic of most crime reporting: the sensational headlines, the melodramatic vocabulary and the deliberate heightening of those elements in the story considered as news. The regular use of phrases such as 'riot', 'orgy of destruction', 'battle', 'attack', 'siege', 'beat up the town' and 'screaming mob' left an image of a besieged town from which innocent holidaymakers were fleeing to escape a marauding mob.

During Whitsun 1964, even the local papers in Brighton referred to 'deserted beaches' and 'elderly holidaymakers' trying to escape the 'screaming teenagers'. One had to scan the rest of the paper or be present on the spot to know that on the day referred to (Monday, 18 May) the beaches were deserted because the weather was particularly bad. The holidaymakers that *were* present were there to watch the Mods and Rockers. Although at other times (for example, August 1964 at Hastings) there was intimidation, there was very little of this in the Brighton incident referred to. In the 1965 and 1966 incidents, there was even less intimidation, yet the incidents were ritualistically reported in the same way, using the same metaphors, headline and vocabulary.

The full flavour of such reports is captured in the following lines from the *Daily Express* (19 May 1964):

There was Dad asleep in a deckchair and Mum making sandcastles with the children, when the 1964 boys took over the beaches at

Margate and Brighton yesterday and smeared the traditional postcard scene with blood and violence.

This type of 'over-reporting' is, of course, not peculiar to the Mods and Rockers. It is characteristic not just of crime reporting as a whole, but mass media inventories of such events as political protests, racial disturbances and so on. What Knopf[2] calls the 'shotgun approach' to such subjects – the front-page build-up, the splashy pictures, the boxscores of the latest riot news – has become accepted in journalism. So accepted, in fact, that the media and their audiences have lost even a tenuous hold on the meaning of the words they use. How is a town 'beaten up' or 'besieged'? How many shop windows have to be broken for an 'orgy of destruction' to have taken place? When can one – even metaphorically – talk of scenes being 'smeared with blood and violence'? Commenting on the way the term 'riot' is used to cover both an incident resulting in 43 deaths, 7000 arrests and $45 million in property damage *and* one in which three people broke a shop window, Knopf remarks: 'The continued media use of the term contributes to an emotionally charged climate in which the public tends to view every event as an "incident", every incident as a "disturbance" and every disturbance as a "riot".'[3]

The sources of over-reporting lay not just in such abuses of language. There was a frequent use of misleading headlines, particularly headlines which were discrepant with the actual story: thus a headline 'violence' might announce a story which, in fact, reports that *no* violence occurred. Then there were more subtle and often unconscious journalistic practices: the use of the generic plural (if a boat was overturned, reports read 'boats were overturned') and the technique, well known to war correspondents, of reporting the same incident twice to look like two different incidents.

Another source of distortion lay in the publication, usually in good faith, of reports which were later to receive quite a different perspective by fresh evidence. The repetition of obviously false stories, despite known confirmation of this, is a familiar finding in studies of the role of the press in spreading mass hysteria.[4] An important example in the Mods and Rockers inventory was the frequently used '£75 cheque story'. It was widely reported that a boy had told the Margate magistrates that he would pay the £75 fine imposed on him with a cheque. This story was true enough; what few papers bothered to publish and what they all knew, was that the boy's offer was a pathetic gesture of bravado. He later admitted that not only did he not have the £75, but he did not even have a bank account and had never signed a cheque in his life. As long as four years after this, though, the story was still being repeated and was quoted to me

at a magistrates' conference in 1968 to illustrate the image of the
Mods and Rockers as affluent hordes whom 'fines couldn't touch'.

This story had some factual basis, even though its real meaning
was lost. At other times, stories of organization, leadership, particular incidents of violence and vandalism were based on little
more than unconfirmed rumour. These stories are important because
– as I will show in detail – they enter into the consciousness and
shape the societal reaction at later stages. It is worth quoting at
length a particularly vivid example from the media coverage of an
American incident:

> In York, Pa., in mid-July, 1968 . . . incidents of rock- and bottle-
> throwing were reported. Towards the end of the disturbance
> UPI in Harrisburg asked a stringer to get something on the situa-
> tion. A photographer took a picture of a motor cyclist with an
> ammunition belt around his waist and a rifle strapped across his
> back. A small object dangled from the rifle. On July 18, the picture
> reached the nation's press. The *Washington Post* said: 'ARMED
> RIDER – Unidentified motorcyclist drives through heart of York,
> Pa., Negro district, which was quiet for the first time in six days of
> sporadic disorders.' The *Baltimore Sun* used the same picture and
> a similar caption: 'QUIET BUT . . . An unidentified motorcycle
> rider armed with a rifle and carrying a belt of ammunition, was
> among those in the heart of York, Pa., Negro district last night.
> The area was quiet for the first time in six days'.
>
> The implication of this photograph was clear: the 'armed rider'
> was a sniper. But since when do snipers travel openly in daylight
> completely armed? Also, isn't there something incongruous about
> photographing a sniper, presumably 'on his way to work,' when
> according to the caption, the city 'was quiet'? Actually, the 'armed
> rider' was a sixteen-year-old boy who happened to be fond of
> hunting groundhogs – a skill he had learned as a small boy from
> his father. On July 16, as was his custom, the young man had
> put on his ammo belt and strapped a rifle across his back, letting
> a hunting licence dangle so that all would know he was hunting
> animals, not people. Off he went on his motorcycle headed for the
> woods, the fields, the groundhogs – and the place reserved for
> him in the nation's press.[5]

Moving from the form to the content of the inventory, a detailed
analysis reveals that much of the image of the deviation presented
was, in Lemert's term, putative: '. . . that portion of the societal
definition of the deviant which has no foundation in his objective
behaviour'.[6] The following is a composite of the mass media inventory:

> Gangs of Mods and Rockers from the suburbs of London invaded,
> on motor bikes and scooters, a number of seaside resorts. These

were affluent young people, from all social classes. They came down deliberately to cause trouble by behaving aggressively towards visitors, local residents and the police. They attacked innocent holidaymakers and destroyed a great deal of public property. This cost the resorts large sums of money in repairing the damage and a further loss of trade through potential visitors being scared to come down.

The evidence for the ten elements in this composite picture is summarized below:

(i) *Gangs.* There was no evidence of any structured gangs. The groups were loose collectivities or crowds within which there was occasionally some more structured grouping based on territorial loyalty, e.g., 'The Walthamstow Boys'.

(ii) *Mods and Rockers.* Initially at least, the groups were not polarized along the Mod-Rocker dimension. At Clacton, for example, the rivalry (already in existence for many years) between on the one hand those from London and on the other locals and youths from the surrounding counties, was a much more significant dimension. The Mod-Rocker polarization was institutionalized later and partly as a consequence of the initial publicity. In addition, throughout the whole life of the phenomenon, many of the young people coming down to the resorts did not identify with either group.

(iii) *Invasion from London.* Although the bulk of day trippers, young and old, were from London, this was simply the traditional bank holiday pattern. Not all offenders were from London; many were either local residents or came from neighbouring towns or villages. This was particularly true of the Rockers who, in Clacton and Great Yarmouth, came mainly from East Anglian villages. The origins of 54 youths, on whom information was obtainable, out of the 64 charged at Hastings (August 1964) was as follows: London or Middlesex suburbs – 20; Welwyn Garden City – 4; small towns in Kent – 9; Sussex – 7; Essex – 4; and Surrey – 10.

(iv) *Motor bikes and scooters.* At every event the majority of young people present came down by train or coach or hitched. The motor bike or scooter owners were always a minority; albeit a noisy minority that easily gave the impression of ubiquity.

(v) *Affluence.* There is no clear-cut information here of the type that could be obtained from a random sample of the crowd. Work on the Brighton Weekend Project and all information from other sources suggest that the young people coming down were not particularly well off. Certainly for those charged in the courts, there is no basis for the affluence image. The average take-home pay in Barker and Little's Margate sample was £11 per week.[7] The original Clacton offenders had on them an average of 75p for the whole

Bank Holiday weekend. The best off was a window cleaner earning £15 a week, but more typical were a market assistant earning £7·50 and a 17-year-old office boy earning £5·12.

(vi) *Classless*. Indices such as accent and area of residence, gathered from court reports and observation, suggest that both the crowds and the offenders were predominantly working class. In the Barker–Little sample, the typical Rocker was an unskilled manual worker, the typical Mod a semi-skilled manual worker. All but two had left school at fifteen. At Clacton, out of the 24 charged, 23 had left school at fifteen, and 22 had been to Secondary Moderns. All were unskilled; there were no apprentices or anyone receiving any kind of training.

(vii) *Deliberate intent*. The bulk of young people present at the resorts came down not so much to make trouble as in the hope that there would be some trouble to watch. Their very presence, their readiness to be drawn into a situation of trouble and the sheer accretion of relatively trivial incidents were found inconvenient and offensive; but if there really had been great numbers deliberately intent on causing trouble, there would have been more trouble. The proportion of those whom the police would term 'trouble-makers' was always small. This hard core was more evident at Clacton then at any of the subsequent events: 23 out of the 24 charged (97 were originally arrested) had previous convictions.

(viii) *Violence and vandalism*. Acts of violence and vandalism are the most tangible manifestations of what the press and public regard as hooliganism. These acts were therefore played up rather than the less melodramatic effect of the Mods and Rockers which was being a nuisance and inconvenience to many adults. In fact, the total amount of serious violence and vandalism was not great. Only about one-tenth of the Clacton offenders was charged with offences involving violence. At Margate, Whitsun 1964, supposedly one of the most violent events – the one which provoked the *Daily Express* 'blood and violence' report – the only major recorded violence consisted of two stabbings and the dropping of a man on to a flower bed. At Hastings, August 1964, out of 44 found guilty, there were three cases of assaulting the police. At Brighton, Easter 1965, out of 70 arrests there were 7 for assault. Even if the definition of violence were broadened to include obstruction and the use of threatening behaviour, the targets were rarely 'innocent holidaymakers', but members of a rival group, or, more often, the police. The number of recorded cases of malicious damage to property was also small; less than 10 per cent of all cases charged in the courts. The typical offence throughout was obstructing the police or the use of threatening behaviour. In Clacton, although hardly any newspapers mentioned this, a number of the 24 were charged with 'non-hooligan' type offences: stealing half a pint of petrol, attempting to steal drinks from a vending machine and 'obtaining credit to the amount of 7d. by means of fraud other than false pretences' (an ice cream).

(ix) *Cost of damage.* The court figures for malicious damage admittedly underestimate the extent of vandalism because much of this goes undetected. Nevertheless, an examination of the figures given for the cost of the damage suggests that this was not as excessive as reported. Table 1 shows the cost of damage at the first four events.

TABLE 1

COST OF DAMAGE TO FOUR RESORTS: EASTER
AND WHITSUN, 1964

Place	Date	No. of arrests	Estimated cost of damage
Clacton	Easter, 1964	97	£513
Bournemouth	Whitsun, 1964	56	£100
Brighton	Whitsun, 1964	76	£400
Margate	Whitsun, 1964	64	£250

SOURCE: Estimates by local authorities quoted in local press.

It must be remembered also that a certain amount of damage to local authority property takes place every Bank Holiday. According to the Deputy Publicity Manager of Margate,[8] for example, the number of deck-chairs broken (50) was not much greater than on an ordinary Bank Holiday weekend; there were also more chairs out on Whit Sunday than ever before.

(x) *Loss of trade.* The press, particularly the local press, laid great emphasis on the financial loss the resorts had suffered and would suffer on account of the Mods and Rockers through cancelled holidays, less use of facilities, loss of trade in shops, restaurants and hotels. The evidence for any such loss is at best dubious. Under the heading, THOSE WILD ONES ARE TO BLAME AGAIN, the Brighton *Evening Argus* quoted figures after Whitsun 1964 to show that, compared with the previous Whitsun, the number of deck-chairs hired had dropped by 8000 and the number using the swimming pool by 1500. But the number using the miniature railway increased by 2000, as did the number of users of the putting green. These figures make sense when one knows that, on the day referred to, the temperature had dropped by 14°F, and it had been raining the night before. This is the main reason why there was less use of deck-chairs and the swimming pool. In Hastings, August 1964, despite a big scare-publicity build up, the number of visitors coming down by train increased by 6000 over the previous year.[9] Newspapers often quoted 'loss of trade' estimates by landlords, hotel keepers and local authority officials, but invariably, final figures of damage fell below the first estimates. These revised figures, however, came too late to have any news value.

Although there were cases of people being scared away by reports of the disturbances, the overall effect was the opposite. The Margate publicity department had a letter from a travel agent in Ireland saying that the events had 'put Margate on the map'. Leaving aside the additional young people themselves attracted by the publicity – they would not be defined as commercial assets – many adults as well came down to watch the fun. I was often asked, on the way down from Brighton station, 'Where are the Mods and Rockers today?', and near the beaches, parents could be seen holding children on their shoulders to get a better view of the proceedings. In an interview with a reporter during which I was present, a man said, 'My wife and I came down with our son (aged 18) to see what all this fun is at the seaside on Bank Holidays.' (*Evening Argus* 30 May 1964). By 1965 the happenings were part of the scene – the pier, the whelks, the Mods and Rockers could all be taken in on a day trip.

PREDICTION

There is another element in the inventory which needs to be discussed separately because it assumes a special importance in later stages. This is the implicit assumption, present in virtually every report, that what had happened was inevitably going to happen again. Few assumed that the events were transient occurrences; the only questions were where the Mods and Rockers would strike next and what could be done about it. As will be suggested, these predictions played the role of the classical self-fulfilling prophecy. Unlike the case of natural disasters where the absence of predictions can be disastrous, with social phenomena such as deviance, it is the presence of predictions that can be 'disastrous'.

The predictions in the inventory period took the form of reported statements from local figures such as tradesmen, councillors, and police spokesmen about what should be done 'next time' or of immediate precautions they had taken. More important, youths were asked in TV interviews about their plans for the next Bank Holiday and interviews were printed with either a Mod or a Rocker threatening revenge 'next time'. The following are extracts from two such interviews: 'Southend and places won't let us in any more. It will get difficult here and so next year we'll probably go to Ramsgate or Hastings.' (*Daily Express* 30 March 1964). 'It could have been better – the weather spoiled it a bit. Wait until next Whitsun. Now that will be a real giggle.' (*Daily Mirror* 31 March 1964).

Where predictions were not fulfilled, a story could still be found by reporting non-events. So, for example, when attention was switched to East Anglian resorts in 1966, the *East Anglian Daily Times* (30 May 1966) headed a report on a play attended by a group of long-haired youths, FEARS WHEN TON-UP BOYS WALKED IN GROUND-LESS. Reporters and photographers were often sent on the basis of false tip-offs to events that did not materialize. In Whitsun 1965, a *Daily Mirror* report from Hastings, where nothing at all happened was headed, HASTINGS – WITHOUT THEM. In Whitsun 1966, there was, a report (*Daily Mirror* 30 May 1966) on how policemen on a 'Mods and Rockers patrol' in Clacton could only use their specially provided walkie-talkies to help two lost little boys. Again, headlines often created the impression that something had happened: the *Evening Argus* (30 May 1966) used the subheading VIOLENCE to report that 'in Brighton there was no violence in spite of the crowds of teenagers on the beach'.

These non-event stories and other distortions springing from the prediction theme are part of the broader tendency which I will discuss later whereby discrepancies between expectations and reality are resolved by emphasizing those new elements which confirm expectations and playing down those which are contradictory. Commenting on this tendency in their analysis of the media coverage of the October 1968 Vietnam war demonstrations, Halloran et al.[10] draw attention to a technique often employed in the Mods and Rockers inventory '. . . a phase or sentence describing in highly emotive terms either the expectation of violence or an isolated incident of violence, is followed by a completely contradictory sentence describing the actual situation'.

The cumulative effect of such reports was to establish predictions whose truth was guaranteed by the way in which the event, non-event or pseudo-event it referred to was reported.

SYMBOLIZATION

Communication, and especially the mass communication of stereotypes, depends on the symbolic power of words and images. Neutral words such as place names can be made to symbolize complex ideas and emotions; for example, Pearl Harbour, Hiroshima, Dallas and Aberfan. A similar process occurred in the Mods and Rockers inventory: these words themselves and a word such as 'Clacton' acquired symbolic powers. It became meaningful to say

'We don't want another Clacton here', or 'You can see he's one of those Mod types'.

There appear to be three processes in such symbolization: a word (Mod) becomes symbolic of a certain status (delinquent or deviant); objects (hairstyle, clothing) symbolize the word; the objects themselves become symbolic of the status (and the emotions attached to the status). The cumulative effect of these three processes as they appeared in the inventory was that the terms Mods and Rockers were torn from any previously neutral contexts (for example, the denotation of different consumer styles) and acquired wholly negative meanings. The identical effect is described by Turner and Surace in their classic study of the 1943 Zoot Suit riots[11] and by Rock and myself in tracing how the Edwardian dress style became transformed into the Teddy Boy folk devil.[12]

In their case study, Turner and Surace refer to this process as the creation of 'unambiguously unfavourable symbols'. Newspaper headlines and interpersonal communication following the initial incidents in Los Angeles reiterated the phobia and hatred towards Mexican American youth. References to this group were made in such a way as to strip key symbols (differences in fashion, job style and entertainment) from their favourable or neutral connotations until they came to evoke unambiguously unfavourable feelings. Content analysis showed a switch in the references to Mexicans to the 'Zooter theme', which identified this particular clothing style as the 'badge of delinquency' and coupled such references with mention of zoot suiter attacks and orgies. Invariably the Zooter was identified with the generalized Mexican group. In the same way, the Mods and Rockers status traits were, in later stages of the reaction, to wash off on the generalized adolescent group. Their 'badge of delinquency' emerged as symbols, such as the fur-collared anorak and the scooter, which became sufficient in themselves to stimulate hostile and punitive reactions.[13]

Symbols and labels eventually acquire their own descriptive and explanatory potential. Thus – to take examples from an earlier folk devil – the label 'Teddy Boy' became a general term of abuse (for example, John Osborne being described as 'an intellectual Teddy Boy'); the devil was seen as a distinct type of personality (drugs were announced to soothe Teddy Boys and make them co-operative for treatment, statements made such as 'some of these soldiers here are just Teddy Boys in army uniform') and the symbols were seen as changing the person ('He was never in trouble before he bought an Edwardian suit'; 'Since my son bought this thing a year ago his personality has changed').

Such symbolization is partly the consequence of the same standard mass communication processes which give rise to exaggeration and distortion. Thus, for example, misleading and inappropriate head-lines were used to create unambiguously negative symbols where the actual event did not warrant this at all or at least was ambiguous. Accounts of certain events in Whitsun 1964, for example, were coupled with a report of a 'Mod' falling to his death from a cliff outside Brighton. Similarly in August 1964 there were headlines, MOD DEAD IN SEA. In neither case had these deaths anything to do with the disturbances; they were both pure accidents. A reading of the headlines only, or of early reports not mentioning police state-ments about the accidents, might have led to a misleading connec-tion. This sort of effect reached its bizarre heights in a headline in the *Dublin Evening Press* (18 May 1964) TERROR COMES TO ENGLISH RESORTS. MUTILATED MOD DEAD IN PARK. The 'mutilated Mod' was, in fact, a man of 21–25 wearing a 'mod jacket'(?) who was found stabbed on the Saturday morning (the day *before* the incidents at the resorts) in a Birmingham park.[14]

Another highly effective technique of symbolization was the use of dramatized and ritualistic interviews with 'representative members' of either group. The *Daily Mirror* (31 March 1964) had (Mick 'The Wild One' on WHY I HURLED THAT CHISEL and another boy who said, 'I take pep pills. Everybody does here.' The *Daily Herald* (18 May 1964) quoted one boy clutching his injured head as the police bundled him into a van saying, 'Carry on with the plan.' Another said, 'We're not through yet. We're here for the holiday and we're staying. Margate will wish it was Clacton when we're finished.' The *Evening Standard* (19 May 1964) found 'The Baron' who hated 'Mods and Wogs' and said, 'I like fighting . . . I have been fighting all my life.' The *Daily Mirror* (8 May 1964) found a new angle with THE GIRLS WHO FOLLOW THE WILD ONES INTO BATTLE, and who said about fighting: '. . . it gives you a kick, a thrill, it makes you feel all funny inside. You get butterflies in your stomach and you want the boys to go on and on . . . It's hard luck on the people who get in their way, but you can't do anything about that.'

It is difficult to establish how authentic these interviews are. In some cases they ring so patently absurd a note that they cannot be an accurate transcription of what was actually said. The *Daily Telegraph* (31 May 1964), for example, carried an interview with a Rocker who said, 'We are known as the Rockers and are much more with it.' If any group had a 'with it' self-image and would even contemplate using such a term, it certainly was not the Rockers. It would be fair to describe those interviews and reports as being composite, not necessarily in the sense of being wilfully faked, but as being influenced by the reporter's (or sub-editor's) conception of how anyone labelled as a thug or a hooligan *should* speak, dress and act. This effect may have occasionally been heightened by a certain gullibility about the fantasies of self-styled gang leaders.[15]

Through symbolization, plus the other types of exaggeration and distortion, images are made much sharper than reality. There is no reason to assume that photographs or television reports are any more 'objective'. In a study of the different perceptions experienced by TV viewers and on-the-spot spectators of another crowd situation (MacArthur Day in Chicago), it was shown how the reporting was distorted by the selection of items to fit into already existing expectations.[16] A sharpening up process occurs, producing emotionally toned symbols which eventually acquire their own momentum. Thus the dissemination of overwhelming public support in favour of MacArthur '. . . gathered force as it was incorporated into political strategy, picked up by other media, entered into gossip and thus came to overshadow immediate reality as it might have been recorded by an observer on the scene'.[17]

In this study, observers recorded how their expectations of political enthusiasm and wild mass involvement were completely unfulfilled. Through close ups and a particular style of commentary ('the most enthusiastic crowd ever in our city . . . you can feel the tenseness in the air . . . you can hear the crowd roar') television structured the whole event to convey emotions non-existent to the participants. This effect explains why many spectators at the Mods and Rockers events found them a slight let-down after the mass media publicity. As Boorstin remarks in discussing the effects of television and colour photography: 'Verisimilitude took on a new meaning . . . The Grand Canyon itself became a disappointing reproduction of the Kodachrome original.'[18]

THE INVENTORY AS MANUFACTURED NEWS

The cumulative effects of the inventory can be summarized as follows: (i) the putative deviation had been assigned from which further stereotyping, myth making and labelling could proceed; (ii) the expectation was created that this form of deviation would certainly recur; (iii) a wholly negative symbolization in regard to the Mods and Rockers and objects associated with them had been created; (iv) all the elements in the situation had been made clear enough to allow for full-scale demonology and hagiology to develop: the information had been made available for placing the Mods and Rockers in the gallery of contemporary folk devils.

Why do these sort of inventories result? Are they in any sense 'inevitable'? What are the reasons for bias, exaggeration and distortion? To make sense of questions such as these, one must understand that the inventory is not, of course, a simple sort of stock-taking in which some errors might accidentally creep in from time to time. Built into the very nature of deviance inventories in modern society are elements of fantasy, selective misperception and the deliberate creation of news. The inventory is not reflective stock-taking but manufactured news.

Before pursuing this notion, let me mention some of the more 'genuine' errors. On one level, much exaggeration and distortion arose simply from the ambiguous and confused nature of the situation. It is notoriously difficult in a crowd setting to estimate the numbers present and some of the overestimates were probably no more than would have occurred after events such as political demonstrations, religious rallies, pop concerts or sporting fixtures. The confusion was heightened by the presence of so many reporters and photographers: their very presence could be interpreted as 'evidence' that something massive and important was happening.

It was a problem for everyone present – police, spectators, participants, newsmen – actually to know what was happening at any one time. In such situations, the gullibility effect is less significant than a general susceptibility to all sorts of rumours. Clark and Barker's classic case study of a participant in a race riot shows this effect very clearly,[19] and in disaster research prospective interviewers are warned, 'People who have discussed their experiences with others in the community can rapidly assimilate inaccurate versions of the disaster. These group versions may quickly come to be accepted by a large segment of the population.[20]

Important as such errors may be in the short run, they cannot explain the more intrinsic features of deviance inventories: processes such as symbolization and prediction, the direction of the distortions rather than the simple fact of their occurrence, the decision to report the deviance in the first place and to continue to report it in a particular way. Studies of moral panics associated with the Mods and Rockers and other forms of deviance, as well as detailed research on the mass communication process itself (such as that by Halloran and his colleagues) indicate that two interrelated factors determine the presentation of deviance inventories: the first is the institutionalized need to create news and the second is the selective and inferential structure of the news-making process.

The weekend of the Clacton event was particularly dull from a news point of view. Nothing particularly noteworthy happened nationally or internationally. The fact that the event was given such prominence must be due partly at least to the absence of alternative news. The behaviour itself was not particularly new or startling.

Disturbances of various sorts – variously called 'hooliganism', 'rowdyism' or 'gang fights' – occurred frequently throughout the late 1950s and early 1960s in coastal resorts favoured by working-class adolescents. In 1958, for example, Southend police had to appeal for outside support after rival groups had fought battles on the pier. In Whitley Bay, Blackpool and other Northern resorts there were disturbances and fighting often more severe than any of the early Mods and Rockers episodes. For years British holidaymakers on day trips or weekend excursions to such European coastal resorts as Calais and Ostend have been involved in considerable violence and vandalism. In Ostend, from the beginning of the 1960s, there was a period of the year referred to as the 'English season' during which holidaymakers and members of amateur football clubs caused considerable damage and trouble, rarely reported in the British press. The Mods and Rockers didn't become news because they were new; they were presented as new to justify their creation as news.

It would be facile to explain the creation of the inventory purely in terms of it being 'good news'; the point is simply that there was room for a story at that initial weekend and that its selection was not entirely due to its intrinsic properties. Labelling theorists have drawn attention to the complex nature of the screening and coding process whereby certain forms of rule-breaking are picked out for attention. Such processes relate to social control as a whole and not just the media. The media reflected the real conflict of interests that existed at various levels: for example, between local residents and police on the one hand and the Mods and Rockers on the other. In such situations the media adjudicate between competing definitions of the situation, and as these definitions are made in a hierarchical context – agents of social control are more likely to be believed than deviants – it is clear which definition will win out in an ambiguous and shifting situation.[21]

NOTES AND REFERENCES

1. Peter Laurie, *The teenage revolution* (London, Anthony Blond Ltd, 1965), p. 130.
2. Terry Ann Knopf, 'Media myths on violence', *Columbia Journalism Review* (Spring 1970), pp. 17–18. See also article by Knopf in this Reader.
3. Ibid., p. 20.
4. See, for example, Norman Jacobs, 'The phantom slasher of Taipei: mass hysteria in a non western society', *Social Problems* 12 (Winter 1965), p. 322.
5. Knopf, op. cit., p. 18.

6. Edwin M. Lemert, *Social pathology* (New York, McGraw-Hill, 1951), p. 55.
7. Paul Barker and Alan Little, 'The Margate offenders: a survey', *New society* (30 July 1964).
8. Interview (23 November 1964).
9. Estimate by Hastings Stationmaster, quoted in *Hastings and St. Leonards Observer* (8 August 1964).
10. James D. Halloran et al., *Demonstrations and communications*: *A case study* (Harmondsworth, Penguin Books, 1970), p. 112.
11. Ralph H. Turner and Samuel J. Surace, 'Zoot Suiters and Mexicans: symbols in crowd behaviour', *American Journal of Sociology* 62 (1956), pp. 14–20.
12. Paul Rock and Stanley Cohen, 'The Teddy Boy' in V. Bogdanor and P. Skidelsky (eds.), *The age of affluence 1951–1964* (London, Macmillan, 1970).
13. During the inventory period, scooter owners and manufacturers frequently complained about the bad publicity that they were getting. After Clacton, the General Secretaries of the Vespa and Lambretta Scooter Clubs issued a statement dissociating their clubs from the disturbances.
14. Newspapers furthest away from the source invariably carried the greatest distortions and inaccuracies. The *Glasgow Daily Record and Mail* (20 May 1964), for example, described Mods as being dressed in short jacketed suits, with bell bottoms, high boots, bowler or top hats and carrying rolled up umbrellas.
15. Yablonsky has provided numerous examples of how outside observers accept at face value the fantasies of gang leaders and members. See Lewis Yablonsky, *The violent gang* (New York, Free Press, 1962).
16. Kurt and Gladys Lang, 'The unique perspective of television and its effect: A pilot study', *American Sociological Review* 18 (February 1953), pp. 3–12. Halloran and his colleagues (op. cit.) report an identical process in their analysis of the TV coverage of the 1968 anti-Vietnam war demonstrations.
17. Ibid., p. 10.
18. Daniel J. Boorstin, *The image* (Harmondsworth, Penguin Books, 1963), p. 25.
19. Kenneth B. Clark and James Barker, 'The Zoot effect in personality: A race riot participant', *Journal of Abnormal and Social Psychology* 40 (1965), pp. 143–8.
20. I. H. Cissin and W. B. Clark, 'The methodological challenge of disaster research', in G. W. Baker and D. W. Chapman, *Man and society in disaster* (New York, Basic Books, 1962), p. 28.
21. The notion of a 'hierarchy of credibility' in regard to deviance is suggested by Howard S. Becker in his paper 'Whose side are we on?', *Social Problems* 14 (Winter 1967), pp. 239–67.

The British press and Northern Ireland*

EAMONN McCANN

British newspapers are wont to congratulate themselves on their high journalistic standards. The British people are encouraged to believe that their press is the best in the world. Phrases such as 'guardians of liberty' have been known not to stick in the throats of leader writers.

During the past three years, while editors and higher executives have whiled away the time in contemplation of their own ethical purity, the job went on of managing and mangling the news from Northern Ireland.

Most British people have a distorted view of what is happening in Northern Ireland. This is because they believe what they read.

There have been honourable exceptions. But examination of reports reveals a clear pattern of distortion. The news has systematically been presented, consciously or not, so as to justify the assumptions and prejudices of British establishment and to serve the immediate political needs of British governments.

Immediately after 5 October 1968 dozens of journalists descended on Northern Ireland. At one point the *Mirror* had twelve people in Derry. Few of these had any detailed knowledge of the situation. Some, mindful of the May days in France that year, spent much of their time trying to identify a local Danny the Red. Others would wander into the Bogside and ask if they could be introduced to someone who had been discriminated against. Most people prominent in the events preceding the October march had experiences such as Miss Rhoda Churchill of the *Daily Mail* coming to their front door seeking the address of an articulate, Catholic, unemployed slum-dweller she could talk to.

During this period the press was generally favourable to the Civil Rights Movement. Reporters and photographers were well received in Catholic areas; harassed and on a number of occasions physically attacked in Paisleyite demonstrations. Editorially, every paper

* Extracts from pamphlet of same title published by the Northern Ireland Socialist Research Centre (London, Pluto Press, 1971).

backed O'Neill, who was projected as a 'cautious crusader'. There was little or none of the cruder distortion which was to come later.

The coverage of Bernadette Devlin's election and entry into Parliament reflected fairly accurately the attitude of the press around this time. She was depicted as 'the voice of the student generation'. (*Sun*, 19 April 1969). The *Daily Mirror* (19 April 1969) said 'Swinging – that's petite Bernadette Devlin'. 'She's Bernadette, she's 21, she's an MP she's swinging . . . the girl whose honesty, vision and courage has made her the most talked of person in Irish politics for a long time.' (*Daily Express*, 19 April 1969). 'Miss Devlin enthralls packed house' (*The Times*, 23 April 1969). There was much more along similar lines. Obviously the press at the time saw no harm in her.

Despite the generally benevolent coverage of the Civil Rights campaign at this stage one could discern already the tendency to blame 'The IRA' for any violence which occurred. It was assumed for example that the IRA was responsible for the explosions preceding O'Neill's resignation. But this was mild and tentative stuff compared to what came later.

The real, sustained and systematic distortion began when British soldiers came on to the streets, and by the middle of 1970 when the troops were in almost constant conflict with Catholic working-class neighbourhoods most papers had in effect stopped carrying the news. They were vehicles for propaganda. Some incidents were ignored. Others were invented. Half-truths were presented as hard fact.

As far as the British press was concerned the soldiers could do no wrong. Residents of Catholic working-class areas in Belfast and Derry could see rubber bullets being fired at point-blank range, the indiscriminate batoning of bystanders and rioters alike, men being seized and kicked unconscious and then let go. As time went on and weaponry escalated some witnessed the reckless use of firearms, the casual killing of unarmed people, sometimes at a range of a few yards. They experienced the offensive arrogance of soldiers on patrol, the constant barrage of insult and obscenity, and in the British press they read of Tommy's endless patience under intense provocation, of his restraint in the face of ferocious attack, his gentlemanly demeanour in most difficult circumstances.

The other side, 'the rioters', got different treatment. They were represented as vicious and cowardly, almost depraved in their bloodlust.

To say that the press distorted the situation beyond all recognition is not to say that those who came on to the streets to fight British soldiers behaved in a manner which liberal opinion would

Modes and models

find admirable. Of course not. Riots are not like that. In the average Northern Ireland riot neither side gives much quarter. Verbal and physical abuse is fairly unrestrained. There are teenagers in the Bogside who, obscenity for obscenity, could match the best, or the worst the British Army could put up. A soldier seized by a rioting crowd would receive much the same treatment as arrested rioters experience at the hands of the army. But the great majority of the British people, dependent on the press to tell them what is happening in the North of Ireland, are by now *incapable* of forming a judgment about it, so one-sided has the reporting been.

The most abiding myth fostered by the press has been the recurrent story that all riots and troubles are organized. Usually the IRA is credited with this subversive activity, but there have been other candidates, some fanciful, some farcical.

On 11 September 1969, the *Daily Mail* splashed a story under the headline: BERNADETTE'S SINISTER ARMY. It explained that:

Revolutionary extremists are now in complete control of the Civil Rights movement in Ulster. Their declared aim is to turn the whole of Ireland, North and South, into a Cuba-style republic.

People's Democracy, the organization that directed the wave of protest demonstrations which brought Ulster to the brink of civil war, is riddled with Trotskyists and their sympathizers who believe in world-wide revolution . . .

The present turmoil in Ulster has been conceived on Maoist-Castroist-Trotskyist lines, planned the same way and carried out with the traditional weapons of street fighters the world over . . .

Posters, leaflets and revolutionary news sheets are also being printed in London for the Ulster militants, often by the International Socialists' own printing company . . .

Money is also being collected for the revolutionaries.

Ford shop stewards are being asked to hold a whip-round this week.

As Mike Farrell commented gloomily at the time, 'I wish to Christ it was true.'

A good example of the farcical approach came from Mr George Gordon who, under the headline, TROOPS FEAR THE CROAK OF THE FROG reported in the *Daily Sketch* (29 June 1970).

Behind the swirling haze of CS gas, the croak of the frog summons Londonderry to riot. It blares above the crash of the gas canisters and rises over the screams of terror. It is a voice the troops in Bogside would dearly love to identify.

They call it the frog and every soldier now recognizes it after 48 hours of almost continual fighting. It moves from street battle to street battle pouring out a continual stream of hate, vilification and obscenities.

When the rioters flag, the voice urges them on, croaking in rubble-strewn alleys and echoing across the 100 yards of no-man's-land that the tired troops have now held for two days and two nights.

Colourful stuff. Many a piece along similar lines has been sucked from the thumb of a reporter desperate for a new angle.

Northern Ireland has been the subject of almost continuous blanket coverage for nearly three years. One would need to write a book (someone should) to deal adequately with every aspect and example of distortion. It is proposed here to direct most attention towards reports in the British national daily papers since mid 1970, and to examine some reports in detail.

One is not concerned with the tendentious editorial comment or with run-of-the-mill journalistic chicanery. Cynics expect such. Nor is it proposed to deal further with reports which, while questionable, have been relatively harmless. For example the *Mail*'s piece on Miss Devlin's Sinister Army and the *Sketch*'s discovery of the Bogside Frog indicate a certain journalistic standard, but such stuff is not uncommon on a slow news day and in the long term probably has small effect.

THE PRESS AND THE IRA

On Sunday, 16 August last year, 24-year-old Barry Burnett picked up a holdall which has been left by someone in Row 'O' of the stalls in the Empire Theatre, Leicester Square. He had the bag with him when he and his girl friend, Anna Korhonen, drove away in a mini. In the Charing Cross Road a time bomb in the bag exploded. Mr Burnett was seriously hurt. Miss Korhonen sustained multiple injuries and burns for which she was later awarded ten thousand pounds.

Within two days the press had managed to suggest that the IRA was almost certainly responsible. It was an enormous story. On 18 August the *Daily Mirror, Sun* and the *Daily Sketch* each gave it the whole front page. Tom Tullet and Edward Vale reported in the *Mirror,* 'Last night Scotland Yard believed that they were the victims of an Irish Republican Army terror bomb attack.'

Other papers not only indicated that the IRA was responsible but quoted anonymous police spokesmen on the possible motive. The *Daily Mail* said on the front page, 'Police investigating the bomb that blew up a car in the West End of London on Sunday night believe the couple in the car were the innocent victims of IRA terrorists. Detectives suspect the bomb was left in the Empire Cinema, Leicester Square, as a reprisal against the arrest of Irish sympathisers.'

The *Daily Telegraph* offered a slight variation. Describing the theory that the IRA was responsible as 'too strong to ignore', it continued: 'the activities of the Yard's Special Branch during the past few months has caused considerable concern to IRA leaders in Britain. It is thought they may have "lost face" and want to hit back.'

The other newspapers followed suit.

'One police theory is that some of the phone calls are part of a move by the IRA to reassert its importance among members discouraged by police action.' (*Daily Express*)

'The terrorists were believed to have planted the bomb in a bid to reassert their importance following police activity in London and Ulster which has made IRA leaders lose face with followers.' (*Financial Times*)

'The explosions, it was considered, could be part of a face saving operation mounted by IRA men in retaliation for Scotland Yard swoops on their leaders and the discovery of arms caches.' (*Evening Standard*)

'The explosions may be the work of angry IRA militants launching a carefully planned reign of terror following the arrests and charges of six men during the weekend.' (*Evening News*)

Thus, millions of people were led to the belief that the IRA had planted the bomb. Since that time speakers at Irish Republican meetings in Britain have constantly been asked 'what you hoped to gain by planting bombs in cinemas?' Yet at no time was there a shred of evidence to link any Irish group to the incident. The police have discovered no useful leads. No arrest has been made. What happened was that the image of the IRA as bloodthirsty gangsters was emphasized and reinforced.

There are those who would object that, whatever the truth of the Empire Theatre incident, some more recent activities of at least one wing of the IRA are not defensible. This is not the issue. The point is that over a period of many months the British press depicted the IRA in a way which was not based on any available facts. No subsequent events can provide retrospective justification for this pattern of reporting.

The coverage of five days of fierce rioting in the Ardoyne area at the end of October and the beginning of November last year was fairly typical of such stories.

The riots started after three men were shot on 29 October. These were some of the bitterest clashes Belfast had known up to that time.

Stones, petrol bombs and nail bombs were used against the troops. One soldier, Marine Michael Wainwright, had his leg shattered by a nail bomb. At least fourteen other soldiers were injured. On Saturday, 31 October the third day of the rioting, the trouble spread to Divis Street, where cs gas was used to disperse crowds, and to the Springfield Road where twenty-nine windows in the local police station were broken by stones.

The *Sunday Times* was quite explicit about what caused the trouble. The front-page headline read 'Eighteen IRA cross border to stir Belfast riots.' The text below by '*Sunday Times* Reporters' told that the 18 infiltrators

> had orders to create a crisis in the North likely to embarrass Mr Jack Lynch ... who faces a vote of confidence in the Dáil on Wednesday. ... Twelve of the infiltrators were born or had lived in the North for a long time. ... They travelled unarmed by car to Belfast where they picked up arms and gelignite bombs. They had an immediate impact on the streets of Belfast.

Colin Brady in the *Sunday Telegraph* had simultaneously discovered that, 'The sudden assault on British troops and the Royal Ulster Constabulary in Belfast last Thursday, which started three days of shooting and bombing, was a calculated plan by militant Irish Republicans to disrupt several weeks of comparative peace in Northern Ireland's capital.' However, Mr Brady did not agree with the *Sunday Times* reporters' contention that the motive was to embarrass Mr Lynch. His information was that 'their [the IRA's] aim is to keep the province boiling and continually focus world attention on Ulster, to the embarrassment of the Stormont and Westminster governments. Men are moving about traditionally anti-British parts of Belfast, stoking up feeling and preparing assault groups which choose their own time and place to strike.'

On Monday, 2 November, the rest of the press followed suit. The *Sketch* reported that 'IRA guerrillas have organized children into stone-throwing gangs'.

The man in the black beret

Eddie McIlwaine reported in the *Daily Mirror* that 'men in black berets were seen giving orders'. The *Daily Express*, too, reported that 'The Special Branch of the RUC and Army Intelligence are investigating reports that a "provocation squad" from an illegal organization wearing black berets were organizing the latest rioting among Catholics in the Crumlin Road and at Divis Street.'

Other newspapers on 2 November reported in similar vein.

On the 3rd a report by John Chartres in *The Times* summed up and extended the press explanation of the causes of the riots. Having pinned responsibility for the previous days' trouble on Provisional IRA agitation, he wrote: 'This is the only interpretation that can be put on any of the Catholic attacks on troops since the beginning of this year.'

The Guardian editorial went further: 'When an Irishman throws a bomb at a Royal Marine he is not simply trying to kill. He wants, through murder, to provoke reprisals. His aim is a Northern Irish Sharpeville.'

There are a number of unanswered – unasked even – questions raised by the reporting of this particular spate of rioting. They are questions which could be asked about the press treatment of many other incidents in Northern Ireland.

For example: when the *Daily Sketch* reporter wrote on 2 November, 'IRA guerillas have organized children into stone-throwing gangs' what exactly did he intend to convey? That he had been on the spot and seen and heard this happen? Presumably not, since there is no dramatic eye-witness account of orders being given and children deployed. Did someone *tell* him that this had happened? Who? If a local person, a fortuitous witness, why no quote, even an anonymous quote? Or did the information come via an army or police briefing?

On the face of it this last is a not unlikely possibility. But if that was the basis of the story why was it not made clear, so that readers could understand that they were dealing with an allegation, albeit an 'official' allegation, rather than a definite fact?

This question is posed even more sharply by the *Sunday Times* report of 1 November, quoted above. '*Sunday Times* Reporters' not only mentioned the exact number of 'IRA infiltrators' – eighteen – but filled in some fairly detailed background. Twelve were either natives of Northern Ireland or had lived for some considerable time there; they were not armed on the journey to Belfast; one of their first acts on arriving in Belfast was to organize the throwing of seven gelignite bombs – again the exact number is given – at Royal Marines in the Hooker Street area.

There were no ifs, buts or attributions in the story. It was set down as a straightforward and detailed account of something that had just happened. Doubtless it was accepted in this spirit by hundreds of thousands of *Sunday Times* readers. One can imagine that most of them found it riveting stuff.

Once again: from where did the '*Sunday Times* Reporters' obtain all this information? From the army or the police? Then why not say so? And how did it happen that the representatives of no other

British or Irish newspaper became aware that the authorities had discovered such dramatically newsworthy facts?

If the security forces were in possession of this wealth of detail it is not easy to understand why they have never made public mention of it. To put no finer point upon it, the arrival in Ardoyne in the midst of bloody rioting of an eighteen-strong squad of IRA organizers from the South is not the type of fact Army and Police spokesmen in Northern Ireland have ever been anxious to conceal.

Could the information have come from an IRA source, perhaps even from one of the eighteen agitators themselves? Hardly. 'Sunday Times Reporters' have never been noticeably reluctant to evidence their 'inside' contacts. Had they got the story 'straight from the horse's mouth' we would most certainly have been told.

On what then was the report based? Take the sentence:

The 18 infiltrators from the South are said to have had orders to create a crisis in the North likely to embarrass Mr Jack Lynch, the Dublin Premier, who faces a vote of confidence in the Dáil on Wednesday.

Are said by whom to have had such orders? By 'Sunday Times Reporters' certainly. Further than that we may never know.

Similar questions could be raised about almost every other report of these particular riots in British newspapers. About Eddie McIlwaine's report in the *Mirror* of 2 November, for example, that 'men in black berets were seen giving orders'. Seen by whom? Himself? Then why not the more convincing and dramatic 'I saw'? About Geoffrey Cooper's report in the *Sketch* of 3 November which referred to a 'highly trained squad of *thirty* IRA infiltrators' who had 'unlimited supplies of gelignite'. Unlimited? How did he know? – Who told him? – Did he see it? If so, what does an 'unlimited' supply of gelignite *look* like?

Curiously no one managed to obtain a photograph of any of these eighteen or thirty black-bereted guerillas despite the fact that reporters apparently could see them. It cannot have been impossible or too dangerous to take such photographs since Mr McIlwaine assured *Mirror* readers that 'photographs of the troublemakers were taken'. Mr McIlwaine did not say in whose possession these dramatic pictures were. No newspaper ever printed one.

Perhaps one clue to the source of many of the reports is contained in the sentence quoted above from John Chartres of *The Times*. The riots must have been caused by IRA agitation, he says, *because there is no other interpretation that can be put on them*. And, indeed, if one is operating on the premise that the soldiers' behaviour is at all times impeccable and that the people of the area involved have no genuine grievance against the army and what it represents, then it would not be illogical to conclude that they would only pitch themselves against the troops if urged, or ordered, or fooled into doing so by some outside agency. It would be the 'only interpretation' which could be put on it. And perhaps rumours, or stories leaked from 'unattributable' semi-official sources, which seemed clearly to confirm this interpretation, would seem so plausible and so reasonable as to be almost certainly true. This is a possibility.

For all that, none of the reporters in Belfast could have been unaware that there was a much simpler explanation for the riots starting.

Late on Thursday evening, 29 October, a crowd of youths threw stones at a police car in the upper Crumlin Road. It was a minor incident. Troops were called up. Some stones were thrown at them. A relatively small crowd was involved. Up to that point the situation would not have qualified for the description 'riot'.

Then Norbert Jan Bek, 27, of No 41 Marine Commando, shot and wounded Kevin McGarry, Samuel Dodds and Sean Meehan. It was not alleged by the police, the troops or anyone else that any of these three was involved in stoning or had been part of the crowd from which stones had come. Shortly afterwards the army announced that the discharge of shots had been accidental and apologized for the injuries inflicted.

This incident sparked off the weekend's rioting. By the time the army apology was made – by an officer through a loud-hailer – crowds had poured out from Ardoyne and the battle, which lasted over the weekend, was joined. No one who was in the Ardoyne area in the next few days could have doubted that the shooting of McGarry, Dodds and Meehan was uppermost in the minds of the rioters. Rioters and bystanders, in the course of the invective they directed at the troops, referred continually to it. Any reporter who, on the Friday or Saturday, asked a local resident what the trouble was about, would certainly have been referred to the incident on Thursday night.

On Sunday, Mr Colin Brady's report in the *Sunday Telegraph* included: 'There was no specific reason why trouble should break out in Ardoyne on Thursday . . .'

Marine Bek was arrested and charged with maliciously wounding three men. He was tried at Belfast City Commission on 30 March this year and found not guilty. He returned to England on 31 March, saying that he intended now to join the Australian army.

The thoughts of Colin Brady

The tendency immediately and without evidence to blame 'the IRA' for any atrocity which could plausibly be represented as their work, was illustrated again by the reporting of the deaths of Arthur McKenna and Alex McVicker in November last year.

Mr McKenna and Mr McVicker were shot dead in Ballymurphy on 10 November. Both wings of the IRA denied responsibility. There was no record of either man being involved in politics.

No one has ever been charged with the murders. No evidence linking the deaths to the IRA or to any other organization has ever been made public. Irish journalists have since suggested that the men may have been killed in a gangland vendetta over a gambling ring.

Whatever the facts of the matter it is demonstrable that there was never a basis for any journalist to write or any paper to print that a particular organization was guilty.

This did not prevent Colin Brady writing in the *Daily Telegraph* of 17 November: 'It is thought' – by whom? – 'that the killers may have been members of the fanatical provisional army council which broke away from the IRA last year.'

The *Financial Times*, likewise, reported that it was 'thought to have been an internal IRA assassination' (17 November). *The Guardian* at least told us who it was had formed this suspicion of IRA responsibility: 'a gangland killing which police believe to an IRA internal assassination' (17 November). The *Daily Express* was in no doubt: 'a boy, aged 10, saw an IRA "executioner" shoot down two men in a Belfast street yesterday'. The *Sun* headline was BOY SEES IRA VENDETTA KILLING. And so on.

A precisely similar pattern emerged in the coverage of the deaths of five men in Co Fermanagh on 9 February this year.

The five men, two BBC engineers and three building workers, were in a landrover on their way to a BBC transmitter along a mountain track at Brougher Mountain, near Enniskillen, when an explosion wrecked the vehicle. All five died instantly.

A few hours later the *Evening News* led with: BBC MEN DIE IN IRA TERROR. The rest of the press took the same line. Both the *Telegraph* and *The Guardian* devoted their main leaders to the incident. According to the *Telegraph* of 10 February this incident and others 'bear clearly the signature of the Irish Republican Army'. *The Guardian* of the same date described it as 'the worst single incident of the new campaign of IRA violence'.

Mr Vale makes a discovery

By this time the image of the IRA as ruthless cut-throats was firmly implanted in the consciousness of the British public. It was an image shortly to be given dramatic reinforcement by the coverage of the triple killing of Scottish soldiers in March, and which was constantly elaborated and strengthened by reports, articles and editorials.

On 6 March, for example, under the headline 29 DIE IN GUN-LAW EXECUTIONS the *Daily Mirror* carried a story by Edward Vale telling that a

> series of twenty-nine horrifying murders have been uncovered in Ulster by Scotland Yard detectives. All the victims had been shot through the head – apparently on orders by the Irish Republican Army . . . The Yard team are hunting three IRA extremists thought to be leading the gang of executioners . . . Within forty-eight hours they had started to link up a series of mysterious deaths – first sixteen, then twenty. Since then nine more murders have been uncovered. All the victims appear to have been shot at close range, most in the back of the head. Some are thought to have been tortured before they died . . . One detective said last night 'the pattern of the killings is too similar to be a series of coincidences . . . They were shot, dragged into cars and dumped on the outskirts of Belfast.'

The story obviously had some basis in a briefing given by an anonymous detective or detectives. It is not clear how many of the gruesome details came from this source and how many were the results of Mr Vale's independent fact-finding. Either way the report has some perplexing implications.

One of the deaths referred to is that of John Kavanagh, found shot dead in Belfast in January: which leaves twenty-eight.

Curiouser and even curiouser
If we assume that all the killings took place after August 1969, when the IRA re-emerged as a real force, we must understand from the report that between then and February 1971 the bodies of twenty-eight murdered men were discovered in or around Belfast. That is, on average, one every three weeks.

The most perplexing thing about this is that no one apparently noticed. Until 6 March no newsman in Northern Ireland had any idea that this wholesale slaughter was in progress. The people who stumbled on the bodies – 'in ditches, hedgerows, derelict houses and on lonely roads' according to Mr Vale – kept quiet about it. More confusing still, the relatives of the twenty-eight victims, their wives, mothers, brothers, sisters, children – maintained an equally tight-lipped silence. One wonders what they told the neighbours.

The funerals, obviously, were in secret.

The behaviour of the Royal Ulster Constabulary raises even more questions. It is not clear from Mr Vale's text how many of the murders they had been aware of prior to the arrival of the assiduous team from the Yard. Manifestly, they had carried out their investiga-

ions with breathless stealth. No pictures of the various ditches,
hedgerows, derelict houses and lonely roads were published. No
appeals for anyone who had seen any suspicious activity in a par-
icular vicinity around the times of the respective murders to come
forward. No pictures of any of the deceased with requests for anyone who may have seen him immediately prior to the crime to
contact the murder-hunt HQ. No house to house questioning.
Nothing.

None of the murderers was ever found. The Scotland Yard
detectives have returned to London. As they left, inscrutable to the
end, they made no mention of the twenty-eight dead men. Presumably the RUC continue their quiet investigations, unannounced and
unnoticed, while twenty-eight Belfast families nurse their private
grief and tell the neighbours that 'he's working in England'.

Indeed the number may now be more than twenty-eight. It
probably is. There is no reason to suppose that the IRA Execution
Squad ceased operations on 6 March. If they have maintained their
previous average they will have killed and dumped in ditches/
hedgerows/derelict houses/lonely roads another dozen by now.
One has no way of knowing. Mr Vale has never returned to the
subject.

Just a few days after Mr Vale's piece appeared, three Scottish
soldiers were killed at Ligoniel, outside Belfast. They were killed in a
manner uncannily foreshadowed by his descriptions – shot in the
head at close range. The general press coverage too echoed Mr Vale's
previous story. The entire British press was seized with anti-IRA
fury. The headlines and intros told their own story.

11 March

The murders reminiscent of the methods of the IRA during the
Irish troubles earlier in this century. (Kenneth Dodd, *The Guardian*)

Three British soldiers were shot dead in an IRA ambush at Ligoniel
a North Belfast suburb last night. (Colin Brady, *Daily Telegraph*)

TROOPS MASSACRED BY IRA GUN GANG (*Sun*)

IRA MURDER 3 SOLDIERS IN AMBUSH (*Daily Mirror*)

IRA EXECUTE THREE ARMY BOYS (*Daily Sketch*)

IRA DEATH SQUAD (*Evening Standard*)

12 March

BRUTALLY MURDERED BY IRA GUNMEN (*Daily Telegraph*)

IRA MURDER MEN SHOT THEM DOWN (*Daily Sketch*)

The last hours of the three young Scottish soldiers massacred by the IRA (*Sun*)

BIG HUNT FOR THE IRA KILLERS (*Daily Mirror*)

THE ANGRY HUNT FOR IRA KILLERS (*Daily Mail*)

All the hallmarks of the work of the militant provisional wing of the IRA (*The Times*)

It was, almost without a shadow of doubt the work of the Provisional violent wing of the IRA (*Daily Telegraph*)

None of the reporters, none of the editors had any evidence that the IRA was involved. No such evidence existed. Indeed there were factors powerfully indicating other culprits. Ligoniel is not a Catholic ghetto, not an area where an IRA unit could move freely or would choose to operate.

Still, on 13 and 14 March the howl of outrage continued. Pressure mounted on both Westminster and Stormont to adopt tougher security measures. On 16 March Chichester-Clark was called to London to confer with British ministers.

The result of the talks, given the press coverage, was inevitable. The public anger made it politically acceptable, indeed expedient to send more troops to Northern Ireland and to declare an intention further to repress Republican dissidence.

17 March

URGENT REVIEW OF ARMY TACTICS (*Financial Times*)

FACE TO FACE PREMIERS GET TOUGH OVER ULSTER (*Daily Express*)

PLEDGE ON FIRMER ACTION (*The Times*)

MORE TROOPS AND TOUGHER LINE OVER ULSTER (*The Guardian*)

CRACKDOWN ON ULSTER TERRORISM (*Daily Telegraph*)

PLANS TO BEAT IRA TERROR (*Sun*)

The advocates of 'law and order' were well satisfied. In the atmosphere of emotional recrimination they gathered strength for the final push, a few weeks later, to topple Chichester-Clark. One wonders as they contemplated the new respectability of their attitudes whether they understood how much they owed to obscure men at desks in Fleet Street and the Grays Inn Road.

Despite the fact that the Scotland Yard team investigating the death of John Kavanagh took over the case, the killers have never been found. No evidence was unearthed to link either wing of the IRA to the incident. The only persons held for questioning, and then released, were extreme 'loyalists'.

A few weeks before the killing of the Scots soldiers some journalists had given a new gloss to one of the standard IRA stories – the one about the IRA organizing riots. This was in its own way as grisly an affair as any other.

Some rioters in Northern Ireland are very young indeed. One sees eight- or nine-year-old children throwing stones at soldiers.

A sociologist could suggest reasons for this. The children are less conscious than adults of the dangers involved and, to some extent at least, regard rioting as play. Northern Ireland in this sense is the biggest adventure playground in the world.

Whatever the explanation, anyone who has observed such children in action will know that it is difficult, well nigh impossible to dissuade them. Almost as common as child rioters are parents seeking desperately to find and to take their children out of the 'firing line'.

The British Press has not always seen it like that. Last Feburary there appeared a spate of stories putting an entirely different construction on the phenomenon – that IRA men were ordering the children to riot. The three tabloids in particular gave the story splash treatment, with a wealth of cloak-and-dagger detail.

The horrified MIRROR

The *Daily Mirror* of 8 February led on the front page with HORROR OF THE CHILD TERRORISTS. Howard Johnson reported

School children are now being pushed into the front line of the terrorists' battle against British troops in Belfast . . . there have been reports of an eight year old boy hurling petrol bombs at troops . . . The tiny terrorists are used as messenger boys for IRA officers. They are also employed to spark off full-scale street battles by baiting and attacking troops.

Under the headline FRONT LINE KIDS Roger Scott reported in *The Sun* the same day that

IRA terror leaders here are now sending shock troops to war – their own children. Bomb-throwing eight year olds are in the front line. They steal out at dusk to play games with death, trained to hate and kill. And the children at war chant obscenities to nursery rhyme tunes as the bullets fly. The sinister parents stay in the shadows firing from behind the ranks of the young in street battles.

The *Daily Sketch* headline on 8 February was KIDS' ARMY GOES TO WAR. George Gordon and James Nicholson wrote that 'Rioters again ordered their children into the front line battle for Belfast yesterday.'

The general picture is one from which the British public must have recoiled in horror and distaste. Millions would have accepted it as an accurate description of the situation – that parents in the New Lodge Road and Ballymurphy were indeed lurking in doorways at night having despatched their eight- and nine-year-old offspring, petrol bombs in hand and matches at the ready, to do battle with the British army.

No one who knows the areas or the people who live there could accept these reports. But the overwhelming majority of the readers of the *Daily Sketch,* the *Sun* and the *Daily Mirror* had no such knowledge. It might not have occurred to them to question Mr Scott's statement that small children were actually being trained to kill. Mr Scott did not indicate where he unearthed this grotesque detail.

Mr Scott, Mr Johnson, Mr Gordon and Mr Nicholson saw small children rioting. What they did not see – what none of them makes any claim to have seen – was these children being ordered to riot. This part of each of the three reports was based either on mere supposition or on allegations from some unnamed source. But in each case it was written as though it were incontestable fact.

As for the more colourful details: one could go through each of the reports clause by clause and question whether the reporter could possibly have known this or that to be true. How could Mr Scott tell that any of the children he saw rioting was the son or daughter of an 'IRA terror leader'? Did he know them by name and actually know whose children they were? Did he notice facial resemblances to acknowledged IRA leaders? Mr Scott's intimate knowledge of Belfast neighbourhoods must make his presence there invaluable to the *Sun*.

It may be coincidence – or it may not – that, according to *Hansard*, Mr Robin Chichester-Clark (Unionist) said in the Westminster House of Commons on 7 February that IRA men were hiring children as 'cover' while they, the IRA gunmen, 'shelter in doorways'.

One could speculate whether news editors in London, particularly news editors of papers locked in a circulation war, might on hearing Mr Chichester-Clark's allegation, have contacted their representatives in Belfast and asked whether it would be possible to put some flesh on this skeleton of a story. This would be mere speculation. One is not certain it happened. One could not therefore state it as fact.

Other, more minor examples of British papers without evidence linking the IRA to atrocities, imagined or real, are legion. On 9 May this year for example someone threw a petrol bomb at the home of Mr John McKeague, militant protestant leader of the Shankhill Defence Association. The premises caught fire and Mr McKeague's seventy-three-year-old mother was burned to death.

Shortly afterwards the RUC issued a statement saying that they did not believe the incident to have had 'any sectarian significance'. In the Northern Ireland context this meant clearly that they did not believe the IRA was responsible. Unimpressed, the *Daily Telegraph* next day carried a headline on the front page, MOTHER DIES IN IRA BOMB FIRE.

The *Daily Telegraph* really warrants a study of its own. At one time this year there was a short period of complete peace. Since the *Telegraph* concluded from almost any week's events in Northern Ireland that the IRA ought to be put down immediately one wondered how, exactly, it would handle this new situation: 'It has always been part of the IRA's tactics to intersperse outrages with periods of relative inactivity, designed to encourage complacency.' Editorial, 1 April 1971.

THE LIE MACHINE

There is no conscious conspiracy to distort the situation. Pressmen do not get around a table and decide to twist the truth in an agreed direction.

Still there is a certain apparent co-ordination and this is not accidental. It happens because the press in general serves a certain interest, and whether individual journalists are conscious of it or not, whether they like it or not, the news as published will tend to support that interest.

In the aftermath of 5 October the central thrust of British government policy was directed towards the 'democratization' of Northern Ireland. The increasing British investment in the Republic, the growing importance of the South of Ireland as a trading partner made dangerously obsolete the traditional attitude of previous governments – one of uncritical support for the Unionist party in the North. For the first time in the history of Anglo-Irish relations it suited the Imperial power to balance between the Orange and the Green. This was automatically reflected in British policy toward the North. It involved a resolution to force concessions to the Catholics.

It was reflected too in the press. It offers an explanation of many pro-Civil Rights editorials, of the curious treatment of Bernadette

Devlin, of the fact that the Catholic case received enormously more coverage than the Protestant case. One can remember arguing with journalists that they ought at least to visit the Fountain Street area in Derry and talk to the Protestants. Few did.

One of the functions of the British army when it came on to the streets was to supervise and to enforce the reforms which had already been promised and those which were to emanate from the Hunt Report. Another of its functions was to see that things did not go beyond that.

The interest of big business required the democratization of the state – i.e. that the Specials be disbanded, the police disarmed, discrimination eliminated. It was not in its interest that, to take a random example, the state be overthrown.

It was quickly clear that there were those within the Catholic community, and with some influence especially in the barricaded areas, who wanted to go much further than British policy dictated, and in the press a very clear differentiation was made between these and the more reasonable elements. The *Daily Mail* story on Bernadette's Sinister Army was an early example of this but it was with the emergence of the IRA as a force to be reckoned with that press attitudes solidified into the outright hostility evidenced by consistent misreporting.

Once 'the IRA' had been identified as the main enemy all concern for fact melted marvellously away. The stories of IRA mass murders, IRA extortion and intimidation, IRA men training children to kill, etc., served to justify increasingly repressive measures to the British public. It was on this basis that *The Guardian*, self-appointed keeper of the British liberal conscience, was able to plausibly support internment. It was as a result of such stories that politically the British government could operate the policy.

The British press is in a constant state of adaptation to the needs of the British ruling class. This happens because the press is not an independent institution. There is no 'free press'. It is locked into the structure of society.

Newspaper owners like to pose as fearless, independent-minded rather swashbuckling characters. Occasionally, in the boozy atmosphere of the annual get-togethers, they have been even known to talk of their 'love' of newspapers.

But a cursory examination of newspaper ownership shows what nonsense this is. Every British national newspaper is, either directly or through its major shareholders, linked to other big businesses, inextricably enmeshed in the capitalist system.

The Daily Mail and General Trust Limited, for example, owns Associated Newspapers Ltd. Through Associated Newspapers it is involved in Television (Southern Television Ltd.), docks (Purfleet Deep Wharf and Storage Co and Taylor Bros Wharfage Ltd.), Transport (W. West Haulage Ltd.), Mining (Rio Tinto/Hamilton Group); in all, in 50 subsidiary enterprises.

The News of the World Organization (*News of the World, Sun*) has interests including engineering, retail newsagents, transport, and betting shops.

The International Publishing Co – the Mirror Group – merged in 1970 with the Reed Group of companies. It is involved in a bewildering multitude of activities. The group has 400 associated and subsidiary companies. It is involved in plastics, engineering, building, transport, wallpapers, TV, films, theatres etc., etc. It has vast city and financial interests. It has overseas possessions in Canada, New Zealand, Australia, Holland, South Africa, Hong Kong, Nigeria, the Republic of Ireland, France, Germany, Italy and the United States.

The Thompson Organization (*The Times, Sunday Times*) has 192 subsidiaries and associated companies. It has substantial holdings in Scottish Television, in package tour companies, and in transport. It has overseas interests in South Africa, the United States, Zambia, Rhodesia, New Zealand, Malawi, Jamaica, Gibraltar, Canada and Australia.

Even those papers which are formally independent have on their boards men who are simultaneously directors of other, outside businesses. *The Observer*, for example, is controlled by a board of trustees and prides itself on its resultant independence. Chairman of the Board is Lord Goodman who has 27 directorships, at the last available count. Others involved included the Hon N. C. J. Rothschild (31 outside directorships, including textiles, property companies and investment companies) and various Astors and associates, all of whom have other business interests.

There is no such thing as an independent national newspaper.

Those who have ultimate control over what is printed and what is not are drawn from a relatively tiny segment of society—the owners of big business. Generally speaking, what is printed tends to support their interests.

The more paranoic members of left-wing groups believe that this happens because press barons order editors, who in turn order reporters, to tell lies. The actual process is marginally more subtle.

In the first place the editorship of a national newspaper is a responsible position and 'responsibility', as understood by the owners of newspapers, would be incompatible with the belief, say, that private ownership of industry is a bad thing. One of the qualifications for editorship is, naturally, a general acceptance of the owners' attitudes.

This is reflected in the editorial 'line' of every paper and it filters through to reporters, sub-editors etc. A journalist who has covered Northern Ireland for a British daily paper explains

> You must remember that every journalist wants what he writes to appear, and in practice all journalists know pretty well what their paper's line is, what is expected of them. There is a fair amount of self-censorship. This happens without thinking. No journalist I have met writes what he knows will be cut. What would be the point? If he has a story which he knows will cause controversy back at the newsdesk he will water it down to make it acceptable.

Most journalists rely heavily on 'official' sources. This explains the sometimes striking similarity of coverage. Stories from 'official' sources will, of course, be eminently acceptable. Moreover, as a former *Mirror* employee writes:

> In a situation like Northern Ireland our people would have to keep in close touch with the Army Press Office. It would be more or less part of their job to get to know the army press officer as well as possible and that in itself would affect their judgement a bit. Then one of their biggest preoccupations is not to be scooped by a competitor. No one on the *Mirror* would be sacked because he didn't come up with a carefully authenticated and researched piece, written from local hard work. You do get sacked if the rival has a sensation about the IRA.'

Nothing one can do?

Even if a reporter does send through copy which is critical of the establishment and its representatives (e.g., the army) it is at the mercy of the news editor and the sub-editors. These are likely to be the most conservative of all the journalistic staff, with years of grinding practice in what is acceptable to the editor and the management. The average senior sub-editor will, as a reflex action, strike out any sentence which jars his sense of propriety. A reporter still working in Northern Ireland for a 'quality' daily says

> . . . However, a few lines cut here and there which can completely alter the tone of the piece is almost impossible to argue about. You get bland apologies that cuts were made for reasons of length and yes, the subs should have referred back to you but after all it was near the edition time and we're all professionals. It is never admitted that the cuts are those sentences which are critical of the army, or which make the point that Faulkner is not entirely accepted by the whole Ulster community. If you push it they tell

you that you are imagining things. You can end up thinking that you are. There's nothing you can do about it.

Reporters who know what is expected of them; news editors and sub-editors trained to recognize and eliminate 'unhelpful' references; editors appointed with 'sound' attitudes; boards of management composed of substantial businessmen: the whole sprawling machinery of news gathering and publication automatically filters, refines and packages the information fed in and works to ensure that the news, as printed, is fit to print. The general picture is enlivened by occasional bursts of maverick radicalism. A 'fearless exposé' every now and then helps to maintain the official myth of the independent press (and can be good for circulation) but does not alter significantly the pattern which emerges.

On dangerous issues – the behaviour of the army, a power workers' strike – the pattern will emerge clear and stark. Newspapers tell lies. The news from Northern Ireland has been a compound lie.

Sir, Writing by candlelight …*

E. P. THOMPSON

Let the power workers dim the street lamps, or even plunge whole districts into utter darkness, the lights of righteousness and duty burn all the brighter from 10,000 darkened drawing-rooms in Chelsea or the Surrey hills.

> Sir,
> May I, writing by candlelight, express my total support for the government in their attempt to halt the unbelievably inflated wage claims now being made?

enquires one correspondent to *The Times* (12 December). Undoubtedly he may and will.

Historians have often paid tribute to this peculiar character of the British. It is in grave adversity, in states of emergency, that they have noted this flaring-up of the British spirit. Only then do those proper guardians of the conscience of the community – the retiring middle classes – shed their usual reticence and openly articulate their values and commitments.

One infallible signal of such a time of bourgeois renaissance is the epistolary *levée en masse* of the readers of *The Times*. Such *levées* are infrequent; when they occur, one senses the presence of History. One such took place in February 1886 after the 'Trafalgar Square Riots', when unorganized unemployed demonstrators – after listening to some exciting rhetoric from John E. Williams, John Burns and H. M. Hyndman of the Social Democratic Federation – broke into a brief rampage through the West End, smashing shop windows, looting and even throwing bricks at select London clubs. Worse riots occurred, in most years, in some parts of the country: but not on such sanctified ground as Pall Mall.

'Sir', wrote one unfortunate gentleman, whose carriage windows were smashed in the rioting: 'I am a subscriber to various charities and hospitals, which I shall discontinue. I have always advocated the cause of the people. I shall do so no more.'

But wounded and long-suffering righteousness, on these occasions,

* From *New Society*, 24 December 1970, pp. 1135–6.

takes second place to the firm disciplinary mode. 'Sir', demanded one correspondent in 1886,

> What is the use of having a highly-paid Commissioner of Police, with proportionately highly-paid deputies, if they are afraid of the responsibility attaching to their posts? . . . When there is a kennel riot in any kennel of hounds, the huntsman and whips do not wait to get the special orders of the master, but proceed to restore order at once.

Another correspondent (11 February 1886) produced an example of the genre so rich that it has to be quoted at length:

> Sir,
> On returning from the Prince's Levée I was walking through Pall Mall, in uniform. It was gradually filling with very suspicious-looking 'unemployed' at that time, two of whom, turning towards me, one said, rather significantly, 'Why, who the —— is this chap?'
> As I passed the War Office entrance, formerly the Duke of Buckingham's, a blind fiddler, led by a little girl, came by . . . playing some odd tune or other, when a young guardsman on sentry stepped out and said, in a commanding tone, 'You stop that noise' . . . I thought, 'Now there is a man of common sense and of action.' It was a little thing to stop at the time, but when the snowball which a child or a blind fiddler could set rolling on the top of the hill reaches the bottom it has become in this country an immovable monster, in other countries a destroying avalanche.
> On the 10 April 1848, I was sworn in a special constable between Buckingham Palace and the House of Commons. At the former we had a battery of Horse Artillery hidden in the stable yard. I asked the officer commanding what he was going to do? His answer was, 'We have our scouts, and if we hear of any gatherings we could run out and sweep the Mall or the Birdcage Walk in two minutes, or command St James Street and Pall Mall in three.' He would not wait till mischief was done. Are those days quite gone?
> Your obedient servant,
>
> Wilbraham Taylor

Such high heroics can rarely be repeated, just as the true, physical *levées* of the bourgeoisie against the plebs (the Volunteers against the Jacobins in 1800, the Yeomanry against the poor of Peterloo, the Specials against the Chartist 10 April, the debs and Oxbridge undergraduates against the General Strike) are too few to satiate the desire dramatically to beat the bounds of class. So the epistolary cry goes out for someone – the government – to discipline *them*, and put them back in kennels.

John E. Williams had been reported, in 1886, as having deplored that the unemployed were not well enough organized – not to riot and destroy property – but to occupy the banks, Stock Exchange and government offices. 'Sir', wrote one *Timesian*, 'if correctly reported Williams must be an atrocious miscreant, compared with whom Gashford in *Barnaby Rudge* is a virtuous person.'

December 1970 has produced little in this genre of comparable quality, perhaps because Electrical Workers' leaders are scarcely typecast as communist or trotskyist fiends. (Perhaps the nearest was the letter – 14 December – from Nicolas Bentley, suggesting that Robert Morley, who had dared to declare his solidarity with trade unionism, must be a 'callous reprobate'.) But the old theme of 'there ought to be a law against . . .' has been fully orchestrated. This was very evident in another vintage epistolary year, 1926.

One mine-owner addressed himself (5 June 1926) to the subject of the mineworkers' officials: 'Their one object is to squeeze as much money out of the industry as it will stand, to the detriment of the proprietors who have taken all the risk incidental to coalmining.' (A rigorous statistical examination of the number of coal-owners killed in mining disasters might not bear this out.) The Bishop of Durham came baying up behind (22 June): 'Trade unions now include in their ranks a great number of young men whose boyhood was spent during the war, when every kind of discipline was weakened . . . These lawless youths are well-fitted to become the janissaries of Communist Revolution.'

Trade unions were 'the mocking caricature of anything . . . democratic', and their rank-and-file were 'the hopeless fools of the ruling clique'. They could only be held down by stronger law. The compulsory secret ballot, then as now, was one grand recipe for the extirpation of strikes, from correspondents pathetically anxious to believe that if only the workers expressed their minds *in secret* they would turn out to be chaps just like themselves – or, rather, chaps *convenient to* themselves, compounded of all bourgeois virtues of prudence, self-help, and deference to property, but emasculated of the bourgeois reproductive system – the drive for *money*.

Such themes, announced in 1926, have, if anything, become more pronounced with the epistolary *posse commitatus* of 1970. Should strikes be forbidden by law? asks Sir H. T. Smith, from Wallingford (11 December). On the same day the 'long-suffering public' found a spokesman in H. P. Rae: deeply perturbed about invalids dependent upon 'continuously functioning kidney machines' (which they aren't), he demanded: 'why the hesitation in putting in troops *now*?' 'The vast majority of the public', he assured *Times* readers from his Chelsea address, 'are sick to death of the squalid attempts by the unions to tyrannize' etcetera. Mr Tennet of Shottermill Ponds, Haslemere, also found (12 December) that the workers were '[mis]-using their monopoly position', and Richard Hughes, from the United University Club, suggested 'a national one-day token lock-out [by employers] in support of the . . . Industrial Relations Bill'.

Mr Flamank of Solihull (also 12 December) wanted to see the formation of 'an emergency service corps', which could, at the Home Secretary's whistle, 'move in and run the services'. Those encouraging industrial unrest, 'be they communists, shop stewards or militant students, are just as much our enemies as were the Nazis'. (Perhaps one can hear an echo of Wilbraham Taylor and the Horse Artillery over Birdcage Walk)?

Such situations tend to make the bourgeois feel, with a sudden flash of insight, their own value in the world: they bear its weight and (*vide* the coal-owner) its risks upon their shoulders. 'Think what the feeling would be', exclaimed Lord Midleton (28 June 1926), 'if any pit were closed for the day and all wages lost to the men because the managing and controlling staff required a day off!' A similar thought occurred to Mr Reade (14 December 1970): 'Sir, If manual workers can work to rule, why not wages clerks too?' Aha! The argument is final: what if we, who *have* the money, stopped letting you rotters have it ! ! !

It is not to be thought that in such national emergencies, the bourgeoisie is solely concerned with such paltry matters as money or comfort or class power. Not at all: the full moral idealism blazes out. Thomas Hughes, the Christian Socialist author of *Tom Brown's Schooldays*, came unhesitatingly to his post in the correspondence column in 1886: these modern socialists he found to be 'notorious ruffians', and 'If Mr Chamberlain will consider where he cannot be getting Messrs Hyndman & Co a year or two's oakum picking instead of "receiving their views in writing" he would be doing all honest folk more service, in my judgment.'

At such moments *Timesian* correspondents always know unhesi-tatingly what are the thoughts and needs of 'all honest folk' or of (see *The Times*, 14 December 1970) 'the welfare of the entire community' (Rose Cottage, Westhumble, Surrey). But it was left to the honest folksman, Sir Alan Lascelles (The Old Stables, Kensing-ton Palace), to come forward as shop steward of 'an immensely larger union – namely, the union of British citizens' (17 December).

In 1926, however, the immediate requirements of the 'entire community' were pointed out to the striking miners in more dulcet tones, since they had made the tragic error of being manoeuvred into a bitter, wasting strike during the summer months, and the readers of *The Times* were suffering, not from empty grates, but from an overfull sense of moral outrage. At such a time the clergy select themselves as the proper admonishers. The Dean of Worcester advised the miners (8 June 1926) that if they capitulated to the coal-owners' terms they 'will have won a great victory – a victory of their nobler over the lower self.' The Archdeacon of Chester addressed the same homily with greater fervour: capitulation by the miners 'would be good Christianity . . . an act of personal self-denial . . . of personal self-renunciation for the sake of others, following the supreme example of the Greatest Figure in history.'

One has yet to notice, in 1970, correspondents congratulating the power workers, who called off their work to rule, on their good Christianity, or likening Frank Chapple to the 'Greatest Figure' in history. (Nor did *The Times* publish such congratulations from rural deans in 1926, when the miners returned to their pits defeated; after all, such letters, if read at the pithead, might have induced moral complacency, and, as events were to show, the nation was to expect a good deal more Christianity from the miners in the coming years.)

But – let us be fair – there has been one change in the genre in recent years: the clergy, generally, do not push themselves forward so obtrusively, nor do they presume so readily to express the conscience of the nation on socially-divisive issues. Their role, as national conscience and admonishers of delinquents, has been passed over, in good part, to David Frost and Malcolm Muggeridge. Some small part, perhaps, has been taken over by that new conscience-bearer, the middle-class housewife, who being out of the hurly-burly and puerility of industrial warfare, can watch all things with a wholly objective eye and instantly detect from her kitchen the national interest. Thus, on 11 December, a correspondent from Prescot, Lancs:

> . . . the radio is dead. The television is dead. The electric heaters are dead. The kettle is dead. The fridge is dead. My washing machine is dead. My iron is dead. All the street lights are dead . . . Goodness knows how many *tragic* deaths may result . . .

It is (she concludes) 'an exhibition of power surely grotesque in its selfishness.'

All dark and comfortless: we stalk the drear world of the psalmist or space-fiction writer: all that inanimate world of consumer goods, animated each quarter by the insertion of money, lies inert, disobedient. All flesh is grass, we know; but what (O ultimate of horrors!) if all gadgets turned out to be grass also? It is the Rebellion of the Robots, recorded by the author of Ecclesiastes.

Grotesque and selfish the power workers' action may have been. How can one know? Facts have been scarcer than homilies. Reading the press one learns that one has been living through little less than cosmic disaster. One had thought that one's neighbours had suffered little more than power cuts for several hours on three or four days, but the mistake is evident. Outside there, in the darkness, the nation had been utterly paralysed for week upon week; invalids dependent upon 'continuously operating' kidney-machines lived two or three to every street; armed robbers prowled the darkness with impunity; not a hospital in the country that was not lit solely by candles, with surgeons operating upon month-old babies by the light of a failing torch.

A comparatively few individuals, wrote a correspondent from Richmond (12 December) were inflicting upon the public 'catastrophic injury'. Why not 'issue an order *withdrawing all legal protection* from the persons and property of the workers concerned', and the officials of their unions? 'Let the community get its own back.' This 'whole community' (another correspondent, 16 December) 'has long been renowned for its patience and forbearance. But surely the time has come,' etcetera. 'We are sick and tired . . .,' 'the time has come,' 'irresponsible' . . . irrespondible *to us*!

What is, of course, 'grotesque in its selfishness' is the time-worn hypocrisy of the bourgeois response to discomfort. Anyone familiar with the Victorian and Edwardian press cannot fail to detect, in these tones of moral outrage, that old bourgeois theme for moralisms: the 'servant problem'. But the servants now are out of reach; an electric light switch is impervious to the scolding of the mistress; a dust-cart cannot be given a week's wages in lieu of notice.

And anyone who has read his E. M. Forster or his Angus Wilson knows the old British bourgeois propensity to moralize his own convenience and to minister to his own comforts under a cloud of altruism. For 95 per cent of the bluster and outrage was the miasma rising from tens of thousands of petty material inconveniences. The electric alarm failed to go off, mummy fell over the dog in the dark, the grill faded with the fillet steak done on one side only, daddy got stuck for half an hour in the lift on the way to a directors' meeting, the children missed *Top of the Pops*, the fridge de-froze all over the soufflé, the bath was lukewarm, there was nothing to do but go early to a loveless bourgeois bed. But, wait, there was one alternative: 'Sir, Writing by candlelight . . .'

But to mention the *real* occasions might seem petty. It was necessary to generalize these inconveniences into a 'national interest'. The raw unlit fillet steak became an inert kidney-machine, the dripping fridge an operating theatre, the loveless bed became a threat to

the 'whole community'. No matter: now the emergency is over these
moral fantasies will shrink back to their proper size. The shivering
old age pensioners (many of whom will continue to shiver all winter
through on their inadequate pensions), the imperilled invalids
(many of whom will continue in peril from inadequate medical
provision) will cease to obtrude themselves in the correspondence
columns of *The Times*.

It has been a notable state of national humbug. It was concluded,
as in an obligatory ritual, by David Frost, at peak viewing hours
on a Saturday night, bullying a few power workers, with a studio
audience, handpicked for their utter insensitive self-righteousness,
baying at his back.

Occasions were found, not only to express moral disapprobation,
but also approval; the audience applauded to the echo nurses who,
underpaid as they are, would never strike because of the needs of
their patients. David Frost who, from what one has heard, does not
face the same financial dilemmas – and the withdrawal of whose
labour would scarcely induce even this government to declare a
state of 'national emergency' – was evidently delighted. The
bourgeoisie has always been ready to acknowledge virtue in the
servant class when it finds it: pliant, loyal, living patiently in the
attic, carrying on dutifully a service to the 'whole community'.
Aubrey Leatham, physician at St George's Hospital, Hyde Park
Corner, saluted the same virtue among the cardiac technicians at his
hospital (*The Times*, 16 December) who, earning 'as little as £415
a year, would like to strike, but they do not, because they are humanitarian'.

And how noble they are, indeed, to pace the hearts of emergency
patients in the acute care area for only £8 a week! But, surely, if
this is so, this also is an outrage, which we should have heard of
before, and insistently, and not only as a stick to beat the power
workers with? Has Mr Leatham taken up his pen before, to press
the astonishing case of his cardiac technicians? Or will he, and the
other militant correspondents to *The Times* and so many other
papers, relapse into silence now that the inconvenience and discomfort is over?

The grand lesson of the 'emergency' was this: the intricate
reciprocity of human needs and services – a reciprocity of which
we are, every day, the beneficiaries. In our re-ified mental world,
we think we are dependent upon *things*. What other people do for
us is mediated by inanimate objects: the switch, the water tap, the
lavatory chain, the telephone receiver, the cheque through the post.
That cheque is where the duties of the good bourgeois end. But let
the switch or the tap, the chain or the receiver fail, and then the

bourgeois discovers – at once – enormous 'oughts' within the reciprocal flow.

But these 'oughts' are always the moral obligations of other people: the sewage workers ought not to kill fish, the dustmen ought not to encourage rats, the power workers out not to imperil invalids, and – this week it will be – the postmen ought not to deny bronchitic old age pensioners of their Christmas parcels from grandchildren in Australia. Why, all these people owe a duty to the 'community'!

What the duty of the community is to these people is less firmly stated. Certainly, those whose lolly is the theme of the business supplements – those whose salary increases (like those of admirals and university teachers) are awarded quietly and without fuss, and which (it seems) create no national emergency and no dangerous inflationary pressures – have little need to compose letters to *The Times* as to their own moral obligations and duties.

It is the business of the servant class to serve. And it is the logic of this re-ified bourgeois world that their services are only noticed when they cease. It is only when the dustbins linger in the street, the unsorted post piles up – it is only when the power workers throw across the switches and look out into a darkness of their own making – that the servants know suddenly the great unspoken fact about our society: their own daily power.

The mass media and racial conflict*

PAUL HARTMANN and CHARLES HUSBAND

Communication between people is possible to the extent that they share common frameworks of interpretation. They need to have similar meanings for the same symbols, and a way of thinking about things in common before they can communicate. Our perceptions are structured by the mental categories available to us for making sense of our world.

Research into attitudes commonly concentrates on differences in attitude between people and groups, and the interpretive frameworks within which such differences occur are either taken for granted or ignored. Where racial prejudice is concerned this emphasis may produce a tendency to seek the origins of prejudice in the personality of the individual or the immediate social situation rather than in the cultural framework itself. This approach was evident in the *Colour and Citizenship*[1] survey and made possible the comforting but misleading conclusion that intense prejudice is a phenomenon rooted in the personality of the individual, an irrational solution to the inadequacies of an undermined personality.[2] But prejudice is not in the first instance the result of immigration, personal pathology or social strain; it is built into the culture. Our whole way of thinking about coloured people, influenced by the colonial past, constitutes a built-in predisposition to accept unfavourable beliefs about them. The very notion of 'tolerance' betrays this cultural bias, for it implies that there is something nasty that requires special virtue to put up with. Even 'authoritarianism', so often cast as the villain of the piece, is not some purely personal aberration; for the beliefs and values that serve to define it are related to our particular social and industrial history and are well embedded in British culture. They have much in common with 'Social Darwinism' and the 'Protestant Ethic'. Only after the underlying cultural predisposition to prejudice had been taken into account does it make sense to ask how variations in prejudice relate to other factors.

*Extracted from Paul Hartmann and Charles Husband, 'The mass media and racial conflict', *Race*, Vol XII, No 3 (January 1971), pp. 268-82 Published for the Institute of Race Relations by the Oxford University Press, © Institute of Race Relations, 1971.

THE MASS MEDIA AND ATTITUDES

A considerable amount of research effort has been devoted to assessing the influence of the mass media on attitudes and opinions. Results, on the whole, have shown that social attitudes, including prejudice, are relatively resistant to influence through the media. What effects have been demonstrated have typically been of a limited kind. Trenaman and McQuail,[3] for instance, in their study of the effects of the 1959 election campaign on television showed that this produced increases in political knowledge, but were unable to find any effects on attitudes or voting behaviour. Blumler and McQuail's[4] important and complex study of the 1964 election campaign found that various kinds of attitude change did occur as a result of exposure to election television, but the particular kind of attitude change depended on the characteristics of the voter, particularly his motivation, and it was not possible to make across-the-board generalizations that applied to the electorate as a whole. In an early study on prejudice, Cooper and Dinerman[5] found that although many of the *facts* presented in an anti-prejudice film did not get through to the audience, this was not associated with change of attitude, and there was even evidence of 'boomerang' effects.

One of the main explanations for findings of this kind is selection. People select what they read and what they view and tend to avoid communications that they find uncongenial. They are also selective in what they perceive and what they remember. Where the 'message' clashes with existing attitudes or beliefs it is typically the existing outlook that remains intact, while the 'message' is rejected, or distorted to fit the outlook. A study of viewers' reactions to a programme in an ITV series, 'The Nature of Prejudice'[6] carried out in 1967 found that prejudiced viewers evaded the intended anti-prejudice message by a variety of means, ranging from becoming hostile towards the interviewer (who was opposed to prejudice) to finding in the programme confirmation of their own views.

In reviewing research on the effects of mass communications Klapper[7] came to the conclusion that they are much more likely to reinforce existing attitudes (whatever the attitude and whatever the 'message') than to change them. Attitudes may be expected to be particularly resistant to change when they are supported by strong group norms or the prevailing cultural climate.

Work of our own confirms that direct effects on attitude following short-term exposure to media material are unlikely. We studied the effects of the six-part television series, 'Curry and Chips' which caused some controversy in November and December 1969. We gave questionnaires to about 200 secondary schoolchildren, both before the beginning of the series and after it had finished. They had no reason to connect us or the questions with television. The question-naires included attitude measures as well as open-ended questions designed to elicit beliefs and information about Pakistanis. On the second occasion they were also asked how many of the programmes they had seen. Differences between responses on the two occasions were analysed in relation to the number of programmes viewed. We expected that children who had seen all or most of the series would show changes in information and attitude not found in those who had seen none of the programmes. We found no effects that could be attributed to viewing the programmes. Even when analysed in relation to initial attitude, to whether the children had discussed the series with others, to how true-to-life they had thought it, and other variables, the data yielded no positive results.

This is not to say that the series had no important effects, but only that it appears not to have had the type of effects studied. We do not know the extent to which children's initial opinions were strength-ened by viewing the programmes, for instance. It may be that the series helped to make it more acceptable for both children and adults to make fun of immigrants. Letters of complaint appearing in the press and anecdotal evidence suggest that for a time at least this was so. And going on press reports and letters, we have the impression that one of the main effects of the series was to affront the Asian communities. A further possibly important effect was that the pro-grammes provided a focus of discussion in which the questions of immigration and race were aired in informal groups up and down the country. Sixty per cent of the children we surveyed claimed to have discussed the series with others. This must at the very least have resulted in greater awareness of race as a controversial topic and greater familiarity with prevailing norms. All that emerges clearly from our study is that to look for effects in terms of simple changes of attitude may be to look in the wrong place.

More generally we should not conclude from the type of research that we have been discussing that the media have no important influence on public opinion or race relations. Part of the reason for the high incidence of null results in attempts to demonstrate the effects of mass communications lies in the nature of the research questions asked and the limitations of the theoretical orientations of the research tradition. Much of this work was influenced by a view of man as an atomized unit of mass society, whom stimulus-response psychology saw as responding in a straightforward way to the stimuli or 'messages' of the media. The tradition is characterized by a search for direct effects, short-term effects, and an over-reliance on attitude as the index of effect.[8] This kind of model of mass media influence is still the basis of much thinking on the subject. It may be that the media have little immediate impact on attitudes as commonly assessed by social scientists, but it seems likely that they have other important effects. In particular they would seem to play a major part in defining for people what the important issues are and the terms in which they should be discussed. Thus the debate surrounding race in Britain has come to be defined as hinging on immigrant numbers and the threat to existing social patterns, rather than on integration, housing, or other issues.

We now present, with some supporting evidence, an outline of one of the main ways in which we believe the mass media influence the race relations situation in Britain at the present time. We are concerned with the news media in particular because these relate directly to the present social situation, have wide circulation and enjoy the high credibility that enhances their capacity to influence how people think.[9] They also provide a steady stream of race-related information. Preliminary content analysis shows that the typical popular national daily contains on average two items a day in which coloured people in Britain or the u.s.a. figure, or that deal with explicitly race-related topics.

THE ARGUMENT

Briefly, our thesis is that the way race-related material is handled by the mass media serves both to perpetuate negative perceptions of blacks and to define the situation as one of intergroup conflict. In communities where there is a realistic basis for conflict (e.g., competition for housing) black-versus-white thinking about the situation will be reinforced by the media and existing social strains amplified. In multi-racial communities where there is no 'objective' basis for conflict, conflict may be created because people come to think in conflict terms. People in all-white communities are particularly liable to accept the interpretation of events offered by the media because they lack any basis of contact with coloured people on which to arrive at an alternative way of looking at things – apart, of course, from the view of blacks provided by traditional culture.

Mass communications regarding race will be interpreted within the framework of meanings that serve to define the situation within any social group. At the same time the way race-related material is handled in the media contributes towards this definition of the situation. Attitudes and interpretations prevailing in a community are therefore seen as the result of the interplay between the on-the-ground social situation and the way race is handled by the media.

'Media influence' is seen as operating on interpretive frameworks – the categories people use when thinking about race-related matters – rather than on attitudes directly. The way the media define the situation is seen as resulting from the definitions prevailing in the general culture and from institutional factors that stem from the media themselves.

The media are social institutions located within the overall socio-economic structure, and they have their own characteristics which influence the form and content of their output. In the first place, the nature of the medium itself, the kind of production ideology this generates, together with simple physical limitations of time and space, and the need to attract readers and viewers, imposes constraints both on what events make the news and on the kind of treatment they receive. The well-known preference for action visuals over 'talking heads' in television production, for instance, means that television coverage of a riot, say, is likely to emphasize the violence to the neglect of the causes and background. This was the major criticism made against the television coverage of the 1967 disturbances in America by the Kerner Commission.[10] The Commission concluded that the type of coverage given contributed to the definition of the disturbances as simple black-white confrontations. This is still the generally accepted view, even though the Commission found that the situation was in fact far more complex. 'In fact almost all the deaths, injuries and property damage occurred in all-negro neighbourhoods, and thus the disorders were not "race riots" as that term is generally understood.'[11]

The cultural legacy
The are two main strands to our argument. They are intertwined but it will make for clarity to illustrate each separately. Briefly, the first is this: The British cultural tradition contains elements derogatory to foreigners, particularly blacks. The media operate within the culture and are obliged to use cultural symbols. Hence it is almost inevitable that they will help to perpetuate this tradition in some measure. The prevalence of images and stereotypes deriving mainly from the colonial experience and at least implicitly derogatory to coloured people may be gauged from the existence of a number of traditions of cartoon jokes. These include the missionary in the pot, the fakir on his bed of nails, the snake charmer, and the polygamous Eastern potentate with his harem. Similar themes and images are to be found in nursery rhyme, idiom and literature.

We do not think that these examples are particularly important in themselves, except as an index of the widespread familiarity with, if not acceptance of, the image of coloured people that they carry.

It does, however, become disturbing to find this kind of outmoded image obtruding itself into the media handling of current events concerning real people; so that elements of the cultural legacy that are at best ethnocentric and at worst racist come to influence reactions to and interpretations of race-related events in Britain today. The tendency may most clearly be seen in headlines and in cartoon comment, where the use of a phrase or image that will evoke a similar set of associations and meanings in virtually all members of the society to which it is directed enables a complex point to be crystallized unambiguously and memorably in a few words or a single picture. In its front page report of the discovery of the forty illegal Indian immigrants in a Bradford cellar last July the *Daily Express* of 2 July used the heading POLICE FIND FORTY INDIANS IN 'BLACK HOLE'. This is an instantly recognizable allusion to the 'black hole of Calcutta', which, by evoking colonial associations suggests that the appropriate attitude to adopt towards these Indians is that adopted towards the natives in the days of Empire. We are not suggesting that this is what the *Express* intended, only that this is the sort of reaction that the heading is likely to have achieved. The importance of headlines in influencing the way news items are interpreted has been demonstrated by Tannenbaum, and by Warr and Knapper.[12] Headlines have a particularly strong influence when the item itself is not thoroughly read. In the illegal immigrant story, a similar effect was created by the cartoon in the *Sun* on 3 July in which an illegal immigrant asking the way addresses a white man as 'Sahib', and in the cartoon in the *Mirror* on 6 July which showed two lovers on a beach, one of whom was saying 'I thought you said this was a quiet beach' while the beach was being overrun by illegal immigrants in turbans, including a man riding on an elephant, a snake-charmer complete with snake, and a man carrying a bed of nails. The reiteration of this kind of image, not merely at the level of joke or fantasy, but in relation to actual events involving real people, can only perpetuate an outlook which is not only outmoded but antithetical to good race relations and likely to influence perceptions of current events. These examples illustrate the way in which a cultural tradition may be at least partly self-sustaining. The image is used because it exists and is known to have wide currency and therefore enables easier communication. By virtue of being used it is kept alive and available for further use.

News value
The second strand of our argument concerns the concept of 'news value' which influences the pattern of coverage of race related topics. We might regard news value as composed of some of the major

criteria by which information about events is gathered, selected and published. Johan Galtung's[13] famous analysis of what factors make events newsworthy includes the concepts of unambiguity, meaningfulness, consonance, continuity and negativeness. Though we shall not use these terms our approach is essentially the same. A similar approach was used by Lang and Lang,[14] who showed that the television coverage of a parade in Chicago bore a closer resemblance to the newsmen's anticipations of what the event would be like, than to what actually happened. Similarly, Halloran[15] and his colleagues in their recent study of the anti-Vietnam war demonstration in London in October 1968 showed how the event came to be defined by the media in advance as a violent one, and once this news framework was established, how it structured the coverage of the event itself so that violence was emphasized, and the issues involved and the predominantly peaceful nature of the march neglected.

For present purposes we may distinguish two kinds of characteristics which make events newsworthy. Firstly, conflict, threat, and deviancy all make news, both because information about these has a real importance to society, and because, for various reasons, people enjoy hearing about them. Conflict is the stuff of news just as it is the stuff of drama and literature. Material that can be couched in terms of conflict or threat therefore makes better 'news' than that which cannot. Hence for the story of the forty illegal Indian immigrants referred to above, the front page of the *Daily Mail* of 2 July 1970, carried the headline 40 INDIANS 'INVADE'. The word 'invade' manages to imply that society is somehow threatened by them. This theme was echoed in the *Sun* of 3 July which headed its story THE INVADERS, and in the *Daily Sketch* of the same date which had the headline: 'INVASION OF MIGRANTS' FEAR IN BID TO BEAT BAN. Similarly, the police were said to have 'seized' the Indians in the same way as drugs, firearms and other dangerous commodities are seized (*Sun* and *Express*, 2 July). This story was big 'news', being carried on an outside page of seven of the eight major national dailies. That it could be made to carry the inference of threat and conflict would seem to be at least part of the reason that it was thought so newsworthy.

A second feature that makes events more newsworthy is their ability to be interpreted within a familiar framework or in terms of existing images, stereotypes and expectations. The framework and the expectations may originate in the general culture, or they may originate in the news itself and pass from there into the culture. The situation is one of continuous interplay between events, cultural meanings, and news frameworks. The way events are reported helps structure expectations of how coloured people will behave and how race relations situations develop. Subsequent events that conform to the expectation stand a better chance of making the news than those that do not. Thus new events may be interpreted in terms of existing images even if the existing image is not in fact the most appropriate. The use of the image of ethnic conflict derived from the American disorders of the 1960s as the framework for reporting the British situation is a case in point.

In January 1970 the Birmingham *Evening Mail* published a series of feature articles on the race relations situation in the Handsworth area, which explained the background to the social problems there. This was a positive attempt to foster better community relations and was rightly commended as such. The first article of the series, which gave an overview of the situation, provides a good example of what we have been discussing. Its first sentence was 'Must Harlem come to Birmingham?' In the subsequent fifty column inches there were four further explicit parallels drawn between Birmingham and the United States. There were also fourteen separate sentences in which explicit reference was made to violence (this excludes generalized references to crime and robbery). Effectively the situation is defined as one of potential riot. Thus the image of black-white confrontation derived from the media coverage of the American disorders becomes the model for thinking about the British situation, both because it is known to be familiar to the audience, and because it fulfils expectations of how race relations situations develop. The question is, is such an image the most appropriate one for Birmingham today, and does its use not have all the elements of the self-fulfilling prophecy? Might it not be that any benefits resulting from the in-depth explanation and pro-tolerance tone of the *Evening Mail* series were bought at the expense of confirming expectations of civil disorder and amplifying conflict in the area? The author of the article himself seems to be aware of the danger, for he writes:

> The trouble about violence in a multi-racial area like those we have in north Birmingham is that it may be dangerous to the community. People start using emotive words like 'race-riot' and take sides according to the colour of their skins. Reports appear in overseas newspapers. Before you know it the community is split into bitter factions. The problems of the Handsworth area are bad enough as it is.

The fact that he is effectively doing with the best of intentions what he fears might be done by others and the overseas press illustrates the apparently unconscious nature of many of the assumptions that go to structure the news.

The numbers game

Public perceptions of the race relations situation depend very heavily on the type of material made available through the media, the relative prominence given to different types of material and the way it is handled. All these factors are influenced by considerations of 'news value'. A comparison of the coverage given to two events by the eight major national dailies provides an illustration of this process in a particularly important area.

The events were the publication on 10 March 1970 of the Registrar General's returns which showed that the birth-rate among immigrants was higher than the national average, and the announcement by the Home Secretary on 14 May 1970 of the immigration statistics which showed that the rate of immigration was decreasing and that the number for the previous quarter was the lowest on record. Our comparisons are of the coverage of the events on 10 March and 15 May respectively, the days on which the news was first carried.

Seven of the eight national dailies carried the birth figures, five of them on the front page. Only four carried the news about the reduction in immigration, only one of these on the front page. The average headline for the birth figures occupied four times as much space as the average headline for the low immigration figures. Altogether there was about five times as much news-space given to the birth figures and reactions to them as to the immigration figures (approximately 250 column inches as compared with about 50). Five of the seven papers carried Enoch Powell's reaction to the birth figures, of which only one, *The Times*, went to the trouble of trying to balance the story by eliciting reactions from other sources. This pattern of coverage meant that almost no one who opened a newspaper on 10 March – or even glanced at his neighbour's on the bus – could fail to become aware that the coloured population was increasing and that this was regarded as a matter of great importance; while only the most diligent newspaper reader on 15 May would have discovered that the rate of immigration was low, and reducing.

Even if we accept that the birth figures were of greater social significance than the reduction in immigration and therefore warranted greater coverage, and allow that Enoch Powell did make a statement, a reportable event, it would still seem necessary to invoke other factors to explain this pattern of coverage.

Specifically, events that carry or can be given connotations of conflict or threat are more newsworthy than others. 'More coloureds' is thus better copy than 'fewer coloureds'. That the threat image was important in making the birth figures newsworthy is clear from the opening paragraph in the *Telegraph*'s front page report where it was stated that 'there was no sign of panic over the fact that nearly

12 per cent of the 405,000 babies . . . were conceived by mothers born outside the United Kingdom'. And the front page of the *Sketch* carried the assertion that 'The report adds fuel to Mr Enoch Powell's previous warnings of the rapid breeding rate among coloured families.' Note the use of the word 'warnings' and the acceptance of the Powell definition of the situation. The idea that coloured people constitute some kind of social threat is simply taken for granted – it has become one of the unspoken assumptions of the news framework. The birth figures made a story that fitted this framework, and so the story got big play. The reduction in immigration didn't fit the framework very well, and so it got little play. But even in the reporting of the immigration figures the framework is evident. All four papers that carried the story also reported the Home Secretary's determination to keep the figures low.

Finally the amount of newspace devoted to Powell's statement must be partly explained by the fact that Powell on race has come to be newsworthy in himself. Once a particular kind of news has hit the headlines there appears to be a lowering of the threshold for subsequent news of a similar kind. With Powell one has the impression that since his first immigration speech his every utterance on the question is now thought worth reporting, even if what he says differs in no important respect from what he said the previous week.

SOME RESULTS

It is one thing to argue from an examination of the media themselves that their handling of race effectively defines the situation in conflict terms, and another to show that this pattern of coverage does in fact influence people's view of the matter. We now present evidence based on a partial analysis of some of the data from our ongoing research that provide support for our general argument. These results cannot be taken as conclusive because our sample is small and confined to white working-class secondary schoolchildren, and the differences we have found do not always reach a high level of statistical significance. A rigorous evaluation of our argument must await the completion of our data collection and analysis. However, the results we have available show a sufficiently coherent pattern to make them worth presenting now.

Unless otherwise stated, the quantitative evidence that follows is based on a combined group of 208 11/12 year old and 14/15 year old children, both boys and girls. Half of them come from areas of high immigration in the West Midlands and West Yorkshire and half from Teesside and Glasgow where immigration has been very low. Schools were chosen in pairs from each area so that one contained an appreciable number of coloured immigrant children (at least 10 per cent, normally 20–40 per cent) and the other few or none. So we have fifty-two children from 'high contact' schools in 'high contact' areas (high-highs), fifty-two low-highs, fifty-two high-lows and fifty-two low-lows. We shall make our comparisons between 'high' and 'low' types of *area*, and our sampling design ensures that the children are roughly equated for amount of personal contact with coloured people, and for social class.

The first thing that has become evident from our interviews is the widespread conviction that the number of coloured people in the country or the rate of immigration is very high and that this poses some kind of threat. This is true even of places where there has been no immigration. In a school in a County Durham village for example (not part of the sample described above) as many as 35 per cent of children expressed something of this kind in response to general open-ended questions. When specifically asked whether they thought anything should be done about coloured immigration to Britain, nearly half (47·4 per cent) advocated restricted entry or more stringent policies. In areas of high immigration the impression of vast numbers is understandably even greater and a clear majority want the numbers limited or reduced. But in an area like our Durham village the only possible major source of this impression is the media. Even apart from that, what is striking is that the idea that 'there are too many here' or 'too many coming in' should be taken as self-evident by such large proportions of children wherever they live. Clearly the message about numbers and their implied threat has got through. It has been equally evident that the message that there is little threat (promoted from time to time, usually in editorials) has not got through. Nor has it got through that whatever threat was posed by unrestricted immigration is now being dealt with. We were confronted with people recommending, as a matter of urgency, the adoption of policies that have been in operation for five years! This is clearly the result of the pattern of reporting about 'numbers' discussed earlier. The inference of threat that any increase in numbers has come to carry is also evident from the fact that when asked how they thought the presence of coloured people in Britain would affect their lives in the future, 23 per cent of all answers referred explicitly to increasing numbers or expressed the fear that the blacks would 'take over'.

Other findings show an interesting pattern. Firstly, children in areas of high immigration are more aware of the major points of 'realistic' competition or conflict between black and white – namely, housing, and employment – than are children in 'low' areas. When asked, 'How do you think the presence of coloured people in Britain might affect your life in the future?', firstly fewer of them foresaw no effect (thirty-eight compared with sixty-one of the 'low' group), and secondly they were more likely to say that their housing or employment opportunities would be threatened (25 per cent of 138 answers given compared with 13 per cent of 117 answers – these include 'no effect' answers. When 'no effect' answers are left out, the percentages change to 35 per cent of 100 answers in 'high' areas, and 27 per cent of fifty-six answers in 'low' areas. Some children gave more than one answer). This fits the commonsense expectation and is also consistent with the pattern of attitude scores which shows that there is more hostility in areas with a realistic basis for conflict.

On this basis we might expect that the ideas of white children in areas of high immigration would be relatively more dominated by the notion of conflict than those living elsewhere. To test this we examined the responses to one of our first questions, 'Can you tell me what you know about coloured people living in Britain today?' Ten per cent of each group gave no answer. Of the remainder we counted the responses having a conflict theme. These fell broadly into three groups: (a) References to direct conflict, e.g., 'They cause trouble.' 'They make riots.' (b) Responses implying incompatibility of interests between black and white, e.g., 'They take all the houses.' 'They take white people's jobs.' 'They'll take over the country soon'; and (c) Responses that showed awareness of hostility of whites to blacks, e.g., 'People dislike them; are prejudiced against them; discriminate against them.' These were counted whether they were said with approval or disapproval. The essential criterion was whether the response explicitly or implicitly contained a definition of the situation in terms of conflict. This is not the same as attitude. Contrary to the hypothesis we found that conflict themes were more common in areas of *low* immigration (29·6 per cent of 159 responses, as compared with 23·0 per cent of 161 responses in areas of high immigration – some gave more than one response).

For each response a child gave we asked him also for the source of his information. 27·4 per cent of the 190 sources mentioned in 'low' areas were media sources, against only 17·5 per cent of 177 sources in 'high' areas. Taking both groups together, 54·2 per cent of the 83 responses attributed to a media source were 'conflict' responses, as against 45·1 per cent of the 62 attributed to other people, and 16·7 per cent of the 222 claimed as personal experience, 'own idea', or 'don't know'. So of all the information children were able to give us, that obtained from the media was more likely to contain the conflict theme than that obtained elsewhere. Looked at in another way, there were 110 responses in all that had the conflict theme of which 45 (41 per cent) were attributed to a media source.

There were 41 answers that mentioned cultural differences (religion, clothing, life-style) of which only five (12 per cent) were attributed to media sources. This suggests that while the media seem to play a major role in establishing in people's minds the association of colour with conflict, their role in providing the kind of background information that would help make the race relations situation, including its conflict elements, more understandable, is relatively small.

The picture seems clear, and is what might be expected if our analysis of the handling of race-related matters in the mass media is correct. Children who live in areas of low immigration rely perforce more heavily on the media for their information about coloured people than do others. Media-supplied information carries the inference of conflict more often than that from other sources. As a result these children are more prone to think about race relations in terms of conflict than are those in 'high' contact areas, even though they (the 'lows') live in places where the objective conditions for inter-group competition or conflict are absent. It would seem that while *attitudes* are responsive to the characteristics of the local situation – i.e., the extent of immigration – interpretive frameworks, ways of thinking, are heavily structured by the mass media, particularly in areas where there are few immigrants.

CONCLUSION

. . . We have argued that a number of factors pertaining to traditional culture, to the media as institutions, the technologies and their related ideologies, and to the interplay between these factors, operate to structure the news coverage of race related matters in a way that causes people to see the situation primarily as one of actual or potential conflict. Blacks come to be seen as conflict-generating *per se* and the chances that people will think about the situation in more productive ways – in terms of the issues involved or of social problems generally – are reduced. The result is that real conflict is amplified, and potential for conflict created. For the media not only operate within the culture, they also make culture and they help shape social reality.

Clearly the factors that we have discussed are not the only ones that structure news coverage. There are obviously others, including the nature of events themselves and editorial policy, but the ones we have discussed do influence what is reported and how it is reported. Although there may be political and other motives at work in the media that influences the coverage of race, it is not necessary to invoke these to explain the kind of pattern we have described. A main point of our argument is that this kind of result may be produced in a quite unintended fashion. The media do not need to *try* to define the situation in terms of conflict. They need merely unreflectingly to follow their normal procedures of news-gathering and selection and to apply their normal criteria of news value.

REFERENCES

1. E. J. B. Rose et al., *Colour and citizenship* (London, Oxford University Press for the Institute of Race Relations, 1969).
2. N. Deakin, *Colour, citizenship and British society* (London, Panther Books, 1970).
3. J. M. Trenaman, D. McQuail, *Television and the political image* (London, Methuen, 1961).
4. Jay G. Blumler and D. McQuail, *Television in politics: its uses and influence* (London, Faber & Faber, 1968).
5. E. Cooper, H. Dinerman, 'Analysis of the film "Don't be a sucker": a study in communication'. *Public Opinion Quarterly*, Vol. 15, No. 2 (1951).
6. The study was carried out by Dr Roger Brown in connection with a production study conducted by Philip Elliott, to be published shortly.
7. J. T. Klapper, *The effects of mass communication* (New York, Free Press, 1960).
8. A good review of work in this tradition is to be found in Klapper (op. cit.). For general reviews and discussion of mass communications research and theory see: D. McQuail, *Towards a sociology of mass communications* (New York, Collier-Macmillan, 1969); M. L. De Fleur, *Theories of mass communication* (New York, McKay, 1966); J. D. Halloran (ed.), *The effects of television* (London, Panther, 1970).
9. See, e.g., Klapper (op. cit.), Chapter V.; C. I. Hovland, I. L. Janis, H. H. Kelley, *Communication and persuasion* (New Haven, Yale University Press, 1953).
10. *Report of the National Advisory Commission on Civil Disorders* (New York, Bantam Books, 1968).
11. Ibid., p. 365.
12. P. H. Tannenbaum, 'The effect of headlines on the interpretation of news stories', *Journalism Quarterly*, Vol. 30, (1953), p. 189–97; and P. B. Warr and B. Knapper, *The perception of people and events* (New York, John Wiley & Sons, 1968).
13. J. Galtung and M. H. Ruge, 'The structure of foreign news', *Journal of Peace Research*, No. 1 (1965). See extract in this Reader.
14. K. Lang and G. E. Lang, 'The unique perspective of television and its effect: a pilot study', *American Sociological Review*, XVIII (1953), pp. 3–12.
15. J. D. Halloran, P. Elliott and G. Murdock, *Demonstrations and communications: a case study* (Harmondsworth, Penguin Books, 1970). See also article by G. Murdock in this Reader.
16. H. Evans, *The Listener* (16 July 1970).

How to be immoral and ill, pathetic and dangerous, all at the same time: mass media and the homosexual*

FRANK PEARCE[1]

Before the emergence of the Gay Liberation Movement, there were few people, in this country including homosexuals themselves, who would claim that to be a homosexual was as desirable as to be a heterosexual. Even those supporting the 1967 Sexual Offences Act in its passage through parliament tended to view them as sick or unfortunate, and less informed opinion has often made even harsher judgments relatively consistently until the last five or so years. In such a climate there was a possibility of prosecution (a danger that still exists if practising homosexuals are under 21 or if their sexual acts do not take place 'in private', or if they are service-men or merchant seamen) losing one's job and a fear of rejection by family, friends and the local community. The fear of social stigma and the dangers of making sexual advances to strangers meant that it was only in the interstices of society that homosexuals were able to create the social life that is a precondition for developing any satisfactory sexual relationships.

The fear of social stigma and police pressure tended to make them concentrate in 'gay ghettoes', hidden from public view. At the extreme it has forced some homosexuals to protect themselves even from each other by only engaging in the anonymous sex that takes place in public toilets, known colloquially as 'cottages' in Britain and as 'tearooms' in America. Under these conditions heterosexuals have little chance of learning through their own experience how essentially similar homosexuals are to themselves. Cases such as child molesting are predominantly the ones presented to the public.

This only serves to reinforce the inaccurate view that homosexuals typically engage in such practices. Little help toward achieving a true picture is given by the innumerable jokes involving 'pansies', 'Nancy-boys', 'brown-hatters', etc. Probably the only source of systematically presented information is the newspapers. But this is made available in a sensational manner in articles with such titles as

* Paper prepared especially for this volume.

EVIL MEN (*Sunday Pictorial*, 26 May, 1 June, 8 June 1952), THE SICK MEN OF HAMPSTEAD HEATH (*The People*, 24 March 1968), and TWILIGHT TRAITORS (*News of the World*, 28 October 1962).

Because of its importance in forming public attitudes it is the press, and particularly the Sunday newspapers, which will be the focus of this article. I am going to examine their portrayal of the nature of homosexuality and its social organization in Britain.

Since reports were infrequent I have tended to concentrate on a limited number of cases that were important news stories and also on feature articles in the Sunday papers. The news stories include those dealing with the trials of Montagu and Wildeblood, the Vassall case and the Wolfenden Report, the feature articles were written in 1952, 1963, 1968, 1972. Although I read accounts in *The Times* and *The Guardian* I have taken most of the examples from the *Daily Mirror*, *Daily Sketch*, and *Daily Telegraph*, *Sunday Pictorial/Sunday Mirror* (changed January 1963), *News of the World*, and *Sunday People*. There is ample justification for such concentration since the *Daily Telegraph* is the most important paper among social grade AB, and, while in 1970, only 45 per cent of this social grade bought the *Sunday Times* and *Observer* (combining the sales), 45 per cent bought the *Sunday Express*, and 49 per cent bought either the *Sunday Mirror*, *News of the World* or *The People*. Needless to say these latter three newspapers are the most widely read by the rest of the population.[2]

Why is homosexuality treated with both fear and scorn? To answer this requires an analysis of its relationship to 'normal' sexuality. What *this* was and what should be done about it has been a major concern of the church in Britain. The Christian tradition tended to view man's sexual urges as part of his baser nature and thus to be controlled. Regrettably complete control was not possible, if for no other reason than that it was only by sexual intercourse that increasing and multiplying could be achieved. Furthermore, different Christian churches at different times in history were more or less optimistic over the degree to which these urges could be regulated and repressed. In Victorian Britain puritanical morality which publicly proclaimed the necessity to repress sexuality was dominant.[3] Sex was publicly referred to mainly when it was being denounced or in the context of reproduction. This functional stress led in the early twentieth century to the sex drive being called the 'racial instinct'.[4]

Such a view was compatible with both the Malthusian pessimism dominant during most of the nineteenth century and the concern with producing healthy workers and soldiers in the early part of the twentieth century. After further concern in the 1930s about a drop in the birth rate, the 1940s saw the beginning of a change in attitude. Fears about underpopulation and the quality of the population were transformed into a worry about overpopulation. Social concern over this and the custom of smaller families led to a decreasing emphasis on marriage as a baby factory. The relationship between husband and wife gained in importance, and sex was credited with a significant role in this relationship.

During the period when the church only tolerated sexuality because it led to reproduction, sexual acts which could not, by their very nature, produce children were condemned as unnatural. Canon Law, Henry VIII's act of 1535, and subsequent legal practice used the term 'buggery' to describe such unnatural acts. These included sodomy, irrespective of whether it took place between members of the same or different sexes, and bestiality, involving sex relations with animals. The rhetoric of M.P.s such as Shepherd, Osborne and Black in the House of Commons debate in 1966 on the Sexual Offences Bill, demonstrated very clearly that in the view of many, 'sex without responsibility' was still viewed as unnatural. Furthermore, the legislative practice of grouping homosexual activity with other kinds of undesirable sexual activity was only ended with the passing of the 1967 Sexual Offences Act. Both the 1885 Criminal Law Amendment Act which created the offence of Gross Indecency between men, and the anti-soliciting and importuning Vagrancy Act of 1888 contained provisions designed effectively to contain heterosexual relations within marriage. Homosexual activity was legislatively acknowledged, in order to more effectively eliminate it *and sex-as-such* from the public consciousness. In fact it was only in the 1950s when sex was openly discussed in the newspapers that it became possible to focus attention on homosexual practices.

I have made clear that official morality's definition of homosexuality has long been one that defined such sexual practices as unnatural. They were viewed as such, since those equipped with penises were expected to comport themselves in a masculine manner which necessarily included heterosexual desires. Men who had sex with other men were seen to be perverted. In the pre-psychiatric versions (still very strongly represented in the 1966 debates over the Sexual Offences Act), these men chose to give in to 'temptation'. In the later clinical versions they were seen as being impelled towards homosexual acts through either physiological deficiency (chromosomal or otherwise) or through psychological immaturity. Whether homosexuals are to be pitied or condemned, this view sees them as defective males. As opposed to this view one might argue that people in this society are potentially bisexual and are brought up in a 'sex-negative' culture, where homosexuality particularly is condemned and is therefore not provided for in any socially accepted way. Exclusive heterosexuality and exclusive homosexuality are not conditions but are rather 'roles' that people commit themselves to, to a greater or lesser extent. In this society the heterosexual role is publicly valued, highly articulated, socially provided for and also associated with gender identity. At the same time men who wish to engage in homosexual practices after adolescence are virtually forced to utilize the organized homosexual network of meeting places which exist in the interstices of the society. Commitment to a homosexual way of life is likely to result, since some kind of minimal involvement is called for in order to learn the skills and cues necessary for this as any other sexual activity. Thus the average male in this society is constantly pushed towards heterosexual involvement and away from homosexual eroticism, and if he experiments with homosexuality he is likely with decreasing age either to abandon it or virtually to commit himself to it completely by adopting a homosexual role. And so exclusive homosexuality is a logical corollary of enforced exclusive heterosexuality and occurs when a homosexual role has been created.[5]

Using Kinsey's American figures as a basis, estimates have been made for the number of committed homosexuals in Britain. This is probably 5 per cent; while the number who have had some homosexual experience to the point of orgasm between adolescence and old age is some 37 per cent; and the number who have experienced homoerotic feelings, some 50 per cent. Thus the inclusive total for males who have had some homosexual feelings probably includes at least some 50 per cent of the male population.[6]

These figures obviously pose a real problem for the belief that homosexuality is 'unnatural'. It helps fracture the coherence of the core gender identities – thought to be necessarily associated with male and female biological equipment. Those men finding other men attractive are anomalies, and 'anomalies' as Mary Douglas points out, endanger the natural moral order of this society: 'in a chaos of shifting impressions each of us constructs a stable world in which objects have recognizable shapes, are located in depth, and have permanence'.[7]

But our categories are constantly confronted in everyday living with a world which they cannot exhaust, and this becomes serious when there are anomalies which question the validity of the very categories themselves. In such cases she suggests that societies have evolved strategies for dealing with the threat to their universality: (1) Negatively we can ignore, just not perceive them or perceiving them, condemn. (2) We can settle for one or other possible interpretation of what they are and thereby reduce ambiguity. (3) We may use the anomaly as a negative reference point – all that something should not be. (4) The anomalous event may be labelled as dangerous and reacted to appropriately, and this may involve violence. I will return to these categories again.

But first, I wish to make a relevant criticism of Mary Douglas! In one place she comments on Sartre's analysis of antisemites as follows: 'This diatribe implies a division between ours and the rigid black and white thinking of the antisemite. Whereas, of course, the yearning for rigidity is in us all. It is part of our human condition to long for hard lines and clear concepts.'[8] In so formulating the problem she fails to recognize that certain social structures are more likely to engender the restriction of human potential than are others. Moreover that the importance given to particular categories depends on how firmly wedded they are to culturally significant and structurally important social practices. As I have argued homosexual practices were condemned because they called into question ideas of masculinity that were tied into the roles men performed in the family, and the economy and the army. Furthermore, the reasons for viewing the family as important depended upon which social class was examined. For capitalists and also for the petit-bourgeois it was intimately linked with the inheritance and consolidation of private property.[9] For most of the rest of society its function was to reproduce a crucial factor of production: the healthy, loyal, obedient worker. Loyalty and obedience are instilled by processes such as those analysed by Laing (in his book *Politics of the family*); as Kenneth Patchen puts it:

No man ever stood up to authority but did so with a sense of guilt. How they have trapped us! That's the secret of their power, for deep in all of us is a sense that they must be right.[10]

Far-sighted capitalists had supported factory legislation because healthy workers were more profitable, being more efficient and more likely to repay the cost of their training. A desire to produce healthy workers and soldiers was a major reason for the general support given to the social welfare legislation at the beginning of this century. A healthy family was seen as most likely to produce healthy men who could contribute to the nation's wealth and protection and reformers such as Beveridge explicitly related productivity and citizenship.[11]

This stress on the family and reproduction was aligned with the dominant aggressively masculine images of men as either rugged individualistic entrepreneurs or as tough manual workers and brave soldiers. Home and work definitions of men tended to stress their differences from women who were seen as:

> inconsistent, emotionally unstable, lacking in a strong conscience or super-ego, weaker, 'nurturants' rather than productive, intuitive rather than intelligent, and if they were at all 'normal' suited to the home and family.[12]

Thus the reasons for the importance given to heterosexuality as a necessary component of manliness are linked both directly and via the family to the structure of our society. With slight structural change, for example in the job market, some of the more clear-cut sex role expectations also alter and developments such as, for example, the open marketing of unisex clothes become possible.

SUPPRESSION OF KNOWLEDGE

It is precisely because of a new flexibility over the masculine/feminine roles that I have concentrated in my analysis of newspapers in the period 1950–68. The 1950s were the time when sex started to be discussed openly; the late 1960s were the time when the social consciousness had started to recognize the implications of changes in employment patterns for masculine and feminine roles. Indeed this, and the changing importance of the family, made possible a re-emergence of a women's movement in this country.

The first method Mary Douglas mentions to cope with anomalies is to ignore the phenomenon. Prior to the 1950s homosexuality was virtually never mentioned and an examination of daily and Sunday newspapers in the 1950s finds that homosexuals are mentioned relatively infrequently. One survey, conducted by the Howard League for Penal Reform, found in an examination of press cuttings covering *all* homosexual cases reported in national or provincial papers, in the period October 1954 and February 1955, that only 321 individuals were reported as charged. The number of reports fell far short of this since pairs of these individuals were often in the same case.[13] My own examination revealed that only some local papers and the *News of the World* regularly devoted space to brief court reports concerning homosexual activities. This and other information was generally bitty and restricted to a minority of homosexuals, feeding stereotypical pictures of their activities. Occasionally, however, there was a news explosion. During most of 1957 the *Daily Mirror* never mentioned homosexuality, then, after the publication of the Wolfenden Report, in September it devoted to it 963 column inches in two weeks. The following two weeks it had already dropped to 45 column inches, and after that there was virtually no reference to the subject at all.[14] The articles of Swarth in the *Sunday Pictorial* of 1952 were seen by Swarth and the *Daily Mirror*'s editor Hugh Cudlipp as an end to this 'conspiracy of silence' about the subject. Cudlipp claimed that these articles

> stripped the subject of the careful euphemistic language in which it has always been concealed. Doctors, social workers and the wretched homosexuals themselves recognized this as a sincere attempt to get to the root of a spreading fungus.[15]

The blatant dishonesty of such a statement is made evident by Swarth's own proud recounting of homosexual fears about the effect of his articles. ' "This will make life dangerous", one of them said and he named three of his revolting friends, who on the strength of my report, took the boat to Guernsey' ('Evil men', *Sunday Pictorial*, 1 June 1952). Gradually the general awareness of sexuality entailed a recognition of homosexuality too.

DEVIANTS AS SOCIAL PROBLEMS

In the stereotypical presentation of deviants' identity, the essential self of the deviants is seen to reside in their deviant activity. There are murderers, cold-blooded IRA gunmen, junkies, homosexuals. They are obsessional about their vice and clearly differentiated from other men. Their supposed essential difference from other men is emphasized by *objectifying* them, using a vocabulary which emphasized that they are *less than* the normal human citizen. Homosexuals are called 'freaks', 'perverts', 'degenerates' and at one extreme they may be given remarkably consistent animal characteristics: Vassall's 'pale eyes flickered like a lizard's towards the domed ceiling and he did not reply. . . . He listened unblinking, emotionless as a newt.' Meanwhile (!) 'Burgess sits in Moscow like a patient toad awaiting his next willing victim' ('Twilight Traitors', *News of the World*, 28 October 1962). They may also be described as 'sick', 'ill' or 'unfortunate'. And it was precisely such labels that were used by those who supported the 1967 Sexual Offences Bill. Yet these also objectify, they express the arrogant pity of the 'healthy' for the 'sick'. Sometimes there is an unintended humour in articles on homosexuality. Vassall was often described as a 'tool of the Russians', and one doctor said that the study of homosexuals was 'still in the groping stage of trial and error' ('Evil men', *Sunday Pictorial*, 8 June 1952).

I have already indicated that all classes read the sensational press. They find deviance an interesting phenomena. A possible reason for this was suggested by Laing. 'There are many pleasurable feelings many people are forbidden to experience, imagine, remember, dream about, and they are definitely forbidden to talk about them.'[16] These pleasurable sensations that we have denied but not annihilated may be lived through again by means of the sensational newspaper. By reading a newspaper we are able to stumble across stories about the unthinkable-for-me, pleasurable deviant acts. We can read the details, be disturbed by the salaciousness of what is written, and then condemn what has taken place. We have thereby broken none of our convoluted rules, and yet lived through the forbidden experiences and gained the additional pleasure of moral indignation. It is for this reason that although people complain about the sensationalism, morbidity and triviality of newspapers, 'Sex, crime, violence, scandal and gossip, the very topics deplored, regularly obtain high "thorough readership" scores'.[17] One popular article on homosexuality provided, in repetitive detail, accounts of what four teams of reporters saw on Hampstead Heath. One team claimed (?) that 'At least one hundred men cavorted among the bushes. Some were naked, some were partly dressed. They embraced. They kissed. They cuddled' (*The People*, 24 March 1968).

To analyse adequately the treatment of homosexuals we must take account of its specificity. Guy Burgess and Oscar Wilde are the ideal-typical models for the affluent homosexuals. One newspaper account of Vassall's life, for example, seems to be closer to such types than what Vassall himself wrote (or at least acknowledged) in the *Sunday Pictorial* (and was, in fact directly based on Peter Wildeblood's autobiography *Against the law*). Furthermore there are constant cross-references to various cases, supporting Galtung's contention that news items are reported in images derived from previous stories. (Galtung's example was of the Norwegian Broadcasting Corporation only reporting those aspects of the Russian invasion of Czechoslovakia which were consonant with its image of the 1956 invasion of Hungary.)[18] Although it may well be true that newspaper reporters and editors do so naïvely, without realizing it, this does not take away their responsibility as opinion formers of trying to be honest and accurate.

AMBIGUITY AND RESOLUTION

The second method of dealing with anomalies is by settling for one or other interpretation. Mary Douglas points out that the Nuer treat monstrous human births as baby hippopotami and lay them down in the river where they belong. Homosexuals violate the natural order – they are men who are attracted to men. They are thought of as being like the hippopotami. However instead of being an animal born to a human they are women born in a man's body. This metaphysical belief that homosexuals are men with women's souls inspires the medical research on the subject. Experiments trying to find evidence of female chromosomes illustrate this belief admirably.[19] This similarly explains the tremendous stress by journalists on their effeminacy – usually emphasized through juxtaposition with normal masculinity.

'Most people know there are such things – "pansies" – mincing effeminate, young men who call themselves queers. But simple, decent folk regard them as freaks and rarities.' ('Evil men', *Sunday Pictorial*, 25 May 1952).

They are seen as working in the 'unvirile' professions:

Homosexuality is rife in the theatrical profession. Dress designers, hat makers, window-dressers have a high percentage of homosexuals in their ranks.

The style and comportment is female. They 'have mincing ways'. ('Evil men', *Sunday Pictorial*, 25 May 1952), call 'each other girls' names openly', are 'painted perverts', (*Sunday Pictorial*, 8 June 1952). They wear women's clothes. This was particularly stressed in the Vassall case ('Secrets of the scented flat', *Daily Sketch*, 24 January 1963). Then: 'I watched effeminate-looking men disappear into the "ladies" to titivate their appearance and tidy their waved, dyed hair before going into the back room to dance and cuddle with their "boyfriends".' ('Do we need pubs like this?', *The People*, 24 March 1968.) Photographs can also be used to give particular kinds of impressions. During the Montagu–Wildeblood case the *Daily Mirror* published a photograph of Wildeblood which made him look extremely effeminate. On close examination the photographs had obviously been touched up so that he looked as if he was wearing lipstick. Finally there is often a stress on a female-like interest in clothes. Vassall had 'nineteen Savile Row suits' (*Daily Sketch*, 23 October 1962).

Having recategorized homosexuals as women in men's bodies resolution can be achieved by uniting the female mind with a female body. The newspapers are very sympathetic when operations are performed to effect just such transformations. Moreover they are often sympathetic during periods of time when they are writing very emotive articles about homosexuality.

Thus the *Daily Sketch* (15 December 1953) had an article entitled 'Sex Change Dilemma' which dealt sympathetically with the problems faced by somebody wanting a sex-change operation. This was in the middle of the stereotypically presented Montagu of Beaulieu case, and just over a month after an article by Donald Soper entitled WHY I WANT A ROYAL COMMISSION TO INVESTIGATE VICE, meaning homosexuality (in which he made the novel prediction 'that a disarmed world would be a world in which homosexuality would die out'.

The *News of the World* (7 October 1962) had an article headlined SEX CHANGE BRIDE and a sympathetic portrayal. Only three weeks later it had a vicious article entitled TWILIGHT TRAITORS. Similarly The *News of the World* (9 November 1969) had a front-page article, LONDON BOBBY TURNS INTO A GIRL: an article stressing that Miss Linda Grant was feminine from the beginning and the *Sunday Mirror* (13 February 1972) had an article entitled HE OR SHE? AGONY OF A TV STAR.

The effeminate are generally viewed as harmless, the world laughs at them but it rejoices with them when they resolve their 'identity' problems and match the right mind with the right body. Thus ambiguity is resolved by recategorizing the anomaly as an example of the production of a hybrid which is in turn put together again properly.

MORAL TALES

Needless to say not all homosexuals are so treated. Their existence may also be used, again following Mary Douglas, as a negative reference point: as an occasion to reinforce conventional moral values by telling a moral tale. Through these means tensions in the social system can be dealt with and 'conventionalized'.[19] Explicit and implicit contrasts are made between the nature and moral career of 'ordinary men' and that of 'perverts', 'degenerates', 'sick men', 'freaks' and the 'abnormally sexed'. These latter inevitably come to a bad end and the whole incident is used as an occasion to preach 'a little sermon'.[20] Nowhere has this been better demonstrated than in the case of Vassall, the rather insignificant spy of the early 1960s. Vassall was discovered to be a spy after a whole series of scandals during the 1950s – Burgess, MacLean, Philby and the Portdown spy ring. There were allegations that his boss at the Admiralty, Galbraith, was emotionally involved with him, although, looking at the evidence, this in fact seems unlikely. However, Vassall was a homosexual and it was through his homosexual activities that the Russians were able to blackmail him. He was finally sentenced to 18 years' imprisonment and was released in 1972. The whole case was used by the press to demonstrate what happened to the unnatural.

To understand how this was done, it is necessary first to construct the implicit model of the career of the 'normal man'. He is born into a normal, stable family. He is given a proper amount of affection by his mother, is not mollycoddled or rejected. His father spends time with him – he takes him 'to see the trains' – and helps him to develop masculine qualities. He then goes to a school befitting his class and intelligence. He works hard there and in particular he plays sports well. He then gets a job fitting his abilities. This job should ideally be in useful occupation – not in the intellectual world, nor in the world of bars or the retail clothing trade. He then marries and has a family. He is proud of his respectable family and his useful job. He respects and is respected by those in other strata. He is patriotic and goes off to war.

Contrast this with the portrayal of Vassall. He had a strong affection for his mother – 'I needed mother love, and after my mother died they felt they could provide it!' (*Sunday Pictorial*, 11 November 1962). At school he didn't work hard academically and avoided sports. 'He was colourless and rather effeminate', Captain Noel Elston, the headmaster at his public school said. (*Sketch*, 23 October 1962). He had 'no moral fibre' – Defence Counsel (*Daily Telegraph*, 23 October 1962). (That peculiar concept compounded of a Christian belief in free will and some kind of genetic determinism.) At school his moral weakness expressed itself in his having homosexual relations with other boys. This lack of moral fibre further expressed itself in failures throughout his life: he failed to gain a commission; he was only an Admiralty clerk; and also he (supposedly) failed with women. (See particularly *Daily Mail*, 23 October 1962.) Vassall also claimed to be what he had no right to say he was. He claimed to be rich (as a schoolboy when his father was only a clergyman) and later (when only receiving a clerk's salary). He matched this presumptiousness with snobbishness. He did not manage his relationships with social inferiors properly.

Homosexuals are often seen to violate such barriers. Oscar Wilde had been virulently condemned for his relation with the lower classes and Wildeblood was criticized during his trial in 1954 for mixing with 'social inferiors', and much stress was placed on those who were given 'lavish hospitality from men who were their social superiors'.

In fact, as Wildeblood points out, the prosecution relabelled the bottle of cider as a bottle of Champagne. Similarly in the 'Evil men' series Swarth wrote, 'In Swansea police consider the vice most rampant among the "socially elevated classes", although they take their unnatural desires down to the dockland (*Sunday Pictorial*, 1 June 1952). The discipline of national life is seen as being endangered and it is precisely in those areas where this is most transparent that homosexuality is most severely attacked. Sexuality involves some kind of equality, hierarchical institutions are threatened by this. Thus the Army, Air Force, Navy and Merchant

Navy are excluded from the provisions of the 1967 Act. The justification for this was perhaps most clearly expressed in an American court case where an officer, Navy Lt Carl R. Pitasi, was convicted of fraternizing with an ordinary rating. On appeal the conviction was upheld because 'Some acts are by their very nature palpably and directly prejudicial to the good order and discipline of the services' (*Los Angeles Times*, 30 June 1971).

It was not surprising then that Vassall failing by normal methods to live the kind of life he wished, should, by the vice that was the strongest expression of this weakness, become a spy – a 'Traitorous tool of the RUSSIANS' as the *Daily Telegraph* expressed it (23 October 1962). For he was blackmailed by the Russians to spy for them through their having photographs of him in compromising positions with other men.

He was following a typical pattern: 'After the Burgess and Mac-Lean scandal, civil servants were urged to report any colleagues they suspected of having character defects such as drunkenness or homosexuality' (*Daily Express*, 13 November 1962).

'Who was for years an uncrowned leader in these garish guilty places? A diplomat called Guy Burgess, who disappeared to Moscow eleven years ago' ('Twilight traitors', *News of the World*, 28 October 1962). But now justice was done: 'Men – ordinary men who were patriotic, with normal feelings towards each other – had placed him in the dock, caged him like a rare trapped reptile.' Thus the moral career of the wicked – punished in the end.

I have already mentioned that, both when characterizing homosexuals as being effeminate and when using them to tell moral tales, a contrast is frequently drawn with 'normal men'. In the Vassall case Colonel John Macafee, Director of Security, was quoted in the *Daily Sketch* (23 October 1962) as saying, 'But if anyone wants to have me sacked, let them try. I walk around with a smile on my face and my shoulders are wide enough to take whatever is coming.' Unfortunately, people who according to this model would not be homosexuals turn out to be so. Particularly problematic are wartime heroes. For if a man is a brave superpatriot, how can he be a 'degenerate'? Here the papers demonstrate their brilliance. There are two solutions. They are either not homosexuals or they are not really superpatriots. In 1962, on December 23, less than a month after the article 'Twilight Traitors' in the *News of the World*, there appeared the following news item.

ARMY HERO CLEARS HIS NAME
Wartime Hero Michael Abbey Osborn who had been sentenced to be dismissed from the Service won his battle to clear his name

in the High Court. Colonel Osborn, holder of the DSO and MC, was accused of indecently assaulting a 15-year-old German boy a fortnight after arriving in Germany as Deputy Chief of Staff to the First British Corps of the Rhine Army. The 44-year-old Colonel, whose home is in the Old Brompton Road, Kensington, London, was found guilty at a Court Martial at Bielefeld. He appealed to the High Court but the three judges could not agree. Then Lord Parker, the Lord Chief Justice, ordered the appeal to be heard again by five judges. This time the appeal was allowed, and the conviction was quashed (*News of the World*, 23 December 1962).

This new item was also reported by the *Daily Mirror* on 23 January 1963 as THE CLEARED COLONEL WHO IS AFRAID TO BE FRIENDLY. This while they were still reporting the Vassall case.

In the *Sunday Mirror* of 7 April 1973, the front page was devoted to another wartime hero, ex-Lieutenant-Commander Christopher Carlisle Swayer. This was headlined WAS JUSTICE DONE? and outlined the dubious evidence on which this man was found guilty in 1956 of indecent assault. Happily he has since cleared his name. One wonders what the verdict would have been of those who followed the *Sunday Mirror*'s guide, 'How to spot a possible homo' – only three weeks later on 28 April.

But what of the clearly homosexual who have performed admirable tasks? This is solved by suggesting that they do not really do so.

They claim successes not only as writers and in the arts, theatre and poetry, but also as generals, admirals, fighter pilots, engine drivers and boxers. The brilliant war records of many homosexuals is explained by the fact that, as the Spartans, they fought in the company of those whose opinions they valued most highly (*Sunday Pictorial*, June 1952).

So it is for lust, not for patriotism that homosexuals behave bravely. Recently on a television programme the head of security operations pointed out that his bravest spy during the second world war was a homosexual. The man in question explained that he was brave in part to show that homosexuals too could be men of courage.

DANGEROUS DEVIANTS

The ways of coping with deviants that I have outlined so far have not particularly viewed them as a threat. When there is a stress on their inadequacies (not really men . . .) then they can be viewed as sick. They are people who require help and providing that they do not offend public decency, they can be more or less ignored. Further, when homosexuals are used in moral tales, the ending of the tale usually involves some kind of natural justice for them – again suggesting that society working normally will catch them if they are being harmful. Thus 'commonsense' precautions at embassies will exclude them as liable to blackmail, etc. However, alongside these views are others, where homosexuality is viewed as far more dangerous than this. This view is one which often involves an emphasis on a rather different stereotype from the effeminate male. This is the view that sees homosexuals primarily as corrupters of youth and is very prevalent despite the evidence to the contrary. Society is seen as clearly divided into three groups: the normal, the vulnerable and the corrupt. The relative size of each group depends on what is being presented, as does its visibility.

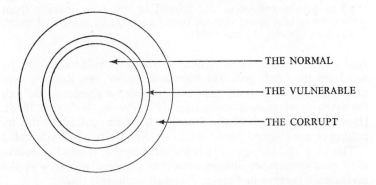

Homosexuals in this view are seen as being above all interested in young children. Thus Swarth bemoans that few parents 'recognize the corrupting dangers of the evil men who, in increasing numbers, pervert youngsters to their unnatural ways'. And he exemplified this by referring to the case of a

> 51-year-old vicar sent to prison for 15 years for ten offences against boys and a little girl of 13. He asked for 27 other offences to be taken into consideration. The police found a little black book in his possession, containing the names of 850 boys. Against the names of 382 of them were various symbols (*Sunday Pictorial*, 28 May 1952).

During the *Mirror*'s coverage of the Wolfenden Report, it juxtaposed on the same page for several days general articles on the topic with articles on a sensational sexual murder case, thus potentially linking this murder in the readers' minds with homosexuality. Information can be received without explicit linking. (One does not have to argue

that this was being done to mislead – the fact that these news items
were viewed as strongly associated is significant.) This model of
homosexuality has the advantage that all homosexuals can be
included. Vassall, for example, was seduced by much older boys. So
there is an unending tale of childhood corruption. Moreover, one
such contact is sometimes seen as enough, as in Swarth's account of
the 'Steamers'. These agency homosexuals were reputed to look out
for youths, job hunting.

> They offer them bed and breakfast, and that, in case after case, is a
> young man's introduction to perversion. Inevitably he drifts to
> the clubs that male prostitutes frequent! [However, not only
> children are vulnerable – if men go to prisons where there are
> already homosexuals . . .] Many men who are not homosexuals
> go to prison and come out tainted in this way, making them
> even more of a social menace than they were before ('Evil men',
> *Sunday Pictorial*, 4 June 1952).

And under extreme circumstances anybody is vulnerable – in the
article on the Leeds pub, *The Hope and Anchor*, one Rugby player
said 'that he was the only man who had been a regular at the pub
for seven years without going bent' (*The People*, 24 March 1968).
(However, in the first of the Swarth articles he contradicts this by
talking of *uncorrupted* young soldiers – who are still heterosexuals.)

This view of homosexuality is a disease model. It sees homosexuality as a contagious disease – much as madness was seen in the
seventeenth century in France. Foucault comments thus:

> Suddenly, in the middle of the eighteenth century a fear arose – a
> fear formulated in medical terms but animated basically by a
> moral truth. People were in dread of a mysterious disease that
> spread, it was said, from the houses of confinement, and would
> soon threaten the cities. They spoke of prison fevers; they evoked
> the wagons of criminals, men in chains who passed through the
> cities, leaving disease in their wake; scurvy was thought to cause
> contagions; it was said that the air, tainted by disease, would
> corrupt the residential quarters. And the great image of medieval
> horror reappeared, giving birth, in the metaphors of dread, to a
> second panic. The house of confinement was no longer only the
> Lazar house at the city's edge; it was leprosy itself confronting
> the town.[21]

This view of madness is not far from some of the views expressed in
the House of Commons during the debate on the Sexual Offences
Bill in 1966; it is close to Swarth's treatment of the gays; and it is
virtually identical to what James Douglas, editor of the *Sunday*

Express, wrote in 1928 on the occasion of the publication of Rad-
clyffe Hall's novel of lesbian love, *The well of loneliness*.

> I have seen this plague stalking shamelessly through great social
> assemblies. I have heard it whispered about by young men and
> young women who do not and cannot grasp its unutterable
> putrefaction. Both aspects of it are thrust upon healthy and
> innocent minds. The contagion cannot be escaped, it pervades
> our social life. Perhaps it is a blessing in surprise or a curse in
> disguise that his novel forces on our society, a disagreeable
> task which it has hitherto shirked, the task of cleansing itself
> from the leprosy of these lepers, and making the air clean and
> wholesome once more (*Sunday Express*, 1928).

Like all the views concerning homosexuality that I have discussed
this helps to solve crucial difficulties caused by the prevalence of the
phenomenon. For if it is widespread then it is difficult to describe
it as unnatural. It may well be that men can as *rationally* choose to
engage in homosexual practices as in heterosexual ones. (Or that
men can be socialists as well as stay within the dominant bourgeois
political culture, or smoke marihuana as rationally as drink beer.
All such deviant activities are on occasion explained by invoking
such a model.) By treating homosexuality in this way it becomes
possible to avoid any confrontation with the real living men who
are homosexuals. They can be *legitimately* hounded, locked away
and even castrated or destroyed; all of which solutions have at
times been advocated. Of course there is a certain consistency in
their view. While these practices are unnatural many may be tempted
but only the morally inferior will succumb. The invocation of a
Christian cosmology is frequent by those who use this model.
Again there may be good reason why some sections of the community readily subscribe to conceptions such as temptation. Many
of the rich and powerful members of this society go to public schools
(where Schofield found that 28 per cent of boys admitted to engaging
in homosexual practices themselves, and 44 per cent said that they
knew that they went on) and may well have 'gone through' a homosexual phase themselves.[22] They can then rationalize these away
by implicitly referring to their own moral strength. And who is there
to question them?

The newspapers' treatment of homosexuality is comprehensible
as an attempt to come to terms with the anomalous nature of the
activity. Homosexual acts call into question the 'natural' order which
has been so necessary for industrial capitalism. I have tried to show
how hard the newspapers have to work to suppress the information
that destroys both their conception of homosexuality and of the

normal moral world. These efforts have been at the expense of
homosexual men who have suffered terrible legal and social persecution, stigmatization and psychological stress. One of the worst
examples of this very persecution involved the murder of a young
homosexual, Michael De Gruchy, on Wimbledon Common on 25
September 1969. Two years later the *Sunday Times* Magazine
covered the incident with a story entitled THE QUEER BASH KILLERS.
(*Sunday Times*, 7 February 1971). In this article they discussed the
urban anomie in the large estates near the common. They quoted
a psychiatrist who thought 'the constraints on violence are missing'.
Everybody was shocked at the conduct of the four youths who
killed De Gruchy. Nobody however related their behaviour to the
attitudes of the wider society to homosexuals. Nobody mentioned
that only a year before, *The People* (1 September 1968) had run
an article about THE SICK MEN OF HAMPSTEAD HEATH, which provided
a perfect rationale for persecuting homosexuals. Nor did they mention that the boys in their explanations of what they did used *identical*
phrases to those used in the original article. 'If they do it in private
that's one thing. . . .' The boys recognized the presence of homosexuals by 'the glow of cigarettes': just as *The People*'s reporters said
that homosexuals could be spotted signalling to each other. Urban
anomie? Surely the opposite! What were these boys if they were not
agents of the 'public consensus' so artfully created by the papers?

NOTES AND REFERENCES

1. I am grateful to Tony Marden, Colin Prescod, Andy Roberts, Paula
   Struhl, Karsten Struhl, Harold Wolpe, and Tony Woodwiss for their
   critical comments on this paper. Any errors, misrepresentation or
   faulty argumentation is my responsibility alone. F.P.
2. See the readership surveys utilized by the *Guardian* newspaper.
3. Rugoff, M., *Prudery and passion* (London, Hart Davis, 1971); Rattray-
   Taylor, G., *Sex in history* (London, Thames and Hudson, 1953).
4. See C. W. Saleeby's contribution to Emmott, A., *The nation's morals*
   (London, Cassell & Co., 1910).
5. Macintosh, M., 'The homosexual role', *Social Problems*, Volume 16,
   No. 2 (Fall 1968). Churchill, W., *Homosexual behaviour among males*
   (Englewood Cliffs, Prentice Hall, 1971).
6. Schofield, M., *Sociological aspects of homosexuality* (London,
   Longmans, 1965).
7. Douglas, M., *Purity and danger* (Harmondsworth, Penguin Books,
   1966), p. 49, pp. 51–2.
8. Ibid., p. 191.
9. See Titmuss, R., *Income distribution and social change* (London,
   George Allen & Unwin, 1962); Lundberg, G., *The rich and the super-*

rich (New York, Bantam Books, 1969). See my discussion of these points in F. Pearce and M. Brake, *Sociology of sex* (forthcoming).

10. Patchen, K., *The journal of Albion Moonlight* (New York, New Directions Paperbacks, 1961), p. 214.

11. Quoted in Stedman-Jones, G. *Outcast London* (London, Oxford University Press, 1971), p. 335; see also Semmel, B., *Imperialism and social reform* (London, George Allen & Unwin, 1960).

12. Weinstein, N., '*Kinder, Küche, Kirche* as scientific law; psychology constructs the female' in Morgan, R. (ed.), *Sisterhood is powerful* (New York, Vintage Books, 1967).

13. During the 12-month period 1955–6 some 5963 men were charged in England and Wales with homosexual offences. In the five-month period reported this would mean some 2485 men were prosecuted. See *Criminal Statistics England and Wales 1969* (London, HMSO, 1970). For the newspaper survey see Tudor Rees, J. and Usill, H., *They stand apart* (London, Heinemann, 1955), pp. 195–7.

14. I am grateful to Tony Marden for these figures.

15. Cudlipp, H., *At your peril* (London, Weidenfeld & Nicolson, 1962).

16. Laing, R. D., *The Politics of the Family* (London, Tavistock Publications, 1971), p. 115.

17. Curran, J., 'The impact of TV on the audience for national newspapers' in Tunstall, J. (ed.), *Media sociology* (London, Constable, 1970), p. 106.

18. Quoted in Halloran, J. D., Elliott, P., and Murdock, G., *Demonstrations and communications: a case study* (Harmondsworth, Penguin Books, 1970), p. 26.

19. Pare, C. M. B., 'Etiology of homosexuality: genetic and chromosomal aspects' in Marmour, J. (ed.), *Sexual inversion* (New York, Basic Books, 1965), p. 73.

20. In a sense the constant reiteration of similar tales is equivalent to, although much less clearly articulated than, anthropologically interesting myths. They provide a mechanism by which contradictions can be discussed and dealt with. See Levi-Strauss, C., *Structural anthropology* (London, Allen Lane, The Penguin Press, 1968), Ch. XI.

21. Foucault, M., *Madness and civilisation* (London, Tavistock Publications, 1965), p. 202.

22. Schofield, M., *Sexual behaviour of young people* (London, Penguin Press, 1965), p. 61.

Mickey Spillane: a reading*

JERRY PALMER

Most sociological analysis of the mass media concentrates upon non-fiction. When sociology turns its attention to fiction it is apt to do so in a simplistic fashion, asking only questions such as: Is the hero always white and middle class? What values does he openly espouse? This type of question omits all reference to what the literary critic and cultural historian see as the central question: How does a given work, or body of works, portray the world? For by proposing to the reader a view of how the world is organized, a work fits into an ideology. For overtly didactic works, like Paton's *Cry the beloved country*, Ellisson's *The invisible man* or Nadine Gordimer's *Occasion for loving*, this is obvious, and nobody would question it. But for books that 'just tell a story', it is not at all clear how they do present a view of the world. What this essay attempts to demonstrate is that Mickey Spillane – a prolific and immensely successful writer and the most widely read thriller writer there is – constructs through his novels what Edmund Leach has called a 'legitimating myth'. Leach was writing about the *Old Testament*, and his analysis of the historical distortions present in the biblical account prompt him to a final conclusion about the ideological function of either historical records or fiction:

> Patterned structures in the surviving historical record (or in the *remembered* historical record) do not embody *intrinsic* moral implications. The patterning is simply a logical ordering of the parts, in itself it is morally neutral. But as soon as moral judgments are injected into any part of the system – as soon as it is postulated that 'A is a good man and B is a bad man' then, automatically, the logical ordering of the system causes the *whole* story to be permeated through and through with moral implication; the structure becomes 'dramatic'. . . .
>
> However we may choose to distinguish between Old Testament history and Old Testament myth, myth and history alike must serve mythical functions. Both must serve to justify the doctrine that the Israelites are the divinely ordained owners of the whole promised land from Dan to Beersheba, both also justify the doctrine that the Israelites, a people of common descent, form an

* Paper prepared especially for this volume.

exclusive religious sect, and both doctrines need to be fitted in
with the tradition of the dual monarchy and with the empirical
fact that the land in question has a very mixed population in
which the Israelites, narrowly defined, are a minority not in full
political control.[1]

This essay will attempt to ascribe a similar function to Mickey
Spillane.

In the opening scene of *The big kill* Spillane's hero, Mike Hammer,
is sitting in a cheap bar somewhere in New York; a girl 'in a dress
that was too tight a year ago . . .' approaches him: '[She] decided
I could afford a wet evening for two and walked over with her
hips waving hello.'[2] Similarly, elsewhere: 'He snapped a light off,
threw a couple of switches and picked up the slugs. While he was
running the photos I walked to the window . . .'[3] When Hammer
refers to a 'wet evening for two' the slangy phrase suggests that
the incident is part of a pattern, with which he is familiar and quite
able to cope, and when he summarizes the girl's manner of walking
with the phrase 'her hips waving hello', the choice of words indicates
both that he understands why she is approaching him and that he is
not taken in by her tactics. Similarly, when Spillane uses words such
as 'snapping' a light off instead of 'turning' or 'switching', and
'running' photos instead of 'developing', the implication is the same:
the actions, simple though they may be, are both thrown into relief
by the eccentric choice of words and are presented to us as being
within the competence of the hero. Thus the style of the novels both
gives presence to incidents and shows that the hero has at his disposal a technique that enables him to deal with the world he sees
around him.

The presence-giving properties of Spillane's style can also be seen
in other forms of presentation:

> The goon who drove the car was still running around loose and
> if I had to go after somebody it'd might as well be him. I stepped
> on the starter, dragged away from the kerb and started back
> across town.[4]

The choice of the verbs 'step' and 'drag' presents an insignificant
action (which could very easily be omitted from the description) in
such a way as to give it a certain degree of significance. In other
words, the mundane has again been given presence. It is this recurrent stylistic trick, rather than the multiplication of dramatic
incidents such as murder, brutality, sexual encounter, which contributes towards the most obvious cause of Spillane's success – the
unflagging pace at which his novels move.

The importance of technique in Spillane's world is reflected in his manner of presenting the most insignificant actions:

> I said, 'If you want me, leave a call at Donniger's'. His mind closed on the name . . .[5]

One might summarize these comments on tough style thus: the intimate structure of this manner of presenting the world consists of the tension between the dramatization of incidents, which places us in the world of the unexpected, and the delineation of technical adaptation to this world, which places us in a world where everything is, if not controlled in advance, at least easily controllable when it occurs. One might describe this world as opaque to the reader but transparent to the hero.

In the same way as incidents are given significance by the manner of their presentation, so are human beings. In an early novel, Mike Hammer meets a prostitute in a café. She is broke, he buys her a cup of coffee and decides that she is a good person. During the conversation a man comes in and starts threatening her. Hammer punches him about, and assumes that the incident is closed; however, the intruder reaches for a gun. The passage continues:

> I let him almost reach it, then I slid my own .45 out where everybody could get a look at it. Just for effect I stuck it up against his forehead and thumbed back the hammer. It made a sharp click in the silence. 'Just touch that rod you got and I'll blow your damn greasy head off. Go ahead, just make one lousy move towards it,' I said.
>
>   He moved, all right. He fainted. Red was looking down at him, still too terrified to say anything. Shorty had a twitch in his shoulder. Finally she said, 'You . . . didn't have to do that for me. Please, get me out of here before he wakes up. He'll . . . kill you!'
>
>   I touched her arm gently. 'Tell me something, Red. Do you really think he could?'[6]

Thus an additional element is inserted into the thriller's structure – the man with heroic stature.

At this point in the analysis, therefore, we have established that in Spillane's fiction the world is presented in a particular fashion, and in this world there is a hero, someone who is supremely competent to deal with all the difficulties and problems he confronts. Now this world, in the ultimate analysis, consists of nothing other than other people – Spillane's novels are remarkable for a more or less total absence of anything except people and their emotions: insofar as the physical world exists it is there solely in order to provoke emotions in the participants, or to further the action they are involved in.

The other inhabitants of the world who are of relevance to the present analysis may be classified as bureaucrats, villains and women. Of these only women are really important, for the villains are either anonymous or women (this point will be analysed at some length), and the only function of the bureaucrats is to make it obvious how inefficient bureaucracy is compared with the hero's unequivocally personal and untrammelled methods.

There are two kinds of women in Spillane's world: those one loves and respects, and those one goes to bed with. However, this statement is somewhat oversimplified, for there are more than two elements in even these grossly naïve portrayals of sexual relationships. The elements are: sexual desire, delay in satisfying this desire, respect/love, and betrayal. *The big kill* is an average example: Hammer desires, and eventually sleeps with, Ellen, who also helps him obtain the information he needs; he also desires and eventually sleeps with Marsha, who appears to be helping him, but who turns out to be the criminal he has been hunting throughout the novel.

The structure is not so simple as it might appear at first sight: desire and respect are by no means mutually exclusive, and the delay in achieving satisfaction is certainly not due to any deficiency in the hero – the women he desires always desire him, and are in the habit of unzipping at the earliest possible opportunity – nor, primarily at least, to a desire to keep the reader on edge, although it undoubtedly fulfils this function too. The hero refuses what is offered him because he has something else to do – an urgent appointment to keep, information to collect, a killer to hunt down. And one should not think that these reasons are intended as excuses: normally there is much at stake in the case the hero is on – a massive plot to subvert the city, or to take over the United States Government, or even to dominate the world. Under these circumstances it is no doubt thoroughly laudable to refuse the pleasures of sex in order to pursue one's duty.

What is less obvious is that there seems to be an element of fear involved in the hero's attitude towards satisfying his desire. Possibly for this reason, one of the recurring endings to Spillane's novels (it occurs in almost half of them) is the discovery that it was the woman the hero was either sleeping with, or in love with, or both, who is the villain of the piece: she uses her sexual attraction to mislead the hero, and ultimately to try to kill him – many of the novels end with an armed confrontation between the lovers. Moreover, there is frequently in the tone of sexual description, or in the lovers' dialogue, an element of this fear, or at any rate of danger:

... high breasts that dared you with every curving line, taut
stomach muscles that ebbed and flowed like a tide into generous
thighs that held a fluid hungry stance unknowingly deliberate ...[7]

... breasts arrogantly thrusting out and upwards from the
athletic grace of her body, their ruby-hued tips like tiny warheads
capable of destroying a man on contact unless they were disarmed
first with a gentle touch.[8]

... lovely Rondine. Beautiful as hell. With the same potential.
Beauty and death inside the same shell.[9]

Ludicrous though the imagery may be, it seems to be based on a
very real sense of threat to the hero's ego. Indeed, in *The by-pass
control*, Tiger Mann and Camille (who turns out to be the villain)
habitually refer to each other as 'spider' and 'fly' – she being the
former – and many of their conversations are little more than
extended elaborations, a series of puns, upon this metaphor.

Similarly, the hero always complains if his lover sees him naked,
regardless of whether they have made love, but adores looking at
her nude:

Then she saw me silently laughing at her, spun round grabbing
for her blouse, then realizing how silly it was, gave me an impatient
stamp of her foot and said, 'How long have *you* been there!'
'Long enough.'
'Well, it isn't polite . . .'
'It isn't polite to undress a guy and put him to bed, either,' I
reminded her.
'That was different.'
'I hope so,' I said. I walked across the room and held out the drink.
'You look better all the time, kid.'
She took the drink, shook her head in feigned annoyance, and
reached for her bra. 'You keep it up and there won't be anything
left for when we're married.'
I gave her a long appreciative stare and grinned. 'With you,
honey,' I told her, 'there's always going to be plenty left over.'
Then before she could throw something at me I went back out-
side.[10]

Seeing his lover in the nude is often referred to as revenge for her
seeing him in the same state previously: it is as if there is a constant
battle between the sexes in which victory for the male consists in
never being seen nude, but in observing nudity in the opposite
sex (whereas for the female it is different: they object to being
caught nude or semi-nude unawares, but frequently choose to
display themselves in this state – there is a pattern of enticement and
avoidance involved, for it is usually on the occasions when the

woman undresses for his benefit that the hero refuses the offer of intercourse).

It is not that fear is omnipresent in the hero's attitude towards sexual desire, for there are many passages in which desire is presented as something quite open and honest, a very genuine expression of the relationship between a man and a woman. On the other hand, the imagery and attitudes mentioned above recur constantly, and the desire to delay consummation is always there. Even in the scenes where intercourse eventually takes place the hero's natural enthusiasm is often mixed with reluctance – he feels he ought to be doing something more germane to his enquiries – and it is always the woman who seduces the man.

It would seem that the structure of sexuality is bipolar: on the one hand the fear and reluctance, and the fact of betrayal by the one one should be able to trust, and has trusted, one's sexual partner, constitute what might loosely be termed a 'praying mantis syndrome'; on the other hand, love, respect and untrammelled consummation are no doubt pure libidinal desire finding adequate expression. During the course of each novel, the relationship which the hero has with any one of the women involved may well contain elements appertaining to both sides of the structure, but by the end all ambiguity is removed: each individual is placed on one side or the other of a line clearly demarcating good from bad.

This is to say that, in the structure of the novels, sexuality is subordinate to that same vision of the opacity of the outside world which is presented by tough style. The 'praying mantis woman', for example, represents very clearly the fear of an uncontrollable external agency, since that is precisely her function in the narrative, to provide the final dramatic shock of treachery by the hero's most intimate colleague: this is especially clear in Spillane's first novel, *I, the jury*, where Mike Hammer refuses to sleep with the girl in question on the grounds that marriage demands virginity (complete trust); in the final chapter he recounts to her how she committed various crimes of which she is guilty while she strips in an attempt to dissuade him; when she is quite naked he shoots her in the stomach and leaves her to die.[11]

Now the praying mantis figure is merely an extraordinarily threatening villain. Elsewhere – especially in the early novels, written during the McCarthy era – the villain is a highly respectable public figure whom the hero trusts implicitly (*One lonely night*, *My gun is quick*, for instance), and in general it is clear that the function of the villain is conspiratorial. Moreover, the villain is not even identified until the closing pages: for the hero, and therefore for the reader, all that is known is that *there is a conspiracy*, which has to be

rooted out. The technique which is used for eradicating the conspiracy which the hero confronts – Mafia, Soviet espionage, sub-
version, etc. – is that violence for which Spillane is so justly famous.
However, while violence is a technical resource in the individual
warfare of which the plot consists, it is the passion with which it is
used that is dominant:

> I didn't watch her walk away. I sat there dreaming of the things
> I'd like to do and how maybe if nobody was there to see me I'd
> do anyway. I was dreaming of a lot of fat faces with jowls that
> got big and loose on other people's meat and how they'd look
> with that smashed, sticky expression that comes with catching
> the butt end of a .45 across their noses. I was dreaming of a slimy,
> foreign, secret army that held a parade of terror under the Mafia
> label and laughed at us with our laws and regulations and how
> fast their damned smug expressions would change when they saw
> the fresh corpses of their own kind day after day.[12]

The dramatic function of this violence is, it would seem, to
exhilarate the reader: involved with the hero, one is intended to
enjoy with him the suppression of the evil men against whom he pits
himself. The violence of the villain, on the other hand, is sickening:

> They had left me on the floor. There were my feet and my hands,
> immobile lumps jutting in front of my body. The backs of my
> hands and the sleeves were red and sticky. The taste of the sticki-
> ness was in my mouth too. Something moved and a pair of shoes
> shuffled into sight so I knew I wasn't alone. The floor in front of
> my feet stretched out into other shoes and the lower halves of
> legs. Shiny shoes marred with a film of dust. One with a jagged
> scratch across the toe. Four separate pairs of feet all pointing
> toward the same direction and when my eyes followed them I
> saw her in the chair and saw what they were doing to her.
> She had no coat on now and her skin had an unholy whiteness
> about it, splotched with deeper colours. She was sprawled in the
> chair, her mouth making uncontrollable, mewing sounds. The
> hands with the pliers did something horrible to her and the mouth
> opened without screaming.[13]

The differentiation, which is established by the tone of the description,
reflects the relationship between the intensity of the experience
involved in this violence and the justifiability of the employment of
these techniques. There would seem to be a connection between
intensity and purity, for the emotion acts as a crucible, refining itself
and by implication refining the motives for giving expression to the
emotion. It is not that this is acceptable as a moral justification, but
the reader's sensibility is so affected by the white heat of hatred that

he may well assume that a person who can be so single-minded in his hatred of something (which is anyway known *a priori* to be evil) cannot but be pure in his motivation, and if Spillane can make his reader accept the purity of his hero's motivation, he has half succeeded in making him accept the justifiability of his actions.

The implication is that physical violence is structurally subordinate to the emotion of hatred, which is aroused by opposition to the hero's world-view:

> That was me. I could have made it sound better if I'd said it. There in the muck and slime of the jungle, there in the stink that hung over the beaches rising from the bodies of the dead, there in the half-light of too many dusks and dawns laced together with the criss-crossed patterns of bullets, I had gotten a taste of death and found it palatable to the extent that I could never again eat the fruits of a normal civilization. . . .
> So he gave me back my soul of toughness, hate and bitterness and let me dress in the armour of cynicism and dismissed me before I could sneer and make the answer I had ready.[14]

In other words, sexuality and violence have the same structure in Spillane's novels: in both cases the outside world is perceived as riddled with threatening entities, which arouse fear and/or hatred, and the connection is made explicit by the case of the 'praying mantis woman' who incarnates both aspects of the structure.

This world is the underworld, the world of criminals, hustlers, spies and policemen, and its distinctive feature is that it is beyond the reach of law and order: in a very real sense it is a jungle, where might is right and the weakest go to the wall. Moreover, it is a world which is superordinate to the ordinary everyday world, for it is the invisible battlefield in the midst of society, where the fate of that society is fought out: the hero confronts a gigantic plot – Mafia, Soviet spy ring, etc. – and eventually destroys it, thus becoming the saviour of society, the preserver of the American way of life. In this jungle the hero is the animal who knows best how to survive, and who is justified by the goals he always successfully attains.

This is a world which is glamorously outside the world of everyday reality, and the hero is suitably an outsider, for he lacks even the elementary protection given by membership of the normal law enforcement agencies: he is variously a private detective (on occasions, as in *The girl hunters*, with his licence revoked), a privately employed spy, or even a gangster. As a result he is always operating completely on his own, which gives him added stature, and this is emphasized by his refusal to contain his activities within the normal limits of detective and espionage work:

... Our groups are highly skilled. Although those chosen to
augment our group are of the finest calibre, the most select,
élite ... they still have certain handicaps civilized society has
inflicted on them. Maybe you can finish it for me.'
    I nodded. 'Sure. Let's try a lucky guess. You need an animal.
Some improver of the breed has run all the shagginess out of
your business-suit characters and you need a downtown shill to
bait your hook. How close did I come?'
    'Close,' he said.
    'I'm still listening.'
    'We need somebody of known talents. Like you. Somebody
whose mind can deal on an exact level with ... the opposition.
We need someone whose criminal disposition can be directed into
certain channels.'
    'An animal,' I said, 'the dirty kind. Maybe a jackal that can
play around in the jungle with the big ones without being caught.'
    'It's descriptive enough.'
    'Not quite. The rest of it is that if he's killed he wouldn't even
be missed or counted for a loss.'[15]

Here he is specifically employed by an official agency to do 'the
dirty work'; more normally, as in all of the Tiger Mann novels, his
excess of initiative is a bone of contention between the lone wolf and
the agencies who are (often perforce) his collaborators.
    In his search for the villain, the hero plunges into this underworld,
offering himself as a target in order to find out who is shooting, and
he gradually works his way up the hierarchy of his enemies, from the
hired hands to the master-mind, whom he eventually kills, in a
single-handed confrontation in a remote or unlikely location, and
usually with the maximum possible violence. In *One lonely night*,
for instance, the climax occurs in a deserted warehouse: Hammer
mows down with a conveniently located machine-gun the three
Soviet spies who are torturing his fiancée, and then sets fire to the
building to cover up the traces of what he has done.[16] The intention
seems to be to create a finale of orgasmic intensity. In *Bloody sunrise*
Tiger Mann blows up, with a fake ball-point pen, the girl Sonia
with whom he has been sleeping, and who is the villain. The novel
closes:

The sun was just coming up in the east, the crescent tip of it a
brilliant orange, reaching out to light the earth with fiery fingertips
of a new day.
    Sonia was still there with me, but she wasn't watching this
sunrise. In essence, she was almost part of it, a sparkling wet,
red splash on the grey rubble of the building that reflected the
glow of a fresh day and a job that was all over.[17]

It must be emphasized that these are recurrent narrative conventions, common not only to each and every one of Spillane's novels, but also to the thriller in general. The world 'out there' is always opaque and threatening, the hero always brings transparency and security to it; the ending is always as climactic as possible, since the reader needs the emotional release provided in order to be convinced that the threats really have been neutralized.

What relationship, therefore, is it possible to trace between the view of the world propounded by Spillane's novels and the wider culture into which they are inserted? And what have we learnt about the mass media?

There is school of thought which would argue with Silbermann that the structure of a work of art is irrelevant to sociological study:

> For it is not the vague concepts 'art', 'painting', 'music', 'literature', etc., that are in the centre of the artistic life: it is characterized by the experience of art. It is this meeting – resulting from conflict or contact – between the producer and the consumer, these social processes and these social actions which concretize and assume a definite shape. Around them the art groups assemble; they alone, in accordance with the methods of empirical sociology, may and can, as sociological facts, be the centre and starting-point of observation and research.[18]

I cannot agree, for it would seem that to establish the content of groups of artefacts, whose appeal is empirically clear, is an essential precondition for an understanding of the social functioning of any work of art: to use Silbermann's terminology, the art groups do not assemble at random: no doubt their composition is influenced by factors which have little to do with the artefacts they contemplate such as income, location of residence, etc., but it is impossible to deny that an important factor in this composition is the nature of the artefact whose existence forms the focus of the group.

In other words, the manner in which a work is consumed by the public is clearly a product of – among other things – the nature of the work. Thus the study of the structure of the work becomes a question, which at the level of theory is separate and to which it is therefore legitimate to devote a separate analysis.

This is not to deny the importance of empirical work, and is interesting that the most stringent statement of this necessity comes from a Marxist critic, who is entirely convinced of the necessity of structural analysis as well as of empirical investigation:

> ... we must keep in mind a principle, characteristic of any examination of the mass communication media (of which the popular novel is one of the most spectacular examples): the

message which has been evolved by an educated élite (in a cultural group or a kind of communications headquarters, which takes its lead from the political or economic group in power) is expressed at the outset in terms of a fixed code or cipher of emission, but it is caught by divers groups of receivers and deciphered on the basis of other codes, ciphers of reception. The sense of the message often undergoes a kind of filtration or distortion in the process, which completely alters its 'pragmatic' function. This means that every semiological study of a work of art must be complemented by checks made so to speak in the field. The semiological examination reveals the implications at the moment of emission; the check on the spot should establish what new meanings have been attributed to the message, defined as a semantic structure at the moment of reception.[19]

In the final analysis, what Spillane's novels are about is the antagonistic relationship between the individual and the environment made up of his fellow men. The antagonism is real because the individual is in competition with his fellows; but this is an unpalatable truth and the thriller is dedicated (so to speak) to rendering it palatable. This is achieved by rendering the process of competition heroic and by making the goal of the heroism the preservation of society. The paradox is clear, and nowhere is it given clearer expression than in this passage, where the intensity of feeling and the apparently illogical flow of the ideas guarantees the importance of what is apparently a luxury extraneous to the structure of the novel:

Who the hell do they think we are? Damn it, we got what we wanted because we took it from those who couldn't hold it and we did it the hard way. You think gooks with blunderbusses and archaic ideas don't know this? So now we walk the road easy because nobody in the capital wants to disturb the status quo. They'd better learn there're still some left who can lift a head on the end of a pole as well as the poor uneducated can. Goddamn, I skinned a guy alive once and he screamed his state secrets with no trouble at all. Sure, he died, but he died like he killed other people and we got the answers. I want to see our eggheads trying that, or the Peace Corps, or the politicos.

Girl we're strictly civilians working to keep this country out of the hands of the garbage heads who want to give it away to the half-asses. We're people who object to punitive income taxes that destroy the brains of the nation and put control in the hands of those who know nothing. Let's say we're right wing . . . like so far right we go through the wall . . . but anything to knock out the destroyers of our country.[20]

This society, which the hero is trying to save, is just the one which is creating a way of life which is incompatible with his ideas of how life should be lived and societies should be run (the well-known conflict between the ideology of free enterprise and the restrictions demanded by the rationalized liberal state). It is only by existing on the fringes of society and by being its saviour that the hero can affirm both his individuality and his sociability.

REFERENCES

The references to Spillane's novels are to the original English Corgi paperback editions. Since these have been frequently reprinted, the edition current on the bookstalls may in fact have different pagination.

1. 'The Legitimacy of Solomon', pp. 53 and 82; in *Genesis as myth and other essays* (London, Cape, 1969).
2. *The big kill* (London, Corgi Books, 1960), p. 7.
3. *Day of the guns* (1966), p. 126.
4. *The big kill*, p. 39.
5. *Man alone,* p. 100; in *Killer mine* (1965).
6. *My gun is quick* (1960), p. 13.
7. *Man alone,* p. 107.
8. *The by-pass control* (1968), p. 84.
9. *Day of the guns* (1966), p. 32.
10. *The by-pass control*, pp. 84–5.
11. 1963, pp. 120–6.
12. *Kiss me, deadly,* p. 33.
13. Ibid., p. 13.
14. *One lonely night* (1960), p. 9.
15. *Me, hood* (1963), p. 12.
16. pp. 205–9.
17. *Bloody sunrise* (1966), p. 159.
18. 'A definition of the sociology of art', *International Social Science Journal*, Vol. XX, no. 4, (1968) p. 583.
19. Umberto Eco, 'Rhetoric and ideology in Sue's *Les mystères de Paris*', *International Social Science Journal*, Vol. XIX (1967), pp. 568–9.
20. *The death dealers* (1967), p. 28.

The myth of the drug taker in the mass media*

JOCK YOUNG

The most amazing quality of mass media reporting of the drug problem is their ability to get the wrong end of the stick. Indeed in *The drugtakers* I formulated, with tongue in cheek, Young's Law of Information on Drugs. Namely, that the *greater* the public health risk (measured in number of mortalities) of a psychotropic substance, the *less* the amount of information (including advertising) critical of its effects. Tobacco, alcohol, the barbiturates, amphetamines, heroin, LSD and marihuana (listed in declining public health risk) would all seem to fit this proposition – apart from those exceptional and short-lived occasions when lung cancer scares occur. It is the explanation of the social basis of this 'Law' with which this article is concerned.

We live in a world which is extremely socially segregated: direct experience of individuals with behaviour different from our own conventions and values is rare. It is in just such a world that we come to rely on the mass media for a sizeable proportion of our information as to the goings on of outsiders to our small discrete social worlds. Criticism of the mass media has centred round the notion that journalists are biased, misinformed or just plain deceitful. The impression is given that if the profession were to revamp its ethics and remove its bias, the body of responsible journalism would be uncovered and the population receive from then on the simple facts of the matter, to interpret as they please. Minor adjustments have to be made to the set after which the picture will focus and the facts be held objectively. I wish to suggest, to the contrary, that 'facts' do not speak for themselves, that they are only given meaning in terms of the frame of reference provided. Further, that the mass media offer an amazingly systematic frame of reference. It is not random bias but a consistent world view which is purveyed. The model of society held by the mass media, and implicit in their reporting of both deviant and normal, I will term consensualist. Its constitution is simplicity itself: namely, that the vast majority of

* A revised version of 'Drugs and the mass media', *Drugs and Society*, Vol. 1 (November 1971), pp. 14–18.

people in society share a common definition of reality – agree as to what activities are praiseworthy and what are condemnable. That this consensus is functional to an organic system which they envisage as society. That behaviour outside this reality is a product of irrationality or sickness, that it is in itself meaningless activity which leads nowhere and is, most importantly, behaviour which has direct and unpleasant consequences for the small minority who are impelled to act this way. The model carries with it a notion of merited rewards and just punishments. It argues for the equitable nature of the *status quo* and draws the parameters of happiness and experience. Specifically, it defines material rewards as the payment for hard work, sexual pleasure as the concomitant of supporting the nuclear family, and religious or mystical experience as not an alternative interpretation of reality but as an activity acceptable only in a disenchanted form which solemnizes (their word) the family and bulwarks the *status quo*. The illicit drug taker is, I want to suggest, the deviant *par excellence*. For his culture disdains work and revels in hedonism, his sexual relations are reputedly licentious and promiscuous, and the psychdelics promise a re-enchantment of the world – a subversive take-on reality.

It is not drugs *per se* which are denigrated – for our culture is historically normal in that drug use is ubiquitous. Rather it is drugs taken for hedonistic reasons. The social drinker who is relaxing between his work bouts, the middle-aged barbiturate addict who needs drugs in order to sleep, the tranquillizer habitué who takes drugs in order to ease his work or marital tensions – or even the physician morphine addict who uses the drug to keep him working under pain or stress: all of these individuals are ignored or treated lightly. It is when drug use is seen as unrelated to productivity, when it leads to 'undeserved' pleasures, when it gives rise to experiences which question the taken-for-granted 'reality', that the forces of condemnation are bought into play.

The mass media carries a mythology of the average man and the deviant – within which Mr Average is seen to prosper and be content in his universe of hard work and industrious consumption and the deviant is portrayed as being beset by forces which lead to ineluctable misfortune. But the real world outside this spectacle differs radically from this. For often the worker doubts the fairness of his rewards, the middle-class housewife surveys her Ideal Home with ambivalence, the husband eyes his secretary and then goes back to his wife, the adolescent Seeker looks at the Established Church and cannot for the life of him see how it refers to the same reality as that of the Christian mystics. For popular consciousness is a collage of contradictions: it is both sceptical and complacent, satisfied and discontented, rational and superstitious, conservative and downright subversive. It is on this base that the mass media acts. For there exists widespread suspicion that the sacrifices made are not worth the rewards received. This is the basis for what Albert Cohen calls moral indignation. Thus he writes:

> ... the dedicated pursuit of culturally approved goals, the adherence to normatively sanctioned means – these imply a certain self restraint, effort, discipline, inhibition. What is the effect of others who, though their activities do not manifestly damage our own interests are morally undisciplined, who give themselves up to idleness, self indulgence, or forbidden vices? What effect does the propinquity of the wicked have upon the peace of mind of the virtuous?[1]

What Cohen is arguing is that deviant activities, even although they may have no direct effect on the interests of those who observe them, may be condemned because they represent concrete examples of individuals who are, so to speak, dodging the rules. For if a person lives by a code of conduct which forbids certain pleasures, which involves the deferring of gratification in certain areas, it is hardly surprising that he will react strongly against those whom he sees to be taking short cuts. This is a partial explanation of the vigorous repression against what Edwin Schur calls 'crimes without victims': homosexuality, prostitution, abortion and drug taking.

The mass media have discovered that people read avidly news which titillates their sensibilities and confirms their prejudices. The ethos of 'give the public what it wants' involves a constant play on the normative worries of large segments of the population; it utilizes outgroups as living Rorschach blots on to which collective fears and doubts are projected. Moral indignation, if first galvanized by the newspapers and then resolved in a *just* fashion, makes a fine basis for newspaper readership. To this extent then newspaper men are accurate when they suggest that they are just giving the public what it wants, only what this represents is reinforcing the consensual part of the popular consciousness and denigrating any subversive notions.

The widespread appeal of the mass media rests, therefore, on its ability to fascinate and titillate its audience and then reassure by finally condemning. This is a propaganda of a very sophisticated sort, playing on widespread discontent and insecurities and little resembling the crude manipulative model of the mass media commonly held in liberal and left circles.

Illicit drug use is custom built for this sort of treatment. A characteristic reaction to drug use is that of ambivalence for, as with so many social relationships between 'normal' and 'deviant', the normal person simultaneously both covets and castigates the deviant action. This after all is the basis of moral indignation, namely that the wicked are undeservedly realizing the covert desires of the virtuous. Richard Blum captured well this fascination-repulsion relationship to drug use when he wrote:

Pharmaceutical materials do not dispense themselves and the illicit drugs are rarely given away, let alone forced on people. Consequently, the menace lies within the person, for there would be no drug threat without a drug attraction. The amount of public interest in stories about druggies suggests the same drug attraction and repulsion in ordinary citizens. 'Fascination' is the better term since it implies witchcraft and enchantment. People are fascinated with drugs – because they are attracted by the states and conditions drugs are said to produce. That is another side to the fear of being disrupted; it is the desire for release, for escape, for magic, and for ecstatic joys. That is the derivation of the menace in drugs – their representation as keys to forbidden kingdoms inside our-selves. The *dreadful* in the drug is the *dreadful* in ourselves.[2]

This is an explanation of the hostility and attraction which drugs evoke. It makes understandable the findings in opinion polls on both sides of the Atlantic which show the drug pusher to be evalu-ated a higher community menace than the property criminal. It is rooted in moral indignation. Alasdair MacIntyre captured the attitude well when he wrote:

Most of the hostility that I have met with comes from people who have never examined the facts at all. I suspect that what makes them dislike cannabis is not the belief that the effects of taking it are harmful but rather a horrifying suspicion that here is a source of pure pleasure which is available to those who have not *earned* it, who do not deserve it.[3]

I want to suggest that the media unwittingly have set themselves up as the guardians of consensus; that as major providers of infor-mation about actions, events, groups and ideas they forge this information in a closed consensual image. Further I want to suggest that the myths generated and carried by the media although based on ignorance are not of a random nature. The myths are grounded in a particular view of society which throws up certain contradictions which they attempt to solve. They contain certain simple structures irrespective of whether one considers the myth of the prostitute, the criminal, the striker, the pornographer, the delinquent, or the drug taker.

The mass media is committed, on one hand, to reporting that which is newsworthy and, on the other, to interpreting it within a consensual frame of reference. This leads to the first major contradiction that the media must face: for it is precisely alternative deviant realities such as the world of the illicit drug user which are simultaneously highly newsworthy and, because they are alternative realities, violations of the consensual image of society. For if different realms of meaning exist, and illicit pleasure is in fact pleasurable then the mass media world of the happy worker and joyful consumer is threatened. The contradiction is resolved by a skilful defusing of deviant action. Namely, that much drug taking is a product of personality disorders and is, moreover, unpleasurable. Illicit pleasure, the tinder of moral indignation, is accentuated in reporting in order to maximize its news value. The forbidden is thus potentially all the more tempting. To circumvent this the myth contains the notion of in-built justice mechanisms. Atypical pleasure leads to atypical pain. Thus premarital sexual intercourse gives rise to v.d., lsd to madness and marihuana to pitiful degeneracy. Whatever the outcome the message is the same: *deviancy is unpleasurable*. No one would voluntarily choose to be a drug user of this sort, because of the sticky fate that awaits him. Only the sick person, impelled by forces beyond his control, would find himself involved in such an activity. Thus initially there is a bifurcation of the world and human nature into:

(a) the normal rational average citizen who lives in well normed communities, shares common values, and displays a well-deserved happiness – he is the vast majority;
(b) the tiny minority of psychologically sick whose actions are determined by their affliction and are probably a product of social disorganization. Moreover, their deviancy has an in-built punishment. They are unhappy because of their deviancy. Normality is seen to be rewarded and deviance punished. The underlying message is simple: the rational is the pleasurable is the handsomely rewarded is the freely chosen is the meaningful is the non-deviant; the irrational is the painful is the punished is the determined is the meaningless is the deviant. See top diagram opposite.

The overtypical 'man in the street' makes free choices to work hard, marry and consume regularly. He relaxes at the right time and place with beer and cigarettes which give him 'luxury' and 'deep pleasure' but do not threaten either the ethos of productivity or the mundane world of taken for granted experience.

Every day attempts are made in the newspapers to lay the ghost

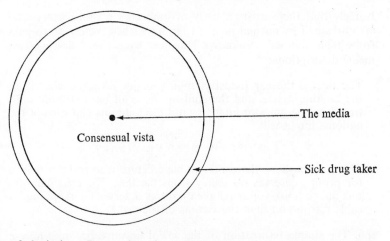

of deviation. Every day the same message is repeated, the same morality play enacted, the same parameters drawn, the same doubts and fears dispelled. But the simple bifurcation model comes in certain instances to face further contradictions which must also be met.

Now and then large numbers of individuals engage in activities which are palpably deviant, e.g., strikes, rioting and marihuana smoking. The simple consensual model would not seem to fit this. For the 'normal' young person, the 'normal' working-class individual, the 'normal' woman, etc., must of necessity embrace the consensus. A significant elaboration of the consensual myth is necessary in order to deal with large-scale deviation. Diagrammatically:

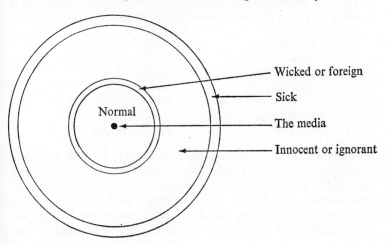

Namely that there exists a body of innocents within society who are corrupted by normal people who are wicked, who seek to gain from their fellows' weakness. Thus we have the following two media descriptions:

> The docks, the car industry, mines, major airports, electricity, the building trade, and the students have all been steadily infiltrated in one guise or another until the militants can disrupt the national life at will.[4]

DRUGS: THE REAL CRIMINALS

> The drug pusher – the contemptible creature who peddles poison for profit – deserves no mercy from the law. The criminal who sets out to hook young people on drugs deserves far more implacable retribution than the victims of the evil.[5]

N.B. The simple bifurcation of the social universe becomes now a fourfold split:

  (a) sick (who can't help it)
  (b) innocent (who are corrupted)
  (c) wicked (who are corrupt)

and a reduced number of (d) the normal

Thus we have the sick who must be treated and cured, the innocent who must be saved, the wicked who must be punished and the normal who must be congratulated and rewarded.

Deviance then does not ever occur out of volition (for after all it is essentially unpleasurable), it either occurs out of sickness or corruption. Indeed for every example of widespread deviance it is possible to detect the intervention of a corruption. Thus:

strikers	agitators
student sit-ins	foreign agitators
prostitutes	pimps
spiritualists	con-men
illegal immigrants	immigrant runners
marihuana smokers	pushers
junkies	junkie doctors

But the mass media sometimes find themselves in a position where a growing body of opinion insists that certain illicit activities are both pleasurable and harmless. As in the case of marihuana, a crisis of confidence occurs. This is solved by what I shall term the nemesis effect. Namely that those individuals who violate the natural law of happiness and productivity ineluctably suffer in the *long run*.

Thus in the long run deviancy must be seen to be unpleasurable. In this mould the stereotype of marihuana has changed. Initially it reflected the exaggerated ambivalence of the mass media towards drugs. Thus, it held promise of uninhibited pleasure, yet plummeted the taker into unmitigated misery. So we had a distorted spectrum ranging from extreme sexuality, through aggressive criminality, to wildly psychotic episodes. The informed journalist, more recently, however, found this model difficult to affix to marihuana usage. He, therefore, switched gear and indicated how the innocuous pleasures of smoking are paid for by the sacrificial few who mysteriously escalate to the nightmares of heroin addiction. Similarly, the American journalist William Braden[6] notes how the press reporting of LSD went through three stages:

1. *Favourable reporting*: in the early 1960s LSD was seen as a therapeutic aid to the mentally ill and the addicted. That is, as a vehicle back to a normality it was in accord with consensual values.
2. *Initial negative reporting:* LSD was simultaneously identified with an ineffable mystical experience and as a cause of suicide, violence and madness. This was concomitant with the movement of LSD out of the hands of the therapists into the psychedelic subculture centring around Timothy Leary.
3. *Secondary negative reporting*: The discovery that LSD *might* result in abnormal chromosome breakage obviated both the sticky problems of mysticism that the psychedelics were giving rise to plus finally providing tangible evidence that LSD was really dangerous after all. As *Chicago's American* put it: LSD: THE 'FLY NOW, DIE LATER' DRUG (the best epithet for the nemesis effect that I've come across). Thus the press found itself armed with a hard 'incontrovertible' fact to use against the growing subculture of pro-LSD advocates.

Every now and then an initially legitimate body of experts will come up with evidence which grossly violates the stereotype. The reception the mass media gave the Wootton Report is fascinating in that we have a government setting up an Advisory Committee to try and elucidate the 'objective' facts about the drug problem which came up with results which violated the political canons that implicitly circumscribed the possible answers that could be accepted as 'objective'! This violation of the consensual myth was dealt with by a flood of invective from the mass media. It:

(a) reaffirmed that corruption was the reason for marihuana smoking – that innocent youngsters had been corrupted by evil pushers;

(b) (most remarkable) suggested that an innocent (ivory-towered) Wootton Committee had been corrupted by a pro-pot lobby.

The corrupter-corrupted imagery was thus used against both the marihuana smoker *and* the Committee that suggested amelioration of their suggestion. As Lady Wootton noted later in the House of Lords:

> The causes of the [hysteria] are familiar to students of social psychology. They occur in other connections as well particularly in relation to sexual crimes, and they are always liable to recur when the public senses that some critical and objective study threatens to block an outlet for indulgence in the pleasures of moral indignation.

To conclude, the mass media portrayal of the drug taker is not a function of random ignorance but a coherent part of a consensual mythology. The mass media are a double-coated pill, for if on the outside they titillate a taste for illicit delights, on the inside, they contain a palliative. They stimulate interest and bromide desire. The myth of the drug user is rooted in moral indignation; it bulwarks the hypothetical world of the normal citizen, it blinkers its audience to deviant realities outside the consensus, it spells out justice for the righteous and punishment for the wicked. Although much of its world view is fantasy, its effects are real enough. For by fanning up moral panics over drug use, it contributes enormously to public hostility to the drug taker and precludes any rational approach to the problem. It also provides a bevy of convenient scapegoats on to which real material and moral discontent can be directed and significant structural changes averted.

References

1. A. K. Cohen, 'The sociology of the deviant act', *American Sociological Review* 30 (1965), pp. 5–14.
2. R. Blum, *Society and drugs* (San Francisco, Jossey-Bass Inc., 1969), p. 335.
3. A. MacIntyre, 'The cannabis taboo', *New Society* (5 December 1968), p. 848.
4. *Daily Express*, 9 December 1970.
5. *Daily Mirror*, 12 March 1970.
6. See W. Braden, 'LSD and the press', reproduced in this Reader.

The press and pop festivals: stereotypes of youthful leisure*

DAMIEN PHILLIPS

I take as a starting point an aspect of deviancy suggested by Matza and Sykes:

> ... the values of a leisure class seem to lie behind much delinquent activity, however brutalized or perverted their expressions may be accounted for by the dominant social order ... The delinquent has picked up and emphasized one part of the dominant value system, namely the subterranean values that coexist with publicly proclaimed values possessing a more respectable air.[1]

Assuming that the pop festival has become a socially respectable means of pursuing certain pleasurable ends – of expressing 'approved' subterranean values – certain societal prescriptions still must be complied with. That is to say, that there may exist certain rules of behaviour at such leisure-times which are implied and reinforced through a consensus represented by the press. The press's constant reference to the police, the organizers, the 'normal' citizen, presents a picture of a higher authority *looking over* and guarding the pop festival youth from 'going too far' in their enjoyment and leisure. The overall message of the press is 'enjoy yourself, but in a certain manner only'. Just as there are dominant values for work, so there are for leisure. In both value systems a degree of obedience is implied. Thus the press laud and reinforce the essential passivity and obeisance of the pleasure-seeker, just as they do the implied qualities of the 'model worker'. Deviations from such leisure values are condemned as a consequence.

Much of press reporting of young people as a 'social phenomenon' is conveyed by reference to extreme actions, events and groups. From the 'drug-taking hippy', the affluence and charisma of the pop star, the violent Mod and Rocker to the young charity walker, a model of youth that embodies extreme polarities is presented. A prevalent image of the young during the past four years has been one of 'the hippy'.

The consensus view of the young at pop festivals portrays 'the hippy' as good-natured, polite, well-behaved, gentle and obedient,

* Paper prepared especially for this volume.

passively enjoying the entertainment provided in the rural open air. The emphasis, then, is upon the hippy's acceptance of and compliance with the official authorities who define and are part of the logic of the event-as-leisure. The hippy is seen as the 'flower child' and the official as a custodian acting as a parent-figure to instruct and guard the young from evil persons and the temptation to go too far in their youthful, but 'so understandable' vigour. However, concurrent with this image of the obedient hippy, is one that portrays him as impolite, violent, gate-grashing, promiscuous and drug taking. Press coverage of pop festivals oscillate between the two stereotypes. It accepts the legitimacy of the youthful enjoyment of leisure and, given its consensual orientation, cannot maintain that such a large body of youth is deviant. Yet at the same time, it is censorious of the emergence of bohemian ideologies amongst the young – of which the image of Woodstock Nation is a major scenario. For these imply the possibility of a radical alternative to the work and leisure patterns of the wider society. It resolves this contradiction by 'normalizing' the phenomenon; that is it portrays the majority of participants as normal decent youngsters enjoying a weekend of deserved leisure and translates the radical alternative into a minority of anarchic troublemakers.[2]

I wish to follow the mass media as they describe the progress of a typical pop festival and tackle the contradictions inherent in their own imagery.[3] To do this I have divided the moral career of the festival into four stages: eccentric invasion, imminent danger, unruly elements, and the fond farewell.

1. ECCENTRIC INVASION

The movement of a large number of young people towards the festival site is portrayed simultaneously as epitomizing the fun-loving spirit of youth and as a potential threat. For it is an invasion and the police are at the ready, just in case. Thus under the headline INVASION OF THE POP PILGRIMS, the *Daily Express*[4] with subheadings of HARMLESS and SEEKING, had this to say on the eve of the festival:

An army of young men that would make the sergeant-major's hair stand on end is camping out at Freshwater, Isle of Wight. Spearhead of a further 200,000 . . . starting tomorrow the 'new-age' heroes will explode into sound!
I can't stand blasting pop music. But I defend anybody's right to rent 300 acres and knock their ear-drums out, if it's their idea of fun.

Under the sub-head of SEEKING, the article is concluded thus:

As film-maker Lemer says: 'You and I don't know what they're at and neither do the kids, I guess. But they're all seeking something, a kind of communal experience that is outside our society. Nobody should want to stop it, or even hope to; because this thing is sweeping a whole generation.'

This general angle is reinforced by the reporter's first-hand experience:

I didn't talk to a single hippy who wasn't friendly, gentle and oddly unworldly.[5]

The overall image of bizarre eccentricity of 'youth' is firmly placed as a *spectacle* by the *Daily Mail*,[6] which plumps for the Woodstock image of hippy subculture.

JUST ONCE IN A LIFETIME WILL I SEE A SIGHT LIKE THIS

This is a once-in-a-life-time sight. The sun is shining and the pilgrims are flocking to the Isle of Wight. . . . You can get a panoramic view of a whole breakaway generation. They arrive in every kind of transportation, as long as it is vaguely eccentric. It is an extraordinary sight, as though some medieval army was on the march.
. . . They seem nice people. I hope they enjoy themselves.

Yet the police at all times are ready for trouble:

POLICE 'HIPPIES' HUNT FOR DRUGS AT FESTIVAL

Drug-Squad detectives in hippy gear mingled with Rock fans streaming to a festival yesterday.
The detectives moved in . . . in a bid to prevent drug peddling among the massive crowds of teenagers.
At last year's festival there were over 150 arrests. Fines and costs totalled more than £1,600.
This year, local magistrates are again standing by in a rota system to impose 'instant justice'.
Forensic scientists are ready at a nearby technical college to quickly analyse possible drug samples taken from fans.[7]

2. IMMINENT DANGER

The actual reporting of the festival in progress is characterized by a continuing stress on the peaceful nature of the events contrasted with a constant play on the imminent likelihood of trouble.
Thus the *Daily Express* described Woburn Abbey as follows:

First there was a false alarm which brought four or five engines dashing up. Then came a bonus hoax – and police cars arrived with sirens sounding. . . .
But through it all, 10,000 Flower Children got on with that 3-day 'love-in' at Woburn Abbey in peace and harmony.[8]

Most of the remarks concerning the good behaviour of pop fans come later as an overall reflection. Much of the 'immediate' reporting focuses upon the hippy as sexually amoral, drug taking, fornicating, and is portrayed in a titillating manner. The press fascinate, allure, titillate but finally condemn certain actions as deviating from the implied norms of enjoying oneself.

For example, the *Daily Mirror*[9] allures the reader with the following headline on the front page: A RIOT THREAT AS DYLAN WALKS OUT.

The article begins:

100,000 fans threatened to riot late last night when folk-singer Bob Dylan suddenly walked out on them.
Security guards with dogs raced to the vast concert arena.
There was near pandemonium as outraged fans asked: 'Has he gone? Where has he gone?'

Two paragraphs later the article states:

. . . But when Dylan himself finally arrived the fans had waited too long.

Continuing on the back page under the headline DYLAN RUMPUS the reader is further fascinated by accounts of manhandling of reporters. The frustration and violence are pinpointed at some group of 'weirdies' and 'hippies' whose label is 'justified' by their behaviour:

Most of the press enclosure was filled with hippies and weirdies who had no official press passes and had simply clambered over the fence surrounding the enclosure.

Under the subhead of STRAIN the article reaffirms the cause of such imminent violence in a minority, not a majority, as the whole article up until now had suggested:

It wasn't ticket-holders who were stopping their view. But the hundreds of freeloaders who had literally gatecrashed.

Being a 'weirdie', then, is equated with gatecrashing. The next sentence, in bold type, returns to the overall violence theme:

'The whole scene was one of chaos.'

But, having headlined its front-page portraying the festival as imminently violent and pandemonious in character, and devoted the whole of the article to chaos and violence, the article is concluded by this final sentence of assurance:

> But in the main, the fans stayed peaceful and calm. While Dylan sang there was serenity – if not overwhelming excitement.

Much of the fascination of the hippy and the pop festival comes as much from a lurid concentration on youthful sexuality as on the event itself. The following comment on American pop festivals is surely pertinent to Britain:

> The media, in their schizophrenic way, at once idealized and denounced rock festivals . . . for a time, festivals became sensational news, worthy of the ultimate American canonization. Like the Haight, festivals were something glamorous, romantic and new, meeting America's need for youth worship. At the same time they were an easy target for attack, for along with the American worship of the youthful image goes the fear of adolescents, the need to bottle them up and suppress their sexuality which is viewed as a threat.[10]

Thus, in an appraisal of the 1969 Isle of Wight festival, the *Daily Mirror*[11] asks:

> Was it the magnetism and magic of Dylan that brought them scurrying in from all over the world?
> . . . But the music lovers may have been only 20% of this fantastic crowd at Pop City.

And then, two paragraphs later,

> But what is the truth of Dylan? Was he the cause of it all? Or was the Isle of Wight Pop Festival a good excuse for a mass orgy?

The allurement by photograph[12] is finally condemned by reference to the police, the organizers and the local resident. In short, having fascinated (photograph) titillated (description and elaboration upon the photograph), the press finally condemns by appeal to this authority. A middle-page photograph/article 'mosaic' of the *Daily Mirror* is particularly apposite.[13]

Under a photograph of semi-naked young people playing in a mass of foam the following appears in bold type:[14]

> Hippie folk-fans waiting for folk-singer Bob Dylan on the Isle
> of Wight watched a public exhibition of love-making by a couple
> of naked teenagers yesterday.

The photograph, the bold type referring to a *public* exhibition of
lovemaking allures and titillates the reader. Assurance is supplied,
however, by pointing out that this open sexuality did not go without
some indignation:

> Some of the audience were obviously shocked . . . Some fans
> stood staring in disbelief at the couple, but most of the crowd
> were obviously in favour of what was happening.

Reassurance finally comes by reference to the authority of the
promoters:

> If we had known the sex act would occur, then we would have
> stopped the happening.[15]

However, such reassurance does not suffice for the newspaper's
crusading spirit. There follows immediately after the above description the following in bold type under the apt subhead of MORALS:

> Last night local residents wanted to know why the happening was
> ever allowed.
> For some of them the weekend had become one long nightmare,
> with the hippies completely changing the face of the exclusive
> Woodside Bay.
> The residents were *sick* of the sound of music blaring into the
> night. *Sick* of their grounds being invaded by some scantily-clad,
> drugtaking hippies. *Sick* of their gardens sometimes being used
> as toilets.

By skilful use of syntax the isolated incidents, blown up to giant
proportions by the paper, are justified as worthy of report by
reference to the 'normal' local resident being plagued and beset
by hippies and their sexual rampagings. Titillation and condemnation is complete by appeal to the normal resident who 'naturally'
abhors seeing (obviously) 'drugtaking' and 'scantily-clad' youth
near *his* home.[16]
A further example of this syntactical leap comes from the *Daily
Express:*

> Shattering too for the sedate island folk who find themselves in
> the middle of this bizarre happening where boys and girls dance
> wildly in the nude.[17]

The two extremes – 'sedate island folk, and nude youth *wildly* dancing' – are syntactically fused in physical space and meaning. The former are to be found '*in the middle of*' such wild dancing. This technique of leaping meaning and location 'brings home' the deviancy of the naked by reference to the normal ('sedate') citizen who is supposedly at the mercy of such youthful vagaries.

Cohen uses the notion of *putative deviation* (as defined by Lemert) to describe these images: 'that portion of the societal definition of the deviant which has no foundation in his objective behaviour'. In this case study, incidents not usually reported or else just described as 'pub brawls' became 'Mods and Rockers' clashes. Ambiguous events were re-interpreted by the use of readily identifiable symbols such as clothing styles.[18]

Similarly, in the foam example, the press took up a minor incident – observed by 100 people at the most, for not more than ten minutes – doted upon it and finally condemned it by a series of syntactical leaps. Local residents became involved and other elements were added in – pissing in gardens, drug taking, nudity, to make up the composite stereotype of the wicked hippy.

Another example of such putative deviation by the ambiguity of the syntactical leap comes from the *Daily Express*.[19] Its report of one day at the festival ends with the following:

A youth was found critically injured at the foot of the cliffs where hippies have been swimming in the nude. 73 people have been arrested for using drugs.

Drugs, nude bathing and a critical fall from the cliffs become (almost) fused in an ambiguous chain of utterly divergent subjects unrelated in time, space and implication.

However, through all the foam copulations and the 'public outcry' the *Express* of the same day (1 September 1969) again plumps for the Woodstock stereotype. In OPINION on page 6 they claim:

No violence! No rowdyism! Instead, compliments from their elders on their politeness and good humour.

3. UNRULY ELEMENTS

The consensus image of the polite, peaceful, loving Woodstock hippy is maintained by asserting that it was a tiny minority that caused all the trouble that was perceived, distorted and magnified by the press. In this fashion, their original ambivalence can be resolved: most kids are decent and law abiding; it is an anarchic fringe which justifies the apprehensive framework within which the events are analysed. Thus the *Daily Express* writes:

'Some of these people are potentially very dangerous,' a senior police officer said. 'Dozens of *fringe groups* have come *just to cause trouble*. They could be a threat all over the country.'[20] (my italic)

The same paper elaborates upon officialdom's imagery and authoritative judgment:

Amongst them are French and Algerian anarchist troublemakers and American anti-Vietnam Revolutionaries.[21]

Having 'successfully' isolated such groups as peripheral and atypical, the *Daily Express* continues in its vituperations:

The Hell's Angels gangs roared on to the Isle of Wight to batter down fences, take over shops and stalls and battle with police . . . The Hell's Angels had succeeded where the foreign extremists from 'Desolation Hill', overlooking the festival site, had failed on Friday.[22]

The Times did not question the imagery:

Security men are blaming Frenchmen and Algerians who, they say, regularly attend pop festivals and attempt to disrupt proceedings in the interests of free music.[23]

The *Daily Mail* elaborated the stereotype.[24]

Twice the corrugated iron fence dividing the paying fans from the free-booters on Devastation Hill was smashed down as foreign anarchists and Hell's Angels rioted in the free section.

The 'threat' to the consensual image of the passive, tranquil festival hippy is preserved by locating the violence in a peripheral group or 'mob' ('fringe elements', 'foreign extremists/anarchists', 'Hell's Angels', 'American anti-Vietnam Revolutionaries'). Final confirmation of this stereotype comes, naturally from the police.[25]

Chief Inspector Osmond . . . said: 'Most of the youngsters were charming and delightful . . . The trouble has come from a lunatic fringe of about *10,000*.' (My italic)

While constantly emphasizing the 'drug-taking' hippies at pop festivals the press manage to suggest that this is a product of corruption rather than volition. As *The Times* reports, the police show a concern over:

> ... older people giving drugs to juveniles. He [Chief Inspector Cutliffe] appealed to anybody under 17 who had been given drugs to hand them to the police.[26]

The *Daily Mail*, under a subhead of POLICE DECLARE DRUG TRUCE FOR TEMPTED FANS, affirms the essential innocence and corruptibility of the young hippy.

> Police at the Isle of Wight pop festival ... declared a drugs amnesty for fans under 17.
> Hampshire Chief Constable Mr Douglas Osmond fears that many young people are being persuaded to try drugs by older hippies at the festival.[27]

The young hippy remains within the consensual image, protected from the dangers of corrupting elders by the custodial police. He does not, according to the above model, *want* to take drugs. He is *tempted* or *persuaded* in his innocence. The deviance of a few and the innocence of the many is confirmed by the *Daily Express*.[28]

> 22 people were charged in connection with drug offences. But this is a tiny element in the huge gathering of youngsters who showed that they can conduct themselves in a responsible manner.

4. THE FOND FAREWELL

The conclusion of the festival is reported as a triumph for the consensual model. In retrospect the press note the overwhelming normality and law-abiding nature of the youngsters involved. The threat implicit in their analytical framework has been placed firmly on the heads of a tiny minority. And so the media – especially if the festival has made it a profit – bid a fond farewell.

> The flower people – or 'children' – have behaved so well at the weekend love-in at Woburn Abbey that the event would 'definitely make a profit'.[29]
> The sleepy town of Shepton Mallet waved a fond farewell to 150,000 pop fans last night.
> And they left this open invitation for the youngsters at the folk and blues festival: 'You're welcome back any time.'
> They feared for the worst at the start of the non-stop pop jamboree – but 48 hours later police were able to report there had *not* been *one* arrest.[30]

REFERENCES

1. D. Matza and G. Sykes, 'Juvenile delinquency and subterranean values', *American Sociological Review*, 26 (1961), p. 712.
2. For a discussion of the defusing of alternative realities and the process of normalization see J. Young, *Media as myth* (London, Paladin, 1973). See also article by J. Young in this Reader.
3. The pop festivals included in this study were Woburn Abbey (1967), Isle of Wight (1969), Isle of Wight (1970), Bath (1970), Reading (1972).
4. 25 August 1970, p. 5. This article appeared next to a humorous rubber-toothed bite at the hippies 'invading' the island.
5. *Daily Express* (26 August 1970).
6. *Daily Mail* (27 August 1970).
7. *Sun* (11 August 1972).
8. *Not even a 'bomb' can halt a love-in*, *Daily Express*, inside page, 28 August 1967. Compare the *Daily Mirror* headline of the same day: *It takes more than a bomb scare to shake the calm.*
9. *Daily Mirror* (September 1969).
10. A. Gordon, 'Satan and the angels: Paradise loused' in J. Eisen, *Altamont* (New York, Avon Books, 1970), pp. 44–7.
11. *Daily Mirror* (1 September 1969).
12. McLuhan's comment on the photograph as 'Brothel-without-Walls' is pertinent here. He says: 'By conferring a means of self-destination of objects, of "*statement without syntax*", photography gave the impetus to a delineation of the inner world. Statement without syntax, or verbalization was really statement by gesture, by mime and by *Gestalt*.' *Understanding media* (London, Sphere Books, 1964), p. 215.
13. *Daily Mirror* (1 September 1969), pp. 12 and 13.
14. The headline shouts: '*The happening – a bunch of teenagers smothered in foam stage a hippy-happy show.*'
15. *Daily Mirror* (1 September 1969). It is ironical, but it was through the *Daily Mirror* that this very happening was financed.
16. The *Sun*, the *Daily Express*, the *Daily Sketch* all featured as their first or second headline and 'angle' this very incident, with startlingly similar condemnation and insinuating syntactical 'leap' to the 'normal' and beleaguered citizen.
17. *Daily Express* (1 September 1969), *A froth for the faithful.*
18. S. Cohen, 'Mods, Rockers and the rest: community reactions to juvenile delinquency', *Howard Journal*, Vol. 12 (1967), pp. 121–30 and *Folk devils and moral panics* (London, McGibbon & Kee, 1972). See also article by S. Cohen in this Reader.
19. *Daily Express* (29 August 1970).
20. *Daily Express* (29 August 1970). *Big security check at pop festival.*
21. 29 August 1970. The entire report of the festival for that day is concerned with such 'fringe elements'.

22. *Daily Express* (31 August 1970), p. 1. '*Free for all as the Hell's Angels move in.*'
23. *The Times* (29 August 1970).
24. *Daily Mail* (31 August 1970).
25. *Daily Mail* (31 August 1970).
26. 29 August 1970. It is worth noting the explanation of the 'lunatic fringe' given by Anthony Haden-Guest (as well as underground papers such as *Friends, International Times*), *Daily Telegraph* Colour Supplement, 30 October 1970. 'The official festival myth is that the walls have been destroyed by crazed bands of anarchists. In fact, eye-witnesses tell me, many of the walls have been pulled down from within to provide windbreaks.'
27. 28 August 1970.
28. 1 September 1969.
29. *The Guardian* (29 August 1970).
30. *Daily Express* (29 June 1970).

PART THREE

Effects and consequences

As we stated in the Introduction, this volume addresses itself primarily to the question of how deviance and social problems are portrayed in the mass media. It is only in this fashion that the derivative problem – the one which is given more immediate attention by the public and the 'experts' – about the effects and consequences of this portrayal, can be clearly comprehended. It should be clear by now that the standard ways in which this problem is posed – for example, in debates about censorship and pornography, research on the effects of television or cinema violence, cases such as the *Oz* trial in 1972 – can frequently be over-simplified and self-limiting. The dominant model is a stimulus/response one: the stimulus (the party political broadcast, the soapflake commercial, the violent drama) is measured against a set of responses (voting behaviour or attitude change, consumer spending, the increase of aggression).

There is a very comprehensive literature in this area, part of which at least is aware of the methodological if not the theoretical problems of talking in stimulus/response terms about such complex social phenomena as deviance and social problems. This literature is sometimes highly technical – for example, on the laboratory studies of imitative aggression – but is easily available in summary form. We suggest references to it at the end of this Part, but don't propose to reprint extracts, concentrating rather on surveying the problem from the particular perspective taken in this volume. The main point of this survey will be to highlight the misleading or incomplete elements in the standard 'effects' literature and to indicate more fruitful ways of approaching the problem.

It might be useful to start by identifying the contrasting perspectives on mass media effects found in the Manipulative and Commercial models. In the Mass Manipulative model, the public are passive absorbers of a set of messages which cannot but influence their behaviour and values. Usually the adherents of this model disapprove of the messages and so – from left- or right-wing positions – the goal of the debate is to identify the effects of the media as being essentially harmful. Sometimes these effects are seen to be short-term and immediate, for example in the charge that TV or cinema violence (assumed or proved to be increasing in content) leads to direct imitation or identification. A typical representative of this position is the psychiatrist Frederic Wertham, who devoted his earlier attention to comic books as the 'seducers of the innocent' and then to TV as the 'school for violence'.[1] His argument is that TV arouses the lust for violence, reinforces it when it is already present, teaches the best method of getting away with it and dulls children's awareness of its wrongness. One might transpose the same set of arguments as that used by Mary Whitehouse and associated pressure groups in this country, apply it to the area of pornography and find it in the legal arguments about 'corruption' used in cases such as the *Oz* trial.[2] In each case 'experts' can be used to give a scientific buttress to the argument, for example, with reference to laboratory or clinical evidence.

The longer-term harmful effects are cited in left-wing critiques of the media in terms of debasing values or mystifying class consciousness. The media are seen to blunt or distort people's perception of reality and create an atmosphere of tolerance for individualistic or competitive behaviour. Similarly, variants of these charges are made from élitist or right-wing positions which lay even greater stress on the supposed debasement of values, standard and morality. Thus in David Holbrook's well known interventions in the pornography debate, such effects as a 'dehumanization of sex' occur.[3]

The Commercial model, most commonly invoked here by social scientists, as well as journalists themselves, is much more cautious about the question of effects. Influenced by 1940s' media research in the United States in such areas as propaganda and voting behaviour, together with their own rather more critical reading of the laboratory studies of aggression, adherents of this position stress that the public is neither so dumb nor so passive as all that. They will only seek out particular messages if they fulfil an existing need or fit into an existing set of opinions. Thus in regard to the TV violence debate, the psychological version of the model works with such concepts as the 'predisposed personality' on whom the media can at the most trigger off violent behaviour. And to repeat the example of the *Oz* trial it is argued that no new converts would be made by reading such material. Sociologists would talk of behavioural and attitudinal change stemming from or being mediated through, primary groups, reference groups and other such influences.

We have to some extent caricatured these two positions by summarizing them in so short a space. For more detailed considerations we refer the reader to our list of suggested readings at the end of this Part.

Our own position – as indicated in the Selection and Models

sections – is at neither extreme. In playing down the more melo-dramatic effects of the media as portrayed in the Manipulative versions – partly because of a liberal democratic opposition to censorship and control – the Laissez-Faire position exaggerates the impotence of the media. Clearly the media must have some influence.

This influence is not monolithic, because some range of choices are made available but these largely remain within a certain narrow perspective on social reality. The audience can perhaps shop around within this framework, but they can rarely escape it. With an ade-quate theory of the 'audience' or the 'public' for the mass media one can direct attention not to a set of straightforward stimulus/ response mechanisms, but a series of human mediations and definitions of the message.

We might use the *Oz* trial as a paradigmatic study of the effects problem. Here the one side was arguing that the contents of the particular edition of the magazine would corrupt its younger readers. Advertisements for homosexual contacts, features presenting a tolerant attitude towards certain forms of drug use, cartoons depict-ing school authority in an obscene and derogatory way, articles and advertisements drawing attention to sexual deviation – all would have a harmful effect on values and behaviour. The opposed position drew attention to the selective nature of the audience (not everyone would buy the magazine) and the unlikelihood that the objectionable messages would actually have any effect on individuals not already committed towards that particular line of action or thought.

Both of us found ourselves involved in this case as potential witnesses for the defence. We had no doubt of the weaknesses of the prosecution's case on both legal and sociological grounds and would have drawn attention to the relevant evidence on such matters as for example, the effects of exposure to explicit sexual material.[4] In addition, our own values made us totally opposed to prosecutions of this sort. We should, therefore, have been ideal defence witnesses. But at some point in our initial briefing by the defence lawyers we realized that we were being put in a somewhat false position. We were being asked to support an extreme Laissez-Faire model which we knew in this case to be patently absurd. Clearly the publishers and editors of *Oz had* intended to change people's values and opinions, otherwise why produce the magazine at all? And if some members of the audience saw the voice of *Oz* as providing an authoritative source of alternative definitions of reality, why shouldn't these definitions affect attitudes to sex, drugs, authority? And weren't the adverts for various sexual couplings precisely designed to attract people or their money? When the defence lawyers saw that we were unable completely to suspend our theoretical doubts about the way they had to argue their case, we were quietly dropped from their line-up. Our doubts – and the scenarios that were enacted in the Old Bailey courtroom – are important only because they exemplify the problems inherent in the effects debate. If we had been called as witnesses, we would certainly have drawn attention to the standard problems in this debate. But we would also – although such matters would hardly look relevant in a court of law – have wanted to make the following points, separating out a series of effects:

1. ON THE INFORMATION STOCK

The master effect of the mass media's portrayal of deviance and social problems is in terms of the quantity and quality of the information which the public receives and uses as a basis for action. In modern urban societies there is an extreme social segregation between different groups. The media are the major and at times the sole source of information about a whole range of phenomena. What McLuhan terms the 'implosive factor' in the media points to continual bombardment by images of phenomena that otherwise could conveniently be forgotten. For reasons we discussed in Part One, many such phenomena are not selected for attention at all, others are given continual exposure (for example, the 'violence problem') while yet others are suddenly thrust into the public consciousness – the housing problem, for example, following the showing in 1966 of *Cathy come home* on television. The quantity of the information, as we have suggested (see Davis and Roshier's articles) has a curious relationship to the real world. In Ben Hecht's often quoted words, 'Trying to determine what is going on in the world by reading the newspaper is like trying to tell the time by watching the second hand of a clock'.

The quality of the information is curious also. In our type of society information about deviance and social problems is invariably received at second hand. This means it arrives after going through the selective filters we have described and after being processed by the media. It tends to be of a flat, one-dimensional quality unlike the multidimensional picture one might have had in societies which could rely more on personal experience. The information is then presented – as our examples in Part Two showed – in a stereotypical manner with elements of fantasy and selective misperception.

This is not to suggest that misperception and fantasy are exclusive attributes of those industrial societies where the mass media are so pervasive. On the contrary, the stereotypical accounts transmitted through such informal processes as rumour and gossip involve parallel distortions and are similar to the moral panics precipitated by mass media coverage. But there remain crucial differences. The manufacture of news is essentially an élitist endeavour whereas the process of rumour formation without the help of the mass media is marked a series of 'democratic' innovations by each person in the chain. It is true, of course, that in order to communicate and persuade, the newsman uses a consensual paradigm which is – at least in part – embraced by large numbers. But the conservative direction of this framework is more structured and the chances of any innovation or alternative interpretations are more severely limited than in face-to-face communication. Rumour can be 'radical' and it possesses a fluidity of structure whereas the media present their audience with a fixed interpretation. When the media themselves trigger off rumour, the message is again more structured and related to the consensual paradigm. Social segregation in advanced industrial societies ensures that the experiential knowledge against which one might measure stereotypes is comparatively poor and restricted. This is not to make the romantic suggestion that pre-industrial man had wider social horizons but merely that *within* small-scale societies social knowledge is more multidimensional and directly experienced, and that the restricted overall *quantity* of such information is less subject to the sudden implosions of concern which allow the mass media to introduce a social problem one day and forget about it on the next.

Students of the mass media, then, before trying to find stimulus/response links or any other such patterns, must look for the master effect which changes the nature of the 'stimulus' – i.e., the information that is actually used to build up society's stock of images.

2. ON THE CONSENSUS

One crucial long-term effect of these images is to reinforce the consensual image of society which the media themselves draw upon. The majority in any society is seen to share a consensus about reality. This involves agreement about what is normal, praiseworthy and acceptable. Those who are abnormal, who deviate or who present problems to the dominant value system are seen to inhabit a territory beyond the boundaries of society. They are allowed no history, no real alternative conception of reality and no status other than objects of social control. They are recurrent objects of attention not just because they entertain and interest us, or fulfil some psychological need for identification but because they inform us about the boundaries of reality. As Erikson notes: 'a considerable portion of what we call "news" is devoted to reports about deviant behaviour and its consequences'.[5] Such news is a main source of information about the normative contours of a society. It informs us about right and wrong, about the parameters beyond which one should not venture and about the shapes that the devil can assume. A galley of folk types – heroes and saints, as well as fools, villains and devils – is publicized not just in oral-tradition and face-to-face contact, but to much larger audiences and with much greater dramatic resources.

It provides, as Hartmann and Husband (Part Two) have elaborated, scenarios by which to understand social problems. They found that the conceptions of race held by children are mainly structured by media images *particularly* in those areas where there was little contact with immigrants. Thus the image of black-white conflict, although basically inaccurate, is accepted as a framework for analysing the problem of race.

The mass media provide a major source of knowledge in a segregated society of what the consensus actually is and what is the nature of deviation from it. They conjure up for each group with its limited stock of social knowledge, what 'everyone else' believes. They counterpose the reification of 'the average man' against the reality of individual group experience. The deviant's own knowledge of how 'most' others perceive him derives from this mass media portrayal; indeed in the case of the isolated deviant, even his knowledge of others involved in the same form of action might derive from this source.[6] This makes each social problem group feel more marginal when facing, what they often presume, is a monolith of agreement. Such a perception is a vital link in the process of deviancy amplification which we discuss later.

In this fashion the mass media present to the population frameworks, grounded in conservative thought, by which social problems are to be interpreted. Laissez-Faire theorists would comment that, if this is so, it is because: (a) such consensual models are the correct interpretations of reality; and (b) they are only taken up by the population because they are, in fact, widely accepted definitions already. In regard to the first point, we can only say that – together with many other sociologists – we find alternative conflict models to work better as interpretations and as strategies for research. The second argument is more subtle and important. It is clearly the case that the mass media in order to communicate must talk in the language of their audience. (See Murdock and Hall's papers in Part Two.) Further, it is evident that the most widespread culture is essentially conservative in nature. But we cannot concede the point completely, because this 'culture' is not the totality of consciousness. All members of a society may understand a culture and partly adhere to it, without this being the only strand of thought in their consciousness. The conservative part of the population's thinking may well be constantly reinforced by the impact of media material, while the radical portion is constantly denied. For consciousness, at least in our society, commonly displays a contradictory mode: our public rhetoric celebrates a world which our private discourse and personal feelings often denigrate. The journalist, as part of such a society, is placed in a role where competence is measured in terms of an ability to write in such an official language, he finds his promotion linked to the notion of 'responsible journalism' which in turn reflects such a way of thinking. It is not necessary, therefore, for him to be machiavellian in his adoption of conservative imagery even though his peace of mind may, at times, be disturbed by the obdurate nature of events. Manipulation, then, can occur, but it is of a more subtle kind than that suggested in the Mass Manipulative model, allowing as it does for a willing journalist and a partially responsive audience.

3. ON MORAL PANICS

The mass media are the main agents and carriers of moral panics. Sociologists have recently devoted increasing attention to the elements involved in the creation of social problems.[7] The presence of a condition about which people feel anxious or threatened, the element of moral indignation,[8] a belief system to legitimate social control and the activities of enterprising individuals who facilitate public awareness of the condition are among the many elements studied. Thus Becker[9] and Gusfield[10] have taken the cases of the Marihuana Tax Act and the Prohibition laws respectively to show how public concern about a particular condition is generated and a 'symbolic crusade' mounted. This, with publicity and the actions of certain interest groups, results in what Becker calls *moral enterprise*: '. . . the creation of a new fragment of the moral constitution of society'.[11]

The student of moral enterprise cannot but pay particular attention to the role of the mass media in defining and shaping social problems. The media have long operated as agents of moral indignation in their own right: even if they are not self-consciously engaged in crusading or muck raking, their very reporting of certain 'facts' can be sufficient to generate concern, anxiety, indignation or panic. When such feelings coincide with a perception that particular values need to be protected, the preconditions for new rule creation or social problem definition are present. The outcome might not always be as definite as the actual creation of new rules or the more rigid enforcement of existing ones. What may result is the sort of symbolic process which Gusfield describes in his conception of 'moral passage', namely a change in the public designation of deviance.[12] In his example, the problem drinker changes over time from 're-pentant' to 'enemy' to 'sick'. Even less concretely, the media might leave a diffuse feeling of anxiety about the situation: 'Something should be done about it.' 'This sort of thing can't go on for ever.'

Such vague feelings are crucial in laying the ground for further moral enterprise. The media play on the normative concerns of the public and by thrusting certain moral directives into the universe of discourse, can create social problems suddenly and dramatically.[13] This potential is consciously exploited by those whom Becker calls 'moral entrepreneurs' to aid them in their attempt to win public support. These campaigns are not, of course, always successful and the media's attempts to whip up a moral panic might not 'take'. Here, for example, is an editorial from the *Sun* (6 October 1972):

> MURDER IN THE WARD: A Jordanian doctor ran amok and killed three children in a Blackpool hospital last February. Now Sir Keith Joseph refuses a formal enquiry. 'The killings were completely unpredictable' he says.
> NOT SO, SIR KEITH.
> PARENTS with children in hospital want to be reassured that there are not any more mad medicos with daggers about.

Whatever the merits of an enquiry in this particular case, it seems hardly likely that the majority of the *Sun*'s readers were consciously worried every time they sent their children to hospital that 'mad medicos with daggers' were lurking about the wards. This particular enterprise looked unlikely to take off and one significant area for sociological research is to uncover the conditions under which the media are or are not successful in creating moral panics.

4. ON SOCIAL CONTROL

Both in their role as purveyors of information and transmitters of moral panics, the media have a crucial effect on society's agents of social control. What Lemert calls the societal control culture, 'the laws, procedures, programmes and organizations which in the name of a collectivity help, rehabilitate, punish or otherwise manipulate deviants',[14] contains not just a set of institutions (courts, prisons, hospitals) and personnel (policemen, magistrates, social workers) but also typical modes and models of understanding and explaining deviance. To a large extent, these modes and models are provided for the control culture by the mass media. There is little reason to suppose that control agents are somehow immune to the messages transmitted by the media and indeed the segregated position of some control agents – such as policemen in regard to the reality of say subcultural drug taking – makes them peculiarly susceptible to the media. We have both shown the powerful way in which the media shape the control culture, particularly in transmitting belief systems which legitimate or justify particular forms of social control.

Once the action against the deviant or social problem is taken, it is the media which provide a commentary on the nature of the 'solution'. Philip Slater has nicely captured the essence of this commentary in his discussion of what he calls the 'compulsive American tendency to avoid confrontation of chronic social problems':[16]

> We are, as a people, perturbed by our inability to anticipate the consequences of our acts, but we still wait optimistically for some magic telegram, informing us that the tangled skein of misery and self-deception into which we have woven ourselves has vanished in the night. Each month popular magazines regale their readers with such telegrams: announcing that our transportation crisis will be solved by a bigger plane or a wider road, mental illness with a pill, poverty with a law, slums with a bulldozer, urban conflict with a gas, racism with a goodwill gesture. Perhaps the most grotesque of all these telegrams was an article in *Life* showing a group of suburbanites participating in a 'Clean-Up Day' in an urban slum. Foreigners are surprised when Americans exhibit this kind of naïveté and/or cynicism about social problems, but their surprise is inappropriate. Whatever realism we may display in technical areas, our approach to social issues inevitably falls back on cinematic tradition, in which social problems are resolved by gesture. Deeply embedded in the somnolent social consciousness of the broom-wielding suburbanites is a series of climactic movie scenes in which a long column of once surly natives, marching in solemn silence and as one man, framed by the setting sun, turn in their weapons to the white chief who has done them a good turn, or menace the white adventurer's enemy (who turns pale at the sight), or rebuild the missionary's church, destroyed by fire.
>
> When a social problem persists (as they tend to do) longer than a few days, those who call attention to its continued presence are viewed as 'going too far' and 'causing the pendulum to swing the other way'. We can make war on poverty but shrink from the extensive readjustments required to stop breeding it. Once a law is passed, a commission set up, a study made, a report written, the problem is expected to have been 'wiped out' or 'mopped up'.

Bombs abroad are matched by 'crash programmes' at home – the terminological similarity reveals a psychological one.

Or – to put Slater's critique in terms of our own model – the peculiar effect on social control of the way in which the media select and present information is simultaneously to direct attention to some conditions (through moral panics etc.) and to selectively avoid others. The tendency to avoid certain conditions is reflected in our way of segregating, particularly through institutionalization, the awkward, threatening or embarrassing elements in our society. This thought pattern is called by Slater the 'Toilet Assumption':

the notion that unwanted matter, unwanted difficulties, unwanted complexities and obstacles will disappear if they are removed from our immediate field of vision. We do not connect the trash we throw from the car window with the trash in our streets, and we assume that replacing old buildings with new expensive ones will alleviate poverty in the slums. We throw the aged and psychotic into institutional holes where they cannot be seen. Our approach to social problems is to decrease their visibility: out of sight, out of mind. This is the real foundation of racial segregation, especially in its most extreme case, the Indian 'reservation'. The result of our social efforts has been to remove the underlying problems of our society farther and farther from daily experience and daily consciousness, and hence to decrease, in the mass of the population, the knowledge, skill, resources, and motivation necessary to deal with them.

When these discarded problems rise to the surface again – a riot, a protest, an exposé in the mass media – we react as if a sewer had backed up. We are shocked, disgusted and angered, and immediately call for the emergency plumber (the special commission, the crash programme) to ensure that the problem is once again removed from consciousness.

The Toilet Assumption is not merely a facetious metaphor. Prior to the widespread use of the flush toilet all of humanity was daily confronted with the immediate reality of human waste and its disposal. They knew where it was and how it got there. Nothing miraculously vanished. Excrement was conspicuously present in the outhouse or chamber pot, and the slops that went out the window went visibly and noticeably into the street. The most aristocratic Victorian ladies strolling in fashionable city parks thought nothing of retiring to the bushes to relieve themselves. Similarly, garbage did not disappear down a disposal unit – it remained nearby.

As with physical waste, so with social problems. The biblical adage, 'the poor are always with us,' had a more literal meaning before World War I. The poor were visible and all around. Psychosis was not a strange phenomenon in a textbook but a

familiar neighbour or village character. The aged were in every
house. Everyone had seen animals slaughtered and knew what they
were eating when they ate them; illness and death were a part of
everyone's immediate experience.

In contemporary life the book of experience is filled with
blank and mysterious pages. Occupational specialization and
plumbing have exerted a kind of censorship over our understanding of the world we live in and how it operates. And when we
come into immediate contact with anything that does not seem to
fit into the ordinary pattern of our somewhat bowdlerized existence
our spontaneous reaction is to try somehow to flush it away,
bomb it away, throw it down the jail.

But in some small degree we also feel bored and uneasy with
the orderly chrome and porcelain vacuum of our lives, from which
so much of life has been removed. Evasion creates self-distaste
as well as comfort, and radical confrontations are exciting as well
as disruptive. The answering chord that they produce within us
terrifies us, and although we cannot entirely contain our fascination, it is relatively easy to project our self-disgust on to the
perpetrators of the confrontations.

This ambivalence is reflected in the mass media. The hunger for
confrontation and experience attracts a lot of attention to social
problems, but these are usually dealt with in such a way as to
reinforce the avoidance process. The TV documentary presents a
tidy package with opposing views and an implication of progress.
Reports in popular magazines attempt to provide a substitute for
actual experience. Important book and film reviews, for example,
give just the blend of titillation and condescension to make the
reader imagine that he is already 'in' and need not undergo the
experience itself – that he has not only participated in the novel
adventure but already outgrown it. Thus the ultimate effect of the
media is to reinforce the avoiding response by providing an effigy
of confrontation and experience.[17]

5. ON DEVIANCE AND SOCIAL PROBLEMS

It is only against the background of such broader effects of the
mass media – the master effect in shaping information about deviance, the effects on the consensus, moral panics, control agents –
that we can begin to think about the effects on groups considered
socially deviant or problematic. Here we must stress, with Chaney[18]
that whatever questions we ask – Is the programme or story likely
to cause the viewer or reader anxiety? Will it be used as a model
for anti-social behaviour? – we must note how it is that a member
of the audience 'at risk' perceives or defines the message, how he
interprets it according to his self and his view of the world: 'We can
no longer be content to speak vaguely of television "reinforcing"

trends in viewers that were already present; the reinforcement only becomes relevant when it is seen by the viewers to be relevant.'

We would argue that any further studies of effects should take this element as central.

To conclude this section we have selected examples from our own work of two typical mass media effects on the development of deviance: *amplification* and *sensitization*.

REFERENCES

1. See Frederic Wertham, *The seduction of the innocent* (New York, Holt, Rinehart & Winston, 1954) and 'School for violence', *New York Times* (5 July 1964), reprinted in Otto N. Larsen (ed.) *Violence and the mass media* (New York, Harper & Row, 1968).
2. For illustrations see Tony Palmer, *The trials of Oz* (London, Hutchinson, 1971).
3. D. Holbrook, *Sex and dehumanization* (London, Pitman, 1972).
4. For a recent authoritative summary of this literature, see the American *Report of the Commission on Obscenity and Pornography.*
5. Kai T. Erikson, *Wayward puritans: a study in the sociology of deviance* (New York, John Wiley, 1966).
6. For an elaboration of this notion of perceived consensus and the effects on deviants, see J. Young, 'The consensual myth' in P. Rock and M. McIntosh (eds.), *Deviance and social control* (London, Tavistock Publications, 1973).
7. Howard Becker (ed.), *Social problems* (New York, John Wiley, 1964) see Introduction.
8. See S. Ranulf, *Moral indignation and middle class psychology* (New York, Schocken Books, 1964) and Albert K. Cohen, 'The sociology of the deviant act', *American Sociological Review* 30 (1965), pp. 5–14.
9. Howard S. Becker, *Outsiders: studies in the sociology of deviance* (New York, Free Press, 1963), Chaps. 7 and 8.
10. Joseph Gusfield, *Symbolic crusade: status politics and the American Temperance Movement* (Urbana, University of Illinois, 1963).
11. Becker, op. cit., p. 145.
12. Joseph Gusfield, 'Moral passage: the symbolic process in public designations of deviance', *Social Problems* 15 (Fall, 1967), pp. 175–88.
13. For further details on the role of the mass media in creating moral panics, see Paul Rock and Stanley Cohen, 'The Teddy Boy' in V. Bogdanor and R. Skidelsky (eds.), *The age of affluence 1951–1964* (London, Macmillan, 1970); Jock Young, *The drugtakers* (London, Paladin, 1971) and Stanley Cohen, *Folk devils and moral panics: the creation of the Mods and Rockers* (London, MacGibbon & Kee, 1972).
14. Edwin M. Lement, *Social pathology* (New York, McGraw Hill, 1952), p. 557.
15. See references in note 13.

16. Philip Slater, *The pursuit of loneliness: American culture at the breaking point* (Boston, Beacon Press, 1970), Chapter 1.
17. Ibid., pp. 15–17.
18. David Chaney, 'Involvement, realism and the perception of aggression in television programmes', *Human Relations*, Vol. 23, No. 5 (1970), pp. 373–81.

The amplification of drug use*

JOCK YOUNG

This section is based on a participant observation study on the relationship between the police and the marihuana smoker in Notting Hill over the period 1967–1969. First it is necessary to introduce the concept of deviance amplification. This process, originally elaborated by Leslie Wilkins[1] must be understood in the context of what we have said about the nature of information about deviance in contemporary society. The argument is that under certain conditions, society will define as deviant a group of people who depart from valued norms in some ways. This negative societal reaction – with its concomitant exclusion and restriction on the possibilities of normal action – might merely serve to increase the possibility that the group will act even more deviantly. If it does so, societal reaction will increase at the same pace, more deviancy will be induced and, in turn, the reaction further escalated. As a result, a deviancy amplification spiral is entered into where each increase in social control is matched by a corresponding increase in deviancy.

Diagrammatically:

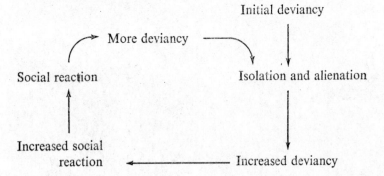

It should not be thought that the deviant group is, so to speak, a pinball inevitably propelled in a deviant direction, or that the

* This is a revised version of part of Jock Young's paper 'The role of the police as amplifiers of deviancy, negotiators of reality and translators of fantasy: some consequences of our present system of drug control as seen in Notting Hill', in S. Cohen (ed.), *Images of deviance* (Harmondsworth, Penguin, 1971).

agencies of social control are the cushions of the machine that will inevitably reflex into a reaction triggered by the changing course of the deviant. Although the notion of deviancy amplification is often used mechanically there is no need for us to limit ourselves to such an interpretation. Thus, the drug-taking group creates its own circumstances to the extent that it interprets and makes meaningful the reactions of the police against it; both the police and the group evolve theories which attempt to explain each other and test them out in terms of the actual course of events: the arrest situation, encounters on the street, portrayals in the mass media and conversations with friends. These hypotheses of the police about the nature of drug use, and of the drug taker about the mentality of the police, determine the direction and intensity of the deviancy amplification process.

It is obvious that a prime factor in this exchange between police and deviant group will be the nature of the information that each has of each other. We must examine how the extent to which the mass media provide this information and by this means threaten to precipitate a deviancy amplification spiral.

THE POSITION OF THE POLICEMAN IN A SEGREGATED SOCIETY

The police occupy a particularly segregated part of the social structure. This is because:

1. A policy of limited isolation is followed, based on the premiss that if you become too friendly with the community you are liable to corruption.

2. Public attitudes range from a ubiquitous suspicion to (in such areas as Notting Hill) downright hostility.

3. In terms of actual contacts, the Royal Commission Survey on the police found that just under half of city police and three-quarters of country police thought they would have had more friends if they had a different job. Two-thirds of all police thought their job adversely affected their outside friendships.

4. A fair proportion of policemen are residentially segregated. Thus a quarter of city police live in groups of six or more police houses.

5. In the particular instance of middle-class drug takers in Notting Hill, the police have very little direct knowledge, outside the arrest situation, of the normal behaviour of middle-class youth.

Because of this segregation the police are particularly exposed to the stereotypical accounts of deviants prevalent in the mass media.

They have, of course, by the very nature of their role, a certain degree of face-to-face contact with deviants; but these contacts are of a type which, because of the policeman's position of power, make for a reinforcement rather than an elimination of mass media stereotypes.

A person in a position of power whose direct empirical knowledge of a group is restricted to situations where he is exerting that authority will tend to elicit stereotypical responses from that group. That is, they will negotiate the situation by telling the police what they want to hear in order to minimize their likely punishment. [2]

THE VESTED INTERESTS OF POLICE AND MEDIA

The police have a bureaucratic interest in apprehending the marihuana smoker to the extent that this avoids public recrimination of failing in their duty. They have also a certain moral indignation about drug use. For the hedonism and expressivity of bohemian drug takers challenges the moral validity of their sense of the work ethic and just reward. They will tend in such circumstances to have an image of marihuana smoking as a pursuit which although pleasurable is dangerous and an appraisal of the bohemian way of life as being a miserable one compared to their own. Drug use is not freely chosen but a result of corruption and innocence. In this fashion they evolve a myth of the marihuana smoker which protects the validity of their own way of life. Their own role is immediately derived from such an ethos: they must save the innocent (i.e. the drug user) in a humanitarian fashion and punish the wicked (i.e., the drug 'pusher'). As suggested in Young's earlier article (Part Two) on the mass media portrayal of drug users, the media have learnt that the fanning up of moral indignation is a remarkable commercial success. They, therefore, play on and continue such distorted imagery. But the relationship between police and mass media is closer and more intricate than this. For a symbiotic relationship exists between the police and the crime reporter: the police providing information and the journalists holding back news in such a fashion as to aid police investigations. Precisely such a cooperative relationship exists over the control of drug use. Robert Traini, the Chairman of the Crime Reporters Association, has indicated how the moral panic over drug use was initiated in this country by the police approaching journalists and informing them that 'the situation had got out of hand'. [3] The mass media responded enthusiastically and police of all ranks become exposed to a playback and subsequent elaboration of their prejudices.

The mass media representing a reified public opinion was a major pressure on the police. The moral panic which evolved in the middle 1960s soon got firmly on its way.

THE FANTASY AND REALITY OF DRUG TAKING

One might contrast the social world of the marihuana smoker in Notting Hill, as it was in 1967, with the fantasy stereotype of the drug taker available in the mass media:

1. It is a typical bohemian scene, that is, it is a highly organized community involving tightly interrelated friendship nets and especially intense patterns of visiting.

The stereotype held in the mass media is that of the isolated drug taker living in a socially disorganized area, or at the best, a drifter existing in a loose conglomeration of misfits.

2. The values of the hippie marihuana smoker are relatively clear-cut and in opposition to the values of the wider society. The focal concerns of the culture are short-term hedonism, spontaneity, expressivity, disdain for work.

The stereotype held is of a group of individuals who are essentially *asocial*, who lack values, rather than propound alternative values. They are prey to wicked pushers who play on their naïveté and inexperience.

3. Drug taking is – at least to start with – irregular. It is not an essential prerequisite of membership. Rather it is used instrumentally for hedonistic and expressive purposes and symbolically as a sign of the exotic 'differentness' of the bohemian. Drugs are thus an important, although not central focus of such groups.

Drugs hold a great fascination for the non-drug taker, and in the stereotype drugs are held to be the primary – if not exclusive – concern of such groups. Thus a peripheral activity is misperceived as a central group activity.

4. The marihuana user and the marihuana seller are not, on the street level, fixed roles in the culture. At one time a person may sell marihuana, at another he may be buying it. This is because at street level supply is irregular, and good 'connections' appear and disappear rapidly. The supply of marihuana at that time derived from two major sources: tourists returning from abroad, and 'hippie' or immigrant entrepreneurs. The latter are unsystematic, deal in relatively small quantities and make a restricted and irregular profit. The tourists' total contribution to the market is significant. Both tourists and entrepreneurs restrict their criminal activities to marihuana importation. The dealer in the street buys from these sources and sells in order to maintain himself in drugs and sustain subsistence living. He is well thought of by the group, is part of the

hippie culture, and is not known as a 'pusher'. The criminal under-world has little interest in the entrepreneur, the tourist, or the dealer in the street.

The stereotype, in contrast, is on the lines of the corruptor and the corrupted, that is the 'pusher' and the 'victim'. The pusher is per-ceived as having close contacts with the criminal underworld and being part of a 'drug pyramid'.

5. The culture consists of largely psychologically stable individuals. The stereotype sees the drug taker essentially as an immature, psychologically unstable young person corrupted by unscrupulous pushers.

6. The marihuana user has in fact a large measure of disdain for the heroin addict. There is an interesting parallel between the marihuana user's perception of the businessman and of the heroin addict. Both are considered to be 'hung up', obsessed and dominated by money or heroin respectively. Hedonistic and expressive values are hardly likely to be realized by either, and their way of life has no strong attraction for the marihuana user. Escalation, then, from marihuana to heroin is a rare phenomenon which would involve a radical shift in values and life style.

In the stereotype the heroin addict and the marihuana user are often indistinguishable, the values of both are similar, and escalation is seen as part of a progressive search for more effective 'kicks'.

7. The marihuana user is widely prevalent in Notting Hill. A high proportion of young people in the area have smoked pot at some time or another.

The stereotype based on numbers known to the police is small compared with the actual number of smokers, yet is perceived as far too large at that and increasing rapidly.

8. The effects of marihuana are mildly euphoric; psychotic effects are rare and only temporary.

The stereotypical effects of marihuana reflect the exaggerated ambivalence of the mass media towards drugs. Thus they hold promise of uninhibited pleasure, yet plummet the taker inevitably into unmitigated misery.

RESULTS OF THE MORAL PANIC

Over time, police action on the marihuana smoker in Notting Hill results in (a) the intensification of the deviancy of the marihuana user, that is the consolidation and accentuation of his deviant values as deviancy amplifies: and (b) a change in the life style and reality of marihuana use, so that certain facets of the stereotype become actuality. That is a translation of fantasy into reality.

I wish to consider the various aspects of the social world of the marihuana user which I outlined earlier and note the cumulative effects of intensive police action:

1. Intensive police action serves to increase the organization and cohesion of the drug-taking community, uniting its members in a sense of injustice felt at harsh sentences and mass media distortions. The severity of the conflict compels bohemian groups to evolve theories to explain the nature of their position in society, thereby heightening their consciousness of themselves as a group with definite interests over and against those of the wider society. Conflict welds an introspective community into a political faction with a critical ideology, and deviancy amplification results.

2. A rise in police action increases the necessity for the drug taker to segregate himself from the wider society of non-drug takers. The greater his isolation the less chance there is that the informal face-to-face forces of social control will come into operation, and the higher his potentiality for further deviant behaviour. At the same time the creation by the bohemian of social worlds centring around hedonism, expressivity, and drug use makes it necessary for the non-drug taker, the 'straight', to be excluded not only for reasons of security but also to maintain definitions of reality unchallenged by the outside world. Thus after a point in the process of exclusion of the deviant by society, the deviant himself will cooperate in the policy of separation.

3. The further the drug taker evolves deviant norms, the less chance there is of his re-entering the wider society. Regular drug use, bizarre dress, long hair, and lack of a workaday sense of time, money, rationality and rewards, all militate against his re-entry into regular employment. To do so after a point would demand a complete change of identity; besides modern record systems would make apparent any gaps which have occurred in his employment or scholastic records, and these might be seen to indicate a personality which is essentially shiftless and incorrigible. Once he is out of the system and labelled by the system in this manner, it is very difficult for the penitent deviant to re-enter it, especially at the level of jobs previously open to him. There is a point therefore beyond which an ossification of deviancy can be said to occur.[4]

4. As police concern with drug taking increases, drug taking becomes more and more a secret activity. Because of this, drug taking in itself becomes of greater value to the group as a symbol of their difference, and of their defiance of perceived social injustices. That is, marihuana comes to be consumed not only for its euphoric effects but as a symbol of bohemianism and rebellion against the unjust system.

Drug taking and trafficking thus move from being peripheral activities of the groups, a mere vehicle for the better realization of hedonistic, expressive goals, to become a central activity of great importance. The stereotype begins to be realized, and fantasy is translated into reality.

5. The price of marihuana rises, the gains to be made from selling marihuana become larger and the professional pusher begins to emerge as police activity increases. Importation becomes more systemized, long term and concerned with large regular profits. Because of increased vigilance at the customs, the contribution of returning tourists to the market declines markedly. International connections are forged by importers linking supply countries and profitable markets and involving large sums of capital. Other criminal activities overlap with marihuana importation, especially those dealing in other saleable drugs. On the street level the dealer becomes more of a 'pusher', less part of the culture, and motivated more by economic than social and subsistence living considerations. The criminal underworld becomes more interested in the drug market, overtures are made to importers: a few pushers come under pressure to buy from them and to sell a wider range of drugs, including heroin and methedrine. A drug pyramid, as yet embryonic, begins to emerge. Once again fantasy is being translated into reality.

6. The marihuana user becomes increasingly secretive and suspicious of those around him. How does he know that his activities are not being observed by the police? How does he know that seeming friends are not police informers? Ugly rumours fly around about treatment of suspects by the police, long terms of imprisonment, planting and general social stigmatization. The effects of drugs are undoubtedly related to the cultural milieu in which drugs are taken. A Welsh rugby club drinks to the point of aggression, an all-night party to the point of libidinousness; an academic sherry party unveils the pointed gossip of competitiveness lurking under the mask of a community of scholars. Similarly, the effects of marihuana being smoked in the context of police persecution invite feelings of paranoia and semi-psychotic episodes. Thus stereotypical effects become in part reality.

7. As police activity increases, the marihuana user and the heroin addict begin to feel some identity as joint victims of police persecution. Interaction between heroin addicts and marihuana users increases. The general social feeling against all drugs creates a stricter control of the supply of heroin to the addict. He is legally bound to obtain his supplies from one of the properly authorized clinics. Lack of personnel who are properly trained, or who even

have an adequate theoretical knowledge of dealing with the withdrawal problems of the heroin addict, results in the alienation of many from the clinics. The addict who does attend either is kept on maintenance doses or else has his supply gradually cut. Either way euphoria becomes more difficult to obtain from the restricted supply, and the 'grey market' of surplus National Health heroin, which previously catered for addicts who required extra or illicit supplies, disappears. In its place a black market springs up, often consisting of Chinese heroin diluted with adulterants. This provides a tentative basis for criminal underworld involvement in drug selling and has the consequence of increasing the risks of overdosage (because the strength is unknown) and infection (because of the adulterants).

But the supply of black-market heroin alone is inadequate. Other drugs are turned to in order to make up the scarcity; the precise drugs varying with their availability, and the ability of legislation to catch up with this phenomenon of drugs displacement. Chief of these are methadone, a drug addictive in its own right and which is used to wean addicts off heroin and freely prescribed barbiturates. As a result of displacement a body of methadone and barbiturate addicts emerges, the barbiturates being probably more dangerous than heroin and cause even greater withdrawal problems. For a while the over-prescription by doctors creates, as once occurred with heroin, an ample grey market of methadone and barbiturates. But the pressure on the doctors restricts at least the availability of methadone, and the ranks of saleable black-market drugs are increased in the process. Because many junkies share some common bohemian traditions with hippies (they often live in the same areas, smoke pot, and affect the same style of dress), the black market of heroin, methadone, barbiturates and marihuana will overlap. The heroin addict seeking money in order to maintain his habit at a desirable level and the enterprising drug seller may find it profitable to make these drugs available to marihuana smokers.

Some marihuana users will pass on to these hard drugs, but let me emphasize *some*, as, in general, heavy use of such drugs is incompatible with hippie values. For full-blown physical addiction involves being at a certain place at a certain time every day; it involves an obsession with one substance to the exclusion of all other interests; it is anathema to the values of hedonic expressivity and autonomy. But the number of known heroin addicts in Britain is comparatively small (only 1555 in 1971), while the estimates of the marihuana smoking population range up to one million and beyond. Thus it would need only a minute proportion of marihuana smokers to escalate for the heroin addiction figures to rise rapidly. Besides, the availability of methadone and barbiturate gives rise to alternative avenues of escalation. Methadone, once a palliative for heroin addicts, becomes a drug of addiction for individuals who have never used heroin. To this extent increased social reaction against the drug taker would make real the stereotype held by the public about escalation. But the transmission of addiction, unlike the transmission of disease, is not a matter of contact, it is a process that is dictated by the social situation and values of the person who is in contact with the addict. The values of marihuana smokers and the achievement of subterranean goals are not met by intensive heroin use. Escalation to heroin (or methadone and the barbiturates) will occur only in atypical cases where the structural position of the marihuana user changes sufficiently to necessitate the evolution of values compatible with heroin use as solutions to his newly emergent problems.[5] Availability of a drug alone is insufficient to precipitate addiction, there has to be a meaningful reason for its use. At the moment, the widespread structural unemployment in Britain may provide – along American lines – precisely such a cause. Increased availability *plus* the desperation associated with exclusion from the means of earning a living is the sort of combination which might spell a serious heroin problem in the future. The irony is that if it comes it will strike hardest amongst the lower-class youth on the edge of the drug culture. The middle-class marihuana smoker will have a degree of immunity to the solution heroin offers.

8. As the mass media fan public indignation over marihuana use, pressure on the police increases; the public demands that they solve the drug problem. The number of marihuana users known to the police is a mere tip of the iceberg of actual smokers. Given their desire to behave in accordance with public opinion and to legitimize their position, the police will act with great vigilance and arrest more offenders. All that happens is that they dig deeper into the undetected part of the iceberg; the statistics for marihuana offenders soar; the public, the press and the magistrates view the new figures with even greater alarm. Increased pressure is put on the police, the latter dig even deeper into the iceberg, the figures increase once again, and public concern becomes even greater. We have entered a fantasy crime wave, where the supposed statistical increase in marihuana use bears little relationship to the actual rate of increase. Because of the publicity, however, the notion of marihuana smoking occurs for the first time to a larger number of people, and through their desire to experiment there will be some real increase in the rate of smoking. We must not overlook here the fact that moral panic over drug taking results in the setting up of drug squads which by their very bureaucratic creation will ensure a regular

contribution to the offence figures which had never been evidenced before.

Police action not only has a deviance amplification effect because of the unforeseen consequences of the exclusion of the marihuana smoker from 'normal' society. It has also an effect on the content of the bohemian culture within which marihuana smoking takes place. The important feature to note is that there has been change, and that this has been in part the product of social reaction. For many social commentators and policy makers, however, this change has merely reinforced their initial presumptions about the nature of drug takers; individuals with near psychopathic personalities, a weak super-ego, an unrealistic ego and inadequate masculine identification. Inevitably these people, it is suggested, will pass on to heroin, and the figures show that this has actually occurred. Similarly journalists and the police, convinced that drug use is a function of a few pushers, will view the deviancy amplification of the bohemian and the emergence of a drug pyramid as substantiation of their theory that we have been too permissive all along. False theories are taken by many to be a proof of their initial presumptions. Similarly, the drug taker, evolving theories as to the repressive nature of the police, finds them progressively proven as the gravity of the situation escalates.

REFERENCES

1. L. Wilkins, 'Some sociological factors in drug addition control', in D. Wilner and G. Kassebaum (eds.), *Narcotics* (New York, MacGraw Hill, 1965).
2. See the discussion in T. Scheff, 'Negotiating reality', *Social Problems*, 16 (Summer 1968).
3. R. Traini, *The work of the Crime Reporters Association* (Paper Read at the 8th National Deviancy Symposium, University of York, 10–11 July 1971).
4. For a discussion of the deviancy amplification of bohemians, see J. Young, 'The hippie solution' in I. Taylor and L. Taylor (eds.), *The politics of deviancy* (Harmondsworth, Penguin, 1973).
5. See J. Young, *The drugtakers* (London, Paladin, 1971).

Sensitization: the case of the Mods and Rockers*

STANLEY COHEN

At each Bank Holiday scene during the peak of the Mods and Rockers phenomenon in the middle 1960s, the mass media operated to reinforce and give shape to the crowd's sense of expectancy and provide the content of rumours and shared definitions with which ambiguous situations were restructured. Although popular commentators on the Mods and Rockers often blamed 'publicity' for what happened (and the press responded with indignant editorials about its 'duty' to publish the 'facts'), the term 'publicity' was used in a somewhat restricted sense. It either referred to the publicity immediately before the event which advertised the disturbances and pinpointed the resorts where they would take place, or to the gratification young people supposedly derived from exposure to publicity during the event.

The first of these factors operated in the gross sense of publicizing the event in such a way that it might look attractive, but it is unlikely to have directly influenced the choice of target: asked where they got the idea from (of going to Margate), 82·3 per cent of a sample of offenders mentioned friends as their source, only 2·9 per cent mentioned newspapers and 2·9 per cent television. Only a handful I spoke to at any stage said that anything in the press or television *initially* decided them on a particular resort. The media more likely reinforced rather than initiated rumours already current. There were certain exceptions, though, when during the weekend a sensational report or TV interview might have directly attracted new crowds. One notorious BBC interview in which two Rockers said that reinforcements would be arriving, was followed by a sudden influx of both Mods and Rockers, large numbers of whom might have been attracted by the excitement the interview promised.

There were also signs of direct publicity-seeking behaviour in the sense that on-the-spot attention from journalists, reporters and

* This is an adapted version of Stanley Cohen, *Folk devils and moral panics: the creation of the Mods and Rockers* (London, MacGibbon & Kee, 1972), Chapter 5.

photographers was a stimulus to action. The following account is by one of the boys arrested at Margate:

> By the railway station a cameraman asked 'Give us a wave'. So me and a group ran about and waved some flags we bought. My picture was in the paper. We were pleased; anybody would be.

If one is in a group of twenty, being stared at by hundreds of adults and being pointed at by two or three cameras, the temptation to do something – even if only to shout an obscenity, make a rude gesture or throw a stone – is very great and made greater by the knowledge that one's actions will be recorded for others to see. The participant in such situations might exaggerate the extent of his involvement and look for some recognition of it. Thus at every weekend, young people could be observed at newspaper kiosks buying each edition of the evening paper as it appeared and scanning it for news of disturbances. The exploitative element in this feedback is reflected in the rumours – which, at least in one case, I am certain were firmly based – that press photographers were asking suitably attired young males to pose kicking in a window or telephone kiosk.

The cumulative effects of the mass media, though, were at the same time more subtle and more potent than simply giving the events pre-publicity or gratifying the participants' need for attention. Through a complex process that is not yet fully understood the mere reporting of one event has, under certain circumstances, the effect of triggering off events of a similar order. This effect is well documented in regard to the spread of crazes, fashions, fads and other forms of collective behaviour, such as mass delusion or hysteria. The main reason why this process has been misunderstood in regard to deviance – particularly collective and novel forms – is that too much attention has been placed on the supposed direct effects (imitation, attention, gratification, identification) on the deviants, rather than the effects on the control system and culture and hence (via such processes as amplification) on the deviance.

The simple suggestibility type effect can be seen even in apparently individual forms of deviance such as suicide. A particularly vivid example is the spread in the self-immolation as a form of suicide following the report in 1963 of a Vietnamese monk burning himself to death as an act of political protest. This is a form of suicide almost completely unknown in the West; in the period 1960–1963, there was only one such case in England, yet in 1963, there were three and in 1964, nine. A similar progression in numbers occurred in the United States. In this case, the effect was in the technique rather than the motivation behind the act and must be explained in terms of what the 'new' stimulus meant and how it was interpreted. Cases where the motive as well as the technique is suggested by mass communication might be the spread of prison riots, prison escapes and racial and political riots. A particularly well-documented example is the Swastika Epidemic of 1959–1960. The contagion effect could be clearly shown in plotting the curve of the 'epidemic'.[1]

An example closer to the Mods and Rockers is the spread during the 1950s of the Teddy Boy riots and similar phenomena elsewhere in Europe. Most commentators on these events acknowledged the role of publicity in stimulating imitative or competitive forms of behaviour[2] and some studies have been made on the mass media coverage of such events.[3] At the time, though, blame was put on 'publicity' in the restricted sense and there was little awareness of the complex ways in which mass communication operates before during and after each event. The causative nature of mass communication – in the whole context of the societal reaction to such phenomena – is still usually misunderstood.

The common element in all these diverse examples of the amplification of violence is that an adequate medium of communication must be present for spreading the hostile belief and mobilizing potential participants. The mass communication of the news of one outbreak is a condition of structural conduciveness for the development of a hostile belief. This, in turn, has to sensitize the 'new' crowd (or individual deviant) to incipient or actual action and lower the threshold of readiness by providing readily identifiable symbols. The symbolization process (see Part Two, page 235) becomes crucial during the event, shaping the content of the rumours[4] spread through the crowd that something was going to happen and locating the targets for action.

The inventory reporting (see Part Two, page 238) can be seen as having a reinforcing effect on already existing tendencies to expect and look forward to trouble. Constant repetition of the violence and vandalism images and reports about preparations for the next 'invasion' generated an atmosphere in which something *had* to happen. Once a dominant perception is established the tendency is to assimilate all subsequent happenings to it. This is how to view the relatively trivial incidents which attracted attention and sometimes triggered off trouble. Through the process of sensitization, incidents which would not have been defined as unusual or worthy of attentions during a normal Bank Holiday weekend acquired a new meaning. Thus:

Two boys stopped to watch a very drunk old tramp dancing about on the beach. They started throwing pennies at his feet. Within

45 seconds there were at least 100 people gathered round and in 60 seconds the police were there. I turned my back on the crowd to watch the spectators gathering on the promenade above and by the time I turned back, two policemen were leading a boy away from the crowd.

(Notes, Brighton, Easter 1965)

The mass media provided the images and stereotypes with which ambiguous situations could be restructured; a stone-throwing incident might not have progressed beyond the 'milling stage' if there were no readily available collective images to give meaning to the activity. These images provide the basis for rumours about 'random' events: so, an incident in which a girl was carried on a stretcher to an ambulance was variously explained by the crowd gathering round as 'this bloke with her must have knifed her', 'too many pills if you ask me', 'these Rockers' birds just drink all the time'.

Different versions of such events are circulated and eventually assimilated into one theme that receives collective sanction. Each link in the chain of assimilation involves preconceptions derived from sources such as the mass media. Without publicity about 'stabbings on the beach' or 'drug orgies' the rumours about the girl being carried to the ambulance would have assumed an entirely different form. Rumours further serve to validate a particular course of action: the deviant, as well as the control agent, uses collective imagery (which may be objectively false) to justify action. Symbolization provides a short-circuited definition of the situation whereby culturally sanctioned signs and symbols are used as a basis for action. The inventory symbols prepared the crowd for action because shared images and objects contribute to uniformity: if a dance hall becomes defined as 'The Top Mod Spot of the South', then the defence of it against invading Rockers takes on a symbolic significance. So not only was the likelihood of deviance increased – one almost *had* to try to see or take part in trouble – but the content of the behaviour influenced. The societal reaction increases the deviants chance of acting and – given his interpretation of the new situation- provides him with some lines and stage directions.

The crucial effect here is the way in which deviant behaviour is shaped by the normative expectations of how people in that particular deviant role should act. Much of the Mods and Rockers behaviour can be conceptualized in terms of a role-playing model. Posing for photos, chanting slogans, making warlike gestures, fantasying about super-gangs, wearing distinctive insignia, making a mock raid on an ice-cream van, whistling at girls, jeering at the 'other side': all these acts of 'hooliganism' may be seen as analogous to the impersonation of mental illness resorted to by those defined as mentally ill. The actor incorporates aspects of the typecast role into his self-concept and when the deviant role is public – as hooliganism is by definition – and the situation increases the chances of mutual suggestibility, then this incorporation is often more conscious and deliberate than in those types of 'private' deviance such as mental illness, homosexuality and drug taking, to which a role-playing perspective has been applied.

New recruits might search for and positively try to exemplify the values and imagery portrayed in the stereotypes. The media created some sort of diversionary sideshow in which all could seek their appropriate parts. The young people on the beaches knew very well that they had been typecast as folk devils and they saw themselves as targets for abuse. When the audiences, TV cameras and police started lining themselves up, the metaphor of role playing becomes no longer a metaphor, but the real thing. One acute observer at the live TV coverage of the Mod Ball at Wembley (a week after the initial Clacton event) described a girl in front of the cameras worshipping a hair salvaged off Mick Jagger's trousers as being like a man acting drunk when he is hardly tipsy, 'acting out this adoration. She sees she is being watched, grins sheepishly and then laughs outright.'[5]

The content of the typecast role was present in the inventory and crystallized more explicitly in the process of spurious attribution or labelling. This is not to say that a new one-to-one link between the labelling and the behaviour was formed. For one thing, the typecast hooligan role was known to the potential actors before the deviance even began; like the labellers themselves, they could draw upon an existent folklore and mythology. The point, however, was that the normative element in the role was reinforced by the societal reaction; although the actors might already have been familiar with the lines and the stage direction, they were now confirmed in their roles. In the same way as the 'chronic' schizophrenic begins to approximate closer to the schizophrenic role, so did the Mods and Rockers phenomenon take on every time an increasing ritualistic and stereotypical character.

Although the hooligan role was ready made and had only to be confirmed by the labelling process, there were other elements in the behaviour which could be directly traced to the societal reaction.

One was the way in which the gap between the Mods and Rockers became increasingly wider and obvious. Although the Mods and Rockers represented two different consumer styles – the Mods the more glossy fashion-conscious teenager, the Rockers the tougher, reactionary tradition – the antagonism between the two groups was not initially very marked. Despite their real differences in life styles – visible in symbols such as the Mods' scooters and the Rockers' motor bikes – the groups had a great deal in common, particularly their working-class membership. There was, initially at least, nothing like the gang rivalry that is supposed to characterize the type of violent conflict gang enshrined in folklore by the 'Sharks' and 'Jets' of *West Side Story*. Indeed, one could not justifiably talk of 'gangs' at all in any meaningful sociological sense. The only structured grouping one could find in the early crowds was based on slight territorial loyalty and it was tenuous enough to be broken up in the crowd situation.

Constant repetition of the warring gangs' image, however, had the effect of giving these loose collectivities a structure they never possessed and a mythology with which to justify the structure. This image was disseminated in the inventory, reinforced through the symbolization process, repeated in opinions which exaggerated the stylistic differences and the degree of pre-planning, used to advantage in the form of commercial exploitation and repeated during the warning phase. Even if these images were not directly absorbed by the actors, they were used to justify control tactics, which still further structured the groups and hardened the barriers between them. Police action, for example, increased the deviance by unwittingly solidifying the amorphous crowd forces into more viable groups for engaging in violence and by further polarizing the deviants against the community. Such solidification and polarization takes place not simply in the face of attack, but attack that is perceived as harsh, indiscriminate and unfair. Even if these elements had not been present the ambiguous crowd situation offered the maximum possible opportunity for rumours of such police action to spread. In the same way that the Mods and Rockers were perceived symbolically and stereotypically by the police, the police too were perceived by the crowd as the 'enemy'. By seeing the crowd as a homogeneous mass, to be controlled on the basis of the visible stigmata of dress, a greater sense of cohesion develops. If subject to indiscriminate harassment or even if only witnessing the use of violence by the police, the crowd could quite easily develop a sense of resentment and grievance. This could be the first step towards a sense of identity and common purpose with the real or imagined 'hard core', with 'police brutality' as a rallying point.

The presence of the media – actually, in the form of cameras and reporters, symbolically in the form of the next day's stories – gave police and courtroom confrontations with the deviants a ritualistic dramatic quality. These were arenas for acting out society's morality plays. And they had to be reported as 'news', so the amplification effects of the control culture were fed back into the mass media, which further exaggerated them, thus producing another link in the sequence. If the policemen did not see themselves as the 'brave men in blue' fighting with the evil mob, nor the magistrates themselves as society's chosen mouthpiece for denouncing evil, the polarizations were made on their behalf by others.

The mass media – and the ideological exploitation of deviance – reinforced the polarization: between the Mods and Rockers on one hand, and the whole adult community on the other. If one is seen as the 'enemy' in the 'war against crime', it is not difficult to respond in similar spirit: one 'rejects the rejectors' and 'condemns the condemners'. The specialized effect of the Lunatic Fringe theme (a derivation of the consensus model which sees most youth as decent and conformist) is to segregate and label those involved by emphasizing their difference from the majority. A striking parallel from a similar form of deviance was the labelling by the motor cycling 'Establishment' of riders identified with the Hell's Angels image as the one per cent who cause all the trouble: the term 'one percenter' was then used by the groups as an honorific epithet, reinforcing their commitment.

In summary then, the societal reaction in general and the mass media in particular could plausibly be thought to have had the following sort of effects on the nature, extent and development on the deviance:

1. Reinforcing and magnifying a predisposition to expect trouble: 'something's going to happen'.
2. Providing the content for rumours and the milling process, thereby structuring the 'something' into potential or actual deviance; such rumours and images facilitated deviance by solidifying the crowd and validating its moods and actions.
3. Creating a set of culturally identifiable symbols which further structured the situation and legitimized action.
4. Spreading hostile beliefs and mobilizing the participants for action.
5. Providing the content for deviant role playing by transmitting the stereotypical expectations of how persons in particular deviant roles should act.
6. Magnifying the Mods–Rockers dichotomy and giving the groups a tighter structure and common ethos than they originally possessed.
7. Polarizing the deviants further against the community and –

through the actions of the police and courts – setting up a spiral of deviancy amplification.

REFERENCES

1. See David Caplowitz and Candace Rogers, *Swastika 1960: the epidemic of anti-Semitic vandalism in America* (New York, Anti-Defamation League of Benai Brith, 1961). A noteworthy feature of this epidemic was that initial reporting indicated other avenues for expressing grievances: at the peak, targets for hostility other than anti-Semetic ones were chosen and, in fact, these general incidents out-numbered the specifically anti-Semitic. This is similar to the ways the Mods and Rockers changed their targets of action. All such processes are heavily dependent on the mass media.
2. See, for example, T. R. Fyvel, *The insecure offenders* (London, Chatto & Windus, 1961) and C. Bondy et al., *Jugendliche Stören die Ordnung* (München, Juventa Verlag, 1957).
3. See Britt-Marie Blegvad, 'Newspapers and Rock and Roll riots in Copenhagen', *Acta Sociologica* 7 (1963), pp. 151–78, and Paul Rock and Stanley Cohen, 'The Teddy Boy', in V. Bognador and R. Skidelsky, (eds.), *The age of affluence: 1951–1964* (London, Macmillan, 1970).
4. For a relevant formulation on the sociology of rumour, see Tamotsu Shibutani, *Improvised news* (Indianapolis, Bobbs-Merrill, 1966).
5. Peter Laurie, *The teenage revolution* (London, Anthony Blond Ltd, 1965), p. 105.
6. See Hunter Thompson, *Hell's Angels* (Harmondsworth, Penguin, 1967) and Robert Shellow and Derek Roemer, 'The riot that didn't happen,' *Social Problems* 14 (Fall 1966), pp. 221–33.

SUGGESTED READING ON EFFECTS AND CONSEQUENCES

ON THE MASS SOCIETY, MASS CULTURE AND MASS MEDIA DEBATE

L. Bramson, *The political context of sociology* (Princeton, Princeton University Press, 1960).

L. A. Dexter and D. M. White (eds.), *People, society and mass communications* (New York, Free Press, 1964).

N. Jacobs (ed.), *Culture for the millions: mass media in modern society* (Princeton, Van Nostrand, 1961).

W. Kornhauser, *The politics of mass society* (London, Routledge & Kegan Paul, 1960).

H. Marcuse, *One dimensional man* (London, Routledge & Kegan Paul, 1964).

D. McQuail, *Towards a sociology of mass communications* (London, Collier-Macmillan Ltd, 1969), Chapter 2.

B. Rosenberg and D. M. White, *Mass culture: the popular arts in America* (New York, Free Press, 1957).

R. Williams, *The long revolution* (London, Chatto & Windus, 1961).

ON THE EFFECTS OF MASS COMMUNICATION (AND OTHER GENERAL BOOKS ON MEDIA SOCIOLOGY)

B. Berelson and M. Janowitz, *Reader in public opinion and communication* (Glencoe, Free Press, 1966).

D. Chaney, *Processes of mass communication* (London, Macmillan, 1972).

J. D. Halloran, *The effects of mass communication* (Leicester University Press, 1965).

J. Halloran (ed.), *The effects of television* (London, Panther Books, 1970).

J. T. Klapper, *The effects of mass communication* (New York, Free Press, 1960).

D. McQuail (ed.), *Sociology of mass communications* (Harmondsworth, Penguin, 1972).

W. Schramm, *The process and effects of mass communication* (Urbana, University of Illinois Press, 1954).

—— (ed.), *Mass communication: a book of readings* (Urbana, University of Illinois Press, 1960).

R. Williams, *Communications* (Harmondsworth, Penguin, 1966).

ON MEDIA EFFECTS IN THE AREAS OF CRIME, DEVIANCE AND SOCIAL PROBLEMS

A. Glucksman, *Violence on the screen* (London, British Film Institute, 1971).

J. D. Halloran, 'Television and violence', *Twentieth Century* (Winter 1964–5), pp. 61–72.

J. D. Halloran, et al., *Television and delinquency* (Leicester, Leicester University Press, 1970).

O. N. Larsen (ed.), *Violence and the mass media* (New York, Harper & Row, 1968).

National Commission on Causes and Prevention of Violence, Various reports (Washington, U.S. Government Printing Office, 1969).

Report of the Commission on Obscenity and Pornography (New York, Bantam Books, 1970).

Surgeon General's Scientific Advisory Committee on Television and Social Behaviour: Various reports, especially 'Television and growing up: the impact of television violence' (U.S. Department of Health, Education and Welfare National Institute of Mental Health, 1971).

PART FOUR

Do-it-yourself media sociology

At various points in this book we have drawn attention to the weakness of empirical material in the field of mass media and deviance. Nearly all our authors could make the same point in relation to their own particular focus of interest. This deficiency is paradoxical in the light of the fact that the mass media are, by definition, widely available and accessible. If we just want to examine the problem of finding out something about the images of deviance and social problems in the mass media (and leave out the more complicated questions of ownership, control and the process of newsmaking behind the scenes), no particularly difficult research problems present themselves. One does not have to struggle to get permission to have access to one's data, the costs are minimal, no massive research teams are needed and there are no particular skills such as interviewing to be learnt.

Yet despite the fact that the media are so wide open to inspection, few sociologists or members of the public have asked the obvious questions which flow out of their day-to-day experience. Every now and then you read a report about an event you personally participated in, scratch your head and say, 'That's not how it was when I was there,' and find that most people who were with you agree. Or you watch a television documentary which has a faint air of unreality. Or get annoyed at the intrusion into someone's private grief in interviews with relatives of disaster victims. Sometimes one is indignant enough to make these feelings public, as Walter Barker did when writing the following letter to the RAP (Radical Alternatives to Prison) *Newsletter* (Vol. 1, No. 6. 1972):

For meanness, prejudice and inhumanity, the *Sunday People* with its lead story of 26 March 1972 must rank among the top contenders. With a four inch deep heading it shouted FANTASTIC – THIS GANG FUNERAL. It went on: 'The most notorious criminals in the country have managed to stage the most opulent underworld funeral Britain has ever known – from their prison cells.'

The paper described the costly floral tributes, covering 90 square yards and estimated at £1,000, sent by some of the most-publicized long-term prisoners to mark the death of a man whom it called 'a faithful friend and brutal henchman to the worst villains of the century'.

When the prison grapevine heard of the death of Freddie Sanson during a soccer match at Hull Prison, 'the master criminals set to work', prisoners sent some tributes direct from prisons 'by permission of the governors', 'messages were sent to friends "on the outside" to buy enormous wreaths and attend the funeral . . .', ' "Mad" Frankie Fraser, serving 20 years for his part in the Richardson gang tortures and the Parkhurst riot of 1969, sent a floral chair (inscribed) "to a great pal, from Frankie Fraser". Fraser must have remembered that Freddie Sanson had given evidence on behalf of the rioters and tried to clear them. . . .'

The Sanson home in Brixton was described as a 'shabby terraced house'. At the graveside 'one of the mourning villains' spoke to the writer of the *People* story. Villains, criminals and other epithets were used with carefree abandon to label various men undergoing long sentences.

Even in death the memory of Sanson had to be smirched. His 12-year sentence for armed robbery was not enough. The scary headlines and savage story probably gained the newspaper a handsome increase in sales, at the price of the dignity of men who are already paying the price that society demands for their crimes.

Is it any wonder that society itself, and a part of the self-styled 'free press', make outcasts and enemies of men who need to be drawn into a mutually understanding relationship with the community? Or must they go on paying indefinitely for their offences, and must part of the press have the right to build circulation and profits by the harsh reputation of the past?

Among the ethical codes of the press, perhaps a place could be found for a ban on the incitement of hostility towards anyone already facing the due process of law. Now. Not in 50 years' time after thousands more have become totally estranged from a society which glosses over its amorality with a sickening moralism towards those incapable of answering back.

But on the whole, people keep such indignation and doubts to themselves and their day-to-day reactions to the media never get documented in a systematic way. Because these doubts and reactions exist and the problem of translating them into concrete empirical evidence is not a particularly formidable one, we have decided to conclude this book with some suggestions for do-it-yourself research. Aside from its intrinsic interest, such research could be used by political and reform groups to monitor their images in the media. These projects – some of which are more suitable for groups or teams rather than individuals working on their own – make no great technical or financial demands. We have confined ourselves to suggesting projects which should be well within the resources available to most groups of students in schools, colleges and universities. Besides some familiarity with the sort of issues we have raised in this volume – as a guide to what questions might be asked rather than an imposed theoretical perspective – the main qualities needed are imagination, resourcefulness and patience.

SUGGESTED PROJECTS

The project you pick depends on how ambitious your aims are. You might want to limit yourself to one form of mass media – for example, the press – and to one form of deviance – for example, vandalism – and you might want to confine yourself to a simple description of the dominant imagery through which this phenomenon is reported. Or you might want to make a series of comparisons. Here is a list of some of the more fruitful ones:

Comparisons

1. Between different products of the same form of mass communication: for example, one newspaper and another, one television channel and another. Try comparing say, the *Sun* or the *Daily Mirror* with *The Times* or *The Guardian* or *The Observer* with the *News of the World*.

2. Between two or more forms of mass communications: for example, television and the press. Note also how these forms feed on each other.

3. Across socially defined boundaries; for example, two regions, the North and the South in England might be compared or between one country and another.

4. Across time: one- or five-year comparisons may be made or a longer time span – say, before and after the war might be used. If there has been a major social change in the area you are studying you should consider a before-and-after design. For example, if you are looking at abortion or gambling, you should compare media images before, during and after the recent legal changes in these areas.

5. Between the mass media and other sources of information and opinion: for example, the public as a whole or the experts (see Nunnally's paper for an example of this sort of research).

6. Between the information channels of the media – the news, features, documentaries etc. – and fictional or fantasy representations. Compare, for example, the image of the policeman in news stories with that in programmes such as *Z cars*, *Softly, softly* and *Task force*.

7. Between the media's representation of certain objects, and the

way those 'objects' as subjects picture themselves. Compare, for example, the image of the hippy in the straight press with that in the underground press such as *Oz* and *I.T.* or the political militant as depicted in the conventional media with his image in the various sectarian left weeklies.

8. Between the media and your own personal experience. If you have taken part in a strike or demonstration compare your own version of what you thought happened with any or all of the media pictures.

The decision on which sort of comparisons to make is partly determined by practical factors – just how much time and resources you have; partly by how ambitious the level of generality or abstractness you are aiming for, and partly by how readily the particular subject you have chosen lends itself a certain type of analysis. You might have chosen to look at, say, the media presentation of environmental pollution as a social problem, but because this is a relatively new problem, you might not be able to establish a 'baseline' of public or expert opinion.

What sort of subject matter should one study? The choice is virtually unlimited and we would suggest any of the following three approaches as being suitable for do-it-yourself researchers. Each offers plenty of scope for following your own particular line of interests.

PICK A PROBLEM

The most straightforward approach is simply to pick a form of deviant behaviour or social problem which interests you and decide on the set of comparisons from our list of possibilities. Any of the areas included in this volume would be suitable and you might in fact prefer to use one of these to follow up any lines of argument which the article raised. Other suitable topics include:

gambling; prostitution; organized crime; political corruption; environmental pollution; traffic problems; poverty – both in your own country and Third World societies – population problems, birth control; students as social problems; pupil power; free school movement, school unions; prisons; mental hospitals; the police; the courts.

The following recent textbooks of readings should give you other examples as well as references to the relevant literature:

Deviance
Marshall B. Clinard, *Sociology of deviant behaviour* 3rd ed. (New York, Holt, Rinehart & Winston, 1968).

Stanley Cohen (ed.), *Images of deviance* (Harmondsworth, Penguin, 1971).

Jack D. Douglas (ed.), *Observations of deviance* (New York, Random House, 1970).

Earl Rubington and Martin S. Weinberg (eds.), *Deviance: the interactionist perspective* (New York, Collier-Macmillan, 1968).

Social problems

Howard S. Becker (ed.), *Social problems* (New York, John Wiley & Sons Inc., 1966).

Russell R. Dynes et al. (eds.), *Social problems* (New York, Oxford University Press, 1964).

Howard E. Freeman and Wyat C. Jones, *Social problems: causes and controls* (Chicago, Rand McNally & Co., 1970).

Judson R. Landis (ed.), *Current perspectives on social problems* (Belmont, Cal., Wadsworth Publishing, 1969).

Edward C. McDonagh and Jon E. Simpson, *Social problems: persistent challenges* (New York, Holt, Rinehart & Winston Co., 1969).

Robert K. Merton and Robert A. Nisbet (eds.), *Contemporary social problems* 2nd ed. (New York, Harcourt, Brace & Co., 1966).

Earl Rubington and Martin S. Weinberg, *The study of social problems* (New York, Oxford University Press, 1971).

S. Kirson Weinberg, *Social problems in modern urban society* (New Jersey, Prentice Hall Inc., 1970).

In addition, see the whole series, edited by Donald R. Cressey for Harper & Row entitled *Readers in social problems* (about 20 volumes published so far in the United Kingdom).

THE EVENT AS NEWS

A good idea for a less time-consuming project is to build your research around the notion of the event as news. This is a good way to understand some of the processes of selection: how the media select certain events as newsworthy and how other events are made into news.

Simple 'one-shot' research can be done around the following sort of events, which you might observe either as a full participant or an outsider: a pop festival, a football match, a strike, a march, meeting, demonstration or other political event, a court hearing, a public speech.

Record your own observations and, if possible, check them with someone else present. If your observations take place over a long period – for example, a sit-in at a college – you need to be more aware of some of the problems of participant observation research in sociology. On these problems see:

George J. McCall and J. L. Simmons (eds.), *Issues in participant observation* (London, Addison-Wesley, 1969).

Your next step is to make your comparisons with the media. Say you have been to a protest march: try to have the TV and radio news tape-recorded and look at every newspaper the next day, asking the following sorts of questions:

1. Which paper ignored the event altogether? Is there any sort of pattern to this inattention? For example, have only the left-wing papers picked up the march?

2. Are there any major discrepancies with your own observations? For example, are the numbers of marchers or strength of the police consistently underestimated? Do such discrepancies occur in all the papers?

3. Which paper/type of paper gives the event most coverage? Look at the size of headline, column inches (not absolute, but relative to paper's whole size); location in the paper (front page or inside), etc.

4. What are the major models and modes of reporting? Can any clear judgement towards the event be detected? (See also checklist of questions below).

An event need not be so dramatic as a march, a pop festival or a demonstration. By definition, 'events' do not happen very often and the media have to create them out of nothing or transform routine everyday matters into events. Thus on the TV news, simple technical aides such as graphs, charts, summarized expert opinions, interviews, reports from special correspondents can add drama to such mundane matters as a completely uninteresting set of monthly trade figures. Such regular monthly or annual 'events' make excellent case studies for do-it-yourself research. Start by finding a media report of one of the following, for example:

sets of annual statistics (crime, housing, divorce, venereal disease, illegitimate births, immigration)
annual meetings (political parties, professional associations, trade union conferences).

Make all the relevant event-comparisons we suggested earlier; in addition look up the papers for at least five previous years to check which particular aspect of the 'event' is picked out as newsworthy and, indeed, whether it is mentioned at all. Taking the criminal statistics, for example, you might find them given the full banner treatment one year (DRAMATIC INCREASES, DISTURBING FIGURES, SHOCK STATISTICS) with very little the year before. You might further find that the statistics for the quiet year in fact showed much the same patterns as the current year's. Why should the treatment be different?

On pp. 378-9 is an example of a comparison which reveals clearly the different pictures which readers of two newspapers received of the 'same' news:

Another approach to the same problem is to start not with a particular event, but with an analysis of one outlet or series of outlets. Look at the whole coverage of say the BBC 9 o'clock news or the ITV *News at Ten* or the *World at One* for a week or your own newspaper for a month. Classify the stories, compare the proportions given to various types of information such as crime or foreign news. (See Bob Roshier's article in Part One for an example of this sort of research.) Here – as elsewhere in your research – you will benefit by learning something about content analysis and other techniques of collecting, and classifying and coding your material. See here the general texts on mass communication we recommended in Part Three and, more specifically:

G. Gerbner, *The analysis of communication content* (New York, Wiley, 1969).

P. R. Holsti, *Content analysis for the social sciences and humanities* (Reading, Mass., Addison Wesley, 1969).

'Content analysis' in G. Lindsey (ed.), *Handbook of social psychology* (Reading, Mass., Addison-Wesley, 1968).

DRAMA AND MYTH

This volume has concentrated on the information and news aspects of the media. The same set of subjects though – say, violence, law and order, political marginality, sexual deviance, alcoholism – might be approached through a study of their fictional representations. Indeed, the feedback between dramatic and real images is an important element in the construction of contemporary modes of understanding deviance. The dramatic form might embody the archetypal consensus about what things are really like or – the opposite – the news might be constructed in terms of traditional dramatic themes: tragedies, heroes, villains, fools, comedies, martyrs.[1]

There is of course a massive literature using this type of analysis – both by social scientists and cultural critics (Jerry Palmer's article in Part Three is one example). We can only offer the simplest suggestion which is to use the genre approach, that is, to take a particular form of dramatic representation and apply to it the same questions

Daily ⚜ Mail

WEDNESDAY, JUNE 7, 1972

3p

Gangs of young thugs link with 'Fagins'

JUNIOR CRIME WAVE SHOCK

By PETER BURDEN, Crime Reporter

INCREASING numbers of youngsters are taking to serious crime. Many operate in gangs. Some link up with Fagin-type adult crooks.

Of all people arrested for serious offences last year, nearly half were under 21.

The figures are revealed in the annual Scotland Yard crime report for the London area, published yesterday.

National figures are still being completed, but reports indicate that they will confirm the London trend : that youth is on a growing crime rampage.

The Yard's figures show :

Age ten to 13 : Arrests for serious crime up 12 per cent. to 10,006 ;

Age 14 to 16 : Up 17·2 per cent. to 15,936 ;

Age 17 to 20 : Up 3·6 per cent. to 17,031.

Violence

Arrests for robbery (theft where violence is used or threatened) in the under-21 group rose by 35·8 per cent. Nearly two-thirds of all robbery arrests were of youngsters between ten and 20.

Another gloomy sign : police have found that many arrested young people have previous records.

A Yard man commented : 'Experience shows that once convicted the chances increase that the boy or girl will go on persuing crime as a "career."

The total arrests in the Metropolitan area in 1971 for serious crimes were 86,287, a 6·6 per cent. increase ; 42,973 were of people under 21.

Gangs

The report, by Sir John Waldron, the just-retired Commissioner, says: 'The tendency for young criminals to operate in gangs, both with others of their own age group and with adults, has continued to grow.'

● At Witham, Essex, children are banned from Mr Michael Jones's toy shop unless accompanied by an adult or they come to buy a specific toy. The reason: £3,000 worth of toys have vanished from his shelves in 12 months.

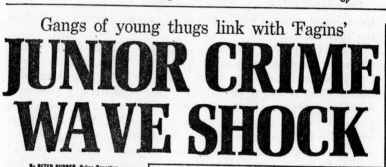

More London po

The number of police officers in London facing serious criminal or disciplinary charges rose last year, though fewer public complaints were made against the police, Sir John Waldron says today in his last annual report as Metropolitan Police Commissioner.

Sir John says he feels bound to comment on this "unwelcome trend," but he also emphasises the small number of officers involved, in view of the false impression which might be pro-

jected by the disproportiona publicity each case attracts.

"It is perhaps indicative the small size of the problem relation to the large numb of police officers in the for that each individual ca remains newsworthy," he say And during 1971, only 3,1 complaints were made again the police by the public—3 (9.8 per cent.) fewer than 1970 and the lowest figure sin 1968.

Sir John explains that in cent years, officers have be promoted at a younger age, ap

Two newspapers' versions
of the 'same' news

On left
Daily Mail, 7 June 1972
Top of front page

Below
The Guardian, 7 June 1972
Bottom of inside page

in trouble but fewer complaints

By PETER HARVEY

able of supervising
I work of the men,
they often had in
perience to identify
of character in sub-
cers. That phase is
says, and there is
a greater awareness
sponsibilities among
officers which
nue to ensure that
ine is exposed.
violence in London
e than 15 per cent
and Sir John says

that violence caused him the
greatest concern during his last
year in office. Robbery and
assault with intent to rob, were
up by 15.1 per cent, to a total
of 2,727 cases. Firearms were
used on almost 400 occasions
and other offensive weapons—
including pickaxe handles ard
noxious fluids, were used 804
times.

But in line with other parts
of the country sexual offences
showed a marked decrease.
During 1970, cases of rape

increased by 29 per cent, to
141. Last year they fell by
24.1 per cent to 107. Other
sexual offences decreased by
12.5 per cent, to a total of
1,833.

Crime in general increased
in London by 6 per cent during
the year, but the clear-up rate
also showed an increase; from
22.3 per cent in 1966 to 29.4
per cent last year.

Sir John's report also refers
to a subject causing growing
discontent in the police: the
number of people given bail in

spite of police objections—thus
"defeating" the value of arrest.

During 1971, 2,094 people
were arrested for indictable
offences committed while on
bail. In 780 of these cases, the
police had objected to bail, and
"by and large we detect only a
third of the crime committed,
so it would be perhaps fair to
assume that at least twice as
many again as the number set
out above commit crime on bail
and get away with it."

you might use for the news. Thus, if you are interested in violence, you might select any of the following obvious forms: the cowboy movie (or any of its subtypes: primitive, intellectual, spaghetti westerns); gangster movies; the James Bond species; TV series such as *Ironside, Callan, Man from UNCLE*; comic books, horror movies; *Man* and *Adventure* type magazines. Here are some examples of studies on fictional violence:

David B. Davis, *Homicide in American fiction, 1798–1860: a study in social values* (Ithaca, New York, Cornell University Press, 1957).
'Violence in American literature' *Annals of the American Academy of Political and Social Science* (March 1966), pp. 28–36.
André Glucksmann, *Violence on the screen* (London, British Film Institute, 1971).
H. A. Grace, 'A taxonomy of American crime film themes', *Journal of Social Psychology* Vol. 42 (1955), pp. 129–36.
James Toback, ' "Bonnie and Clyde": style as morality', *Dissent* (January–February 1968).
Robert Warshaw, 'The gangster as tragic hero' in *The immediate experience* (New York, Doubleday, 1954).

A CHECKLIST OF QUESTIONS

Whatever set of comparisons you make or whichever of the three approaches you choose, there is a similar series of questions to look out for. Items on the following checklist obviously have to be modified according to the particular problem you have chosen.

1. What patterns of selection are immediately apparent? Is this a subject which has just been picked up by the media and if so, why? What significant aspects of the phenomena might have been left out? What ideological, ideational or bureaucratic factors might have been operative? See Part One, particularly the readings by Cirino, Roshier and Rock, for ideas on what sort of questions to ask about selection.

2. What model is being transmitted of the particular form of deviance or social problem you are examining? In particular:
   (a) Is the phenomenon explained in terms of a free will or a deterministic model?
   (b) Are notions such as sickness, pathology, disease being used? (See Pearce, Linsky, and Young for the variations applied to homosexuality, alcoholism and drug taking.)
   (c) Are conspiracy theories or their variants invoked?
   (d) Are the actors involved seen to passively accept society's definitions of them or actively fight such definitions?

3. Are there any contradictions apparent in these dominant

models? Either contradictions within the model itself (see Phillips and Palmer for examples of this) or between the model and reality?

4. Are any obvious recurrent myths being unfolded – (for example, 'Crime doesn't pay', 'All decent people would condemn this . . .')? And are there identifiable heroes and villains – such as the 'handful of brave men in blue' versus 'the screaming mob'? (see McCann).

5. Is the whole phenomenon personalized – for example, the Northern Ireland conflict reported in terms of Bernadette Devlin and the Rev. Ian Paisley – or seen in more structural terms?

6. What hidden biases can be detected in the actual techniques of reporting? (See Cirino for examples.) Try detecting hidden bias in a presentation deliberately set up to present 'both sides', for example, a TV confrontation or debates on programmes such as *Midweek*, *Panorama* or *Man Alive*. If you can find a clear spectrum on issues such as abortion and euthanasia, where on the spectrum do the sides come from? Thus, in the following diagram is the debate A versus Z or really G versus T or A versus T?

$$\longleftarrow \qquad \qquad \qquad \longrightarrow$$
A   G   T   Z

7. What elements of spurious or putative deviation are present? That is, what properties are assigned to a phenomenon, with little or no evidence of their actual existence? (see Cohen, Knopf, McCann for examples). And why should these particular properties be chosen?

8. Is there evidence of a parasitic or symbiotic relationship between the media? That is, does the story or model in question originate primarily from other mass media outlets? For example, see the documentation of how the media's handling of the 1968 Grosvenor Square demonstration was heavily influenced by an initial story in *The Times*.[2]

9. Can a particular moral panic be charted? That is, can one trace in the media the creation and definition of a problem through the fanning up of public indignation?

10. In regard to each question, look for:

(a) comparisons: see list on p. 273 and note examples, such as the straight versus the underground press, picture of drug takers (Young) and the media versus the experts on mental illness (Nunnally).

(b) changes over time: for example in reporting the Northern Ireland situation, a switch from personalization towards a more structural treatment of the issues or, the change in the image of the alcoholic from a free will to a deterministic conception (Linsky).

GUERRILLA RESEARCH

If the media contain elements of the mythical, why not observe the
process of myth making from the beginning? Here are ideas for
some more active research projects:

1. Try to get a story into the media about some event you have
participated in or know something about. This could be as dramatic
as witnessing a bank robbery or as mundane as attending a school
prize-giving. Phone newspapers directly (asking for the news desk
or a special correspondent), local stringers if you know them,
news agencies, TV stations etc. Keep a careful record of their response
– for example, do they immediately say they're not interested? How
much care is taken to check your story? – and then analyse what
eventually appears.

You can vary:
  (a) the number and type of media outlets you contact;
  (b) the angle or content of the story;
  (c) your own involvement;
and then see how each of these variations affects the final story. Say,
for example, that you hear about a pupil from a school in your area
being expelled or not allowed to write his exams because his hair is
too long. Find out some background details, then phone a number
of newspapers emphasizing one set of details to half of them and
another to the other half. Now see what happens.

2. Find a story about an event, group or organization and then
check on what sort of selection and what distortions, if any, have
taken place in the report. Then – with the permission of the group
or organization if this is relevant – contact the news' source and try
to get them to correct their original report. See how far you get –
if anywhere. A good example would have been the publicity given
to the foundation of PROP, the prisoners' union, and the demonstrations they organized in the middle of 1972. A large proportion of
the 'news' – including especially numerous cartoons – emphasized
PROP's demands for conjugal visits: one might have gathered from
some stories that 'More Sex for Prisoners' was the unions *only*
demand. If one had contacted PROP or even looked over one of its
official publicity handouts (from which most of the news stories
were derived) quite a different picture would have emerged.

3. Our final example is the use of the 'Cohen–Young Letter-
Scale Test'. Take an issue on which opinions are highly polarized –
say, abortion, euthanasia, Enoch Powell's stand on immigration,
the legalization of marihuana – and at an appropriate time, draw
up say 20 letters, carefully scaled from an extreme pro through to

an extreme anti position. Now using fictitious names and addresses, send all the letters to each national newspaper. Which ones will they print? There are endless variations on the Letter-Scale Test: for example, varying the name and status of the 'writer' as well as the opinion expressed.

REFERENCES

1. See Orrin E. Klapp, *Symbolic leaders* (Chicago, Aldine, 1965) and *Heroes, villains and fools* (Englewood Cliffs, N.J., Prentice Hall, 1963).
2. James D. Halloran, Philip Elliott and Graham Murdock, *Demonstrations and communications: a case study* (Harmondsworth, Penguin, 1970). See also article by G. Murdock in this Reader.

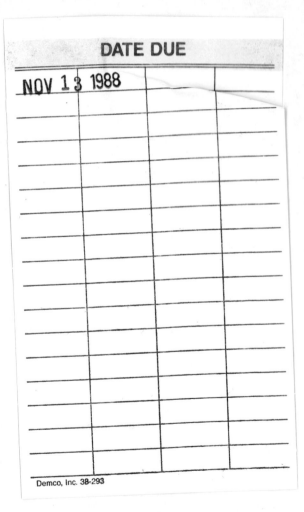

DATE DUE

NOV 1 3 1988			

Demco, Inc. 38-293